STUDIES IN IMPERIALISM

general editor John M. MacKenzie

When the 'Studies in Imperialism' series was founded more than twenty years ago, emphasis was laid upon the conviction that 'imperialism as a cultural phenomenon had as significant an effect on the dominant as on the subordinate societies'. With more than sixty books published, this remains the prime concern of the series. Cross-disciplinary work has indeed appeared covering the full spectrum of cultural phenomena, as well as examining aspects of gender and sex, frontiers and law, science and the environment, language and literature, migration and patriotic societies, and much else. Moreover, the series has always wished to present comparative work on European and American imperialism, and particularly welcomes the submission of books in these areas. The fascination with imperialism, in all its aspects, shows no sign of abating, and this series will continue to lead the way in encouraging the widest possible range of studies in the field. 'Studies in Imperialism' is fully organic in its development, always seeking to be at the cutting edge, responding to the latest interests of scholars and the needs of this ever-expanding area of scholarship.

'The better class' of Indians

MANCHESTER
1824

Manchester University Press

'The better class' of Indians

SOCIAL RANK, IMPERIAL IDENTITY, AND SOUTH ASIANS IN BRITAIN 1858–1914

A. Martin Wainwright

Manchester University Press
Manchester and New York
distributed exclusively in the USA by Palgrave Macmillan

Published by Manchester University Press
Oxford Road, Manchester M13 9NR, UK
and Room 400, 175 Fifth Avenue, New York, NY 10010, USA
www.manchesteruniversitypress.co.uk

Distributed in the United States exclusively by
Palgrave Macmillan, 175 Fifth Avenue,
New York, NY 10010, USA

Distributed in Canada exclusively by
UBC Press, University of British Columbia, 2029 West Mall,
Vancouver, BC, Canada V6T 1Z2

British Library Cataloguing-in-Publication Data is available

Library of Congress Cataloging-in-Publication Data is available

ISBN 978 0 7190 8908 4 paperback

First published by Manchester University Press in hardback 2008

This paperback edition first published 2012

Printed by Lightning Source

To Christine

CONTENTS

Acknowledgements — ix
General editor's introduction — xi
List of abbreviations — xiii

1 Ranjitsinjhi's Britain 1

Part I Institutions

2 The India Office 27
3 The National Indian Association 47
4 London's inner-city missions to Indians 69

Part II Interactions

5 Imperial subjecthood and legal identity 99
6 Patterns of compassion: aiding Indians in need 124
7 Scholarships and the civilising mission 157
8 Assimilation and ostracism in education 195
9 Conclusion: a hierarchical empire 233

Bibliography — 245
Index — 257

ACKNOWLEDGEMENTS

This book began with a Spencer Foundation Small Grant to spend summer 1997 in Britain researching the education of Indians there during the late nineteenth and early twentieth centuries. Thereafter it grew into a more general examination of social rank in the colonial encounter in the United Kingdom. The University of Akron funded further archival research in England in 1999 and 2004. My work draws on numerous collections, and I am grateful to many archivists for their help in my research: in particular, the staffs of the Oriental and India Office Collection of the British Library; the National Archives of the United Kingdom; the Special Collections of University College Library, London; the University of Birmingham Library Special Collections; the University of Chicago Special Collections, and the Council for Legal Education; Dr John Nicholls, Director of Recruitment and Training at the London City Mission, for providing me with publications and minutes of that organisation; Michael Underwood for showing me Indian students' application forms to St John's College, Cambridge, and Sarah Akers and John Ball at the University of Akron's Bierce Library for their tireless efforts to acquire material through interlibrary loan. The Gilchrist Education Trust, the University of Birmingham Library, and the Institute for Advanced Legal Studies have kindly granted permission to cite material from their collections, and material from the India Office Records and United Kingdom National Archives are cited under the rules of Crown copyright.

I am also indebted to friends, colleagues, and relatives. Shelley Baranowski, Michael Carley, Jeffrey Cox and Stephen Harp commented on my manuscript, and provided me with many useful suggestions. My parents, Arthur and Betty Wainwright, have been a constant support, logistically, emotionally, and intellectually, as I have refined my ideas and pursued my research. My greatest debt is to my spouse, Christine Wainwright, who in living and travelling with me as I have researched and written this book, has entered into the world I have been studying. I have benefited incalculably from her knowledge, repeated manuscript readings, and partnership in life as we have raised a family during my years of work on this book. Finally I must thank my children, Elizabeth and Alexandra, for reminding me constantly that this book was not the most important thing in my life.

GENERAL EDITOR'S INTRODUCTION

The British in India were notorious for the complexity of their social hierarchies and obsession with ceremonial precedence. It was almost as if they wished to replicate what they perceived as the complicated system of castes and other forms of ordering within Indian society. As is well known, they theorised much about caste, often creating unreal straitjackets in the process. Yet if the Indian reality was often different from the suppositions of their imperial rulers, so too was the sense of strict categories which the British created for themselves. India actually afforded opportunities for class destabilisation. Individuals who would be classified as working class in Britain could aspire to higher, sometimes considerably higher, status within the Empire. Moreover, the British seemed to seek practical ways in which Indian caste and social hierarchies could be translated into the British class system. Through these efforts at reconciliation, apparent rigidities could be shaken out into new structures. And this happened most notably within Britain itself.

Martin Wainwright's study examines in illuminating detail the multifarious ways in which the British not only attempted to create class comparabilities, but brought their sensibilities about social pretensions and proprieties to bear on many practical situations. Many different sorts of Indians visited Britain: lascar seamen, ayahs, craftspeople at exhibitions and other shows, performers of various sorts, high-born visitors, curious travellers, petitioners, women, and of course, most notably, students. The India Office and other agencies frequently had to make decisions about such people: how they should be received, how disputes were to be settled, what should be done with the indigent, whether they should be repatriated at public cost or not. As Wainwright demonstrates, such decisions were made on the basis of various criteria, including loyalty to the British Empire, potential for success within the processes of the 'civilising mission', and perceptions about supposed social position within a class pyramid. Invariably, such criteria were more important than those of race or religion, while in the gendered sphere Indians were judged according to how well they fitted the concepts of 'gentleman' or 'lady', categories which were themselves heavily imbued with class overtones. To aspire to these, it was necessary to fulfil requirements of 'breeding', 'manners', education (private), as well as the capacity to alternate between city and country (with a particular emphasis on the latter), to participate in the hunting, shooting and fishing fraternity, and to value 'character' over educational attainment.

Yet the British seemed to have no desire to create some kind of évolué class along French lines. Deculturation was not part of their mission. Indeed, on the contrary, they preferred Indians to continue to look like Indians, represented by their dress and other aspects of visual and cultural affiliations, even down to a willingness to accept ancient oriental languages in the place of Latin and Greek. In attempting processes of social assimilation and rapprochement, members of British and Indian elites developed a similar anxiety about the social orders 'below' them. But to all of this we must add further complications of ethnicity. Just as Indians came from many parts of the sub-continent, so too did the British represent a variety of nations within the United Kingdom. It is inevitable and appropriate that for a pioneering study like this much of the evidence comes from England and the 'golden triangle' of educational institutions at Oxford, Cambridge and London. But some day we need a related study of Indian experiences in Scotland, Wales and Ireland. These were undoubtedly different. There were many Indian students at Scottish universities such as Edinburgh and Glasgow and these institutions (as one example) were providing full access to degrees for women from the 1890s, almost three decades before Oxbridge permitted their formal taking of degrees. Social rankings and codes might be seen as somewhat distinctive in the 'Celtic fringe' and an examination of whether the Indian experience was consequently variable outside of England would be exceptionally interesting. But for the moment, Martin Wainwright's book offers many suggestive pointers to further research as well as to the further conceptualisation of these processes.

John M. MacKenzie

ABBREVIATIONS

BCINC	British Committee of the Indian National Congress
CMS	Church Mission Society
CIS	*Report and Minutes of the Committee Appointed by the Secretary of State for India to Inquire into the Position of Indian Students in the United Kingdom.*
EIA	East India Association
GOI	Government of India
ICS	Indian Civil Service
IM	*Indian Magazine*
IMR	*Indian Magazine and Review*
INC	Indian National Congress
IOR	India Office Records, British Library, London
JNIA	*Journal of the National Indian Association*
LCM	London City Mission
LCMM	*London City Mission Magazine*
NIA	National Indian Association
PRO	Public Record Office, National Archives of the United Kingdom, Kew
UCL	University College Library, London

CHAPTER ONE

Ranjitsinjhi's Britain

The cricketer prince

It was mid-July 1896 and cricket fans were flocking to Old Trafford in Manchester to watch England's second test match against Australia. But more was on their minds than simply who would win the match. Indeed, given England's miserable performance in the first test at Lords in London, British fans had little reason to hope for victory. What brought out twenty thousand spectators the first day, and eighteen thousand the second, was England's newest player, noted for his unusual batting that repeatedly sent balls to the boundary. Perhaps he could save England in this second match. If so, England's saviour would be most unusual, for he was Indian, the first person of colour to play for a British national sports team, or even a local one. His name was Kumar Shri Ranjitsinjhi, and to this day he is regarded as one of the greatest cricketers of all time.

By the time he played for England Ranjitsinjhi's fame and popularity preceded him, due to his competence as a fielder and a bowler, and his superb qualities as a batsman. Playing for Sussex against London's Marylebone Cricket Club (MCC) the previous year, he was twice instrumental in getting out W. G. Grace, considered the greatest cricketer of the age. During the same match he scored 150 runs in the second innings, nearly closing the gap with the MCC in what had earlier appeared a hopelessly wide margin.

Such achievements were built on a batting stroke, the 'leg glance', that he had refined as a student at Cambridge University, and they helped overcome the racist attitudes of many in Britain toward this Indian resident. Indeed, Ranjitsinjhi secured membership on the English team only at the insistence of the Lancashire County Cricket Club, which, as the host of the second test match between England and Australia, was entitled to choose the team members. The MCC, which had hosted the first test, had not invited him to join, because its president, George Canning, the fourth Baron Harris and recent Governor of Bengal, considered Ranjitsinjhi's inclusion in the English team inappropriate. According to Harris, Ranjitsinjhi was 'a bird of passage' who had not been born in England and would not be living there permanently. He therefore did not qualify to play for England. The fact that Lord Harris had himself been born in Trinidad made his remark appear at least partly hypocritical. He later confirmed his prejudice, remarking: 'To wear down good bowling, and patiently wait for many overs for a run here and a run there, is easier for the phlegmatic Anglo-Saxon than for the excitable Asiatic.'[1] Ranjitsinjhi also encountered cruder forms of racial prejudice. In 1892, while he was still a student, players at a match in Bridlington mocked him to his face, because they thought that he did not understand English. Later, following Ranjitsinjhi's debut on the England team at Old Trafford, a former Gentleman player for the MCC took umbrage at journalist Home Gordon's praise for the Indian's performance, saying that he wished Gordon could be expelled from the MCC for having 'the disgusting degeneracy to praise a dirty black'.[2]

Furthermore, Ranjitsinjhi's prowess at this English sport caused some confusion, even among his admirers. On the one hand, observers took comfort in the knowledge that Ranjitsinjhi was assimilating into English society by making one of its greatest pastimes the centre of his life. Very few knew that the latest phenomenon in cricket had initially learned the sport, not from Englishmen on the Cambridge 'Backs', but from a Parsi in Rajkot.[3] Crowds flocked to his games, and reporters followed him wherever he went. The *Star* declared: 'if Prince Ranjitsinjhi had any ambitions in the political line, he would have no difficulty in securing a nomination from some enthusiastic constituency, for at this moment he is the most popular man in England'.[4] On the other hand, sports commentators and players heightened the exotic imagery surrounding England's most unusual player and attributed his success to supposed characteristics of his culture and race. Typical of this imagery were the remarks of Neville Cardus that: 'His style was a remarkable instance of the way a man can express personal genius in a game – nay , not only personal genius but the genius of a whole race. For Ranjitsinjhi's cricket was of his own country; when he batted a strange light was seen for the first time on English fields, a light out of the East.'[5] Part of the exotic allure was also Ranjitsinjhi's status as the heir to the throne of Nawanagar, which made him, according to the title of one of his biographies, the 'prince of cricketers'. The very novelty of an Indian prince playing for England appealed to many, in part because of the symbol it served of imperial loyalty and unity.

Yet Ranjitsinjhi's status as a prince was more than mere exoticism, because it enabled him to use Britain's most entrenched hierarchical social system, class, to overcome its less prominent one, race. This was possible because, given the absence of a large minority of people of colour in Britain, the most common form of social stratification among Britons on their home island was class. Although ethnic concepts and imagery circumscribed Ranjitsinjhi's position as one of England's greatest cricketers, they did not present an absolute barrier to his participation in the sport. While excellent cricketing helped in part to overcome racial barriers, so did British perceptions of his rank in India's social hierarchy. British society still admired amateur 'gentlemen', who played sports for their own sake, over professional 'players', who played for money. In English cricket, amateurs entered the field first, and professionals second. As an amateur, Ranjitsinjhi entered the field with fellow English 'Gentlemen' followed by the other English, professional 'Players'. He also participated on the Gentlemen's side of 'Gentlemen versus Players' matches.

An Indian cricketer's social precedence over an Englishman was possible in Britain, because with a few exceptions such as those noted above, the leaders of Britain's cricketing institutions recognised the validity of ranks in an Indian social hierarchy which they attempted to translate into British equivalents. Clearly the heir to the throne of a princely state was a gentleman according to the terms of late Victorian British society. The Australian player, Frank Iredale, noted this fact when he contrasted British perceptions of Ranjitsinjhi with those common in his own country: 'Australians will never know a man of his blood, because so few people in this country rightly understand what the blue-blood of India really means. The people here view all people not actually white as alien, and they think that the proper conversation to indulge in when they address them is pidgin English.'[6] By contrast many of Britain's elite, and many below them, perceived Ranjitsinjhi as a 'blue-blood'. Ranjitsinjhi knew that such a perception was an essential component in the willingness of British cricketing institutions to accept him into their fold, and for this reason he hid the fact that their perceptions of his status were exaggerated, if not completely wrong.

In reality Kumar Shri Ranjitsinjhi was neither a prince nor the heir to any throne. He had come close to achieving this status as a child when, in 1878, Vibhaji, the Jam Sahib of Nawanagar, having earlier disowned his only son for conspiring to murder him, accepted Ranjitsinjhi, a distant relative, as his heir. The birth of another son to Vibhaji ended Ranjitsinjhi's prospects for the throne, and the Jam Sahib continued to fund Ranjitsinjhi's education at the princes' college in Rajkot, and later Cambridge University, only as an act of kindness.

It is uncertain how necessary it was for Ranjistsinjhi to be perceived as a prince in order for him to play first-class cricket in England. As a member of the Rajput aristocracy, and a graduate of Rajkot College and Cambridge University, he could claim the stature of a gentleman in British society without actually being a prince. Nevertheless, to be a prince certainly increased his marketability, and England's first, first-class Indian cricketer saw an opportunity that he could exploit to his advantage. Although initially Ranjitsinjhi did not purposefully spread disinformation regarding his claim to the throne of Nawanagar, neither did he attempt to set the record straight when others referred to him as a prince. In the context of his financial difficulties, his prowess at cricket became a means of escaping his dependence on the Jam Sahib and remaining in England.

Initially, Ranjitsinjhi had played the prince in order to gain the acceptance of England's cricketing institutions and receive the highest acclaim they could offer. After becoming a player for England in 1896, he used this acclaim to turn the fiction of his Indian social status into reality. The fact that Vibhaji's biological son, Jaswantsinjhi, ascended the Nawanagar throne in 1895 did not deter Ranjitsinjhi. Returning in 1898 from his tour with the England team in Australia, he spent a year in India staking his claim to the Nawanagar throne. In this effort he found allies among leaders of other Rajput clans and administrators of the British Raj. Many purity-conscious Rajputs objected to the fact that Jaswantsinjhi was the son of Vibhaji by a Muslim concubine. They preferred Ranjitsinjhi, whose Hindu Rajput lineage was incontestable. British administrators were now divided on whether to support his claim, but they gradually yielded under pressure from businessmen, sports enthusiasts, and politicians who argued that 'Ranji', as the British press affectionately called him, was too great a public relations asset to imperial unity for the Raj to discard his claim to the throne. Thus within thirteen years of becoming the first person of colour to play county cricket in England, Ranjitsinjhi ascended the throne of Nawanagar. That he would have played for England without being perceived as an Indian prince is possible, but less likely. That he would have ascended the Nawanagar throne without becoming a legend in the British sporting world is inconceivable.

The British context of Ranjitsinjhi's success

Ranjitsinjhi's achievement was truly an imperial one, combining as it did the cultures and societies of India and Britain to propel him to a prominence that he would not otherwise have attained. He was hardly typical of Indians living in Britain at the turn of the twentieth century. Few could claim to be either princes or sports stars, let alone both. Yet because it tested the limits of acceptance into British society, his career illustrates the complexities of the interaction among the British Empire's many social hierarchies and the importance of manipulating perceptions among Britain's institutional elite. While celebrities such as Ranjitsinjhi are not the focus of this book and do not represent the experience of most Indians in Britain, his career reveals the background contextual story that is. Ranjitsinjhi understood that while his race was a liability in a world dominated by Europeans, he could, at least partly, overcome its negative effects by forcing British authorities to focus on his status in the alternative hierarchy of class. This effort was most likely to be successful in Britain for a couple of reasons, one born of strategic necessity and the other of less conscious assumptions about social stratification.

First, more than any other part of the Empire, Britain maintained the forms (albeit less often the substance) of openness and equality toward people of colour. If the British Empire was supposed to be a civilising institution as its supporters claimed, then it must theoretically allow its subjects, regardless of the colour of their skin, to achieve whatever civilising potential British culture could provide. In his recent analysis of Ranjitsinjhi's career, Satadru Sen notes that in late Victorian Britain:

> Mobility across the lines of race, geography and social status was encouraged, because seeing the native as 'one of us' (who might experiment with being 'one of them') was an immensely pleasurable experience for the metropolitan observer. At the same time this mobility needed to be contained within ideological, discursive and spatial parameters that would preserve the order – i.e., the moral meanings and relative locations – of race, class and gender in the empire.[7]

Ranjitsinjhi demonstrated excellence at one of the most celebrated aspects of British civilisation: cricket – and in spite of some resistance, he attained the highest rank possible as a cricketer: to play for England's national team. To have formally denied him the right to pursue his potential on the basis of his race would have exploded the myth that the British Empire's most important mission was a civilising one.

To recognise that the imperial metropole's official openness to people of colour was greater than that of its dominions or India should not be taken to imply that British society was colour blind. Recent scholarship has established conclusively that racial prejudice and bigotry were present at all levels of British society. Nevertheless, institutions in late Victorian and Edwardian Britain were less prone than those elsewhere in the Empire to define Britishness in ethnic terms. The governments of Australia, Canada, and New Zealand were in the process of restricting the full rights of citizenship to Europeans. By 1914 they prohibited people of non-European descent from becoming residents and in some areas denied the franchise to people of colour who were already resident. Even before becoming a dominion in the aftermath of the Boer War, the Boer republics and British colonial authorities of southern Africa were creating a system that foreshadowed apartheid. Perhaps more galling to Indians than their treatment in the dominions was the official denial of their rights in their own country. Indian judges could not hear cases involving people who were wholly of European descent unless half the jury was European, and Indian soldiers could not become officers in the Indian army. Moreover, India was governed almost exclusively by British administrators who were not responsible to Indian voters (because there were no elections) and lived in segregated suburbs, known as 'civil lines'. Such official discrimination helped to spawn the Indian nationalist movement in the late nineteenth century.

Yet in Britain Indian men could vote (if they met the property qualification), become Members of Parliament (twice in the 1890s), and receive peerages (the first in 1919). Indians studied in British universities and occasionally held positions on their faculties. Such official acceptance, was just that – official (and arguably token) – for as we shall see, in practice Indians often encountered racial discrimination in housing, hiring, and education. Moreover, even official colour blindness went only so far. For instance, and very significantly, during this period the War Office banned people of colour from commissions in the British army, a policy to which it made exception in only a few instances. Nevertheless, although the level of unofficial racism in British society was considerable, the response of many British institutions to the presence of Indians in Britain was at least officially more inclusive than it was in other parts of the Empire.[8]

Furthermore, Indians exercised these rights because as British subjects they were legally considered British. The Merchant Shipping Act of 1858 and the Indian Emigration Acts of 1874 and 1883 required employers to return Indians whom they had hired to their homeland.[9] Apart from the provisions of these acts, Victorian and Edwardian Britain had no legislation restricting the migration of people of colour into the United Kingdom. The British Government imposed further restrictions on 'coloured' seamen in 1925. Nevertheless, it confined such restrictions to the labouring classes until the Commonwealth Immigration Act of 1962 established quotas favouring applicants from predominantly white countries, whatever their social rank. Nevertheless, such racial inclusiveness did not guarantee equal opportunity for most Indians in the United Kingdom. Rather, as with native Britons of the period, it offered access to society's upper echelons mainly to those who already came from privileged backgrounds. Thus, members of India's elite in Britain fared better with British institutions than did their compatriots located lower in the Indian social system. They also fared better than did native Britons located lower than they in Britain's social hierarchy.

The second reason for Ranjitsinjhi's success, therefore, lay in the influence of the British class system over the way in which Indians residing in Britain related to the rest of the population. Because they lived in a profoundly class-conscious society, Britons judged others according to the perceptions that they held of their class ranking. Although their presence was significant, few people of colour lived in Britain. Comprehensive statistics on their number do not exist, but they probably did not number much more than ten thousand during the period under discussion.[10] The considerable literature and imagery of Indians in India portrayed them in a wholly different environment, in many ways alien to the daily experience of Britons at home. There was, therefore, little competition in the consciousness of native Britons to this class hierarchy in its domestic setting. Unlike the dominions, Britain was ruled by its indigenous population. Unlike their counterparts in the colonies of Africa, Asia, and the Caribbean, whites in Britain vastly outnumbered people of colour. The geographic, demographic, and cultural context of Britain's institutional response to the presence of people of colour was, therefore, unique in the British Empire. The existence of an ethnically different empire overseas may have played an important role in the development of a British (as opposed to English, Irish, Scottish, or Welsh) national consciousness,[11] but the presence of non-Europeans in Britain was too small to alter significantly the primary system of social stratification in Britain, at least until the First World War. Elsewhere in the Empire institutions erected legal walls of separation between Europeans and the members of all other ethnic groups, and only afterward applied class ranking. In the dominions, this practice often amounted to a form of social levelling that recognised only the lowest classes among people of colour. By contrast, in Britain institutions often attempted to translate the hierarchies of non-European peoples into British social equivalents which provided comprehensible categories that they could manipulate and manage. The result was a process of interpretation, through which British institutions and Indian residents established the ranks of the latter in British society, with the attendant advantages and disadvantages that the resulting status implied.

Themes and organisation

This process of interpretation is the central theme of this book. It focuses on an issue which existing scholarship has treated only tangentially: the ways in which British institutions and Indians residing in

Britain used social hierarchical rankings, particularly those of class, to identify and relate to one another. Such forms of ranking have received little attention among scholars concerned with the culture and society of the British Empire, because these scholars have tended to assume that race, sometimes defined in gendered terms, was the primary linguistic register of the relationship between British administrators of the Empire and the people of colour whom they ruled. To focus on social rank is not to deny the importance of race in this encounter. Rather, I argue, class did the ideological work among institutions in Britain that race often did in other parts of the empire. Thus in Britain class tended to incorporate race and gender in defining the 'Other' as a means of establishing a cohesive identity for the elite. In the case of South Asians this process involved the complex interplay of race, caste, class, and social behaviour, all of which helped to determine an Indian's acceptance into British polite society. Britons did not simply put caste and class in the service of defining South Asians as a racial 'Other', an opposite against which they created their own British identity. Rather they excluded some Indians and included others in their society on the basis of their understanding of Indian society and their interactions with these Indians as individuals.

Only recently has David Cannadine focused on class as a form of stratification as important as race in governing the British Empire, and on British imperialism as 'the domestication of the exotic – the comprehending and the reordering of the foreign in parallel, analogous, equivalent, resemblant terms'.[12] Cannadine has received considerable criticism for a number of reasons. First, by focusing almost exclusively on the 'ornamental', or symbolic, aspects of empire, he pays little attention to the mechanics by which this process of social ranking actually affected the fate of the people of colour concerned, in other words the power dynamic involved in imperialism. Although the process of interpreting social rank was the creation of analogy between the metropole and India, it was simultaneously an exercise in 'othering' within the resulting imperial society. It was therefore still the exertion of power, albeit vertically within society rather than horizontally between societies. Class and race could easily reinforce each other in the imperial setting. Moreover, British polite society clearly played the dominant role in this exercise. It was the gold standard to which Indians were held, and they shed their appearance of difference only inasmuch as their cultural practice, however foreign it appeared, seemed analogous to that of the elite in the imperial metropole. Perceptions of difference through race and culture continued to be a significant issue, but the interpretation of social rank often determined how serious they were.

Another criticism of Cannadine is one that could be levelled at many scholars of the colonial relationship, including Edward Said, from whom Cannadine draws marked distinctions – his tendency to focus on the Empire outside Britain, rather than Britain as a constituent part of the imperial experience. A central premise of this book is that the Empire was a very domestic concern, and that the Indo-British encounter in the imperial metropole actually affected official concepts of British identity – albeit in ways contrary to those highlighted in recent scholarship. This assertion does not mean that the Empire impinged upon British society unaffected by local context. The institutional response to the presence of Indians in the United Kingdom was not a simple matter of transposing the racial attitudes of the Raj's Anglo-Indian community back to Britain. Rather those attitudes, hardened in the context of a heavily outnumbered governing minority, contended (sometimes within the same person) with the overwhelming presence of class ranking in the context of Britain's domestic social order.

Unlike many other scholars, therefore, I draw sharp distinctions between the Indo-British relationship in the imperial metropole, which provided a unique zone of encounter, and elsewhere, where the interpretation of social rank did not afford Indians the same opportunities to mitigate the prevalence of racial prejudice. Race, class, caste, and gender interacted together in often ad hoc and transactional ways, that differed markedly across the Empire in the contexts of its varied social dynamics. In order to explain Indo-British encounters in the imperial metropole, therefore, I pay close attention to the ad hoc nature of institutional behaviour, which was contingent more on the social context of geographic location and individual circumstance than on any attempt to interact with Indians within a theoretical framework. Thus my argument applies to polite society *in the United Kingdom alone*, because this group less than any other felt threatened by the presence of people of colour, and could therefore more easily use the register of class to identify rank and even Britishness through analogy and difference. This book does not attempt to argue a grand synthesis of racial and class attitudes at the imperial level. Nevertheless, to the extent that it provides a theoretical framework for understanding the relationship of social rank in Britain to imperial racism elsewhere, the framework is that local social contexts in the various parts of the empire precluded the existence of a truly empire-wide system of ranking. Space considerations preclude an attempt to deal with those other contexts outside the United Kingdom, and this book does not set out to make a systematic comparison between them. Rather it relies on primary sources to bring to light evidence that questions and complicates the current master narrative regarding race relations in Victorian and Edwardian Britain that has developed over the last few decades. In doing so it explains the interaction of the contradictory forces involved.

The local context of the encounter did not, however, prevent it from having empire-wide consequences, particularly regarding the evolution of British identity. So central was the application of social hierarchy to the presence of South Asians in Britain that it shaped official policy toward British legal identity generally. The desire to assimilate Indians into British polite society encouraged the Imperial Government to define Britishness dynastically rather than ethnically, adhering to pre-industrial and pre-national concepts of allegiance as they did with class. The Indo-British encounter in the United Kingdom, therefore, demonstrates that just as empire could be a catalyst for the creation of national identity, as Benedict Anderson and Linda Colley have shown, so could it exert a brake on the development of ethnically-based nationhood through its emphasis on class-based dynastic allegiance.[13] In the Indo-British encounter in the imperial metropole, therefore, class served as the linguistic register for determining nationality.

While the process of interpretation was important in India, where British administrators sought to understand Indian society at least partly in order to rule it more easily, it was absolutely essential in Britain, where Indian social ranks would have been meaningless unless translated into British equivalents. Terms such as Brahmin, Rajput, maharaja, and *zamindar*, embodied recognisable, albeit geographically variable, meanings in their local contexts in India. British administrators of the Raj dealt with the bearers of such titles and social identities in the context of dialogues that balanced the ambitions of the Raj with the locally established prerogatives that such titles implied. In Britain, however, such titles carried no local meaning. They became comprehensible only when interpreted into British equivalents. The key issues therefore, were the identity and motives of the interpreter. British administrators applied their own understandings of Indian society in their search for equivalent ranks to assign to Indians residing in Britain, but Indians tried to guide their British hosts in this process.

The effort to interpret social rankings was an essential aspect of the interaction between British institutions and Indians in Britain, because it perpetuated the notion of an ideal hierarchy of class, under which the Empire's various ethnic groups were supposed to relate to one another, rather than the hierarchy of race, which pervaded so many imperial interactions in reality. It also served as a language with which British institutions and Indian residents could negotiate the status of the latter in British society. This process served the interests of British administrators, because it enabled them to place Indians in British society, and it provided the comfort of order which so appealed to the elite. It also often served the interests of Indians. For those from the upper echelons of Indian society an emphasis on class categorisation, which placed them in a position of social superiority, was far preferable to one based on racial or ethnic categorisation, which in a European-dominated world would place them in a position of inferiority. Furthermore, Indians of all social rankings could exploit the relative absence of knowledge regarding their own hierarchical systems that the geographic distance between Britain and India provided. Thus Ranjitsinjhi could exploit the ambiguity in the meaning of 'Kumar Shri' to his advantage and achieve a higher social standing in both Britain and India than he would have done had he remained at home.

The encounter of Indians with institutions in the United Kingdom provides an unusually rich source of information on the interaction of social strata in the British Empire, because both Britain and India had long-standing traditions of pronounced social ranking. Both societies used hierarchical social categories as means of defining who their members were and how they should behave. Yet in spite of the apparent rigidities of the categories that they created, both groups used geographic space as means of moving through social space. Many British officials had visited India and used their careers there as a means of promoting themselves socially in Britain. Likewise, many Indians residing in Britain sought to use their sojourn there as a way to promote themselves socially in India. Such attempts to reinvent one's social pedigree at a location too distant, or under circumstances too confused, to invite close scrutiny of one's background were nothing new in British or Indian society. Whether they were 'nabobs' returning to England with fortunes from India or Rajputs acquiring the aura of a warrior-prince through their relations with Mughal emperors, travellers from both India and Britain had for centuries attempted to elevate themselves by controlling the process of interpreting ranks from one social hierarchy to another.

In this sense what occurred in late Victorian and Edwardian Britain was an extension of both British and Indian social behaviour. Because it involved the interaction between the two societies in the peculiar context of imperial Britain, however, it affected both significantly. Indian residents in Britain included many members of the subcontinent's elite, and Indians residing in Britain were the only Indians whom the administrators of British institutions encountered when they were working at the centre of the Empire. It is, therefore, hardly surprising that the translation of these categories from Indian to British hierarchies reflected and affected the Indo-British imperial relationship. Britain's class hierarchy was, however indirectly, a polite expression of differences in power, and often wealth. Its extension to Indians in the United Kingdom was, therefore an extension or denial of power, depending on the individual. This book shows how rank mattered in practical terms that affected people's careers, financial well-being, and even health.

Nevertheless, social rank was a manifestation of imperial power. Although Indians exploited the process of interpretation as much as Britons did, the process itself was unequal because it was built on British terms. Since the centre of imperial power was Britain, Indians visiting it had to advertise their ranking in British equivalents. Furthermore, because Britain occupied India and not vice versa, British administrators assumed that they knew enough about Indian society to interpret it into British equivalents. It was India's hierarchies that were made to fit uneasily into the British version, and not the other way round.

In order to explain the process of interpretation, I begin, in Part I, by examining the backgrounds of British administrators and Indian residents in the United Kingdom. Chapter 2 examines the most important government institution to interact with Indians in Britain: the India Office. It shows how the educational and social backgrounds of the men who ran this government agency caused them to interpret Indian social ranks as classes and translate them into British equivalents. Chapter 3 looks at the most popular forum for interaction among Indians in Britain and Britons interested in India: the National Indian Association. Its journal shows that educated Indians visiting and residing in Britain, and the British hosts who welcomed them, measured society by class, and class by adherence to the ideals of Victorian polite society. This chapter also highlights the continuing importance of the civilising mission in the late nineteenth- and early twentieth-century British Empire. Chapter 4 analyses the two most important inner-city missions to reach out to Indians in London: the London City Mission and the Strangers' Home for Asiatics. Although the primary purpose of both missions' contacts with Indians was to convert the latter to Christianity, both (particularly the Strangers' Home) provided material aid to poor Indians in the capital, much of it in the context of paternalistic class-based assumptions. Both organisations served in sometimes uneasy partnerships with the British Government and private corporations. Chapters 2 to 4 introduce us to the largest institutions that had the most frequent dealings with Indians in Britain. Since these institutions, or significant portions of them, focused on Indians in their midst, many of their administrators considered themselves, and were considered by other British institutions, to be experts on Indian culture and society. They were often described as 'orientalists', disseminators of knowledge about the Orient, many of whom had spent time in India.

The same could not be said for many of the other institutions that

Indians encountered in Britain. From workhouses to royalty, knowledge of India was usually less direct and far more murky. Administrators of these institutions often relied on the advice of the 'orientalists' or of Indians themselves to gain the knowledge they needed in order determine how to act toward Indians whom they encountered. Rather than devote entire chapters to these administrators and their institutions, I address their backgrounds (when they are known) inasmuch as they applied to specific encounters discussed in Part II. Moreover, I do not cover all institutions that Indians encountered in the United Kingdom. One reason is the availability of records. For instance, the Ayahs' (Indian nannies') Home received probably dozens of Indian women every year. However, its records have not survived, whereas a small portion of those for the Strangers' Home and the overwhelming majority of those for the India Office have. But because the Ayahs' Home appears to have dealt with the needs of ayahs well enough to discourage them from approaching the India Office for aid, and because the Strangers' Home did not accept women, ayahs rarely show up in the available records. Another reason is that some institutions were simply more active than others in the lives of Indians in Britain. The East India Association and the Northbrook Society both claimed to welcome Indians residing in Britain, but by 1900, neither organisation appealed sufficiently to middle-class Indians (for reasons explored in Chapter 3) to justify much attention to them here. Obviously, institutions with overt racial barriers to membership, such as the British officer training academy at Sandhurst, did not serve as significant venues for interaction with Indians, and therefore are not a focus of analysis here, even though their exclusion of Indians tells us much about the limits of British tolerance.

Part II focuses on interactions, the actual *application* of perceptions about Indian and British society to the encounter between administrators of institutions in Britain and Indians living there. Indeed, this book focuses on institutions in order to demonstrate the application of social rank to Indians in Britain, a practice that would be less easy to trace, for instance, in an examination of their portrayal in popular culture. Each chapter deals with a major theme regarding these encounters. For this reason some specific encounters appear in more than one chapter, since they illustrate more than one theme. Chapter 5 explores the extent to which British institutions treated Indians as British subjects, sharing a common legal and imperial identity with the inhabitants of the British Isles. The flip-side of this issue is the extent to which these institutions treated Indians as members of a distinct nation or ethnic group that was alien and inferior to the British. These issues are important for this study, because they show the importance of class as a register for defining legal

Britishness. Chapter 6 identifies patterns of compassion among Britain's elite when interacting with needy Indians in the United Kingdom. It focuses on the tendency to translate Indian caste and land-usage ranks, as well as religious activities, into supposedly equivalent classes in British society. It also shows how charity toward Indian destitutes could serve as a means of reinforcing one's own high social rank and membership in British polite society, whether one was British or Indian.

Finally, Chapters 7 and 8 deal with institutional behaviour toward Indians receiving educations in Britain. This issue is the focus of two chapters, partly because the Indians involved wrote about their experiences and testified before government committees. Chapter 7 establishes the central role of education in the civilising mission, particularly through scholarships to study in Britain. Because late Victorian British officials continued to believe that this mission required the mediation of India's elite, they put a premium on identifying which Indians belonged to it and encouraging them to visit the imperial metropole. Chapter 8 focuses on the ambiguous responses of British institutions to Indian students in the United Kingdom, ranging from accommodation of Indian culture to acquiescence in British bigotry. Both chapters argue that class prejudice played no small role in racial hostility to Indians, and in the willingness of British students and institutions to accept Indian visitors as full members of British polite society. These chapters also show that education lay at the heart of the civilising mission, which, British officials believed, only India's elite could convey to its masses.

Indeed, this entire book argues that to take the civilising mission seriously as a sincere purpose of British administrators explains much of their behaviour toward Indians whom they encountered in the United Kingdom. In doing so it questions a master narrative that for decades has dominated the historical scholarship of British India: that in the wake of the Indian Rebellion of 1857–58, British authorities drifted away from a culturally-chauvinist, social improving policy toward India and adopted instead what one of the most popular textbooks on Indian history describes as 'The postmutiny separation of "races"'.[14] However valid a description this narrative is for the behaviour of British officials in India, it works far less easily for their actions toward Indians in the United Kingdom. The motives and guiding goals of administrators of institutions that Indians in the United Kingdom most frequently encountered often reflected the purpose of the institutions that they served. Imperial security and fiscal responsibility were prominent concerns for India Office administrators. The spread of the Christian gospel was the ultimate goal of inner-city missionaries. The social improvement of India was the primary focus of the National

Indian Association. Yet for the most part, the administrators of all of these institutions shared a belief in the actual or potential benefits that Britain's occupation of India could achieve. Such attitudes and their resulting behaviour were certainly imperialist, but they often interfered with the biological racism that many scholars have highlighted in their studies of Indo-British relations during this period. In fact so complex was the interplay of these apparently contradictory perspectives that many members of Britain's elite held them simultaneously.

Recent scholarship on the Indian presence in Britain has pointed to contradictions and tensions in the imperial system by emphasising the use of race as the filter through which Indo-British encounters occurred. I do the same by emphasising class as the filter. Class, after all, was the officially acceptable form of social ranking in Britain, and it was through this hierarchy that British officials invited Indians to participate in British society. The tensions arose when racial hierarchy interfered with Indian placement and progression in the class hierarchy to the extent that it prevented Indian participation in British society. Yet the class-based social ranking was more than mere window dressing to hide racist policy. It had its own reality that race limited only in specific circumstances. Indeed, racism became a more prominent feature of Indian encounters with British institutions when British officials perceived the Indians concerned to hold low social rank in their own society. Conversely, these officials could hardly regard the racial separation between Indians and Britons as absolute, when so many of Britain's elite believed that the class differences of their own society arose in part from biological difference. Since the focus of this book is the interpretation of rank, it highlights class in the colonial encounter in the metropole. This emphasis is not, however, an effort to privilege class over race, gender, or any other hierarchy in this encounter. Rather it is an exploration of a neglected theme and an argument against privileging other aspects of the relationship. In reality class, caste, religion, race, and gender reinforced one another in a variety of ways, many of which this book explores. Among these were the racialisation of class and the gendering of race, processes on which other scholars have focused at length. These themes appear in this book, particularly regarding Indian students seeking acceptance in university society and entrance into professions. Nevertheless, the focus of this book is to highlight the ways in which race, gender, caste, and religion could be interpreted in terms of British social rank, because these themes remain relatively unexplored. Although class was inextricably intertwined with other aspects of the colonial relationship, it was a paradigm for contemporary understanding of Indians in Britain that carried as much force as race, gender, or religion. While class was a matter of power and wealth, since it partially determined who had access to them and who did not, it was as much a cultural as an economic relationship – which helps to explain how it could interact so closely with other discourses of hierarchy in the imperial relationship.

If the methodology of this study differs from that of earlier historians of class, who emphasised the economic nature of class, so does the focus, because the generation of social historians who examined class in Britain paid scant attention to the presence of non-Europeans in the metropole. For them this population was too small and marginal to merit close examination.[15] However, unlike recent scholarship on the presence of people of colour in Britain, which often emphasises the role of race in perceptions of class, this book does the opposite by highlighting the role of class in perceptions of race. By applying an emphasis on social rank to a post-colonial awareness of colonial encounters in the imperial metropole, this book attempts a synthesis of both scholarly traditions that encourages a new perspective on this important aspect of British and Indian history.

There is a danger here in applying models from the dominions or the United States of the late nineteenth and early twentieth centuries to Britain during the same period. Recent scholarship has shown the Empire's influence on British culture and explored the racial dimensions of British society. Adapting a model pioneered by historians of the United States, such as Noel Ignatiev, historians of Britain, such as Alastair Bonnett, John Marriott, and Zine Magubane have described the application of racialised concepts, often imported from the colonies, to ethnic and class differences in late nineteenth-century Britain. For these scholars, race formed a hierarchical continuum stretching from sub-Saharan Africans at the bottom, through Indians, and even Irish Catholics, before reaching the category of 'whiteness' – the colour and behaviour considered the social norm against which supposedly inferior counterparts measured. Such efforts to 'bring the empire home' are a welcome change from the earlier tendency to treat the social histories of Britain and India (or any other part of the Empire) as totally distinct. At its extreme, however, such scholarship can fall into a reductionism that attributes all aspects of society in late nineteenth- and early twentieth-century Britain to race – a development through which Douglas Lorimer warns 'Victorians have come to stand for the racist Other in binary opposition to our implicit nonracist Self'.[16] Although racial assumptions were often applied to class, in the British context the opposite was just as frequent – British understandings of class affected many encounters across racial divides, and perpetuated a dynastic British identity that rivalled the ethnic one described in so much historical scholarship. The United Kingdom was considerably different from the white-settler territories, whose land Europeans had only recently wrested from indigenous populations in often brutal conflicts that resulted in the near genocide of the latter. Britain by contrast was the homeland of the population that governed and lived in it. Its relationship to Indians was as much bureaucratic – that of the imperial centre to the colonial periphery – as it was racial – that of an expanding European population to a subjugated non-European one.

If one danger in analysing the Indian encounter with institutions in the United Kingdom might arise from the incorrect application of other contemporary societies' experiences, another might from reading the conditions of Britain's present into its past. In her analysis of Indian students in Britain, Shompa Lahiri argues that British society became more racist as time went on. I agree. What this assertion must not lead us to assume, however, is that the behaviour of British institutions and British people toward people of colour in 1900 was much the same as it is today. Lahiri leans in this direction when she points to 'continuity' between British authorities before and after the Second World War, particularly in their paternalism and their desire to restrict the numbers of Indians in the United Kingdom.[17] This book finds paternalism aplenty. It also highlights the construction of difference as a means of securing and preserving power. But the basis of this paternalism and the differences that it highlighted were at least as much those of class, age, and gender as race and culture.

In this context, class becomes a means through which British institutions viewed Indians in analogous terms, as Cannadine points out. But, equally important, class also serves as a form of 'othering' in which, for British polite society and Indians partaking in it, the 'Other' is the lower orders of both Indian and British society. Indeed, in order to take part in polite society, Indians often found it essential to highlight their superiority to the lower orders. Moreover, I question the extent to which British authorities sought to restrict Indian visits to the United Kingdom, a tendency that is the focus of Lahiri's work. While institutions in Britain sought the return of working-class Indians, such as ayahs and lascars, to their homeland, and monitored the activities of potential dissidents, they actively encouraged supposedly loyal Indian scholars and professionals to study in the United Kingdom, as part of Britain's effort to 'civilise' India and simultaneously discourage dissent among its elite. In all areas of interaction British institutions sought to balance their desire to maintain imperial dominance with their idealistic missions, which were much more than mere covers for economic exploitation, to deliver to India what they considered to be the benefits of British rule. In short, British officials in the United Kingdom often believed their own imperialist rhetoric.

A final danger to avoid is an anachronistic understanding of terms used during the late nineteenth and early twentieth centuries. Much of this study deals with the interpretation of Indian terms into British equivalents. It therefore examines the meaning of Indian terms that may be unfamiliar to readers unacquainted with Indian history. In its attempt to explain the interpretation of Indian ranks, therefore, this book itself interprets their meaning, albeit with the hindsight of late twentieth- and early twenty-first-century scholarship. However, some English terms are sufficiently vague to require further definitions to an English-speaking reader. This vagueness is particularly evident if we look at the different usage of terms a hundred years ago.

No word is more problematic in the context of this book than 'race'. Many people today regard it as a physiological/biological category, even though most current physical anthropologists argue that the term is meaningless in this regard. Yet in practice, even today many governments use the term to describe ethnicity, which includes many cultural features. This tendency was certainly the case among British institutions of the late nineteenth and early twentieth centuries. British officials used the term 'race' to describe biological traits, ethnic affiliation, and religious belief, often conflating all three. They sometimes used it to distinguish Celtic ethnic groups from one another and the English. Derogatory physical traits were sometimes used to describe Irish Catholics as well as poor Londoners. Much recent scholarship has attempted to reconcile the ambiguity of race's meaning in the nineteenth and early twentieth centuries by focusing on its proximity to or distance from 'whiteness', albeit not without sparking criticism.[18] This book discusses similarities in such language, although explicit comparisons to Africans or Irish Catholics rarely arise in the records I examine. However, this book argues that one can often just as easily interpret such linguistic similarities as the application of class analogies between 'races' as the 'racialisation' of class. As an analytical term 'whiteness' presumes that the primary register of a society's discourse is racial. Since I argue otherwise regarding the United Kingdom, I often use other phrases, particularly 'polite society' and Britishness (which drew on a complex mix of physiological, cultural, and class attributes), to describe the ruling group and normative standard and values against which Britain's elite measured other supposedly inferior social groups. Both perspectives have validity and neither should be seen as the sole template for understanding social variety in the British context. Nevertheless, I do highlight the racialisation of class where it becomes an issue in the interpretation of Indian social rank.

If 'race' was a nebulous concept, so also was 'class'. Administrators of institutions in the United Kingdom were acutely aware of social rank, even if the language they used to describe it was often vague. Indeed, the only debatable issue is precisely how they ranked the society around them. Mid-twentieth-century scholars, applying Marxist concepts of class struggle, tended to emphasise a three or two-tiered approach to Victorian and Edwardian society, which highlighted the difference between those who held political and economic power and those who did not. This system of production-based class consciousness had supposedly replaced the pre-industrial hierarchy of occupational ranking which had discouraged the development of political action among the disenfranchised and dispossessed. More recent scholarship, however, has focused on the perpetuation into the early twentieth century of occupational rank, either instead of, or coexisting with, a simpler hierarchy of industrial classes. Although such ranks were occupational, however, among the labouring classes in particular they did not necessarily imply political organisation in the Marxist sense. As Patrick Joyce points out, 'the consciousness of *a class* need not be the consciousness of *class*'.[19]

Nevertheless, industrial Britain's social hierarchy differed from its pre-industrial predecessor due to the rapidly changing economic context of the former. The elite of pre-industrial Britain had explained and justified a plethora of social ranks as manifestations of a divinely, or naturally, created hierarchy. Not only did Victorian and Edwardian British society contain whole new ranks emerging from the country's urbanisation and mechanisation, it also emphasised new justifications for differences among these ranks. Nowhere was this change in perception of, and behaviour toward, social rank more obvious than in the evolution of the term 'gentleman'. In eighteenth-century Britain 'gentleman' was an economic descriptor with political implications. Gentlemen did not work for a living. Rather they lived off revenue from their property, usually fixed property. Furthermore, this property entitled them to vote, thus including them in the country's political culture. Although property certainly helped to include its owners in the gentlemanly categories of Victorian and Edwardian society, other aspects of their personal profiles became equally important. Much more than in the eighteenth century, demeanour, behaviour, and education entitled a man to the term. Moreover, the increasing importance and organised influence of professions in political life forced Britain's elite to treat their members in gentlemanly terms. The term 'gentleman', therefore, came to have a much broader meaning in late nineteenth- and early twentieth-century Britain than it had in the mid-eighteenth century. This broader meaning bore moral implications as well, for a man might cease to be treated as a 'gentleman' if he did not behave according to the norms of Victorian or Edwardian polite society. The same was true for the term 'lady', which no longer necessarily meant a woman married to a landowner. A 'lady', however, rarely worked for money, the most common exception being the education of children and other women, which appeared to be a slight, and often temporary, extension to the public sphere of laudable female behaviour in the private.

The result of this evolution was a vague and confusing language of British hierarchy that habitually interchanged the words 'class' and 'rank' and defined key concepts, such as 'lady' and 'gentleman' in both the broad modern sense of respectability and education, and the narrow traditional sense of property ownership and independent economic means. In addition to behaviour and education, occupation determined membership in respectable society. Indeed for British men and women who knew nothing of an individual's personal life, occupation was the easiest way to determine a person's social rank. In practice Britain's elite applied these terms inconsistently, sometimes fairly broadly, sometimes rather narrowly. Often almost any educated man or woman who exhibited social graces common among the middle and upper classes could earn his or her respective appellation. Almost all professionals and property owners (along with their spouses) were addressed in this manner. In this sense, the terms 'gentleman' and 'lady' set off the middle and upper classes from the lower ones in British society. On the other hand, as Chapters 7 and 8 demonstrate, regarding education, British administrators tended to use the word 'gentleman' to describe a man who had received an education at one of Britain's elite 'public' schools. As Geoffrey Best has pointed out, 'anyone was a gentleman who had been to a public school or who successfully concealed that he hadn't'.[20] In this sense, therefore, the term 'gentleman' distinguished the upper and upper-middle classes from the middle and lower-middle classes. Professional men who had received only technical training or apprenticeship often did not qualify. I try to explain the varying uses of these terms as they occur in context.

If terms connected with race and class deserve close analysis, so do those connected with gender. We have already seen above the ways in which the word 'lady' was loaded with class and gender implications. Since so much of gentlemanly behaviour was defined in terms of polite behaviour toward women, the term 'gentleman' was equally loaded with gendered meanings. But as the scholarship of the last few decades has shown, the gendered use of language was not confined to the obvious socially constructed and biological differences between the sexes. Like the continuum of a racial hierarchy between whiteness and blackness, in settings of power relationships, masculinity often served as a privileged norm in a continuum of behaviour that extended from its opposite ideal of femininity. Indeed, these two continua and class hierarchy often reinforced one another. Terms such as 'virile' and 'manly' often defined the right to rule or, in the theme on which this book focuses, the eligibility of Indian men for gentlemanly status.[21] Thus masculine language often described the traits of elite male education in contrast to that of lower-middle-class aspiring professionals. Where relevant, such language receives attention alongside that of race and class.

Terms are very important in this book, because it focuses on interpretation. The act of interpretation determined the way Indian visitors to Britain fitted into the prevailing discourse of British society. This discourse in turn determined the moral playing field on which Indians competed for a place and a voice in that society. It also established the rules for the competition between Indian nationalists and British authorities in the first half of the twentieth century. The focus of this book, therefore, is an issue which was at the centre of Britain's imperial culture, and, ultimately, the collapse of its imperial power.

Notes

1 Lord Harris, 'Introduction', in J. M. Framjee Patel, *Stray Thoughts on Cricket* (Bombay: Times Press, 1905), xiv–xv. The following discussion of K. S. Ranjitsinjhi is based on Simon Wilde, *Ranji: A Genius Rich and Strange* (London: Kingswood Press, 1990) and Satadru Sen, *Migrant Races: Empire, Identity and K. S. Ranjitsinjhi* (Manchester: Manchester University Press, 2005). For Wilde's description of the match against Grace see 53–4.

2 Sir Home Gordon, *Background to Cricket* (London: Arthur Barker, 1939), 157.

3 Cowasjee Desai, Ranjitsinjhi's cricket coach at Rajkumar College, Rajkot. See Sen, *Migrant Races*, 21.

4 Quoted in Wilde, *Ranji*, 80.

5 Neville Cardus, *Good Days* (London: Rupert Hart-Davis, 1948), 2nd edn, 61.

6 Quoted in Wilde, *Ranji*, 95.

7 Sen, *Migrant Races*, 4.

8 Only in the 1980s did historians turn their attention to Indians living in Britain before the Second World War. Scholarship on this topic since then has stressed the pervasiveness of racism in British society. There are two reasons for this emphasis. First, the evidence is overwhelming that unofficial racial discrimination was common in Britain. Second, historians studying the history of Indians in Britain have felt it important to dispel two myths: one that racism was not a problem in Britain and the other that people of colour are only recent arrivals. The major publications that make this point are Shompa Lahiri, *Indians in Britain: Anglo-Indian Encounters, Race and Identity, 1880–1930* (London: Frank Cass, 2000), Rozina Visram, *Ayahs, Lascars and Princes: Indians in Britain, 1700–1947* (London: Pluto Press, 1986), and Ron Ramdin, *The Making of the Black Working Class in Britain* (Aldershot: Gower Publishing Company, 1987). Paul Deslandes explores the overt racism of British university culture in '"The foreign element": Newcomers and the rhetoric of race, nation, and empire in "Oxbridge" undergraduate culture, 1850–1920', *Journal of British Studies*, 37 (January 1998): 54–90. These studies are replete with examples of racial prejudice against Indians in Britain during the period under discussion. For comparative purposes see Jeffrey Green, *Black Edwardians: Black People in Britain, 1901–1914* (London: Frank Cass, 1998).

9 Significantly these acts did not require Indian sailors to leave Britain. They simply

required shipping companies to offer return passage. The Coloured Alien Seamen Order, 1925, on the other hand, prevented sailors, on the basis of their race, from residing in the United Kingdom. See Laura Tabili: 'The construction of racial difference in twentieth century Britain: The Special Restriction (Coloured Alien Seamen) Order, 1925', *Journal of British Studies*, 33 (1993): 54–98; and Laura Tabili, '"Keeping natives under control": Race segregation and the domestic dimensions of empire, 1920–1939', *International Labor and Working-Class History*, 44 (Fall 1993): 64–78. In the latter Tabili acknowledges the theoretical equality of all British subjects under British law, but points out that agreements between the Home Office and the Elder Dempster cargo liner company 'were frankly designed to impede West African seamen from claiming their rights as British subjects in order to deny them access to the British labor market' (66).

10 By 1913, Indian students in Britain numbered between 1,700 and 1,800; see Lahiri, *Indians in Britain*, 5. In 1914 Britain's merchant marine numbered about 51,000 lascars (Asian sailors) – see Rozina Visram, *Asians in Britain: 400 Years of History* (London: Pluto Press, 2002), 54 – but the number who actually resided in British ports at any one time is unknown. Nor are the numbers of ayahs (Indian nannies) who had accompanied their employers to Britain. The four or five hundred Indians residing in charitable shelters were almost certainly a small percentage of the total of their number in Britain. Add to this the Indian business community, and the African, Caribbean, and Southeast Asian counterparts of all the Indian groups mentioned above, and the number might exceed ten thousand. But this figure is pure conjecture. Antoinette Burton has similar difficulties arriving at a number. See Antoinette Burton, *At the Heart of the Empire: Indians and the Colonial Encounter in Late-Victorian Britain* (Berkeley and Los Angeles: University of California Press, 1998), 28–9.

11 See Linda Colley, 'Britishness and otherness: An argument', *Journal of British Studies*, 31:4 (1992): 309–29.

12 David Cannadine, *Ornamentalism: How the British Saw Their Empire* (Oxford: Oxford University Press, 2001), xix. In emphasising analogy over difference, Cannadine acknowledges his differences with Edward Said and those whose work Said has influenced. See Edward Said, *Orientalism* (New York: Pantheon Books, 1978). For criticisms of Cannadine's work see the *Journal of Colonialism and Colonial History*, 3:1 (2002). The entire volume is devoted to critiquing his book.

13 See Colley, 'Britishness and otherness'; and Benedict Anderson, *Imagined Communities: Reflections on the Origins and Spread of Nationalism*, 2nd edn (New York: Verso, 1991).

14 Stanley Wolpert, *A New History of India*, 6th edn (Oxford: Oxford University Press, 2000), 245. It is also implicit in the chronological boundaries of Michael H. Fisher's *Counterflows to Colonialism: Indian Travellers and Settlers in Britain, 1600–1857* (Delhi: Permanent Black, 2004) and explicit in his assertion that the 'events of 1857 ... clearly altered the situation of Indians in Britain' (429). See also Judith Brown, *Modern India: The Origins of an Asian Democracy* (Oxford: Oxford University Press, 1985), 98–9; and Thomas R. Metcalf, *Ideologies of the Raj* (Cambridge: Cambridge University Press, 1997), x; although Metcalf argued earlier that 'the liberal ideology ... persisted throughout the later nineteenth century'. See Thomas R. Metcalf, *The Aftermath of Revolt: India, 1857–1870* (Princeton, NJ: Princeton University Press, 1964), 326.

15 This scholarship, too voluminous to list here, includes the contributions of historians such as Asa Briggs, E. J. Hobsbawm, Gareth Steadman Jones, Harold Perkin, E. P. Thompson, and F. M. L. Thompson.

16 Douglas Lorimer, 'Reconstructing Victorian racial discourse: Images of race, the language of race relations, and the context of black resistance', in Gretchen Holbrook Gerzina (ed.), *Black Victorians/ Black Victoriana* (New Brunswick, NJ: Rutgers University Press, 2003), 187. See also Noel Ignatiev, *How the Irish Became White* (New York: Routledge, 1995); Alastair Bonnett, 'How the British working class became white: The symbolic (re)formation of racialized capitalism', *Journal of*

Historical Sociology, 11:3 (September 1998); John Marriott, *The Other Empire: Metropolis, India and Progress in the Colonial Imagination* (Manchester: Manchester University Press, 2003); and Zine Magubane, *Bringing the Empire Home: Race, Class, and Gender in Britain and Colonial South Africa* (Chicago: University of Chicago Press, 2004).

17 Lahiri, *Indians in Britain*, 217–19.

18 For a critique of 'whiteness' as a category in American history, see Eric Arnesen, 'Whiteness and the historians' imagination', *International Labor and Working-Class History*, 60 (Fall 2001), 3–32 and the accompanying responses. For a critique of arguments asserting the colonisation and racialisation of Ireland and the Irish, see Stephen Howe, *Ireland and Empire: Colonial Legacies in Irish History and Culture* (Oxford: Oxford University Press, 2000).

19 Patrick Joyce, *Visions of the People: Industrial England and the Question of Class, 1848–1914* (Cambridge: Cambridge University Press, 1991), 15. See also Geoffrey Crossick, 'From gentlemen to residuum: Languages of social description in Victorian Britain', in Penelope J. Corfield (ed.), *Language, History and Class* (Oxford: Basil Blackwell, 1991), 150–78; David Cannadine, *The Rise and Fall of Class in Britain* (New York: Columbia University Press, 1999), 51–108; and Walter L. Arnstein, 'The myth of the triumphant Victorian middle class', *Historian*, 37:2 (1975): 205–21. For works arguing for the emergence of politically conscious, simplified classes, see E. J. Hobsbawm, *The Age of Revolutions, 1789–1848* (London: Weidenfeld and Nicolson, 1962); Asa Briggs, *The Age of Improvement, 1783–1867* (London: Longmans, Green, 1959); and E. P. Thompson, *The Making of the English Working Class* (London: V. Gollanz, 1964).

20 Geoffrey Best, *Mid-Victorian Britain, 1851–1875* (London: Weidenfeld and Nicolson, 1971), 254.

21 For the general theory behind gender as an analytical category see Joan W. Scott, 'Gender: A useful category of historical analysis', *The American Historical Review*, 91:5 (December 1985): 1053–75. Anne McClintock extends gender to the analysis of empire's impact on European culture in *Imperial Leather: Race, Gender, and Sexuality in the Colonial Contest* (New York: Routledge, 1995). Mrinalini Sinha uses gender as the basis for her analysis of British rule in India in *Colonial Masculinity: The 'Manly Englishman' and the 'Effeminate Bengali' in the Late Nineteenth Century* (Manchester: Manchester University Press, 1995). Gender also figures prominently in Antoinette Burton's analysis of three Indians' sojourns in Britain in *At the Heart of the Empire*.

PART I

Institutions

CHAPTER TWO

The India Office

Of all the organisations that Indians encountered in the United Kingdom the most important was the India Office, because more than any other institution in Britain this one handled issues relating to the Indian communities on British soil. Since the India Office was involved with a broader cross-section of the Indian population in Britain than was any other institution, its members and their attitudes deserve close examination at the outset.

Collectively, the social background of India Office administrators, the ways in which they expressed and transmitted knowledge about Indian society, and the response of educated Indians in Britain to this body of knowledge, had a profound effect on the behaviour of British institutions toward Indians in Britain. India Office administrators promoted the idea that, although India's society was markedly different from Britain's, it was, nevertheless, possible to translate Indian social rankings into British equivalents and treat them accordingly. This emphasis on analogy over difference was particularly strong in Britain, because of the necessity of judging Indians in the United Kingdom in terms of the society of which they were currently a part, and because of the social context in which British administrators lived and worked. Britain's elite formed its identity mainly in contrast to Britain's lower classes. It is this social context that is so important in understanding the pivotal role that the India Office played in the encounter between British institutions and Indians in the United Kingdom.

The India Office in its social and political context

As members of the respected profession of civil service, India Office administrators had the greatest impact in shaping British elite perceptions of Indians in the United Kingdom. Harold Perkin has observed:

'The professional class produced most of the social thinkers who supplied the concepts and terminology in which the three major classes, the landed aristocracy, the capitalist entrepreneurs and the manual workers, thought about themselves and achieved class consciousness.'[1] If this was the case generally of the professional class, which, Perkin asserts, 'played a role in Victorian class society out of all proportion to their numbers', then how much more disproportionate was the impact of the small number of men who ran the India Office on British perceptions of Indians in their midst? It was to the India Office that other institutions turned most often for expertise on India, and it was the India Office alone that dealt with and advised on matters pertaining to all classes of Indian subjects residing in the United Kingdom.

The political situation in Britain only enhanced the disproportionate influence of the India Office regarding matters pertaining to all things Indian, including the presence of Indians in the United Kingdom. Of all the cabinet offices the India Office received the least attention from Parliament. The geographical distance of India, the seemingly unfathomable chasm between its culture and Britain's, and the arcane knowledge required to understand its society and governance, encouraged an almost deserted chamber when the House of Commons debated Indian issues. The sheer complexity of India Office responsibilities further discouraged much parliamentary oversight. More than any other cabinet office it resembled a government in its own right, because it had to manage the paperwork of the Raj, a regional empire subordinate to the administration of the global British Empire. The India Office, therefore, contained correspondence departments that reflected the needs of an imperial government, which focused primarily on issues arising on the Indian subcontinent. It dealt with matters regarding Indians in Britain only as a by-product of its responsibilities regarding the administration of the Raj.

The two departments most concerned with Indians in Britain were the 'Judicial and Public' and 'Political and Secret' Departments. As the name of the former suggests, it oversaw the execution of justice and public policy in India. It also dealt with questions of the India Office's jurisdiction relating to other cabinet offices. Thus, when British local authorities or charitable organisations referred an Indian visitor to the India Office for financial assistance, it was the Judicial and Public Department that determined initially whether the India Office should handle the case. The Political and Secret Department dealt with intelligence and external affairs aspects of the Raj. It supervised the British Government's relations with Indian princes and monitored the activities of Indians outside India, particularly if their behaviour bore the potential to undermine British authority in India. It therefore arranged receptions for Indian princes visiting Britain and monitored Indian organisations in the United Kingdom.

If the expertise of India Office administrators made them unusually powerful in matters regarding Indians in Britain, so did their ministry's financial independence. Unlike most other cabinet offices (the major exception being the Colonial Office) the people whom the activities of the India Office most affected – Indians – were not those to whom it was responsible. The Home Office and the War Office drew on taxes from the British public and had to answer to its propertied male members in parliamentary elections, but the India Office drew on revenues from Indian taxpayers, who had no ability to change its policy through the ballot box. Thus, whereas the British Treasury, through the operation of disbursing money and questioning accounts, exerted a check on all other ministries, it did not do so over the India Office. The Indian Government operated as an autocracy within an increasingly democratic British Government, and although the India Office provided parliamentary oversight of this autocracy's behaviour, the danger existed at its very inception that there would be little or no oversight of the India Office itself. The Indian Rebellion provided sufficient evidence to most Members of Parliament of what could go wrong when the British Government did not restrain the activities of its citizens in India. Although almost everyone in Britain condemned the rebels, many also held the East India Company responsible for any misrule that led to the war. Parliament's solution was the India Act of 1858, which replaced the East India Company with direct rule from Britain through the India Office.

In order to restrain the autocratic powers of the Secretary of State for India, the India Act created a branch of the India Office that could overrule him. This was the Council of India, which consisted of fifteen members who served for ten-year terms. These members were men who had extensive experience of India and had ceased to reside there no less than ten years before assuming their office. They rotated responsibilities for serving on seven committees whose names and functions mirrored those of the correspondence departments within the India Office, discussed at greater length below. Each member usually sat on more than one committee at once. It was the council's duty 'to "conduct" Indian business transacted in the United Kingdom'.[2] Since the activities of Indians appeared to qualify in this regard, members of the Council frequently took part in decisions regarding them. The influence of the council may have waned in the late nineteenth century, but this was the case more with high political decisions than with policy regarding the treatment of Indians in Britain.[3] The signatures and initials of its members are frequent in correspondence relating to them.

Before or after their terms on the council, some members also served in civil service capacities as chairs of correspondence departments or assistants to the Secretary of State for India. Sir Philip Perceval Hutchins, for instance, served briefly as secretary of the Judicial and Public Department before becoming a member of the council in 1893, and both Sir Owen Tudor Burne and Sir William Lee-Warner held the secretaryships of the Political and Secret Department before becoming member of the council in 1886 and 1902 respectively. On the other hand, Sir Louis Mallet became Permanent Undersecretary in 1874, after serving for two years on the Council.

If the Council of India served as an official check on the policies of the Secretary of State, the Permanent Undersecretary and his staff performed a less formal but equally important counterweight to the political appointments surrounding and including the Secretary of State. Governments came and went at the whims of political realignments and the ever-expanding electorate. These shifting forces account for the numerous secretaries of state for India, nineteen in all, who officially directed the office from 1858 to 1914. The politically appointed parliamentary undersecretaries were even more numerous, with thirty-one serving from 1858 to 1910. Civil servants, however, held tenured appointments and were supposed to be above partisan politics. Only five permanent undersecretaries, therefore, directed the office's daily business during the same period. One of them, Sir Arthur Godley, ran the office for twenty-six years (1883–1909). Trusted by leaders of both the Conservative and Liberal parties, Godley became an institution in the late Victorian and Edwardian governance of India. Responsible for the day-to-day control over hiring and expenditure, his sheer longevity at his post enabled him to mould the India Office to his own liking, systematically favouring the appointment of loyal civil servants, often with little or no experience of India, to replace the more maverick and reputedly lazy India hands, who had dominated the office at its inception (and the East India Company before it). So powerful was Godley within this influential cabinet office that some politicians considered him the 'real Governor of India under a succession of Viceroys and secretaries'.[4] Indeed the Permanent Undersecretary occasionally exercised plenipotentiary powers in important matters of state, when the Secretary of State was unavailable. Normally, however, it was over more mundane issues, among which numbered many matters pertaining to Indians in Britain, that the Permanent Undersecretary wielded *de facto* authority.[5]

In the company of so many colleagues with such extensive Indian experience, the permanent undersecretaries were something of an anomaly, since they did not owe their positions to experience in India.

Sir Louis Mallet (Permanent Undersecretary, 1874–83) transferred to the Council of India only two years earlier from the Board of Trade, where he had served as Private Secretary to the President. Godley, who never even visited India, served twice as Private Secretary to Prime Minister William Ewart Gladstone before his generation-long tenure in the India Office. Yet in spite of the differences in experience of India that set apart some of the India Office clerks and permanent undersecretaries from most of its other senior officials, the vast majority of its administrators shared common experiences that set the context of their approach to social ranking. Most important among these were class and education.

The presence of social rank was ubiquitous for India Office personnel. Senior administrators, and even many junior clerks, lived as gentlemen. A survey of the 1881 census shows that administrators at all ranks had servants. Typical of junior clerks was Henry Williams, thirty-six years old, whose Fulham home included his wife, four children no older than six, a nurse, and a 'general servant'. The same year Frederick Thompson, another junior clerk, lived with two siblings, and his mother and father. The latter was a retired army officer. Their household included a cook, a parlour maid, and a housemaid. Administrators at higher ranks had more impressive households. Sir Arthur George Macpherson, legal adviser to the Secretary of State and soon-to-be secretary of the Judicial and Public Department, lived in Paddington with his wife and three children. He employed a cook, a parlour maid, a schoolroom maid, and a kitchen maid. Godley, who would soon become Permanent Undersecretary of State, lived with his wife, four children, and five servants. The situation was similar in 1901, with the decision-makers living in households with many servants. Colin G. Campbell, Assistant Secretary of the Political and Secret Department, and Richmond T. Ritchie, the Secretary of State's Private Secretary, each lived with his wife and daughter and paid five and four servants respectively to maintain their households. Horace Walpole, the Assistant Undersecretary of State, and head of a family of four, had six servants. Most notable was Alfred Lyall, member of the Council of India, who although living only with his wife, required seven live-in servants to maintain his Kensington residence.[6]

This sense of hierarchy was so obvious to India Office administrators that it received little comment in their correspondence. Since professional ethics discouraged these men from drawing their personal lives into official communications, the absence of such discussion in government records is hardly surprising. More striking, however, is its absence from private correspondence. Although servants were an important, even essential, presence in India Office administrators' domestic lives, they are virtually invisible in these officials' private correspondence and personal reminiscences. Yet consciousness of social rank pervades much of the official and private correspondence regarding these administrators' encounters with Indians. This consciousness arose from the social context in which these administrators lived and worked in Britain.

If social rank was a daily presence for India Office administrators, so was gender, for although modern 'gentlemen' might work for money in certain respectable professions, such as their own, only under exceptional circumstances would a woman working for money be considered a 'lady'. One reason for this assumption was that household servants were overwhelmingly female. Only the India Office's wealthiest members, such as Council of India member Sir Henry Maine, could afford a butler or a footman. Even Maine had four female servants to his two male ones. The female character of the domestic workforce reinforced the separation of social spheres that was so characteristic of distinctions between the sexes in Victorian and Edwardian Britain. As administrators of middle- to upper-class households, the wives of India Office personnel supervised the work of these employees while their husbands governed the Empire. India Office administrators, who more than any others served as experts in the encounter between Britons and Indians in the United Kingdom, commuted between two hierarchical spheres. One was the office in Whitehall, whose personnel held professional rankings from lowly staff and clerks to senior secretaries. The other was home, where rank and difference occurred according to gender and class.

Significantly, women were virtually absent from the India Office premises. Only in 1889 did the Office hire women, as typists, and even then they were segregated from the men in a separate room on the top floor, thus reinforcing the India Office's aura of a men's club. This was particularly significant given the number of officials who had prior experience in India, since as Mrinalini Sinha points out, clubs in India were 'more vulnerable to the "infiltration" of women than their counterparts in Britain'.[7] If 'clubbability' was an important feature of the workplace for India Office administrators, it followed the British model more than the Indian one.

Nowhere was the British context of the India Office's working environment more apparent than regarding race. For if gender was a common feature of class hierarchy in India Office administrators' experiences, race was not. The lack of Indian servants among senior administrators is surprising, especially considering the time that many of them had spent in India. Their absence is evidence of how small the migrant servant population from India to Britain was in relation to the number of servants native to the British Isles. Undoubtedly, these officials had employed many servants while they lived in India. But evidently they did not encourage these servants to accompany them to England. Such behaviour may have resulted from their knowledge of the fate that befell many destitute ayahs, whose employers had dismissed them after arriving in Britain. Moreover, after 1883 employers of Indians who took them outside the subcontinent were required to repatriate them at their own expense. Hiring British servants was, therefore, less of a financial risk than bringing Indian servants to Britain. The 1881 and 1901 censuses provide no evidence that Indians continued to serve their British masters in England. Nor does the India Office list indicate the presence of Indian servants on its premises. Indeed the first Indians to work in the India Office may well have been Syed Husain Bilgrami and Krishna Govinda Gupta, who joined the apex of its governance, the Council of India, in 1907. As Council members they would have ordered British staff members, not vice versa. The domestic demographic context of India Office administrators' lives in England, therefore, did not encourage the type of racially based social levelling that, for instance, the servant status of African-Americans in the United States did. Nor did it serve to perpetuate assumptions of white superiority which occurred in the context of British India, where the servants were almost never of European descent. What the domestic experience of India Office administrators provided during their years of service in England, however, was the context of class hierarchy within their own ethnic group.

Into this context came the political beliefs of the administrators. Civil servants were supposed to be strictly neutral, and Godley confirmed this rule when he rejected a friendly proposal for an 'India Office Magazine' which would highlight the work and ideas of India Office administrators.[8] Yet it was impossible for them to ignore ideology completely. In fact, most India Office administrators had decided political views on Britain's occupation of India. Economic beliefs informed India Office administrators' views regarding class, and may also have sprung from them. Mallet was a proponent of Richard Cobden's classical liberal approach to free trade. Long before joining the India Office he had published pamphlets opposing government intervention in the economy and supporting the notion that self help was the surest way for people to raise themselves out of poverty. Mallet's successor, Godley, espoused similar views. Reflecting in 1917 on the political implications of serving as Gladstone's Private Secretary in the early 1880s he remarked: 'It will be borne in mind that the Liberal doctrines of that time, with their anti-socialist spirit and their strong insistence on the gospel of thrift, self-help, settlement of wages by the haggling of the market, and non-interference by the State, were not very different from those generally held by the Conservatives of the present day.'[9] Late in life Godley joined the Conservative party.

Complementing the common context of social hierarchy in which they lived were the shared educational experiences which set India Office administrators apart from the lower classes. All civil servants had attended university and passed exams to qualify them for their careers. Many members of the Council of India had attended Haileybury College, the training institute for East India Company administrators and had passed Indian Civil Service (ICS) exams. Both sets of exams emphasised a knowledge of the European classics, with ICS exams also expecting proficiency in an Indian language. The training of India Office administrators, therefore, emphasised the importance of antiquity and literate civilisation that applied generally to Britain's professional class. Most of the senior administrators of the India Office had also attended one of the elite public schools. These schools and the colleges of Oxford and Cambridge perpetuated friendships in professional life. For instance, as an alumnus of Rugby, Godley examined the son of the viceroy, Lord Cross, who was also an old Rugbeian. Another example arose in 1887, when Maine ran into trouble with Cambridge University over accepting a professorship of law there while retaining his seat on the Council of India, thus requiring his residence in Cambridge and London simultaneously. Fearing embarrassment over the issue he asked Godley, an alumnus of Cambridge, to 'act as a sort of arbitrator between him and the University'. Maine's death in 1888 spared Godley this unenviable role, but his appointment at Cambridge and his request of the Permanent Undersecretary demonstrate the close connections that India Office personnel maintained with educational institutions.[10]

With such high academic standards for entry into the civil services of Britain or India, it is hardly surprising that many India Office administrators were either scholars themselves or greatly admired the scholarly life. Godley won classics awards in his youth, and Sir Algernon West remarked that it was 'an insoluble problem indeed which his ever ripe scholarship cannot answer in a trice'.[11] Godley's love of the classics is evident in his casual notes to colleagues in the India Office.[12] Other members of the India Office were accomplished scholars in terms of publication and were considered some of the foremost specialists in Eastern cultures. In an age when the term 'orientalist' was an unambiguous compliment, the India Office claimed several of note. Among them was Maine, a highly regarded Cambridge law professor (1847–54), who as member of the viceroy's council (1862–69), applied his knowledge of British and Roman law to the Indian context. After returning to England he became a member of the Council of India (1871–88) and published *Village Communities in the East and West* (1880), which focused on the interaction of customary and statute law in the context of rural society in British and Indian history. As a member of the Political and the Judicial and Public Committees of the Council of India, Maine was in a position to influence decisions regarding Indians visiting Britain. A member of both committees during the years immediately following Maine's death was Sir Alfred Lyall, whose *Asiatic Studies: Religious and Social* (1882 and 1907) focused on the importance of religion in the organisation of Indian society. Joining Lyall on these committees was Sir John Strachey, the author of *India* (1888 and 1904), which commented on a whole range of issues pertaining to the British presence in India.[13]

Scholarship permeated these men's lives, and sometimes instilled in them a sincere appreciation of non-Western cultures. Sir Charles Lyall, secretary of the Judicial and Public Department, 1898–1910, and no relation to Alfred, was an Arabic specialist, who helped to found the University of London's School of Oriental and African Studies and took part in three congresses on world religions. In Lyall's obituary in the *Proceedings of the British Academy*, Reynold Nicholson remembered him reciting Arabic verse:

> I felt constrained to interrupt him with the lament that I could not understand a single word. But he would not stop! I was assured I should enjoy the marvellous beauty of the rhythm, and though I could not do so very much it was impressive to see and feel the genuine pleasure that the music of the cadences gave to him as he recited the long rolling lines.[14]

Given the training of the India Office's entire senior staff and the scholarly pursuits of many among them, it is little wonder that these men valued education so highly and, as later chapters will show, used it as one of their primary methods of determining social rank. Edward Said has shown how such 'orientalist' scholarship reinforced Western rule over much of Asia and Africa by highlighting the inferiority of these continents' cultures to Europe's. But while it often served to highlight differences between East and West, this scholarship also promoted the perception that Indian social ranks were analogous to those of Britain.

Indeed, Charles Lyall's academic interests may be regarded as a metaphor for the process that is the central focus of this book, for as a translator of Arabic poetry he was aware of the problems that one encounters in dealing with an unfamiliar language. In the preface to his *Translations of Ancient Arabian Poetry* (1890), he explained the reasons for his system of transliterating Arabic names:

> The language contains many sounds the right pronunciation of which is

> difficult for a European ... But neither can Arabic poetry be translated, nor stories about Arabs told, without the frequent use of Arabian names; and the only satisfactory course is to give them on a consistent system.[15]

Just as Lyall sought analogous letters in the Western alphabet that produced near equivalents of Arabic sounds in English, so he and his colleagues at the India Office sought analogous terms in English for ranks in Indian society that, they believed, described near equivalents in British society.

The men who ran the India Office lived in a society ranked by class. Their lives at work and home, their elite education, and the government's official recognition of their social rank all reinforced assumptions instilled early in life that class was the normal and appropriate way to divide a society. As the British Government's official experts on India, these men used class ranking as a way of ordering Indians in Britain. But in order to do so, they had to understand the complex hierarchical systems of Indian society. Given the intellectual hubris that often accompanied their orientalist knowledge, few in the India Office feared that they were unequal to the task.

India Office perceptions of Indian social hierarchies

The specifically orientalist education of many members of the India Office placed them in an unusually powerful position in British society to speak with authority on social rank in India and its meanings in British terms. Their published opinions provided guides for understanding Indian society to other India Office administrators and institutions in Britain. That these publications attempted to present Indian society in terms that were meaningful to British readers is significant for two reasons. On the one hand, they provided a means of controlling Indian society by categorising it in comprehensible terms. In many instances, these publications emphasised the difference between India and Europe and the inferiority of the former to the latter. On the other hand, by comparing aspects of Indian society to European counterparts, either past or present, they often implied a rough hierarchical equivalence between parallel social ranks in India and Britain. Complicating the India Office's transmission of knowledge to other institutions in the United Kingdom was the obvious disagreement among orientalist scholars who served it regarding the origins and behaviour of India's social ranks.

Nowhere were these aspects of official attitudes toward Indian society more apparent than regarding caste. Since the eighteenth century, orientalist scholars and British administrators (sometimes the same person) had based much of their understanding of Indian society on misleading information that they had received from Indian religious and social leaders. For instance, under the governor generalship (1774–85) of Warren Hastings, company administrators based many of their legal reforms on information supplied by *brahman* pundits and Muslim *ulema*, who purported to provide an accurate description of customary law. Similarly, Herbert Risley, the 1901 Indian census commissioner and later secretary of the India Office's Judicial and Public Department, consulted Indian community and religious leaders regarding their castes and occupations when preparing the ethnographic section of his report. Both processes arose from imperial pragmatism and intellectual curiosity. Orientalist scholars were fascinated with Indian culture and wanted to learn more about it for academic purposes. British authorities wanted such information to help them rule the subcontinent.

In both cases, however, the process presented a flawed image of Indian society, because it was the version told by groups at its apex, who had a vested interest in portraying social ranks and the laws that supported them as immutable. The opinions of pundits, clerics, princes, and local notables carried weight with British administrators, in part because the opinions of their equivalents in Britain would have borne similar authority, and in part because their rigid, static portrayal appealed to the desire of Britain's elite to see an ordered world that was easily comprehensible. Since, through the classics curriculum, British administrators had learned of the value of ancient authorities in Western society, they recognised the authorities of ancient texts as descriptions of Indian society. Thus British authorities often saw the Hindu scriptures' *varnashramadharma* (colour/caste ranking system) of *brahmans* (priests and teachers), *kshaitryas* (warriors and rulers), *vaishyas* (farmers and merchants), and *shudras* (labourers), along with outcastes or untouchables, as a description of contemporary Hindu society rather than simply an idealisation of ancient India. Within these four *varna* and the untouchables beneath them, British authorities also recognised *jati* (birth groups/subcastes), endogamous, geographically-localised groups that bore unique combinations of characteristics, such as forms and objects of worship, mores, dress, and diet. They also recognised the existence of smaller groups within *jati*, sometimes called *gotra*, which British scholarly literature often referred to as clans. Many British scholars and administrators treated these divisions as fundamental to Indian society, even though the interaction of *varna*, *jati*, and *gotra* varied considerably from one region to another and among different ethnic groups. For instance, the Rajputs might claim to be a *kshaitrya jati*. Yet most Rajput clans would not intermarry with other Rajput clans.

Nineteenth- and much of twentieth-century Western scholarship on Indian society has received considerable criticism over the last twenty years for portraying it as far more rigidly stratified than it actually was. Bernard Cohn, Nicholas Dirks, and Ronald Inden, among others, have shown how British administrative machinery, through its penchant for categorisation, made caste boundaries more fixed than they had been in earlier years.[16] Nevertheless, British administrators and scholars were aware of many of the complexities and fluidities of caste. They simply did not agree with one another on how to understand them as a whole. Some emphasised the differences between Indian and British societies, others the similarities. Often the same author wrote in terms of both.

India's caste system provided abundant opportunities to apply racial theories that were becoming ever more popular in the late nineteenth and early twentieth centuries. Such theories helped to justify British dominance of India by emphasising the presence of supposedly inferior Dravidians alongside the superior Aryans. In some cases the willingness of British scholars to acknowledge greater fluidity in Indian society only served to reinforce the perception that India's inhabitants were inferior to those of Britain. Thus Alfred Lyall observed, somewhat ambiguously, that 'we might make out roughly, in central India, a graduated social scale, starting from the simple aboriginal horde at the bottom, and culminating with the pure Aryan clan at the top; nor would it be difficult to show that all these classes are really connected, and have something of a common origin'.[17] Risley was more explicit and detailed, arguing that castes were manifestations of race, being relics of waves of conquest in which bands or armies of Aryan men, unaccompanied by their women, had produced children by the women of the conquered race. The result was 'the formation of a class of half-breeds ... who marry only among themselves and are to all intents and purposes a caste'.[18] Successive migrations of men from the resulting castes repeated this process, creating new castes ever less Aryan in composition. But, according to Risley, the resulting plethora of *jati* did not develop as *varna*. *Brahman* scholars borrowed the four-tiered system from Persia in order to fix their vaunted status. The *varna* system, therefore, had 'no foundation in fact, but is universally accepted in India'.[19] Risley's racialisation of the caste system has provided recent scholarship with evidence of the focus that British administrators placed on the differences between Indian and European societies. By portraying castes as radically different from European classes, Risley was able to argue that democracy was unsuitable for India, because combined with caste, it would create 'government by social ostracism', in which a caste's elders would pressure all its members to vote according to their wishes.[20]

Nevertheless, while such racial gradations of Indian society emphasised the differences between India and Britain, they were not devoid of analogous implications, since similar explanations were in vogue for differences in wealth, intelligence, and culture in the United Kingdom. As Marouf Hasian points out, these explanations sometimes manifested themselves in a concern that 'the birthrate of the higher classes was dwindling at the same time that the paupers and other unfit classes sprang up like "weeds"'.[21] So powerful was the belief that inferior hereditary elements might undermine the British nation that a clause providing for the 'feeble minded' to be taken into custody in order that 'they should be deprived of the opportunity of procreating children' only narrowly avoided inclusion in the Mental Deficiency Act of 1913, because a handful of Liberal Members of Parliament killed it in committee.[22] No less a political authority than Winston Churchill, as home secretary, supported the bill in its initial stages, because the 'multiplication of the unfit' presented 'a very terrible danger to the race'.[23]

Racial stereotypes were also common for the ethnic groups that constituted the United Kingdom. Sir Owen Tudor Burne, secretary of the Political and Secret Department (1874–76 and 1878–86) and member of the Council of India (1886–89), wrote of the Irish: 'They are the best fellows in the world when quiet, but, like others of the Celtic races, are savage and revengeful when roused by reckless agitators or stirred by fancied wrongs.'[24] As a result they were considered no more amenable to democratic institutions than were Indians. Although the India Office Records pertaining to Indian social rank contain remarkably few comparisons to Celts, such remarks were part of a British elite tendency to express the class and religious differences between England's elite and the Irish peasantry increasingly in terms of nation, conceived as race, in the late nineteenth century.[25]

Rather than treating racial explanations of Indian social hierarchy as setting it apart from Britain, it is therefore equally appropriate to regard them as an extension of British tendencies to racialise class and ethnicity, even among the indigenous inhabitants of the British Isles. Viewed from this perspective, class was not so much a rival hierarchy to that of race as an extension of it, and vice versa. Furthermore, to the extent that racial variation figured in administrators' understandings of Indian society, it encouraged them to distinguish strata in it rather than to level Indians uniformly at the bottom of British society. In this respect their sense of racial hierarchy did not compete with deeply held notions of class. Rather it reinforced them.

While British scholars often focused on caste, because it appeared to be unique to India, it would be inaccurate to assert, as does Thomas R. Metcalf, that 'Class, by contrast, which Victorian Englishmen regarded as the great divide in their own society, was nowhere to be found in

British accounts of India's peoples.'[26] On the contrary, class was implicit in much Victorian and Edwardian analysis of Indian society and explicit in attempts to explain many of its functions in terms comprehensible to the British public. Strachey used the term to describe people by their relationship to the land,[27] and the concept was apparent in the analogies that India Office scholar/administrators made between Indian and European societies, albeit backward in time. Alfred Lyall and Henry Maine regarded Indian society as a sociological fossil analogous to Europe's past, but they disagreed on which portion of the past it was. For Maine it was ancient and tribal, because the 'Village Community of India exhibits resemblances to the Teutonic Townships which are much too strong and numerous to be accidental'.[28] Unlike Risley, he regarded castes as equivalents of European phenomena: 'As a rule, every trade, every profession, every guild, every tribe, every class, is also a caste.'[29] Lyall's analogies were more contemporary. Discussing the social mobility of Indian tribes he declared:

> If a lower group multiplies and acquires wealth, it begins at once to ape the fashions of the group immediately above it, precisely after the manner of English society; if a family belonging to the higher groups has ill-luck, or shocks public opinion irredeemably, it subsides perforce and herds with its inferiors.[30]

Moreover, Lyall compared the fate of India's aristocracy under Muslim rule to that of France's under Louis XIV, lamenting in both cases the virtual extinction of its oldest noble lineages, but crediting 'the tradition of common ancestry' which 'has preserved among them the feeling which encourages a poor Rajpút yeoman to hold himself as good a *gentilhomme* as his Chief, and immeasurably superior to a high official of the professional class'.[31]

Although scholars serving the India Office regarded Teutonic society as primitive, they did not treat it with contempt. If anything they romanticised it as the predecessor of a great civilisation. In an intellectual climate where many regarded the societies of northern Europe and northern India to have sprung from the same Aryan roots, Lyall's and Maine's idealisations of the village community encompassed India. Although they portrayed Indian societies as timeless, such idealisations of its rural communities invited rankings of its social hierarchy in the terminology of Britain's. Thus Lyall could use the term 'yeoman' to describe a Rajput farmer, when, as we shall see below, the social and economic relationships that such a term implied were problematic in the Indian context. However, these comparisons made sense to the late nineteenth-century British elite, because, as Cannadine points out, 'the growing cult of the village in the imperial metropolis came to embody the very essence of "Englishness"'. They were, therefore, 'analogical sociology at work'.[32]

This tendency extended even to Risley, who described some aspects of Indian society in Western terms and provided analogies to European experience. His appendix to the 1901 Census exhibited a fascinating combination of racial and class discourse. It portrayed Rajputs in a Social Darwinian 'struggle for existence', but their failure to maintain dominance resulted from their rejection of 'book learning' rather than natural selection. Furthermore, Risley likened Rajput values, which place 'governing and bearing arms' above education, to those of a European 'medieval warrior'.[33] Like Lyall, he conjured up the image of genteel poverty for many Rajputs, an image familiar to Britain's elite, many of whose landowning members had suffered from the collapse of property prices in the 1870s. Equally important to such discursive analogies were those implicit in the brief translations of Indian tribes and castes that Risley provided at the heading of each section of his appendix on Indian sayings in his *People of India*. These descriptors were overwhelmingly occupational. Thus a Brahmin was a 'priest', a Rajput a 'warrior and landholder', a Baidya a 'physician', a Kayasth a 'clerk', and a Jat a 'Punjab cultivator'.[34] Such references tended to undermine his assertion elsewhere that 'the analogy between Indian caste and the trade guilds of medieval Europe ... is misleading', since, in practice, they provided a shorthand method which he employed in order to help British administrators understand Indian social groups.[35]

If caste and tribe could be understood, at least partly, in historical terms of British class, so could the land revenue system, for social differentiation in India did not rest solely on caste and tribe. Administrative and economic categories existed outside this hierarchy. For instance the Mughal Empire's revenue system relied on the services of local notables called *zamindars* (Persian for 'landholder') who collected money or goods in kind from groups of villages (each described collectively as a *pargana*) and passed a share on to a *taluqdar*, who in turn paid imperial administrators above him. Although in theory such offices were merit-based, in practice they continued to be hereditary, increasingly so after the collapse of Mughal rule. In fact these offices were never part of an imperial bureaucracy, as tax agents would be in a modern state. Rather the relationship of *zamindars* and *taluqdars* to one another and their superiors was transactional and based on personal alliances that Mughal officials had built with families that wielded considerable local influence.

Yet finding a precise, English definition or translation of the term '*zamindar*' is difficult for a number of reasons. First, before the rise of

Company Raj, India's revenue systems were not based on private ownership of property. Rather, *zamindars* had financial propriety over some of a *pargana*'s wealth as did the *ryots* (peasants) who tilled the land communally. Neither class had the right to sell or divide the land, and *zamindars* could not dispossess the peasants who farmed it. This arrangement did not preclude some sale of rights over land. But India's elite did not emphasise or develop concepts of private ownership. If anything their idealisation of the communal aspects of land usage obscured the reality of practices that often operated in a manner very similar to those of a property owner, such as a *zamindar* selling his right to use a well. By contrast Britain's elite extolled property ownership, which the philosopher John Locke had virtually sanctified as one of the three basic rights of existence. This too was an ideal which only imperfectly reflected the reality of mortgages, long-term leases, and eminent domain. Thus, the term '*zamindar*' was not easily translatable as 'landowner' or 'gentry', nor did *ryot* mean 'tenant', as some late eighteenth-century East India Company officials argued.

Second, although the Mughals employed the language of their revenue system wherever their sovereignty extended, its ad hoc and transactional nature allowed for great geographical variations. The idealised form of the system described above was most coherently established in Bengal, where, not coincidentally, the East India Company first began governing India as an empire. The system was not prominent in Rajputana, where the pre-eminence of warrior-lords precluded the security that *zamindars* needed. Nor did the system flourish in hill country where agriculture was more tenuous. In Punjab the Sikh Maharaja, Ranjit Singh, ended the power of the *zamindars* in the late eighteenth century. In some regions people claiming to be *zamindars* were often little more than prosperous peasants who tilled the soil themselves but did not share their wealth in a village community. On the other hand, in the south of India, where Mughal administration had either never reached or lasted only briefly, the term '*zamindar*' was virtually unknown.

Third, the financial status of *zamindars* and *ryots* changed under British rule, partly because of British land reforms and partly because of India's increasing integration into the global economy of the British Empire. Through these reforms British administrators attempted to reshape India's agrarian economy into the image of Britain's on the theory that the latter was more congenial to capitalism and more productive of wealth than the former. This process distanced the new landowners from the land. Unable to pay off their loans on their *parganas* some *zamindars* sold their property to Indian or European businessmen who had little interest in their tenants and focused instead on export crops for the imperial economy. In order to remain solvent, existing *zamindars* emulated these absentee landlords.

Yet although in the past scholars have made much of these reforms, more recently they have come to question whether their form may have exceeded their substance. Even the most ambitious reforms, such as those of Lord Cornwallis in Bengal at the end of the eighteenth century and Thomas Munro in the Madras Presidency at the beginning of the nineteenth century, turn out in practice to have been more negotiations with local magnates than sweeping implementations of Britain's economic and social hierarchy. Nevertheless, the British Raj was far less forgiving of financial insolvency than its Indian predecessors had been. It auctioned off many *zamindars'* rights to land revenues, often held in their families for many generations, simply because they were temporarily unable to pay the taxes assessed on their property. Such circumstances arose often due to droughts and poor harvests. Whereas Indian rulers responded to such misfortunes frequently through temporary reductions of revenues assessed on particular properties, the Raj maintained a remorseless consistency in its levies, which it used in part to fund irrigation projects that opened up arable land, albeit primarily for export rather than subsistence crops. The Indian response to famine had been a renegotiation of social obligations. The British response was a reliance on technology.[36]

India Office administrators recognised many of these nuances and, occasionally, the negative impact of the Raj's failure to appreciate them. For instance, regarding the use of English landowning categories as translations of Indian terms, Strachey wrote:

> Such terms as 'property in land', 'proprietor', and 'tenant', have to be used in default of others more appropriate; but since private proprietorship in land has hardly existed in India in the form in which it exists in England, misconception easily arises. It has happened not unfrequently that English ideas of property, derived from a different condition of things, have exercised a pernicious influence on the interests of the actual occupants of the land.[37]

Indeed the debate over land reform in India and its implications for social hierarchy cut across the India Office in the late nineteenth century, as strongly held beliefs about the political and economic behaviour of the elite toward the poor in Britain spilled over into differences of opinion about how to deal with poverty in India. Like many members of the Indian Government and the India Office, Major General Richard Strachey, a Council of India member (1875–79), supported major government engineering projects in India supposedly designed to reduce poverty. By contrast, Mallet objected to such 'feverish impatience to cover India with railroads and waterworks'. As to the reasons for Indian poverty, Mallet argued that it was 'certainly not from the want of food or of public works, these are the effect and not the cause of poverty'. The underlying problem was India's land system, so 'he who first recognises and introduces the great principle of private property in the soil will be the founder of an institution which will give a new force to Indian civilisation'.[38] Of course, unlike Indian nationalists such as Dadabhai Naoroji, both the supporters of 'state landlordism' and those of private enterprise agreed that India's problems were home grown. Few in the India Office suggested, as did John Strachey, that they might result from the economic distortions of British imperialism. The circumstances of their lives only reinforced these administrators' established view of Indian social stratification and its underlying causes.

The body of knowledge about Indian society that influenced the India Office and, through it, other institutions, was varied and inconsistent. It presented Indian social rankings at once as alien and yet roughly translatable into British equivalents, static yet fluid, racial yet economic. The imperial context of India Office administrators' world views meant that, no matter what they were, they rarely questioned the need for Britain's occupation of India. Yet at the same time, this body of scholarship provided the basis for institutions in the United Kingdom to assess the background of Indians whom they encountered by seeking British analogies to their ranks in India. They were encouraged to do so, not only by the India Office, but by Indians in Britain who operated outside the government, for the community of educated Indians living in Britain had much to say about their origins. If the India Office was ready to speak with authority on Indians in Britain, so were they.

Notes

1 Harold Perkin, *The Rise of Professional Society: England Since 1800* (London and New York: Routledge, 1989), xii.

2 Arnold Kaminsky, *The India Office,1880–1910* (Westport, CT: Greenwood Press, 1986), 26. This discussion draws on chapter 1 of Kaminsky. I am also indebted to Dr Kaminsky for the advice he provided regarding the India Office administration.

3 Kaminsky, *India Office*, 15–16.

4 Quoted in Kaminsky, *India Office*, 6. For the permanent undersecretaries' control of the purse, see Lord Kilbracken, *Reminiscences of Lord Kilbracken* (London: Macmillan, 1931), 191.

5 For the Permanent Undersecretary's powers as plenipotentiary Secretary of State, see Kilbracken, *Reminiscences*, 174–6.

6 Census data for 1881 comes from the *1881 British Census and National Index: England, Scotland, Wales, Channel Islands, Isle of Man, and Royal Navy*, CD-ROM set (Salt Lake City: Church of Jesus Christ of Latter Day Saints, 1999). The Public Record Office references for each entry respectively are Godley, RG11/145 f. 76, p. 21; Macpherson, RG11/15 f. 122, p. 28; Thompson, RG11/162 f. 60, p. 9; and

Williams, RG11/72 f. 13, p. 19. The 1901 census data is from the United Kingdom National Archives website at www.1901census.nationalarchives.gov.uk. Reference numbers for respective census entries are: Campbell, RG 13/84 f. 156, p. 24; Hutchins RG 13/38 f. 152, p. 2.; Lyall, RG 13/19 f. 58, p. 53; Ritchie, RG 1313/77 f. 196, pp. 514–5; and Walpole, RG 13/22 f. 96, p. 19.

7 Kaminsky, *India Office*, 20–1; and Mrinalini Sinha, 'Britishness, clubbability, and the colonial public sphere', in Tony Ballantyne and Antoinette Burton (eds), *Bodies in Contact: Rethinking Colonial Encounters in World History* (Durham, NC: Duke University Press, 2005), 186.

8 British Library, London – Asia, Pacific, and Africa Collections – India Office Records (hereafter IOR) MSS Eur F 102/2, Arthur Godley to A. F. T. Campbell, 9 January 1903, fos. 78–9. Citations from the India Office Records are under Crown copyright.

9 Kilbracken, *Reminiscences*, 83. For Mallet's views, see Bernard Mallet, *Sir Louis Mallet: A Record of Public Service and Political Ideals* (London: James Nisbet and Co., 1905), ch. 1.

10 Kilbracken, *Reminiscences*, 162–3, 173.

11 H. G. Hutchinson (ed.), *Private Diaries of the Rt. Hon. Sir Algernon West, G. C. B.* (London: John Murray, 1922), 133. See also the Earl of Oxford and Asquith, *Memories and Reflections, 1852–1927* (London: Cassell and Co., 1928), II, 202 regarding Godley's classical knowledge.

12 See for instance his handwritten note to Ritchie regarding Tim Evans' *Life of Tacitus*, IOR MSS Eur C 342, 23 February 1894.

13 Sir Henry Sumner Maine, *Village-Communities in the East and West: Six Lectures Delivered at Oxford to Which Are Added Other Lectures Addresses and Essays* (New York: Henry Holt and Company, 1880); Sir Alfred C. Lyall, *Asiatic Studies: Religious and Social*, (London: John Murray, 1907) 1st and 2nd series; and Sir John Strachey, *India* (London: Kegan Paul, Trench, Trübner and Co., 1894).

14 Reynold A. Nicholson, *Sir C. J. Lyall, 1845–1920* (London: Oxford University Press, n. d.), 1. This pamphlet was taken from vol. 9 of the *Proceedings of the British Academy* and published later in the form quoted here.

15 Charles James Lyall, *Translations of Ancient Arabian Poetry: Chiefly Præ-Islamic*. Reprint (New York: Columbia University Press, 1930), viii.

16 See Bernard Cohn, 'The census, social structure and objectification in South Asia', in *An Anthropologist Among the Historians and Other Essays* (Delhi: Oxford University Press, 1987), 224–54; Nicholas Dirks, 'The invention of caste', *Social Analysis*, 25 (1989): 42–52; and Ronald Inden, 'Orientalist constructions of India', *Modern Asian Studies*, 20:3 (1986): 401–46. By contrast see Susan Bayly, *Caste, Society and Politics in India from the Eighteenth Century to the Modern Age* (Cambridge: Cambridge University Press, 1999), upon which I base much of my description of caste structure and colonial views thereof.

17 Lyall, *Asiatic Studies*, 1st series, 176.

18 Herbert Hope Risley, *The People of India*, 2nd edn (1915; reprint, Delhi: Oriental Books Reprint Corporation, 1969), 273.

19 *Ibid.*, 277.

20 *Ibid.*, 286.

21 Marouf Arif Hasian, *The Rhetoric of Eugenics in Anglo-American Thought* (Athens, GA: University of Georgia Press, 1996), 75.

22 Quoted in G. R. Searle, *Eugenics and Politics in Britain, 1900–1914* (London: Noordhoff International Publishing, 1976), 110. *Hansard*, 5th series (Commons), 41, col. 710, 19 July 1912.

23 Churchill to Asquith, December 1910, quoted in Searle, *Eugenics and Politics*, 107.

24 Sir Owen Tudor Burne, *Memories* (London: Edward Arnold, 1907), 74.

25 See Ed Lengel, 'A "perverse and ill-fated people": English perceptions of the Irish, 1845–52', *Essays in History* 38 (1996): http://etext.virginia.edu/journals/EH/EH38/Lengel.html: 7–8.

26 Metcalf, *Ideologies of the Raj* (Cambridge: Cambridge University Press, 1995), 114.

27 Strachey, *India*, 266.

28 Maine, *Village-Communities*, 12.
29 Quoted in Strachey, *India*, 232–3.
30 Lyall, *Asiatic Studies*, 1st series, 176–7.
31 *Ibid.*, 248.
32 Cannadine, *Ornamentalism*, 43.
33 Risley, *Census of India*, Vol. 1, *Ethnographic Appendices: Being the Data Upon Which the Caste Chapter of the Report is Based* (Calcutta: Office of the Superintendent of Government Printing, India, 1903), 83–4.
34 Risley, *People of India*, 305–33.
35 *Ibid.*, 270.
36 Which did not work. See Ranajit Guha, *A Rule of Property for Bengal: An Essay on the Idea of Permanent Settlement* (Durham, NC: Duke University Press, 1996); P. J. Marshall, *Bengal: The British Bridgehead: Eastern India, 1740–1828* (Cambridge: Cambridge University Press, 1987), 137–79; Thomas R. Metcalf, *Land, Landlords, and the British Raj: Northern India in the Nineteenth Century* (Berkeley and Los Angeles: University of California Press, 1978) for the effects of such economic and social experiments. For the British response, or lack thereof, to the famines that often resulted, see Mike Davis, *Late Victorian Holocausts: El Niño Famines and the Making of the Third World* (London: Verso, 2001), 25–59.
37 Strachey, *India*, 264.
38 Mallet, *Sir Louis Mallet*, 120–1 and 118–19.

CHAPTER THREE

The National Indian Association

Among non-governmental organisations whose major purpose was the reception of Indians in Britain, perhaps the most important were the Strangers' Home for Asiatics, Africans, and South Sea Islanders, and the National Indian Association (NIA). The former provided temporary accommodation for sailors and destitutes respectively and is a focus of the next chapter. The latter served as an important forum for social interaction among Britons and Indians claiming membership in polite society.

Goals and roles

The NIA was important because it pursued goals and served functions that were acceptable to both the Imperial Government and its critics. It provided venues for wealthy Indians and Britons interested in India to mix socially and discuss topics related to the subcontinent. Not only were its members well educated, many being students in British universities, but they were in many cases prominent orientalist scholars and members of the British administration of India. The NIA's 1880 membership list, for instance, boasted the Viceroy and his two predecessors, one former, four current, and two future members of the India Office's Council of India, the political *aide-de-camp* to the Secretary of State for India, two Sanskrit professors resident in England, and several Indian princes.[1] Many were also members of the East India Association (EIA) and the Northbrook Society, which also sought to provide venues for Britons and Indians to meet socially and discuss Indian issues. Little wonder, therefore, that the India Office worked so closely with these organisations to meet the needs of Indians visiting the United Kingdom and monitor their activities. Although the EIA, NIA, and Northbrook Society were independent of the government, they constituted officially approved venues for Indian activity in Britain. As such their public statements often repeated the assumptions of orientalist administrators whom Indians frequently encountered in Britain. Yet, unlike the India Office and institutions that catered to poorer members of Britain's South Asian community, these organisations provided a public voice for Indians either to confirm or dispute the statements of Britain's elite.

Their effectiveness, however, depended on their ability to maintain legitimacy simultaneously in the eyes of Indians and British authorities. When the balance shifted far enough in one direction or the other for an organisation to lose legitimacy in the eyes of either group, its use as a venue for dialogue between rulers and ruled diminished seriously. For instance, British authorities never consulted such obviously dissident organisations as the British committee of the Indian National Congress, created in 1889; or India House, established in 1905. Indeed the association of the assassin of the India Office student adviser, Sir W. H. Curzon-Wyllie, with the latter enabled British authorities to close it in 1909. While the Indian National Congress's voice became impossible to ignore after the First World War, these organisations exerted little influence on British understanding of the United Kingdom's Indian community, because Indian Government and India Office administrators held them in contempt. On the other hand, the EIA and the Northbrook Society became too closely associated with British authorities to command the respect of an increasingly radical Indian intellectual community in Britain. The Indian nationalist, Dadabhai Naoroji, played a major role in the formation of the former in 1866, and as late as 1883 the socialist, H. M. Hyndman, argued that British rule was 'positively injurious to India', and that the British 'ought to think how we can best retire from the country'.[2] Nevertheless, by this time the EIA was already well on its way to becoming what Rozina Visram describes as 'an Anglo-Indian debating society'.[3] Over the next quarter of a century its tone became so conservative and imperialist that in 1910 a group of fifty-nine self-described 'members of the British Indian community resident in Great Britain' submitted a petition to the Secretary of State for India objecting to the India Office's proposal to have it participate with the Northbrook Society and the NIA in the governance of a centre for Indians in London.[4] Regarding the Northbrook Society, which the former viceroy of the same name had founded in 1880, initially as a 'gentlemen's' reading room associated with the NIA, the petitioners claimed that 'Its constitution shows a distrust of members, as they are given no voice or votes in its affairs.'[5]

Significantly, the NIA, founded in 1870 by the social reformers Mary Carpenter and Keshub Chunder Sen, was fully acceptable to these petitioners. The NIA's vitality lay in its journal, to which Indians and Britons contributed, and which, Antoinette Burton points out, 'served as a public space where Indian men and occasionally Indian women could speak to, engage with, and in many cases contest the interpretations of Indian society and culture that apparently well-meaning English reformers offered as unalterably true'.[6] First published in January 1871, *The Journal of the National Indian Association* (*JNIA*) changed names twice, to *The Indian Magazine* (*IM*) in 1886 and *The Indian Magazine and Review* (*IMR*) in 1891. Under all three titles it reflected the goals of its parent organisation.

From its very inception the cultural paternalism of the organisation was clear. 'Hindus', a term including Indians of all beliefs, were 'fellow subjects', but they needed 'enlightenment and improvement' that only contact with Western civilisation could provide. The achievement of this goal required the British 'to cooperate with enlightened natives'. In order to do so, however, the 'wants of enlightened natives must be known'.[7] This paternalism applied to another major focus of the NIA, to 'promote friendly intercourse with Native gentlemen now in England, and to introduce them to a knowledge of such institutions in our country as may benefit theirs'. Indians residing in Britain could be voted honorary members and 'English and Native gentlemen and ladies resident in India' were invited to become 'correspondents'.[8] In practice Indian correspondents in India had often, at some time in the past, resided in the United Kingdom. The NIA and its journal were, therefore, particularly important venues for encounters between Indians and Britons in the United Kingdom, because they served as forums in which Indians in Britain could negotiate their own social ranks and those of their fellow expatriates.

The correspondence and social contacts between Britons and Indians in these organisations implied terms of negotiation which involved two acts of recognition. On the one hand, Indians in Britain had to concede the superiority of Britain's culture to India's, although they could limit the aspects of Indian culture to which such concessions applied. On the other hand, Britain's elite had to accord Indian correspondents and members ranks within British society, and the privileges that accompanied them, although they could limit their approval of such privileges in certain exceptional situations, the most important of which involved interethnic sexual relations, to be examined in a later chapter. Class distinctions existed among these organisations in the very relationship which they bore to one another. Burton notes this relationship when she observes that the NIA occupied 'the middle ground between the West End Clubs', such as the Northbrook Society, which catered to some of the wealthiest Indian visitors to London, 'and the East End docks', which was the location of the Strangers' Home.[9] As in British society generally, the higher an Indian's rank in the British social system, the more of a voice he or she had in determining the structure of that system. To most members of the NIA, the inmates of the Strangers' Home had no such voice, although the next chapter will argue that the reality was otherwise. By contrast the *JNIA* and its successors labelled Indian correspondents and members of the association repeatedly as 'native gentlemen'. It was to such 'gentlemen', and the occasional 'lady', that Britain's elite looked to affirm its knowledge of Indian society.

Since the assumption of British cultural superiority underlay the NIA, discussion of Indian social hierarchy revolved around ways in which it was an obstacle to India's progress and the methods by which India's elite, with the help of Britain's, could effect social reform. The two aspects of India's social structure that received the most discussion and criticism were caste distinction and the seclusion of women, because many Indian and British reformers believed that they were inherently unjust and discouraged education and innovation. The ways in which they received criticism, however, implied the presence of equivalent and more acceptable social divisions that could replace them, those of class distinction and the appropriate separation of spheres between the sexes. Both were quintessential British Victorian distinctions, yet members of these organisations often assumed that the basis for such hierarchical relationships existed in their inferior Indian equivalents and could be applied to Indians living in Britain, where the context of caste and female seclusion did not predominate.

Perceptions of hierarchy in the NIA

Orientalist scholars employed by the India Office would have found much to agree with in discussions and articles that appeared in the *JNIA* and its successors. Much of the discourse focused on attempts to understand caste in terms analogous to Western experience. Although most writers or discussants assumed that caste was unique to India, they rejected the notion that it was something *sui generis* that could not be understood in terms of the development of social ranking in Western experience. The discussion surrounding caste focused on whether it was a manifestation of racial, religious, or class distinctions. The argument for its functioning in racial terms often came from scholars who regarded human interaction as inherently competitive and regarded some races (inevitably including their own) as superior to others.

Nowhere was such analysis more popular than in theories regarding the origins of caste. In 1878, for instance, Pramatha Nath Bose described the origins of caste in terms that Risley would echo a generation later. Like Risley, Bose thought caste represented successive layers of miscegenation between 'the fair (Aryans) and the black (Dasyuite, or

Dasā)', which the author also labelled 'Turanian'. The superiority of the former to the latter accounted for the dominance of the current upper caste, because, 'The numerical superiority of the Āryas was probably vastly inferior to that of the Turanians, but the intellectual and moral superiority of the former was in almost inverse ratio.'[10] If castes reflected their racial origins, they also provided the rough equivalents of a class system which modern India inherited from its ancient predecessor. Thus the 'higher classes, the original Āryas, or, as they now style themselves, *Dvijas* (twice-born), especially the Brahmans and Kshatriyas, became rich at the expense of the poor Sūdras'.[11] Some of the twice-born, however, maintained their Aryan purity better than others, and caste system reflected this development:

> The intermarriage of the Brahmans, Kshatriyas, and the Vaisyas amongst themselves, and with the Sudras, resulted in a number of mixed castes. In this intermixture of Aryan and Turanian blood, the Kshatriyas and the Vaisyas came gradually to be confounded, as it were, with some of the impure castes. Besides, they and especially the Vaisyas, intermarried more freely with the lower castes than the Brahmans. Thus the prestige and purity of the second and third castes were gradually all but lost.[12]

Bose helpfully provided a chart illustrating the results of such intermarriage by cross-referencing different combinations of *varna* between parents and showing the offsprings' resulting castes with their requisite occupations. These varied according to the gender of the parent involved and stigmatised severely the children of women who married below their caste. Thus the offspring of a *brahman* man and a *shudra* woman was a 'Nishāda', whose occupation was that of fisherman, but the offspring of a *shudra* man and a *brahman* woman, was a 'Chandāla (the lowest caste)'. As a result of this process, by the reign of the Mughal emperor, Akbar (1556–1605), 'no true Kshatriyas were to be found. The Vaisyas are now all but extinct. The *brahmans* alone succeeded in preserving the purity of their blood to any considerable extent. They inherited the whole of the sacred literature of the Āryas, as well as the traditions of Aryan learning and Aryan wisdom.'[13] The certitude with which Bose described India's caste rankings exceeded that of India Office orientalists, but it also ascribed to one group of Indians a racial identity on a par with Europeans.

Bose's account of caste was, in many respects, non-judgemental of the system itself. As a scholar who accepted racial hierarchy he saw it as the result of miscegenation, which he appeared to condemn through his assertions of Aryan racial superiority and the purity of the *brahman* caste. Yet, given that miscegenation had presumably occurred, Bose implied that the resulting social stratification was inevitable and proper. This attempt to recruit European racial science to maintain the social elevation of upper-caste Indians was not just a ploy of sycophants of imperialism. The British Committee of the Indian National Congress (BCINC) used similar reasoning when it called for an extension of full citizenship rights in South Africa to Indians, but not Africans. Naoroji's assertion that 'Indians were not a race of savages' implied that some ethnic groups were, and the BCINC's contrast between 'ignorant and lawless Kaffirs' and 'educated and highly civilised Indians' underscored the willingness of India's elite in Britain to participate in the discourse of racial hierarchy, even to the detriment of other non-Europeans.[14] Such arguments, however, were dangerous, because, having conceded the existence of a racial hierarchy, they relied on persuading Britain's elite that their authors resided at its apex. These Indians knew that, as long as Britain ruled India, racial ranking would be used more often to assert the former's superiority to the latter than the equality of the two. Some Indians in Britain, therefore, regarded racial distinctions as an evil, and inasmuch as caste resembled race, they regarded it as evil too. Aziz Ahmed implied as much to an NIA meeting, when he explained that he 'had travelled much in America, and thought that nowhere was caste so strong as in that country'.[15]

Indeed many Indian members of the NIA and EIA were more critical of caste than were their British colleagues precisely because they thought it differed markedly from class. This sentiment was apparent in responses to the attempt of Robert Needham Cust, a former administrator of British India and current scholar of oriental languages and religions, to treat the two forms of social hierarchy on a par in a paper he presented to the NIA. Most Indians in the audience, particularly those of Muslim and Parsi heritage, sought to distance themselves from this aspect of Indian society by pointing out that it was peculiar to Hinduism. No Indian voice came to the defence of caste, and several condemned it. Although an evangelical Christian and Church Missionary Society (CMS) activist, Cust concluded with a culturally relative, if somewhat condescending, approach to how to deal with caste:

> I recognise the existence in different nations of an infinite variety of family customs, habits and tendencies, and, where they are prejudicial to the better interests of the human race, the work of amelioration may be left to time, education, intercourse with other nations, and general intellectual development.[16]

To this Krishna Nath Mittra objected that caste was 'the greatest of all

Indian evils', and that 'the government should legislate for its extirpation'.[17] In a written response the following month, Syed Hassan declared that although caste shared the same origins as class, 'caste distinction, as it now exists is essentially different from the distinction of *class* observed in all countries'. In this regard, he believed, the English class hierarchy was vastly superior to India's caste system. Hassan acknowledged that the 'portals of English aristocracy are, socially speaking firmly and hopelessly closed against a man who honestly earns his bread by the *work of his hands*', but he went on to argue in contradiction, that 'Merit and education can make a Mr. A. a Lord Alpha, or Mr. B. an Earl of Beta. On the other hand, a gentleman who neglects the education of his son may find him employed in working a mill.'[18] If an individual's class membership was mobile, it was education that provided the fuel for the mobility. The centrality of education in the negotiation of class rank among Indians in Britain is a theme that we will explore later.

Yet British and Indian commentators alike recognised that class divisions already existed in India, because they so often described the upper castes of India in the terminology of Britain's upper classes. This was particularly conspicuous in discussions regarding *brahmans*, around whom existed an aura of respectability. For Cust 'A gentleman is a gentleman, and the long hereditary culture of the Brahmins has told upon their appearance and manners'.[19] Certainly the *JNIA* advertised *brahmans* as the equivalent of English gentlemen. For example, it praised Krishanara Gopal Deshmukh on being called to the English bar by reminding readers, not only of the gentlemanly credentials that his achievement bestowed, but also of the elite family from which he came: 'This gentleman is perhaps the first high caste Marathi Brahmin from that part of India who has obtained this distinction. The family to which he belongs, the Deshmukhs, originally from Poona, has held a distinguished position in various parts of the Presidency; as many as six judges being found among them.'[20] In this case British education, which had presumably been an essential component in establishing the judges' careers, confirmed the rightful position of a man who already held high social standing by virtue of his caste.

JNIA editors were similarly impressed by the arrival of Sasipada Banerjee and his wife, 'the first Hindu Brahmin lady who has crossed the ocean and trodden on British ground'.[21] Since the couple were social reformers, the journal reported on aspects of their stay in Britain, including the birth of their son, 'the first Brahmin subject of her Majesty Queen Victoria born on British ground', whom the couple named 'Albion, in commemoration of the event'.[22] The mystique surrounding *brahmans* only enhanced the sense of respect that the journal's editors regarded as the couple's due. Sasipada Banerjee's preparations for the journey to England highlighted the *varna*'s quasi-religious qualities by including a 'long-course of self-denying and devoted effort for the improvement of his town's-people'.[23] Such behaviour combined the *brahman* mystique of exotic otherworldliness with the respectability, more recognisable in British society, of *noblesse oblige*. Taboos discouraging upper-caste Hindus from leaving the Indian subcontinent only enhanced the aura of social superiority, by reminding people in Britain that to some segments of Indian society, the apex of imperial power was ritually polluting. So serious an issue were these taboos that the *IMR* repeated a suggestion raised in a letter to the editor of *The Times* that 'a "hall" should be started by wealthy merchants in London or Manchester, at which "Hindu travellers could put up". In that building all the arrangements would be such as to enable its inmates to keep their caste in the matter of food.'[24]

The *brahman* mystique complemented another facet of social analysis well: the cult of the village that Maine and Lyall were so instrumental in expanding from an English to an Indian setting. Indeed the model existed within the pages of the *JNIA*, because occasionally it held an article that extolled the simple, and quasi-medieval, life of the English village in which, for instance, the baker kept credit accounts 'by means of chalk lines or similar primitive devices', which harkened back to a system used in 'the early days of the English Exchequer'.[25] In the competition for rural quaintness, however, Indian villages were not to be outdone. 'Nothing is more dear, more congenial to the heart than the native charms, the verdure of the fields, the beautiful prospect of the distant hills, the abundant vegetation all around, and the cool shades of the noble trees', wrote N. J. Ratnagar rhapsodically of Indian village life. If 'even in the midst of poverty' an Indian village could be described in bucolic terms different from, yet equivalent to, that of its British counterpart, so could its leader, 'the Patel', whom Ratnagar claimed was 'like a member of Parliament who stands for a constituency'.[26] Significantly, Ratnagar assigned a caste, the *brahman*s, to his upper class, because in village India, 'there are two distinct classes – the Brahmins and those who are not Brahmins'.[27]

From the pen of Indians this emphasis on the rural, the traditional, and the ancient could serve to remind the readers of the greatness of Indian civilisation. Thus the Corpus Christi, Cambridge student, S. Satthianadhan, acknowledged the benefits of British rule but concluded that it was India's due, because the West's 'religion, her science, her philosophy, her art, all come from the sunny lands of Asia, and it is now time that the West should give at least something back to her from whom she has received so much'.[28] Cecil Bendall, professor of Sanskrit at Cambridge University, acknowledged the effectiveness of such an approach when he declared that 'it is impossible for anyone who knows anything of Sanskrit to feel contempt for the Hindu even in his present condition, humiliated though he has been by long centuries of intolerance and tyranny', a statement duly reported in the *IMR*.[29] Indeed, educated Indians referred so often to the glories of their past, often noting their individual racial and caste pedigree, that one British writer complained that: 'It is utterly useless for a native to tell us that he is an Aryan and his forefathers were civilized when ours wore blue paint.'[30]

Yet, if anything, this emphasis on the ancient, which Indians used in an attempt to establish credentials of racial and cultural equality with their condescending British rulers, further encouraged the understanding of India's social hierarchy in terms of Europe's past. This focus on the past and village India led British contributors to distinguish between peasants and gentry, and thus to discuss a class system that was analogous at least to pre-industrial, if not contemporary, Britain. J. B. Phear, wrote of the 'everyday life of a Bengali village proprietor', and contrasted it to 'life in a cultivator's family' which was 'of course very different from that of the bhadralog [Bengali for 'gentle people'] just described'.[31] There was little doubt that the former had the natural right of authority over the latter, because the relation between the *ryots* 'and the zamindar is eminently feudal in its character. He is their superior lord, and they are his subjects (ryots) – both by habit and by feeling "adscripti glebœ" [tied to the land]'.[32] Even when it focused on commercial and industrial aspects of India, the *JNIA* often treated the upper castes as managerial and professional classes. Its frequent coverage of reforms in prisons and factories, and education among the working class, often depicted these efforts as the work of British administrators and reformers, but when the effort was an Indian one, it drew sharp distinctions between classes. While railing against the 'tyranny of caste', one article nevertheless praised 'a high caste Brahmin gentleman' for organising a 'pleasure excursion of working men', the implication being that the *brahman* had behaved in a manner uncharacteristic of caste rigidity but characteristic of class-based *noblesse oblige*.[33]

Of course, such descriptions often portrayed India as a static society, and this tendency became a topic of discussion in the NIA long before scholars of the last few decades criticised orientalists for fostering such assumptions. Speaking to fellow members of the NIA in 1905, Yusef Ali, the ICS officer who later translated the Quran into English, criticised Maine's portrayal of Indian village society as 'an archaic system' that 'showed in its primitive structure a stage of human development which the Indo-Europeans had left far behind'. By contrast, he argued: 'We can trace the continuous growth of modern from ancient forms, and within the last few years there has been a complete remodelling of many of the old village customs and institutions, which have got stereotyped in the imagination of persons who have made the "unchanging East" their fetish.'[34] Yet Ali's portrayal of contemporary village life focused on occupational hierarchy, particularly as it applied to the political structure of society. He drew extensively on analogous occupations in British society to describe those of the Indian village. The *chaukidar* was watchman, policeman, and (although usually illiterate) registrar rolled into one. The accountant by contrast was 'an educated man' whose rank was usually reflected by his caste as 'a Brahmin or Kayasth'. Higher than either of these, however, was the 'Lambardar', who 'represents the more comfortable classes in the village and of course belongs to the land-owning class'.[35] Whether or not members of the NIA regarded Indian society as static, therefore, they certainly perceived it as divided according to class, which they often saw as identical to caste.

The most interesting aspect of the *JNIA*'s coverage of caste and class is the assumption that class distinction was 'ordinary', as Hassan put it, and therefore the acceptable register of social discourse.[36] When writers or discussants claimed that caste was similar to class, it was to argue that the former was not the social curse that most in the Indo-British and Anglo-Indian communities believed it to be. When they contrasted it to class, it was to imply that the latter was the ideal form of social hierarchy, to which Indians should adapt the former. Only rarely did anyone condemn class, as did Raja Ram Pal Singh when he 'considered that caste exists just as much in England, only that it is called *class*'. The major difference was 'that India was more free from caste than England'.[37] But the raja's remark was the exception that illustrated the rule. Class was the discourse through which Indians in Britain could aspire to acceptance on a par with their British counterparts. Although the supposed Aryan heritage of many Indians could serve to equate them to Europeans on a racial basis, it was a much more dangerous approach to follow. As we shall see, most Indians preferred to assert their class status in the context of Victorian and Edwardian Britain. Of course, Indians did not use the discourse of the class system in order to occupy its lower ranks. But in order to advance in British society, they had to adopt behaviour commensurate with the class rank that they sought.

Womanhood and polite society

Central to such behaviour was the role of women in helping to define the polite society of the middle and upper classes. British critics of Indian culture often drew attention to what they regarded as the feminine features of Indian society. Their attempts to emasculate Indian males figuratively in a world where women were considered unfit to rule further justified Britain's occupation of the subcontinent and has been the subject of considerable analysis. Some India Office administrators fitted the 'manly English' mould very well, having hunted tigers or fought battles.[38]

Nevertheless, the tendency to emasculate Indian culture did not diminish the civilising value that Britain's elite placed on supposedly feminine virtues. Many of its members argued that the reluctance of Indian men to allow their women to mingle in mixed company, as did their European counterparts, was a major obstacle to social interactions between Indian and British families and thus to upper- and middle-class Indians receiving recognition of their proper rank in British society. Indian men's treatment of women formed a core trait of what modern scholars might describe as their Britishness and masculinity. Discussing the lack of social interaction between ruler and ruled in India, James J. Wilson told the NIA: 'So long . . . as this idea of restraint on women prevails in India, free social intercourse is not within the practical range of present realisation'.[39] Although most educated Indian men in Britain had left their wives at home, many of them supported the NIA's emphasis on the education of Indian women and the loosening of purdah restrictions. K. G. Deshmukh, a *brahman* law student in Britain and son of an Ahmedabad judge, argued that India's future depended on its embracing of the Victorian cult of female domesticity. Indian universities were 'sending forth' men who were 'as educated as their brother graduates in the West',

> but until the wives and the sisters of these educated natives of India are also educated, and are thus rendered fit companions to them throughout life, sympathising and sustaining them in all their laudable efforts for the reform and the regeneration of that vast country, helping them and rallying them by their gentle influence, training up and preparing the infant mind, when it is by reason of its tender age beyond the reach of the schoolmaster, – till this is accomplished half the force of their energy and the result of their endeavours is lost.[40]

The solution was the education of women and the ending of female seclusion and arranged marriages. To R. Mittra the last of these social ills was 'monstrous' but not an essential feature of Indian society, since it occurred because 'social customs of the Hindus' had 'really been degenerating' since ancient times when 'women selected their partners and the parents only aided them with their advice'.[41] These papers expressed the NIA's tone from its very inception regarding the role of women in the reform of India. Its first annual report listed the 'education and improvement of women' as one of the four immediate 'wants of India'.[42] Almost every issue contained an article describing the plight of women in India or calling for attention to their education, and Carpenter established a 'ladies' sewing party' in connection with the association's Bristol branch, in order to receive information 'respecting the progress of female education in that country'.[43]

The *JNIA* thus served as one of the voices that used the subjugation of women in India as, to quote Burton, 'a useful explanatory device for Britain's imperial presence ... and a rationale for Britain's civilizing mission'.[44] But in doing so, it also connected the fate of women inextricably with the class aspirations of educated Indians. One contributor, identified only as J. E. C., claimed that, because 'women give the tone to society, ... society, in the narrower sense in which we speak of London society, or the English society of an Indian station, has as yet no existence in India, and cannot until education – intellectual, domestic and social – has reached the ladies of India'.[45] Society 'in the narrower sense' was high society, the society of the upper middle and upper classes of Britain. Its absence was an obstacle to Indians engaging with Europeans on an equal basis. 'Before there can be much intercourse between English people and Indians, the latter need to adopt, in their own social relations, some of the principles that underlie Western habits', wrote an editor of the *JNIA* in an introduction to a letter by a Parsi woman that had appeared originally in the Gujarati journal, *Rast Goftar*. The letter's author, who signed it simply 'Shereen', complained, 'You can hardly find more than half dozen [*sic*] Parsi ladies who can with due regard to their dignity or self-respect avail themselves of the benefit of English society'. The solution was assimilation: 'According to European style tea parties, music, reading, badminton, croquet parties, converzasiones [*sic*], &c., should be introduced among our people to begin with.'[46] In a letter to the *IMR*, an Indian reader went even further to argue that female Indian students in Britain should behave with the forthright openness commonly seen only in American polite society, especially when dealing with other Indian students, whether they be male or female: 'Ladies need not wait for an introduction; they can introduce themselves.'[47]

A more moderate form of this argument agreed with the need for assimilation but asserted that this would in fact bring Indian society closer to its own roots. This line of thinking appealed to the assumption, common at the time, that the essence of a society was to be found in its earliest forms. Indians and Britons alike, therefore, appealed to the authority of Hindu scriptures to demonstrated that seclusion was un-Indian. Mrs P. L. Roy argued that ancient Hindu scriptures indicated a high society much more amenable to Victorians than the contemporary one that they encountered: 'Great ladies came out in public, took part in festivities and witnessed tournaments – as, for instance the great tournament which was held to commemorate the finish of the education of the Kurus princes in arms and archery. Sita, the heroine of the "Ramayana", travelled openly with her husband all over India, visiting hermits and received her husband's guests in her woodland home.'[48] Such sentiment accorded well with one of the NIA's most prestigious orientalist scholars, Sir Monier Monier-Williams, Boden Professor of Sanskrit at Oxford University, who, citing seclusion and child marriage, declared: 'Well, then in India, I regret to say, there is no such thing as a home.' This lamentable absence of the domestic sphere, however, had not always been so, since seclusion and child marriage 'did not apply to even the upper classes *in ancient times*', when the 'purely spiritualistic', 'root-dogma of true Hinduism' developed the concept of a 'personal Creator, with a double essence, half male and half female'.[49]

Those who questioned the need for assimilation often argued against the idea that purdah was so pervasive in India. Disputing the impression that hardly any women took part in Indian polite society, an 'Indian Traveller' claimed: 'The Purdah system, which prevails in many parts, does not exist among Hindus of Western India.' The writer described 'a Hindu house in Bombay' belonging to a modern middle-class family whose husband was a professional working at the office while his wife oversaw the servants, tended to the house, and debated with neighbouring women the advantages of sending her son to study in England.[50] In a lecture delivered to the NIA, Yusef Ali argued similarly for upper caste women of rural India: 'The usual gossip of the women, morning and evening, is around the village well. It is the ladies' club, as exclusive as the aristocratic clubs of London. The higher castes have wells to which no lower class people are allowed to go to draw water.'[51] Similarly, while lecturing on the subject in Manchester, Mersha Chinnappa, the English teacher at the Maharani of Mysore's high caste school and daughter of the manager of Mysore's Educational Department, argued that 'domestic life is everywhere the same where there is humanity'. She extolled the hospitality of women in even the poorest Hindu households and asserted that wives made themselves beautiful for their husbands not out of 'slavish adulation, but a warmth of domestic love, unsullied by the sins of society life'. Chinnappa argued that an Indian version of the Victorian cult of domesticity had existed since antiquity and drew its 'highest ideal' from the *Ramayana*'s account of Sita, 'the eminent life of that virtuous woman during her exile with Rama'.[52] Such arguments, however, conceded that seclusion, where it existed, undermined the development of the feminine sphere of society and therefore its polite and genteel aspects. They simply questioned the extent of the problem or its peculiarity to India by arguing that it had either not existed in a supposedly pure Indian past or that it occurred only rarely in their own day.

Even the rare voice of dissent from the condemnation of seclusion accepted the importance of upper- and middle-class women in setting the moral tone of polite society in both Britain and India. Perhaps the most prominent Indian woman in Britain to argue along these lines was the wife of the Parsi industrialist, Sir Jehanghir Cowasji Jehanghir. She claimed that seclusion made Indian women 'nearer to the divine beginning of all things for happily we still recognise throughout the historic East that the true Sovereignty of Woman is based, as alone it can be securely and most beneficently based, on Motherhood – that is on the eternal miracle of The Mother, and her pure-born Child'.[53]

The question debated in the NIA, therefore, was not whether middle- and upper-class women should properly be the guardians of public morality through their dominance of domestic life. Almost all writers in the *JNIA* and its successors agreed with this proposition. Rather the question was whether and to what extent the practice of seclusion interfered with the ability of Indian women to assume this role by depriving them of an education adequate to the task and by preventing them from communicating the values of polite society beyond the home. Since almost all of the NIA's members agreed on the role of women as guardians of the moral standards of polite society, both critics and defenders of the status of women in India supported the compromise solution of bringing women together socially in order to educate them and allow them to reinforce one another's values. Such gatherings usually took the form of 'purdah parties', in which women could gather without exposing themselves to the gaze of men. Reform-minded British women, such as Mary Carpenter, occasionally attended such gatherings when visiting India. However, as Flora Annie Steel, the writer of romantic novels set in India, pointed out when addressing the NIA's annual meeting in 1904, most wives of British administrators and officers in India did not try to socialise with middle- and upper-class Indian women.[54] They therefore undermined one of the central goals of Britain's imperial mission in India as understood by the founders of the NIA – the empowerment of women to create a middle- and upper-class domestic sphere analogous to Victorian Britain's that could have a civilising influence over the entire subcontinent. The stereotypes of class as much as those of gender underlay such assumptions, since it was to be middle- and upper-class, educated women who must establish and maintain the domestic sphere in both Britain and India that would preserve a polite and civilised society. The role of women, therefore, lay at the heart of the imperial class hierarchy.

Since polite behaviour toward women of high social standing was a *sine qua non* of the Victorian gentleman, it is hardly surprising that British and Indian men accused one another of failure to observe it when they questioned one another's class credentials. This type of acrimony surfaced most publicly in an essay entitled 'Social Intercourse Between English and Indians in India' and the angry responses that it prompted. Perhaps more than any other contributions to the *JNIA* these exhibited what Ann Laura Stoler terms 'the lexicon of bourgeois civility, self-control, self-discipline, and self-determination', which 'clarified notions of "whiteness" and what it meant to be truly European'.[55] The essay's author, a British administrator in Bombay who used the signature 'Misanthrope', claimed that one of the many obstacles to greater friendship between ruler and ruled was the ungentlemanly behaviour of educated Indian men toward European women: 'Most of us have seen the educated cad with his feet upon a bench in some public place staring at a European lady who cannot find a seat.'[56] Responses were quick and biting. 'In an English crowd I have seen women and children pushed about and ill treated in a way the like of which I have never seen in India', protested Dinsha Davar in the following issue.[57] N. S. Ginwalla argued that in reality it was British rulers who treated Indian women with contempt:

> When our 'Misanthrope' and other European gentlemen of his stamp try to extol the gentle sex of their own nationality, do they ever perceive that many Europeans do not regard a native lady ... worthy of the attention, respect and care they want native gentlemen to bestow upon European ladies? Some time ago I happened to read in the Bombay dailies a pithy account of a respectable and sufficiently known Parsi lady of reformed views and more than ordinary grace, who had great difficulty in getting a seat at the time of the University Convocation ... and does this speak well of many European gentlemen who quietly retained their seats when the lady was so eagerly seeking for a seat before their very eyes?[58]

The behaviour of, and attitude toward, women was central to Victorian and Edwardian understanding of membership in polite society, for it was in the traditionally feminine, domestic sphere that British polite society believed the basis of social order lay.[59] The behaviour of Indian men toward women in general and toward Indian women in particular, signified the eligibility of these men for inclusion in polite society. British reformers, who were often the members of British society most keenly interested in India, usually disapproved of the practice of purdah. Indian men, therefore, had at least to appear to adapt to Western values regarding appropriate female behaviour in order to maintain or advance their standing in British polite society. One of the easiest and most explosive ways in which these men could lose moral, and therefore social, status in the eyes of Britain's elite was to behave inappropriately in their relationships with women. Yet this requirement cut both ways.

First, it was possible to demonstrate that the traditional behaviour of Indian women met British expectations of polite behaviour. This argument emphasised the underlying similarities of purpose and outcome, such as the maintenance of a morally virtuous domestic sphere, between the codes of female behaviour. These underlying similarities, so the argument went, were far more important than the superficial differences of clothing, diet, ritual, and skin colour. Such important differences as existed were to be found in the lower level of education and literacy among wives of middle-class Indians. But this problem could be solved through the combined efforts of British and Indian reformers, such as those who were members of the NIA. For most of these members, the inoffensive trappings of Indian womanhood need not change so long as Indian women were allowed to interact, and were capable of interacting, in polite society.

Furthermore, as the 'Misanthrope' correspondence demonstrates, Indian men could point to inappropriate British behaviour toward Indian women. If chivalrous behaviour toward women was the mark of a Victorian or Edwardian gentleman, then British administrators in India needed to demonstrate it in their dealings with Indians. That they often failed to do so provided further ammunition for critics of Britain's presence in India – for if Indian behaviour toward women generally was a sign of their membership in British polite society, British behaviour toward Indian women was a sign of the respect that British authorities accorded Indian men. The keen sense of insult that men from both countries felt when women supposedly under their protection were not treated as members of polite society was potentially explosive since it hit at the core of class, gender, and ethnic identity. Significantly, however, it was through the register of class and gender that 'Misanthrope' directed his racial barbs at Indians.

The boundaries of hierarchical discourse

Whether the topic was women, education, or a combination of two, contributors to the *JNIA* and its successors were reluctant to attribute social behaviour primarily to race. For instance, in attributing negative stereotypes to the behaviour of Indian professionals and students in the United Kingdom, 'Misanthrope' focused on their class: urban professional as opposed to rural gentry. He complained that the supposedly educated Indians whom he encountered in the cities lacked the aesthetic appreciation to indulge in conversation with their British counterparts: 'Photographs they pretend to look at, but do not understand; music of course they despise.' He contrasted these Indians with the 'higher class of natives whom Europeans sometimes meet in up-country towns'.[60]

These remarks outraged the Indian readers of the *JNIA*, many, if not most, of whom were following professional careers that placed them in the category of 'Misanthrope's' 'native cads' rather than his 'up-country' gentlemen. They responded with three types of argument, sometimes in the same letter. On the one hand, they asserted that polite behaviour was culturally relative. 'The etiquette of the Eastern countries vastly differs from that of the Western,' wrote the law student Syud Sharfuddin, '[b]ut it is absurd to expect any one to appreciate music foreign to his taste.'[61] Ginwalla protested that 'the natives of India are reared up as it were in music'.[62] On the other hand the same respondents unanimously accused 'Misanthrope' of engaging in social levelling. Davar asserted that '"Misanthrope" could not possibly have had much intercourse with that class of educated natives of whom he talks. His experience seems to be derived from a very low grade of Indian society.'[63] Turning the tables on 'Misanthrope', Sharfuddin remarked: 'I would be the last man to level all Englishmen to the class of society who inhabit the east end of London. It seems to me that Mr. Misanthrope had had no occasion of cultivating friendship with the higher class of Indians.'[64] Ginwalla went so far as to question the orientalist knowledge on which Western assumptions about Indian society were based, because European administrators 'presume to learn a difficult Oriental language in six months which it would take six years for a native to learn'.[65] Perhaps most important, the respondents labelled 'Misanthrope's' class rhetoric as racial prejudice. Concluded Ginwalla, 'Let our "Misanthrope", true to his nature and man-hating principle, cloak his real dislike of colour and race under the pretence of want of good and polished manners of the natives.'[66] Significantly, whereas 'Misanthrope' blamed the want of social graces among educated Indians for the diminution of interethnic contact, some of the respondents blamed the increasing, self-imposed segregation of British rulers for this phenomenon. Noted one writer, who may have been British, 'in the cities you are engrossed with your own exclusive coterie, how can you come to like the native, from whom you keep aloof, and where, if you see your "higher class of native from upcountry", you would pretend not to see him and would not salaam him?'[67]

The significance of 'Misanthrope's' essay and the responses to it are not simply further evidence of racism among British administrators in India. (It would be difficult to argue that Ginwalla's criticism of

'Misanthrope' was far off the mark.) They also embody the assumption that the discourse of class is acceptable, whereas that of race is not. 'Misanthrope' was careful, albeit not careful enough, to assert that '[n]either colour nor race can be obviously in the least objectionable',[68] and to accuse Indians, not of belonging to an inferior biological group, but of failing to adopt the social graces that were the hallmark of the British middle and upper classes. His critics argued that he was attributing the crass behaviour of the lower orders to educated Indians and thus depriving them of their social status – in other words, he was guilty of social levelling. Moreover, implied 'Misanthrope's' critics, to treat educated Indians as such was an injustice in itself. Just as the BCINC was willing to accept a racial hierarchy as long as Britain's elite ranked them at its apex, so did Indian correspondents of the *JNIA* approve of a class hierarchy as long as they occupied its upper ranks. Just as the BCINC was willing to recognise the 'savagery' of the South African 'kaffir', so were educated Indians in Britain and India alike willing to share in the British elite's disdain for the unmannered East-Ender or Indian 'coolie'.

In fact, the blunt prejudices of 'Misanthrope' were unusual for the *JNIA* and its successors. More common among British writers were claims that the presence of compatriots in India had allowed the subcontinent's middle class to flourish where it would have withered under Indian rule. Such was the contention of J. Long in his essay, 'The Old Families of Calcutta', in which he managed to combine respect and admiration for that city's Indian managerial class with praise for the Empire that had enabled them to succeed. For instance, he extolled 'Ran Dulal Ray, the Bengali millionaire, who born when his parents had to fly from the Mahrattas, began life as a common clerk on eight rupis [*sic*] a month, and rose to be another Rothschild – he bought large estates, but his money was not made by squeezing the rayats [*sic*]'.[69] This laudatory remark attributed moral and financial virtue to an Indian and placed him on a par with one of Europe's greatest businessmen. Yet the supposed source of adversity in his life, at the time, was the most viable Indian alternative to British rule. Given the realities of British power over their land, such self-congratulatory respect was the best that Indians were likely to receive from British institutions.

Class was, therefore, the language that Indians usually used to negotiate their rank in British society. Apart from committed socialists, which few of them were, they saw nothing offensive in this language. Indeed, in the context of British rule, it was far preferable to the alternatives, such as the language of race, which were less likely to allow Indians to command respect in the upper echelons of British society. Most Indians knew too well that such alternatives existed. In his advice to fellow Indians contemplating a visit to England, one writer warned of the difficulties in gaining admission to a boarding house:

> But there are some houses where they do not *willingly* take Indians; others there are where they do not *readily* take foreigners. They do not take Indians perhaps for two reasons: one is that their dusky colour destroys the charm of the fair society (and yet an Englishman may believe that he is above any kind of prejudice); the other is that some of my countrymen ... have badly figured in the papers here. They do not like to take foreigners because John Bull does not particularly seem to care for an alien, if he can avoid him.[70]

In a society in which groups tended to identify themselves in contrast to others, educated Indians wanted to persuade authority figures in Britain to identify with them rather than in contrast to them. Far better for those others to be the lower orders of both Britain and India than all Indians as opposed to all Britons. Perhaps more than any other voice in Britain, it was the *JNIA* and its successors that offered this vision of the relationship between British institutions and Indians in the United Kingdom. Although it was born out of the assumption of Britain's cultural superiority to India, from its very inception it insisted on giving educated Indians a voice. In doing so, it accorded them a level in Indian society equivalent to that of reformers in Britain.

As for the British administrators who encountered Indians through the NIA, the social setting of their interaction encouraged them to order Indians by class. Certainly, many British administrators stereotyped and 'essentialised' Indians in Britain, but this tendency in no way diminished their willingness to, and even their inability to do other than, rank Indians according to the social system that surrounded them and with which they were most familiar. The difference between the social environments of British administrators in England and in India was so marked that Ratnagar commented on it: 'An Englishman by traversing the ocean does not indeed lose his caste, but is certainly freed from the atmosphere of the public opinion at home.'[71] The concept that the change of social environment altered British administrators' perceptions of Indians deserves further scrutiny. At the theoretical level, these administrators, some of whom were scholars, may not have been any more or less racist depending on their locations. In practice, however, the British social environment encouraged them to distinguish among Indians according to its rules rather than those prevailing in India. Officials in British institutions were going to order the Indians they encountered according to British concepts of class. The problem was how to determine the rank of individual Indians on the basis of their Indian social backgrounds. They had access to a body of knowledge that

British orientalist administrators had provided but that the Indian community in Britain and India had both affirmed and modified. The theory was accessible. The challenge lay in the application.

Notes

1 Membership lists are at the end of every issue of the *Journal of the National Indian Association* (cited hereafter as *JNIA*). My figures are based on the one in no. 116 (August 1880).

2 'Social intercourse between Europeans and natives in India', *JNIA*, 147 (March 1883): 145. Like many Marxists, Hyndman explicitly connected the exploitation of Britain's lower classes with India's. Writing to Naoroji in 1882, he declared: 'The mass of the people here are in a deplorable state and worse, I sometimes think, than your starving ryots and famished labourers of Bombay and Madras – for they have at least the sun.' But he believed that 'Nothing can be done for India unless we have a revolution here.' Thus even his vision of socialist revolution and colonial liberation was Eurocentric. See Cshushichi Tsuzuki, *H. M. Hyndman and British Socialism* (Oxford: Oxford University Press, 1961), 48.

3 Visram, *Ayahs, Lascars and Princes*, 77. See S. R. Mehrotra, *The Emergence of the Indian National Congress* (Delhi: Vikas Publications, 1971), 225.

4 IOR L/PJ/6/977 No. 4647, Petition 'to the Right Honourable Viscount Morley, P. C., M. O. etc., Secretary of State for India', 6 June 1910. Two of these petitioners had English last names. Among the others were eight 'Indian students in Leeds', several merchants, and Shapurji Saklatvala, who in 1926 became a communist member of Britain's Parliament.

5 Petition to Morley, 6 June 1910.

6 Antoinette Burton, 'Institutionalizing imperial reform: *The Indian Magazine* and late-Victorian colonial politics', in David Finkelstein and Douglas M. Peers (eds), *Negotiating India in the Nineteenth-Century Media* (Basingstoke: Macmillan Press, 2000), 25–6.

7 'Objects of the Association', 3, attached to *JNIA*, 1 (January 1871). Italics in original.

8 *Ibid.*

9 Burton, *At the Heart of the Empire*, 57.

10 Pramatha Nath Bose, 'History of the caste system in India – I. Origin of the caste system and its first phase', *JNIA*, 87 (March 1878): 98–9.

11 *Ibid.*, 100.

12 Bose, 'History of the caste system in India – III. Buddhist-Hindu, and Hindu periods', *JNIA*, 89 (May 1878): 195–6.

13 *Ibid.*, 196.

14 Quoted in Jonathan Schneer, *London 1900: The Imperial Metropolis* (New Haven: Yale University Press, 1999), 194 and 195.

15 'National Indian Association', *JNIA*, 103 (July 1879): 340.

16 *Ibid.*, 335. Such relativism was not unusual for Cust, who did not take a literal view of all scripture and, according to a recent biographer, 'prided himself on a scientific understanding of the development of different religions'. See Katherine Prior, 'Cust, Robert Needham (1821–1909)', *Oxford Dictionary of National Biography*: www.oxforddnb.com/view/article/32685?docPos=9 (accessed 19 November 2004).

17 *Ibid.*, 339.

18 Syed Hassan, 'Caste in India', *JNIA*, 104 (August 1879): 391–2.

19 'National Indian Association', 328.

20 'English intelligence', *JNIA*, 26 (February 1873): 275.

21 'Intelligence', *JNIA*, 7 (July 1871): 136.

22 'English intelligence – Bristol', *JNIA*, 11 (November 1871): 244.

23 *JNIA*, 13 (January 1872): 4.

24 'Travelling and caste', *IMR*, 367 (July 1901): 174.

25 Wegeulin Greene, 'English rural life', *IMR*, 425 (May 1906): 112 fn.
26 Nasarvanji J. Ratnagar, 'Village life in India', *JNIA*, 98 (February 1879): 63 and 65.
27 *Ibid.*, 62
28 S. Satthianadhan, 'Is India civilized?', *JNIA*, 127 (July 1881): 419
29 Cecil Bendall, 'Aims and methods of recent Indian research: The professor of Sanskrit's inaugural lecture at Cambridge', *IMR*, 396 (December 1903): 319
30 'Misanthrope', 'Social intercourse between English and Indians in India', *JNIA*, 101 (May 1879): 237
31 J. B. Phear, 'Peasant village life in India', *JNIA*, 76 (April 1877): 103
32 *Ibid.*, 98.
33 'The elevation of the working classes', *JNIA*, 38 (February 1874): 35
34 Yusef Ali, 'Village life in India', *IMR*, 420 (December 1905): 328. Ali was on furlough in England at the time. See M. A. Sherif, *Searching for Solace: A Biography of Abdullah Yusuf Ali, Interpreter of the Qur'an* (Kuala Lumpur: Islamic Book Trust, 1994), 21–7.
35 *Ibid.*, 314–18.
36 Hassan, 'Caste in India', 392.
37 'National Indian Association', 339.
38 See Sinha, *Colonial Masculinity*. For a discussion of hunting and imperial masculinity, see John M. Mackenzie, 'The imperial pioneer and hunter and the British masculine stereotype in late Victorian and Edwardian times', in J.A. Mangan and James Walvin (eds), *Manliness and Morality: Middle-Class Masculinity in Britain and America, 1800–1940* (Manchester: Manchester University Press, 1987), 176–98; and John M. Mackenzie, *The Empire of Nature: Hunting, Conservation and British Imperialism* (Manchester: Manchester University Press, 1988), 26–51 and 168–99.
39 'The present practicable range of social intercourse in India', *JNIA*, 107 (November 1879): 611.
40 Krishnarac Gopal Deshmukh, 'On female education, and the progress of thought in India', *JNIA*, 5 (May 1871): 80.
41 R. Mittra, 'On Hindu marriage', *JNIA*, 8 (August 1871): 152 and 153.
42 'Objects of the Association', 3.
43 'English Intelligence', *JNIA*, 15 (March 1872): 53.
44 Antoinette Burton, *Burdens of History: British Feminists, Indian Women, and Imperial Culture, 1865–1915* (Chapel Hill, NC: University of North Carolina Press, 1994), 11.
45 J. E. C., 'About Indian ladies', *JNIA*, 128 (August 1881): 481.
46 'How to learn European manners', *JNIA*, 117 (September 1880): 534–5.
47 S. V. Ketar, 'Unnecessary formality among Indian students', *IMR*, 492 (December 1911): 334.
48 P. L. Roy, 'Sita, the heroine of the "Ramayana"', *IMR*, 471 (March 1910): 71.
49 Monier Monier-Williams, 'The women of India', *IMR*, 331 (July 1898): 170–1. Italics in original.
50 An Indian Traveller, 'Life in a Hindu home', *IM*, 162 (June 1884): 259–60.
51 Ali, 'Village life in India', 323.
52 Mersha Chinnappa, 'The home life of the Hindu', in 'Hindu ladies in Manchester', *IMR*, 417 (September 1905): 243 and 244.
53 Lady Cowasjee Jehangir, 'Woman in the East and West', *IMR*, 392 (August 1903), 217.
54 See E. T. C., 'Friendly intercourse between English and Indian ladies', *IMR*, 404 (August 1904): 201.
55 Ann Laura Stoler, *Race and the Education of Desire: Foucault's History of Sexuality and the Colonial Order of Things* (Durham, NC: Duke University Press, 1995), 8.
56 'Misanthrope', 'Social intercourse', 236.
57 Dishna D. Davar, 'Social intercourse between English and Indians in India – Reply No. I', *JNIA*, 102 (June 1879): 296.
58 Nusserwanjee Sheriarjee Ginwalla, 'A reply to Misanthrope', *JNIA*, 104 (August 1879): 414.

59 For the origins of separate spheres, see Joan Perkin, *Victorian Women* (London: John Murray, 1993), 86–8; and Pat Hudson, 'Women and industrialization', in June Purvis (ed.), *Women's History: Britain, 1850–1945* (New York: St Martin's Press, 1995), 38–40. For discussions of the ideology of Victorian womanhood see also, Shani d'Cruze, 'Women and the family', in *Women's History*, 53–5; Duncan Crow, *The Victorian Woman* (London: Allen and Unwin, 1971); and Jean Bethke Elshtain, *Public Man, Private Woman: Women in Social and Political Thought* (Princeton, NJ: Princeton University Press, 1981).

60 'Misanthrope', 'Social intercourse', 237.

61 Syud Sharfuddin, 'Social intercourse between English and Indians in India – Reply No. II', *JNIA*, 102 (June 1879): 300 and 302. Sharfuddin later served in various offices of the Colonial Provincial Governments of Bengal.

62 Ginwalla, 'Reply', 415.

63 Davar, 'Social intercourse', 298.

64 Sharfuddin, 'Social intercourse', 301.

65 Ginwalla, 'Reply', 416.

66 *Ibid.*

67 C. D. F., 'Difficulty of social intercourse with the people of India', *JNIA*, 105 (September 1879): 476–7.

68 'Misanthrope', 'Social intercourse', 235.

69 J. Long, 'The old families of Calcutta', *JNIA*, 127 (July 1881): 383.

70 A. M. K. D., 'An Indian view of the modes of living in England – II', *IMR*, 270 (June 1893): 299. Emphasis in original.

71 Ratnagar, 'Difficulty of social intercourse with the people of India', *JNIA*, 107 (November 1879): 585.

CHAPTER FOUR

London's inner-city missions to Indians

The front covers of successive annual reports of the Strangers' Home for Asiatics, Africans, and South-Sea Islanders from the late nineteenth century depict Britannia seated by the sea with sun rays penetrating the clouds behind, beneath which a distant ship's masts stand out against the horizon. Britannia's head forms the keystone of an arc of Biblical text that proclaims: 'Be not forgetful to entertain strangers'. Beneath her, and standing beside a drawing of the Home and its name, are five figures, probably intended to represent men from Africa, the Middle East, Persia or India, Oceania, and East Asia. Two, on the right, are engaged in conversation, perhaps underscoring the Strangers' Home as a meeting place for people from diverse lands. One, who wears attire that many Britons would have immediately recognised as Muslim, is kneeling with his head and arms raised in apparent supplication, though whether it is to (an unseen) God or to Britannia is unclear. At the bottom of the cover are coastal cliffs with a Union Jack flying at their top and two ships, one of them a steamer, plying the waters nearby and underscoring Britain's role as the centre of a polyglot commercial empire.[1] This cover depicts remarkably well the impulses of those who founded, directed, or supported the two major organisations that interacted with India's poor in London: the Strangers' Home and the London City Mission (LCM). For if Britannia's commercial empire formed the economic and politic context of the presence of people of colour in the United Kingdom, it was British Christianity that provided the ethical context for the founders and directors of the organisations that catered to those whom commerce discarded. The result was an often contradictory attitude toward the place of Indians in British society. The full Bible verse from which the quote on the cover of the report comes is: 'Be not forgetful to entertain strangers: for thereby some have entertained angels unawares.'[2]

For impoverished Indian men in London, the Home's ministry was

Figure 1 Front cover of The Strangers' Home Annual Report, 1887.
Reproduced with permission of The National Archives of the UK, ref. MT 9/362/M1067.
Image edited by J. Wade Wilcox, The University of Akron.

most obvious in food, shelter, and religious programmes offered by the Home itself on West India Dock Road in Limehouse and in the proselytising efforts of the LCM's special missionary, based at the Strangers' Home, to Asians and Africans. For much of the period between the Indian Rebellion and the First World War, these organisations cooperated in helping lower-class Indians. At the same time, they also formed an often uneasy alliance with the India Office as their missions to assist and proselytise Hindus, Muslims, and Sikhs, converged with and diverged from the desire of British administrators to control a subordinate, alien population in the imperial capital. In encountering members of India's labouring classes, inner-city missionaries and social workers also drew sharp distinctions between the Indian poor whom they helped and the genteel class of Indians residing in Britain from whom they solicited aid for their humanitarian projects. The inner-city missionary effort to India's poor, therefore, reinforced in its British setting not only the supposed norms of lower-class Indian society but also those of their middle- and upper-class counterparts. By identifying an Indian lower class in Britain, these organisations helped to clarify the existence of the Indian classes above it, whose behaviour was in turn defined in part by its sense of *noblesse oblige*, a form of class-consciousness in itself, toward its inferiors.

The Strangers' Home

Founded in 1857, the Strangers' Home was an interdenominational Protestant organisation that complemented the major British missionary societies' schools and hospitals in Africa, Asia, and Oceania. The Church of England's Church Missionary Society (CMS) played a leading role in establishing the Home, as did the royal family and the recently converted Duleep Singh, Maharaja of Punjab, who contributed £200 and £500 respectively to start up the project. The Wesleyans and Baptists also made donations. The board of directors governing the Home consisted of the representatives of the contributing missions. In keeping with CMS director Henry Venn's policy toward missions elsewhere in the world, the Home was self-supporting and promoted self-sufficiency among its inmates. Residents who were able, therefore, paid two pounds per month in return for board and lodging, although the Home regularly admitted destitute people of colour who had no money. In such situations it was up to the Home's secretary to determine whether an applicant was truly indigent. Along with food and shelter, however, came religious instruction from a Protestant missionary, who actively sought destitute Indians in the docklands of London and Britain's other major port cities. From its inception, the Home's supporters recognised that it required a staff with orientalist expertise in order to minister effectively to its non-Western charges.

This expertise focused mainly on India, because so many of the Home's inmates and potential converts came from the Indian subcontinent. Comprehensive statistics on the Strangers' Home are lacking, because only a few reports remain, but those available suggest that the presence of Indians as a proportion of total residents rose markedly toward the turn of the century. Of the 525 inmates in 1882, 160, or about a third, came from India. A similar proportion held in 1896, for which we have a more detailed ethnic breakdown. That year the Home admitted 744 applicants, of which 209 came from India and 49 from Ceylon. Of the remainder 165 came from Japan, 153 from China, 70 from Arabia, and 54 from Africa. In 1900, Indians numbered 454 of the 876 applicants admitted. Even during the mid-1880s, when the number of inmates dropped dramatically, the number of Indians remained high: 156 out of 356. In that year, the Home's missionary distributed 261 gospels to current and prospective inmates. Of these 158 (about sixty per cent) were in Indian languages.[3] Indians, therefore, came to constitute the largest presence in the Strangers' Home. Furthermore, they were by far the largest group of residents from the British Empire, since many of the Chinese inmates may have come from outside Hong Kong.

With a mission tied so closely to the fate of Asians in London, it is hardly surprising that the Strangers' Home depended heavily for its funding on institutions dealing in Asia. Occasionally, the Home could look to foreign governments for expertise and assistance with inmates who originated outside the Empire. Most notable was the cooperation of the Japanese Government, which donated ¥500 (£55 6s. 9d.) in 1896, and whose ambassador spoke at the Home's annual meeting in 1901.[4] Nevertheless, most of the Home's contacts with governing authorities were with those of the British Empire. In this respect it served as a quasi-official shelter for branches of Britain's colonial government that wanted to minimise the supposedly negative impact of lower-class people of colour on the streets of London. In 1900 eight of them – Ceylon, Gambia, Hong Kong, Lagos, the Strait Settlements, British Guiana, Mauritius, and Trinidad – provided £10 10s. The India Office, however, donated £200, five times the amount of the second largest contributor, the British India Steam Navigation Company, and eight times that of the third, the Maharaja of Travancore. The India Office's contribution amounted to nearly a third of the Home's total charitable receipts of £615 11s. 10d. Even the second and third largest contributors gave primarily because of their jurisdiction over many of the Indians who used the Home. Add to this the sum of at least £30 (roughly £20 from India Office administrators) donated by Britons connected with the administration of India, and close to, if not more than half the contributions to the Home were aimed primarily at covering the costs of Indian inmates.[5] The full title of the Strangers' Home included most men of colour, but with Indians amounting to the plurality, and sometimes the majority, of the Home's residents, and with India's rulers officially and privately contributing so much to the Home's operation, it was primarily a home for lower income and destitute Indians, the overwhelming majority of whom were lascars (Asian sailors) who were waiting for employment on ships returning to India.

Indeed, for much of its existence the Home served in some official capacity. The Port of London designated the Home's Honorary Secretary as a Lascar Transfer Officer, officially empowered to demand compensation (under the Merchant Shipping Act of 1854, and its successors) from shipping companies for the maintenance and repatriation of lascars whom they hired in Asia for the journey to Britain but refused to rehire for the return. Furthermore, for the first thirty-three years of its operation, an officer of the Home held a licence from the Board of Trade's Mercantile Marine Department empowering him 'to supply coloured seamen for merchant ships'. This meant that the Home served as an official agent of the Board of Trade in seeking employment and negotiated wages for lascars with shipping companies. So important did India Office and Strangers' Home administrators consider this official imprimatur that they caused Mercantile Marine officers to wonder whether 'the existence of the Home is imperilled by the withdrawing of the licence', when in 1890 the Mercantile Marine Office ended its licencing programme for all agencies other than those pertaining to boys in training.[6]

The Home's tendency to operate in concert with government authorities, particularly the India Office, might have disturbed missionaries out in the Empire, because the missionary societies who contributed to and staffed the Home were examples of what Jeffrey Cox has called 'voluntarist religion', that is organised religion whose members preferred to operate apart from the state. Yet so much of the Home's financing came from colonial government agencies, and so much of its existence depended on it serving government interests, that such a separation between imperial and missionary activity was impossible and led the Home's mission to fall into 'a giant imperialist trap' that Cox sees as the result of most missionary efforts abroad during this period.[7] This trap was perhaps more immediate and effective in the case of the Strangers' Home than with most missionary establishments in the colonies, because, in contrast to colonial missions, there was no consideration of handing over control of the Home to people of colour – no potential 'Euthanasia of a Mission', which Venn regarded as the ultimate success for any evangelical effort abroad.[8] The tension that might have resulted from the Home's dual role of religious mission and government-sponsored shelter did not arise, because the two staff members in charge of the Home's primary missions – spiritual and material – rarely interfered with each other's jurisdictions. The missionary preached to Hindus and Muslims on the streets of London and encouraged those in need to seek assistance from the Strangers' Home. The Honorary Secretary, who bore 'the chief burden of all the anxious and successful labours connected with the undertaking',[9] determined who would stay in the Home and maintained discipline within it. As with much British missionary activity overseas, therefore, this ministry manifested itself spiritually and materially. Yet the Home's two missions complemented each other, as did the men who directed them. For the missionary and the Honorary Secretary often, though not always, reinforced each other's perspectives regarding the Indians whom they encountered and the society from which they came.

Joseph Salter's critique of Indian culture

For many British missionaries the spiritual side of their activities was the more important, and the missionary societies that set up the Strangers' Home could conceive of it only as part of their evangelical mission. Unlike meetings of the India Office or the National Indian Association, therefore, those of the Strangers' Home made frequent reference to scriptural passages to justify and inspire their proselytisation. Unlike traditional missionary endeavours, however, the Strangers' Home existed, not to send emissaries of Christ to other nations, but to minister to the nations that Britain's economic and military activities had brought to the heart of the Empire. In order to support the spiritual side of its mission, the Strangers' Home maintained a full-time missionary, who actively sought out men of other faiths from Africa and Asia, and urged them to attend Bible studies and religious services at the Strangers' Home. Rather than train its own missionaries, however, the directors of the Strangers' Home recruited from missionary organisations. Most notable among these was the LCM, whose primary goal was to spread the gospel to London's poor. It seconded at least two missionaries to serve the Strangers' Home. They were able to serve both organisations at once, because their role as religious instructors to inmates of the Strangers' Home complemented so well their role as missionaries to London's Asians and Africans.

Most influential among these missionaries was Joseph Salter, who served as the LCM missionary to Asians and Africans from 1853 to 1893 and as the religious instructor for inmates of the Strangers' Home from its foundation in 1857 to 1876. Since he served the Strangers' Home for so many years, his perception of Indians had a significant influence on its policy toward them. It was, after all, Salter who in many cases recruited destitute Indians to enter the Home and receive religious instruction during their stay. Although one historian has described the social composition of LCM missionaries as 'gentlemen to a man',[10] Salter did not start out that way. The LCM's examining subcommittee described him as 'a ladies' shoemaker', whose 'educational advantages in youth were exceedingly small'. Nevertheless, the minutes observed, 'he has since become quite a leader, for a man in his station in life, and he is shrewd and intelligent'.[11] What is perhaps most remarkable about the decision to hire Salter was his lack of experience in the Empire. He had never travelled to the lands whose inhabitants he sought to convert, nor initially did he know their languages. According to R. Marsh Hughes, the Strangers' Home's first Honorary Secretary, Salter learned Hindustani during the early years of his appointment, but, according to Salter, it was during the years immediately preceding his appointment, while he was in the company of visiting Indian princes and their ministers.[12] Yet Salter was one of only seven agents that the LCM directed specifically toward ethnic groups. As such he acted as an expert who performed what Donald Lewis describes as one of many 'specialized forms of evangelism' sponsored by the LCM.[13] Salter's knowledge of India was, therefore, strictly through the words of others rather than personal experience.

In some respects this lack of experience made him less critical of Indian character, since he had not been exposed to the racism inherent in British rule over India. On the other hand, the overwhelming presence of Hinduism and Islam among the Indian community in London evoked his sweeping condemnation of Indian culture as heathen. This religious argument for the superiority of Britain's culture to India's was an old one that predated the biological aspects of late nineteenth-century racial theory and even the secular civilising mission of the early nineteenth century. Since the central goal of missionary activity was to proselytise, it allowed in theory for the full admission of Indians into civilisation through conversion.

However, like so many missionary endeavours abroad, this domestic mission to Hindus and Muslims tended to identify so many aspects of Indian society with the supposedly erroneous doctrines and practices of its members, that it became difficult to separate conversion to Christianity from Westernisation.[14] For instance Salter contrasted the hospitality awaiting Asians since the Home's foundation to the lack of it before, 'when they were allowed to perish unknown and uncared-for; when no European voice broke the monotony of Oriental gloom'.[15]

Elsewhere he implied at least a cultural inferiority of Indians when he declared that 'the Oriental mind runs in a channel, and is prone to follow example'.[16] In one passage he confessed his personal distaste for an aspect of Indian culture that could hardly have offended any doctrinal principle of Christianity. Regarding the music of destitute Indians he complained: 'The noisy dhool was about to follow the song, but, not wishing my ear to be further deafened, I offered to tell them about a King's Son of greater splendour or renown than the rajah of their song.'[17] If India's music was noisy, its cuisine was malodorous: 'The smell of Indian ghee, garlic, sweetmeats, and jagree, were all as novel as the language and would have been unbearable, had they not been the means to an end' – spreading the Gospel.[18] Yet paradoxically, Salter argued that one of the reasons for establishing a home for Asians was because they 'have an aversion to the Union [workhouse], for eating and drinking are part of their religion, and they would rather huddle twenty or thirty together in a small house, where they can cook and eat and drink and smoke, *a la mode Orientale*, amid the fumes of opium and joggree, each defraying his own small portion of the rent'.[19]

Much of Salter's criticism of other religions included general aspects of their adherents' characters and cultural practices – moral weaknesses which he considered to emanate from misguided religious values. Significantly, however, his portrayal of decadence on the basis of religion is more pronounced in his description of upper- than of lower-class Indians, because the moral depravity of the latter was less distinguishable from that of Britons of equivalent social standing. For instance, in his discussion of the Begum of Oudh's visit to England to appeal against the East India Company's annexation of her kingdom, Salter follows a description of a courtier's clandestine conversion from Islam to Christianity with the following remarks:

> Such was the state of anarchy, jealousy, and deadly enmity towards each other in which they lived, even plotting against one another! so that whilst the royal household was conflicting with Parliament, they were at war amongst themselves, till law-suits and counter claims disorganised the whole establishment.[20]

Similarly, in his discussion of experiences among other Indian princes residing in London's prosperous West End, he declares of Muslims that 'their existence is centred in worldly pleasure'.[21] Such criticisms extended to the behaviour of the poor: 'Why do not these Mahommedans fly to the rescue of their suffering brother? The Moslems are stoic fatalists, and are moved by nothing that does not immediately affect their own interest.'[22]

However, much of the fault that he found in the behaviour of India's poor in London was similar or identical to behaviour that he disapproved of among the metropolis's indigenous poor. His books contain many descriptions of public houses, gambling dens, and houses of ill repute, that are virtually indistinguishable from their English counterparts apart from the exotic attire and paraphernalia of the participants. While his focus on opium dens highlights the distinctly oriental flavour of his mission, it does not set Indians off as wholly 'other' from the London poor among whom they lived. However condescendingly he does so, Salter recognises a similarity between the depravities of the East and the West in his condemnation of London as a source of corruption among many of its poorer Asian inhabitants:

> The heathens of the heathen land associate here with the heathens of Christian London, and, truly, they both dwell in the valley of the shadow of death . . . The heathen mind is dark, and the vices of the various heathen systems in which the Asiatic is so brought up as to form part of his nature, are bad enough when unmingled with European sin in his own land of superstition; but here is an interchange of sin and an unholy compound of both.[23]

Certainly, Salter considered unconverted Asians to be heathen and therefore naturally sinful, not because of their biology but because of how they were 'brought up'. But Indians did not so much corrupt London's poor as vice versa. In condemning London's moral environment, Salter was echoing the sentiment of some of the Home's supporters, one of whom complained that Asians 'were allowed to leave our shores and return home as heathens, perhaps more corrupt and depraved than when they left their native land'.[24] Another wrote: 'Many of them settled in England among the worst surroundings, and those who returned to their own lands carried with them an evil impression of our Christianity, being, in reality worse heathens than when they came.'[25] While revealing the arrogance of those carrying out the mission of the Strangers' Home, such declarations show the complexity of their condescending attitudes – for they considered the moral turpitude of Britain's lower orders to be even worse than that of the Indians. Moreover, the former they held to a higher standard, since the Gospel had been within easy access of them all their lives, whereas the latter they considered relatively innocent, having never encountered the teachings of Christ.

Cox has pointed out that the 'spread of Western civilization was a providential opportunity, but it was an opportunity that Christians had to exploit vigorously in order to prevent un-Christian influences in the west from corrupting the heathen'.[26] Nowhere did missionaries regard such un-Christian Western influences as more dangerous than at the heart of Britain's Empire, for the middle-class leaders of British Protestantism considered the inhabitants of London's East End to be as wayward spiritually as were those of Banares or Delhi. To England's inner-city missionaries, apathy and indolence led the former astray as surely as false gods did the latter, and the distance of class cut many native Britons off from the values of Victorian polite society as effectively as the distance of geography did the inhabitants of India. Indeed, Cust, whose remarks regarding caste were discussed in the previous chapter, observed in the *JNIA* that the location of the Strangers' Home on West India Dock Road, Limehouse, was 'a very long way off from civilised London'.[27] Such a remark may have racialised the difference between Britain's respectable and lower classes, but it certainly complicated any attempt to construct a uniform Britishness in distinction from an oriental Other.

Furthermore, amid the sin that Salter assumed to have shaped the character of these 'heathens', he also detected a core of righteousness:

> These are no idle vagrants, so many of whom prowl through the length of our island, preferring rather to beg than work. These are all sons of honest toil, and each one has worked his way to our shores and has landed in our midst with a bright eye and a merry heart, because he had Queen Victoria's golden coins hidden in a corner of his gaudy puggree; enough, in his own estimation and ours, too, should he fall into right hands, to supply all the scanty wants of Oriental life, till he finds another ship that will take him back again to his family and friends rejoicing.[28]

Similarly, in his second book, Salter declares:

> Yet many of these unhappy beings were honest men. They had wives and families of their own in the far-off lands; some had parents whose long-cherished hope of fain seeing their children had yielded to despair. Most of the Eastern exiles were anxious to return to their native homes, but a subtle system of bondage kept them here enslaved.[29]

The juxtaposition of these passages and the earlier ones highlighting London's corrupting influence show well the tension in the attitudes of Salter and his sponsors toward Indian culture. The earlier passages emphasise the 'heathen' basis of Indian society, which makes it fundamentally immoral and different from polite society in Britain, but not from the degraded state of Britain's lower classes, which are also very different from Britain's elite. If these passages emphasise difference, the last two imply similarity. For these visitors are deserving of help because of their innocence. Indeed, India's poor may have possessed an advantage in this regard, because Britain's elite imagined them to come from village communities, whereas the British workers and street people they encountered in London were decidedly urban. Since the cult of the village contrasted the simple purity of the rural with the deceitful vice of the urban, inner-city missionaries may have subconsciously transferred such values onto the Indian and British poor in London respectively. The penultimate passage seems to point toward such a conclusion. Like upstanding Englishmen, Indians were 'sons of honest toil', loyal to the Queen, and optimistic (perhaps overly so) about the opportunities that the British Empire offered. Like their British counterparts they had families and friends, examples of the domestic sphere that Victorians considered so essential for a moral society, who would rejoice at their return. Salter's assessment of Indians in Britain, especially the poor, was consistently condescending. Nevertheless, by writing positively about some of their character traits, and by hinting at domestic analogies that served to humanise them to his readers, he created analogies as well as dichotomies between Britain and India.

Seen this way, Ruth Lindeborg's assertion that Salter employed 'metaphors of contamination and fears of hidden similarities between East and West' needs to be reassessed. The same applies to her claim that 'Salter makes "English" a continuous construct', and that one of the central missions of the Strangers' Home was 'to reproduce belief in the irremediable difference between the English and their colonial subjects'.[30] The elite who ran and worked on behalf of the Strangers' Home were indeed concerned about the potential for contamination, but as much from lower-class Londoners to their counterparts in the East as vice versa. The similarities that these men feared between East and West were among the lower orders, from whom they considered themselves separated by a vast social and moral gulf. Furthermore, it is simply inaccurate to argue, as Lindeborg does, that 'by shifting responsibility' for the 'partial failures of his missions . . . to the Asiatic and the latter's baseness, ... Salter's texts thus erase any causal relationship between English imperial practices and lascar vices'.[31] In addition to Salter's own identification of London's poor as a source of corruption for Asians, and thereby many of the difficulties under which he labours, Hughes, in his introduction to Salter's *The Asiatic in England* made explicit the connection between Britain's commercial empire and the degrading environment, both economic and moral, in which many people of colour lived. He reminded his readers that 'this great and wealthy nation' is 'so deeply indebted to India, China, and its Colonies in the East for its prosperity and riches'.[32] And to the business community he issues this challenge with its implicit criticism:

> You may have amassed a fortune in India; or have been an Employer of ORIENTALS, who assisted you in bringing merchandise to this Christian country; you have doubtless given them their just dues, but have you done anything to rescue them from the harpies that infest our seaports, or used means to prevent their being robbed of their money or stripped of their clothing, or have you used any endeavour to give them the Bread of Life?[33]

Such criticism of London's sinful environment even figures into Salter's 'dislike to an Oriental settling down in England'. Given his obvious unease elsewhere regarding miscegenation, this remark clearly has a racial context. Yet even this statement, which would be wholly unacceptable to modern ears, also implies a condemnation of London's moral environment, since his reason for holding this opinion is that 'with very few exceptions, I have never known them to be morally benefited by it'.[34] Such statements only portray a 'continuous construct' of Englishness set against the wholly 'Other' that the 'Asiatic' represented, if one confines 'Englishness' to polite society. But there is no sign that Salter did, since he referred to London's poor and 'ill-mannered' as English[35] and himself came from a humble background. Rather, Salter's remarks indicate a complex matrix of similarities and differences informed by ethnic and class biases that ranked the societies of India and Britain in comparison with and in contrast to the gold standard of Victorian British polite society.

Missionary critique of empire

Nowhere is this matrix more apparent than in the recognition that Salter and his sponsors accorded to differences between classes of Indians. In his first book Salter devoted an entire chapter, entitled 'West-End Visitation', to his mission among 'natives of the highest rank' who had 'made their way from India to the metropolis of the West'.[36] In his introduction to Salter's *The East in the West*, Henry Morris, a retired officer of the Madras Civil Service, wrote that Asian visitors to England could 'be divided broadly into two classes – the lower orders who have come here as Lascars or seamen on board our great steam vessels, and performers at exhibition; and Hindu and Mahommedan gentlemen who visit this country in order to improve themselves in their positions or professions, and noblemen paying homage to the Queen'.[37] Moreover, he praised Salter for not confining 'his attention exclusively to Orientals of the lower classes', but having 'availed himself of every opportunity that has come in his way of approaching men of better caste or position'.[38] Like many other Victorians, Morris used caste and class interchangeably. While portraying upper-class Hindus and Muslims as immoral, Salter nevertheless respected certain aspects of their ethics, which he called 'Oriental etiquette', particularly those that he regarded as complementary to Christianity, and criticised Englishmen who flouted them. For instance, he described as 'profane' and 'ill-mannered' an Englishman who violated the Begum of Oudh's purdah by gazing upon her while she walked from her palanquin to a train carriage.[39] This recognition of the existence of alternative forms of polite society to those of Britain does not necessarily mean that Salter considered the British version to be on a par with its Indian counterpart, but it does imply that he regarded the Indian version of gentlemanly behaviour, like the British one, to be a marker of social status.

Furthermore, ethnic distance combined with class distance in the perceptions of the Home's supporters to create graduated levels of condescension in their attitudes. This is particularly evident in the remarks of H. C. Squires, the vicar of Holy Trinity Church, Richmond, at the Home's annual meeting in 1901. While the vicar implied that Indians were basically innocent, as with Salter's, Hughes's, and Morris's remarks concerning lower-class Indians, this innocence was born of naivety more than virtue. But the naivety of middle and upper classes did not arise from Indianness itself. Rather it emerged from the context of their surroundings, the fact that Indians were 'strangers' to London. Squires made this point explicit by comparing the experience of socially respectable Indians in London to his own as a missionary in India: 'Having then been a stranger in a strange land, and knowing the difficulties of that position, I am thankful for an Institution in this great city that provides a Home with its doors always open to those strangers from Africa and the East who need assistance.'[40] If, however, Squires tempered his condescension toward middle- and upper-class Indians with sympathy by recognising a rough equivalence between their experiences and his own, a similar level of self-identification is lacking in his attitude toward India's poor. For here the equivalence is with 'a fine-looking specimen of an English navvy' whose injury had prevented him from supporting his family for several weeks, and to whom Squires gave money to tide him over.[41] For both the upper and lower echelons of Indian society there are equivalents in Britain, but Squires clearly regards his own station in life as comparable to the upper.

In this setting, a crucial marker of membership in polite society was the willingness to give to the poor. If, as Saloni Mathur observes, 'The travel of poor Indians to London was ... a problem for the British and Indian elite alike',[42] it was also an opportunity. Not only was assistance to the poor one's Christian duty, but it also established one's credentials as a gentleman or lady. We have already seen how officers of the Strangers' Home criticised British businessmen who profited from the Empire but refused to alleviate the negative consequences of their trade. Consistent with this approach, the Home's British supporters encouraged wealthy Indians to give to it as a means of demonstrating their membership in Victorian polite society. In his *JNIA* article on the Home, Cust appealed to Indian readers for support in terms of their obligations as middle- or upper-class citizens of the British Empire: 'If the natives of India desire to rank on an equality with the people of England – and they justly may desire to do so – they must come forward and take part in associations to alleviate suffering, such as hospitals; and protect the unwary and friendless, such as this Home for Strangers.'[43] The implication was that to behave as a member of British polite society reinforced one's Britishness, in the dynastic-imperial sense (to be discussed in the next chapter).

In fact many Indians gave generously to the Home, which recognised their charity by according them gentlemanly status. The most generous of these benefactors was Duleep Singh, Maharaja of Punjab, whose £500 donation was more than twice the sum that the royal family gave, to found the Home. This prince, who had converted from Sikhism to Christianity as an adolescent, seemed to be the very model of what Salter hoped to achieve at lower social levels through his ministry. Accordingly, Salter dedicated *The Asiatic in England* to the Maharaja, commending him for his 'princely liberality'.[44] By the time that Cust published his article, however, Duleep was a problematic example, because he had renounced Christianity to return to Sikhism. Worse still, he had forsworn his loyalty to Queen Victoria and was in contact with Sikh nationalists hoping to end British occupation of their land. Still, other Indians continued to serve in the role of gentlemanly benefactor, even if they were not all Christians. The Home's report for 1900 records that the Maharaja of Travancore, a Hindu, donated £25, more than any other individual that year. But long before Cust's appeal, wealthy Indians had paid off most of the Home's mortgage. Among them were four princes and 'other Parsee and Hindoo gentlemen of Bombay'.[45] As Hughes noted, 'the debt was speedily effaced; ... not by an appeal to the benevolence of Christians at home, but almost exclusively by the unsought liberality of natives residing in India'.[46]

The involvement of non-Christian Indians as sponsors of the Strangers' Home presented problems for its directors. Not all Indians were happy to give to the Home while it pursued its evangelical Christian mission. Indeed, the contributions that paid off the Home's mortgage followed an incident in which its directors turned down a generous offer, because it would have compromised the Home's religious mission. The Parsi firm, Cama and Company, offered to pay off £4,000 of the Home's mortgage on 'the condition of the present Rule ... (so far as it provides for communicating Christian instruction to

Asiatics who require its protection and aid) being now and forever abolished'.[47] In the conclusion to Salter's *The Asiatic in England*, Hughes pointed proudly to the directors' rejection of this offer and struck a note of victory, and possibly divine intervention, in the gifts of wealthy Indians that soon followed. In the preface, however, Henry Venn emphasised the 'principle ... that there should be nothing like forced proselytism'.[48]

In reality the approach may not have been quite so low-key as Venn described. Yet in keeping with the emphasis of many missions abroad on ministry through charity, it was the Home's material mission that came to take priority. From June 1900 to March 1901 the Home was without a missionary, and the minutes of the 1901 meeting show a realisation and concern that the spiritual mission might seem unimportant or irrelevant to the greater task of material aid. Marshall Lang, the lay secretary of the CMS reminded the meeting: 'Christian instruction, dear friends, we do desire shall be always connected with this blessed Home.'[49] But Squires followed Lang with pragmatic suggestions for eliciting donations beyond the major Protestant missionary societies and their supporters. Significantly, he did not suggest appealing to contributors on the basis of the Home's evangelical activities. Rather he emphasised the social pedigree and orientalist knowledge of its directors and managers. These names formed a list 'that any philanthropic society might well envy, and especially any philanthropic and Christian society that carries on its operations among Asiatics and Africans'.[50] For Britain's elite, considerations of class and education were apparently more persuasive than those of religious conscience.

Abraham Challis: dissident missionary

Ironically the person who filled the Home's vacant missionary post demonstrated that, in the encounter between British institutions and Indian visitors to the United Kingdom, religious instruction could go in both directions. He also demonstrated how destabilising to Victorian values was behaviour that respected Indians of the lower classes. Born in 1857, Abraham Challis entered the service of the LCM in 1884. His social and educational background is a mystery, but unlike Salter he spent up to five months in India in 1896 as part of his training for his position as missionary to London's Asian and African communities. Salter had trained Challis in Hindustani and Swahili during the late 1880s and Challis also acquired a working knowledge of Arabic. In 1900 he filled the position, previously held by Salter, as missionary to the Strangers' Home. By this time he was encountering a challenge almost unique among inner-city missionaries in London, because, unlike the unchurched masses of British poor who were the most common target of the LCM servants, London's Asian visitors often held well-developed beliefs from alternative religions.

The large Indian presence in the Strangers' Home may have made its spiritual mission unusually challenging, since India's culture embraced organised religions that proved historically to be more resistant than many to proselytisation. One reason for this resistance was the tendency of Indians to define their ethnic identity partly in religious terms. Hindus, Muslims, Sikhs, Jains, and Parsis were usually acutely aware of the religious traditions that underlay their ethnic identities. Because the religious beliefs of these ethnic communities had evolved in the context of their relationship to one another, their members were practised in rebutting attempts from adherents of other religions to convert them. This was particularly the case among Muslims, whose scriptures made specific reference to Christianity. Salter noted that 'Mohammedans have a decided dislike to attend Christian services which are intended for themselves. They have sometimes looked in on the Bible classes, and when invited to be seated, have run away, apparently from a fear of Christian influence.'[51] Muslim resistance to Christian proselytising was particularly pronounced among the educated, and Salter records many debates with them in which it is far from clear that he got the upper hand.

The contrast between Salter's and Challis's responses to such arguments is striking. Forty years of service in this unusual mission field provided Salter with the experience and confidence that he displayed in an article for the *LCM Magazine* late in his career.

> Our visitors are very various. Here is a diamond seeker, ready to buy or sell. I told him where to get the pearl of great price. Also an Arab with wonderful charms, credited with the power to quell storms, scare evil genii, and cure all manner of diseases; but he had not the charm that would take away sin. We exchanged the Living Word for his vaunted storm charm, and told him how to obtain pardon for sin.[52]

For those who came to him 'ostensibly to make enquiry about the Truth, but really to establish their own error', he 'recommended ... the more comfortable creed supplied in the Word of Life'.[53] The ability to dismiss the doctrines of other religions with phrases borrowed from the gospels came more easily to Salter than to Challis. Although Salter acknowledged a certain level of moral innocence among his congregation, he regarded their religious beliefs as depraved. For instance he wrote 'how firmly Satan was enthroned within' a 'neo-Buddhist' who remained unresponsive to his preaching.[54]

Challis, on the other hand, praised Hindus and Muslims for the integrity of their faiths. Of lascars, who were overwhelmingly Muslim, he wrote:

> I like them for the stand they make for what they believe to be the truth in their religion. But I like them also because they are very keen about knowing what kind of a foundation Christianity rests upon before they are willing even to give it friendly consideration. If one is not prepared to be criticised through and through, and if one is not also prepared to submit to the criticism of all that we believe, and the manner in which that belief is or is not lived out, it is not much good to expect their interest, even though we had twice as fine a Mission Institute as we now possess. The typical Lascar is a far shrewder person than many give him credit for, and if he is not over-ready to embrace Christianity, he can, if called upon, give some forcible reasons for not doing so, and reasons that are not easy to combat.[55]

Challis's remarks were unusual because they show respect for lascars in spite of their class. Perhaps he credited his audience with the ability to raise challenging arguments for their own beliefs because he was reconsidering his own. If so, his encounter with advocates of other religious beliefs may have reinforced his questions regarding Christian doctrine. Such a process had precedents among encounters between missionaries and non-Christians elsewhere in the Empire. Perhaps most famous among these was the case, fifty years earlier, of John William Colenso, bishop of Natal, whose encounter with African beliefs led him to question the authenticity of biblical accounts. Ultimately, his application of textual criticism led to his excommunication from the Anglican Church.[56] In Challis's case the future of his connection with the LCM was at stake. In the absence of any detailed account, it is impossible to know for certain what led Challis to resign from the organisation in July 1903 after serving as the missionary to the Strangers' Home for less than three years. The LCM Committee minutes record only that 'he had expressed the opinion that he felt it impossible to prosecute his work amongst the Asiatics any longer with success, and that he had quite made up his mind to seek another field of labour where he thought he might do more good'.[57] Had Challis experienced a crisis in his faith? When three months later he applied for re-admission to the Mission, the subcommittee interviewing him recorded that 'he now manifested a much more humbled spirit than he had at first shown'.[58] The LCM had invested much time and money in training Challis, and its leaders likely valued a man who had the necessary orientalist expertise for the mission to London's Asian communities. They re-admitted him with the loss of ten years' service toward his pension. He resumed his activities among London's Asian population but beginning in 1906 devoted his full attention to the creation and maintenance of a home for lascars in Tilbury.

Challis's spiritual odyssey had not ended, however, for in the meantime he began to associate with religious and intellectual groups outside the LCM's evangelical circle. He attended the City Temple during the ministries of Joseph Parker and Reginald John Campbell, of whom the latter held theologically liberal views and regarded other religions from a more relative perspective than did the evangelical activists of the LCM. Claiming that 'what I have to say leads back . . . to the wise men who lived and taught in the East ages before Jesus was born', Campbell preached that 'all life is fundamentally one' and 'the ultimate Self of the universe is God'.[59] Equally disturbing, from the LCM leadership's perspective, was Challis's association with the Unitarian Church and the League of Progressive Thought. These connections came to the LCM Committee's attention in the autumn of 1909, just as his remarks praising lascars, quoted above, appeared in the *LCM Magazine*. Challis appeared before the Mission's Discipline Committee to answer charges of unsound doctrine that might have led to his dismissal. He defended his attendance of the City Temple, arguing that 'Mr. Campbell's teaching had helped him, and better fitted him for his work among Muhammedans'.[60] Nevertheless, under the threat of severance from the LCM, he agreed to end his connection with these organisations, and 'expressed his regret at having been associated with these errors'.[61]

Establishing a causal relationship between Challis's liberal theological leanings and the beliefs of the people to whom he preached is problematic. On the one hand, his association with theologically liberal organisations may have satisfied a longing to reconcile his Christian beliefs with the persuasive arguments of Hindus and Muslims he encountered in the streets of London. On the other hand, his liberal theological beliefs may have simply encouraged him to treat the recipients of his message with more respect. Whatever the case, Challis had adopted an approach markedly different from Salter's. For Challis was willing to use the Quran as an authority, albeit from a Christian perspective, for persuading Muslims to adopt Christian values: 'The Quran is a much-used book in the Institute, and gives the Missionary some of the finest opportunities he can wish for, especially when it comes to the interpretation of its meaning, and the application of it to the lives of men to-day.'[62] Such details of his thought are unavailable, but it is clear that his drift toward a more liberal theology and his encounters with people of other faiths complemented each other.

Having returned for a second time to the evangelical fold, Challis turned his attention to the material plight of his congregation, which now consisted entirely of lascars. But as his sympathy with their condition grew, he crossed the line between taking advantage of the imperial system in order to spread the gospel to criticising specific agents of that system for exploiting labour from the Empire. In October 1912, in a letter addressed to the Undersecretary of State for India, Challis outlined the P&O (Peninsular and Oriental) Shipping Company's abuses against lascars. The Board of Trade investigated the matter, but the P&O Company reacted to these charges by withdrawing permission for Challis to visit sailors on board its ships. From the perspective of the LCM leadership Challis's concern for the lascars' material welfare was undermining the more important effort to secure their spiritual welfare. Indeed, such a restriction may have been disastrous to the mission. The Strangers' Home statistics for 1888, the latest we have regarding this matter, indicate that, of the 208 visits that the Home's missionary made that year, 124 were to P&O ships. If twenty-five years later, the same were true for Challis's mission, then denial of access to P&O ships would have been a crippling blow to the LCM's outreach to Asians. The minutes of the LCM Discipline Committee record its concern that 'to that extent his usefulness [was now] limited'.[63] The outbreak of war, however, soon created a new mission field for Challis, under the pay of the YMCA, among Indian soldiers in France. When in 1924 Challis died while still serving the LCM, the committee's minutes noted that he was a 'man of much force of character ... and greatly interested in the Muhammedan peoples to whom he ministered'.[64]

From the LCM's perspective, however, Challis had exhibited too much force of character in his dealings with British authorities and his own superiors. In reaching out to lascars he had challenged their position at the base of Britain's imperial racial and class hierarchy. His respect for their religious arguments had raised them from the lower-class objects of condescension that they had been to Salter, and tested the assumption of doctrinal and ethical superiority inherent in proselytising. His protests regarding their working conditions highlighted the exploitation on which Britain's commercial success depended. In short, Challis contested the power structure which debased lascars in terms of their class, race and religion. In showing how a British missionary could transcend these barriers, he highlighted the extent to which British authorities did not.

F. E. A. Chamier and the Strangers' Home's material mission

Challis's career demonstrated a fact that had already become apparent from Protestant missionary activity elsewhere in the Empire: that an emphasis on the material over the spiritual aspects of the mission to Asians in Britain's inner cities was less controversial for the theologically unorthodox, so long as they did not denounce the businesses that profited from the exploitation of Indians. Indeed, in his 1881 celebratory retrospective of the LCM, John Matthias Weyland provided a twenty-eight-year chronology of one missionary, Michael Parfitt, that focused almost exclusively on his deeds rather than the number of people he had converted. It is a list of foundations of study groups, ragged schools, and chapels, plus the occasional record of publications. Implicit in the chronology was the effectiveness of this material activity in bringing souls to Christ. Yet nowhere in it was there a numerical indication of the ministry's success, such as numbers of baptisms or professions of faith. When Weyland cited numbers, they were too vague to be of much use. For instance, he quoted Parfitt's number of 30,000, presumably lower-class Londoners, attending 'Mothers' Meetings', but there was no indication as to whether these congregants were converts to Christianity, women who were already attending church, or mothers who simply attended the meetings without making a formal commitment to Christ.[65] The assumption here, and in the accounts of Salter and Challis, was that to offer material aid or social gatherings in an evangelical Christian setting would inevitably bring in converts. Of course, these evangelicals also understood the spiritual and material missions of Christianity to be inseparable, and the LCM's practice of both was typical of Victorian churches at home and in the overseas Empire.[66] Nevertheless, given the obstacles facing the LCM's mission to London's Asians, the material aspects of mission received greater emphasis than the spiritual ones, transforming in practice the nature of the encounter between inner-city missions and Indians in London. In spite of the Home's evangelical efforts, Indians remained overwhelmingly indifferent or hostile to Christian proselytising but took a much keener interest, either as beneficiaries or benefactors, in the Home's efforts to provide a secure environment for Indians of limited financial means. For the latter, the Home served as a means of controlling and limiting the presence of India's lower orders on the streets of London.

Key to these functions was the Home's Honorary Secretary. This man was responsible for interviewing applicants for admission to the Home, organising their board and lodging, maintaining discipline, and evicting inmates who had overstayed their welcome. He was also his charges' banker, and took care of a 'deposit account' through which roughly £2,000 of their 'cash and valuables' passed in the fiscal year 1883–84.[67] Upon entering the Home 'inmates' were required to make such deposits as they could, from which the Honorary Secretary covered their expenses at the Home. Most important, however, was the secretary's quasi-official status as the man to whom the India Office referred destitute Indians whom it was unwilling to repatriate. The frequent correspondence between the Home's secretary and the secretary of the India Office's Judicial and Public Department is replete with mutual consultation on the fate of Indian applicants for assistance. If the Home's secretary brought a case of destitution to the attention of the India Office it was usually he who provided the initial description of the petitioner's social background and the circumstances of his or her plight. The secretary of the Strangers' Home, therefore, wielded considerable power over the fate of Indians who passed under his jurisdiction. He determined whether they deserved assistance, often on the basis of information that they and other Indians supplied. In order to judge this information, the secretary tapped into his knowledge of India. In some cases he received this knowledge from India Office administrators and officials in the Government of India. Most often, however, he drew on his own knowledge, because the men who directed the Strangers' Home during the late nineteenth and early twentieth centuries had experienced India themselves. Cust remarked that 'The Committee of Management consists to a great degree of retired servants, civil and military, of Her Majesty in British India'.[68] This was certainly the case with F. E. A. Chamier, the Home's secretary during the 1890s and 1900s.[69] The son of a Madras civil service officer, he served General Sir James Outram as an interpreter of Persian during the British Raj's expedition into Persia in 1857, and saw action later that year in the Indian Rebellion. He honed his perceptions of Indian society in his decisions regarding the settlement of land revenues in the Bara Banki district of the United Provinces in the 1870s. The very circumstances of his administrative task encouraged Chamier to see Indians in terms of social rank, because he had to categorise the people of his district by occupation for purposes of assessing revenue. For instance, he recorded that cultivators were 'required to pay according to the custom which prevailed in the Nawábí' that preceded British rule. Their revenues were determined as a portion of what they produced to be paid in kind. Examples of these taxes were 'one head-load of straw', 'one basket of chopped straw', or 'one vessel of sugarcane leaves' to be paid annually. Fixed property, such as a sugar mill, required payment of currency, in this case one rupee. Chamier underscored the occupational nature of these revenue obligations by pointing out that 'the tenant only pays the dues fixed for the different crops; he would not give five seers of gram if he had only sugarcane'.[70] In order to assess the capacity of a village to raise revenue, Chamier investigated the inhabitants' standards of living and their social practices. He therefore indulged in ethnic stereotyping according to religion and occupation. Fundamental to his assessment of

Indian society was his belief that Hindus were morally superior to Muslims. The weakness of Muslim society, he asserted, resulted from polygamy, which promoted moral depravity:

> The low ideal of morality which is set before the Mahomedan in his youth is the bane of his after-existence. Though his first wife be 'one whose beauty claims no worse a husband than the best of men', still he forsakes the paths of domestic peace because a plurality of wives is lawful to him, or because his co-religionists and associates have set him the example.[71]

For Chamier, as for many contributors to the *JNIA*, the role of women as the bastions of the cult of domesticity was central to the moral health of any society. Since he regarded polygamy as a practice whose main purpose was to satisfy the lust of men, it could only destroy the social and ethical order of the Muslim domestic sphere, creating 'a life of constant worry and distress'. The disruption of domestic order undermined the morality of Muslim men in the public sphere. Therefore, although 'Mahomedans may be described as an intelligent race . . . their intellects are too often employed in machinations and intrigues'.[72] Chamier's antipathy toward polygamy may, indeed, as he asserted, have resulted from his experience. But his experience of the practice was in the negative setting of inheritance disputes, the intricacies of which he delineated in a chart.[73] It is easy to imagine this settlement officer arriving at a negative view of the Muslim domestic sphere, when his most frequent encounter with it was in civil cases where it had broken down amid acrimony among a deceased householder's wives and children.

If polygamy, an institution supposedly central to Muslim society, weakened its moral standards by undermining domestic tranquillity, caste, an institution supposedly central to Hindu society, did the opposite by strengthening its home life: 'From the strict rules which govern their domestic relations they are a far happier race than Mahomedans with whom they have no manner of sympathy.'[74] Chamier's use of the term 'race' to describe religious communities is indicative of the nebulous approach to classification that permeated even those whose official task it was to classify. By conflating race and religion he indulged in stereotypes of Muslim and Hindu society and did not recognise that many, if not most, Indian Muslim men were monogamous. Nor did he acknowledge the evidence of his own chart that some Hindus were polygamous, or from other statements of his that Muslims were organised into castes. To read the words of an administrator of the Raj approving of caste, even implicitly, may seem surprising, but it is not if one takes into account his treatment of it as an occupationally-based social hierarchy. The order that it provided, therefore, not only bolstered the domestic sphere through monogamy and arranged marriage, but also regulated the public sphere by providing clear divisions and regulations between social classes. The result was that: 'As public servants, especially in the higher offices, Hindús are according to my experience not so liable to lead dissolute lives as Mahomedans.'[75]

Chamier's stereotypes of workers by occupation confirmed his personal approval of a social hierarchy based on it. Like many Victorians, he considered menial labourers to be morally or physically inferior to the educated classes. These assessments applied to Muslims and Hindus respectively, particularly when it interfered with the production of wealth for landholders. Among Muslims, therefore, he declared, 'Weavers are of all castes the most difficult to manage, they lead improvident lives, are ever ready to combine in resisting any new demand, and during the mohurum [Islamic new year] resort to violence at the slightest provocation.' Although Hindu 'cultivators' were 'industrious ... and frugal in their habits', they were 'capable of undergoing considerable fatigue if left to serve in their own slow way'.[76]

By contrast, in spite of the moral differences that Chamier attributed between Muslims and Hindus, class, defined as respectability, was an even greater indicator of reliability than religion: 'If respectable men are selected and then treated with kindness and discriminate confidence, both races [i.e. religious communities] furnish many excellent public officials.'[77] This assessment did not mean that Chamier ranked all high-born Indian men as gentlemen. The social behaviour of *zamindars* and *taluqdars* greatly influenced his assessment of their respectability. Whereas he regarded loyal, educated servants of the British Raj favourably, he considered many of the local notables in his district to be decadent and incapable of good government. The exceptions are consistently those 'rajahs' who have demonstrated their loyalty to the Raj or have assimilated British culture. For example, 'Rájah Farzand Ali is a very intelligent man, and may well be able to manage his estate with prudence and circumspection.' He also served Britain 'during the mutinies'.[78] Another prince, Ram Ibrám Ballí, found favour with Chamier, because: 'Unlike a vast number of kanungos this t'alukdár is an exceedingly well-conducted man.'[79] Similarly, Chaudhri Enáyat Rassul was 'a thorough gentleman', because he served as 't'alukdár of the summary settlement' that Chamier supervised for the district.[80]

Chamier's report reveals three standards that he used to assess Indian society: domestic virtue, social order, and loyalty. He could have used these standards equally well in British society. Indeed, it was from the polite society of Victorian England that they came. The very nature of his mission as the settlement officer for the Bara Banki district distorted his view of some of its social institutions, such as polygamy, but it was the standards of Victorian polite society that he applied to them. Inasmuch as the Indians whom he encountered met these standards, he approved of them and accorded them gentlemanly status. Inasmuch as they did not, he criticised them in his report. Chamier's standards were informed in part by religion. For him society was ranked according to occupation, and to the extent that caste reflected these ranks, he approved of it. Polygamy, on the other hand, contradicted the teachings of the Christian church, and for good reason in his estimation – because it undermined the moral fabric of the domestic sphere which was so essential to the preservation of social order. Loyalty was one of the primary benefits of an ordered society and a moral domestic environment. Chamier's three standards were therefore inextricably linked. This linkage in his mind would be immensely important to destitute Indians in London during the coming decades, when he used it to assess their applications for assistance in his capacity of Honorary Secretary of the Strangers' Home.

The institutions that interacted the most with India's poor in London were the London City Mission, the Strangers' Home, and the India Office. In many respects the Strangers' Home served as a bridge between the spiritual idealism of the first and the political pragmatism of the last. Its administrators were former servants of the British Raj, who held their positions in the Home because of their expertise. As such, their opinions were valuable to a variety of institutions in London that dealt with Indians, but whose administrators had little knowledge of India. Most important, however, the Strangers' Home served as a domestic branch of the India Office, catering at once to the needs of that cabinet ministry and India's poor on the streets of the imperial metropolis. Because of its quasi-official function, the Strangers' Home could not be an effective critic of the system that created the population that needed it. No matter how much Hughes or Salter objected to the commercial aspects of imperial power, they would not attack the organisations, such as shipping companies, that abused their charges. P&O's response to Challis's lone attempt to do so underscored the ideological dilemma facing administrators of charitable organisations serving the Indian poor in the imperial metropolis. Indeed it was through private donations rather than government action that those who felt moved by the plight of destitute Indians sought to ameliorate their position. As we shall see, charity to Indians in late Victorian and Edwardian Britain evolved in ways that reinforced class hierarchy but sent mixed messages regarding racial order.

Notes

1 IOR L/PJ/6/64 No. 1872, Strangers' Home for the Natives of India, Arabia, Africa, China, Straits of Malacca, the Mosambique, and the Islands of the South Pacific, *Annual Report for 1900* (London: Edwin Sears and Co., 1901), front cover.

2 Heb. 13:2 (Authorised Version).

3 For statistics for 1882, see Robert Cust, 'Strangers' Home', *JNIA*, 162 (June 1884): 255. For those for 1896, see University of Birmingham Special Collections, Church Missionary Society Archives, G AC 4/4157a, *The Fortieth Annual Report of the Working of the Stranger's Home*, 1, attached to F. E. A. Chamier to Rev. H. E. Fox. I am grateful to the University of Birmingham for permission to use the Church Missionary Society Archives. For those for 1900 see the Strangers' Home *Annual Report for the Year 1900*, 3. Statistics for 1886 come from the Strangers' Home *Annual Report for the Year 1886*, 10 and 17, in the United Kingdom National Archives: Public Record Office, Kew (hereafter PRO) MT 9/362 M.1067/1890 'Board of Trade's refusal to grant a licence to the Strangers' Home'. Citations from UK public records are under Crown copyright.

4 Strangers' Home, *Fortieth Annual Report*, 1, and *Annual Report for the Year 1900*, 20–1.

5 Strangers' Home, *Annual Report for the Year 1900*, 24–6. The total contributions are calculated on the basis of the monthly subtotals. My estimate of the minimum amount donated by individuals connected with the Indian Government is based on names of contributors whose Indian connections I could verify. Others on the list may have had connections.

6 See Godley to Messrs. Charles Taylor & Company, 2 January 1907, PRO BT 15/62, File F/28218; a note dated 7 March 1890 on a Board of Trade circular memorandum, entitled 'Strangers' Home for Asiatics, West India Dock Road, Limehouse', and draft letter accompanying it, PRO MT 9–362, File M/4861. From 1868 to 1890 the Strangers' Home Officer holding this licence was William Whitmore.

7 Jeffrey Cox, 'Religion and imperial power in nineteenth-century Britain', in Richard Helmstadter (ed.), *Freedom and Religion in the Nineteenth Century* (Stanford: Stanford University Press, 1997), 340 and 371.

8 Max Warren, *To Apply the Gospel: Selections from the Writings of Henry Venn* (Grand Rapids, MI: William B. Eerdmans, 1971), 63. As Warren points out, however, Venn's ideal rarely became reality overseas either. (*Ibid.*, 26.)

9 Henry Venn's preface to Joseph Salter, *The Asiatic in England: Sketches of Sixteen Years Work Among Orientals* (London: Seeley, Jackson, and Halliday, 1873), vi.

10 David B. MacIlhiney, *A Gentleman in Every Slum: Church of England Missions in East London, 1873–1914* (Allison Park, PA: Pickwick Publications, 1988), 107.

11 London City Mission (LCM) Committee Minutes, 31 October 1853, 217. I am grateful to Dr John Nicholls, Director of Recruitment and Training at the LCM, for providing me with a typewritten copy of passages in the minutes that relate to Salter and Challis.

12 See Hughes's introduction to *Asiatic in England*, 14, and Salter's own account, *ibid.*, 71, and Joseph Salter, *The East in the West, or Work Among the Asiatics and Africans in London* (London: S. W. Partridge and Company, 1895), 138.

13 Donald M. Lewis, *Lighten Their Darkness: The Evangelical Mission to Working-Class London, 1828–1860* (Westport, CT: Greenwood Press, 1986), 205–6.

14 For a discussion of early modern European attitudes toward Asia see Michael Adas, *Machines as the Measure of Men: Science, Technology, and Ideologies of Western Dominance* (Ithaca: Cornell University Press, 1989), 21–68. For the Westernising tendencies of nineteenth-century missionaries see Brian Stanley, *The Bible and the Flag: Protestant Missionaries and British Imperialism in the Nineteenth and Twentieth Centuries* (Leicester: Apollos, 1990), 157.

15 Salter, *Asiatic in England*, 286.

16 *Ibid.*, 277.

17 Salter, *East in the West*, 21.

18 Salter, *Asiatic in England*, 42.
19 *Ibid.*, 24.
20 *Ibid.*, 63.
21 *Ibid.*, 256.
22 Salter, *East in the West*, 23.
23 Salter, *Asiatic in England*, 22.
24 Rev. George Smith to the *Evangelical Magazine* (November 1842) quoted by Hughes in *Asiatic in England*, 4.
25 Henry Morris, Preface to *East in the West*, vi.
26 Cox, 'The missionary movement', in D. G. Paz (ed.), *Nineteenth-Century English Religious Traditions: Retrospect and Prospect* (Westport, CT: Greenwood Press, 1995), 212–13.
27 Robert Cust, 'Social and philanthropic institutions in the West – VI. The Strangers' Home for Asiatics, Africans, and South Sea Islanders', *JNIA*, 162 (June 1884): 255.
28 Salter, *Asiatic in England*, 22.
29 Salter, *East in the West*, 16.
30 Ruth Lindeborg, 'The "Asiatic" and the boundaries of Victorian Englishness', *Victorian Studies*, 37:3 (Spring 1994): 387 and 390.
31 Lindeborg '"Asiatic"', 387.
32 Hughes, Introduction to *Asiatic in England*, 10.
33 *Ibid.*, 16–17.
34 Salter, *Asiatic in England*, 51.
35 See his description of the 'profane Englishman' in *ibid.*, 54.
36 *Ibid.*, 255.
37 Morris, Preface to *East in the West*, v.
38 *Ibid.*, viii.
39 Salter, *Asiatic in England*, 54.
40 Stranger's Home, *Annual Report for the Year 1900*, 19.
41 *Ibid.*, 17.
42 Saloni Mathur, 'Living ethnological exhibits: The case of 1886', *Cultural Anthropology*, 15:4 (November 2000), 494.
43 Cust, 'Strangers' Home', 256.
44 Salter, *Asiatic in England*, frontispiece.
45 Hughes, Conclusion to *Asiatic in England*, 299. For the Maharaja of Travancore's donation in 1900 see Strangers' Home, *Annual Report for the Year 1900*, 24.
46 Hughes, Conclusion to *Asiatic in England*, 295.
47 Cama and Company to Lt.-Col. Hughes, 15 Sep. 1863, quoted in *Asiatic in England*, 296.
48 Henry Venn, Preface to *Asiatic in England*, iv.
49 Strangers' Home, *Annual Report for 1900*, 12.
50 *Ibid.*, 16.
51 Salter, *Asiatic in England*, 91.
52 'Mission to Asiatics and Africans', *London City Mission Magazine* (hereafter *LCMM*) 1 March 1892, 58.
53 *Ibid.*, 59.
54 *Ibid.*
55 'The Society's work amongst lascars: Growing usefulness and appreciation of our Tilbury Institute', *LCMM*, October 1909, 200.
56 See Gerald Parsons, 'Rethinking the missionary position: Bishop Colenso of Natal', in John Wolffe (ed.), *Religion in Victorian Britain*, Vol. V *Culture and Empire* (Manchester: Manchester University Press, 1997), 135–75.
57 LCM Committee Minutes, 20 July 1903, 14.
58 *Ibid.*, 26 October 1903, 45.
59 R. J. Campbell, *The New Theology* (New York: Macmillan, 1907), 22, 33, and 34.
60 LCM Discipline Committee Minutes, 15 November 1909, 20.
61 LCM Committee Minutes, 22 November 1909, 332. See also the Discipline Committee Minutes for 8 November (p. 16) and 15 November (pp. 20 and 329).

62 'Society's work amongst lascars', 202.

63 LCM Discipline Committee Minutes, 7 April 1913, 35. For the 1888 statistics on missionary visits, see Strangers' Home, *Annual Report for 1888*, 15, in PRO MT 9/362, M4861. I was unable to trace Challis's letter to the Undersecretary of State in the India Office Records.

64 LCM Committee Minutes, 14 July 1924, 68.

65 John Matthias Weyland, *Our Veterans: Life-Stories of the London City Mission* (London: S. W. Partridge and Co., 1881?), 58–63.

66 For examples see Jeffrey Cox, *The English Churches in a Secular Society: Lambeth, 1870–1930* (Oxford: Oxford University Press, 1982), 41–2, and Jeffrey Cox, *Imperial Fault Lines: Christianity and Colonial Power in India, 1818–1940* (Stanford: Stanford University Press, 2002), 74–5.

67 Cust, 'Strangers' Home', 255.

68 *Ibid.*, 256.

69 Correspondence indicates only three honorary secretaries of the Strangers' Home during the late nineteenth century. The third was J. H. Fergusson, mentioned earlier in connection with the Board of Trade's refusal to renew the Home's licence as its representative. Unfortunately, the dates of these administrators' tenures are as difficult to ascertain as are those of their missionaries.

70 F. E. A. Chamier, *Report of the Regular Settlement of the Bara Banki District* (Allahabad: North-Western Provinces and Oudh Government Press, 1879), 49. This limited publication is available at the University of Chicago Special Collections under the British Library call number, IS. UP 108/3.

71 Chamier, *Report of the Regular Settlement*, 50.

72 *Ibid.*, 50–1.

73 *Ibid.*, 52.

74 *Ibid.*, 51.

75 *Ibid.*

76 *Ibid.*

77 *Ibid.*

78 *Ibid.*, 60.

79 *Ibid.*

80 *Ibid.*, 64.

PART II

Interactions

CHAPTER FIVE

Imperial subjecthood and legal identity

> We hold ourselves bound to the natives of our Indian territories by the same obligations of duty which bind us to all our other subjects, and those obligations, by the blessing of Almighty God, we shall faithfully and conscientiously fill . . . And it is our further will that, so far as maybe, our subjects, of whatever race or creed, be freely and impartially admitted to office in our service, the duties of which they may be qualified by their education, ability, and integrity duly to discharge.[1]

With this proclamation in 1858, Queen Victoria assured the inhabitants of the territories, hitherto directly ruled by the East India Company, that the British Government would treat them on a par with the inhabitants of the United Kingdom. That India's culture was different from that of Britain's or its white-settler colonies was implicit in the proclamation's insistence 'that none be in any wise favoured, none molested or disquieted, by reason of their religious faith or observances, but that all shall alike enjoy the equal and impartial protection of the law', and that 'in framing and administering the law, due regard be paid to the ancient rights, usages, and customs of India'.[2] Having maintained their control over India through the brutal suppression of a bloody rebellion, British authorities sought to legitimise their rule in terms of equality before the law and a common allegiance that transcended ethnic diversity. In order to achieve this goal, they perpetuated the dynastic concept of subjecthood to a monarch at the expense of the concept of citizenship of the state, which was becoming ever more common in other Western countries during the late nineteenth century. As with so many other aspects of British governance, including the domestic political constitution and the acquisition of empire, much of this trend occurred on an ad hoc basis as British institutions responded to the new imperial connections that their expansion abroad created. Nowhere were the boundaries of these connections tested more than in the encounter between British institutions and Indians in the United

Kingdom. The institutional response to the presence of Indians on British soil revealed the tensions between ethnically based concepts of nationality and dynastic traditions of subjecthood which fitted together awkwardly in the context of the imperial metropole. Yet at the same time official attempts to define Indians as British subjects and fit them legally into British society provided opportunities for upwardly mobile visitors from the subcontinent. Equally important, the Indian encounter with institutions in the United Kingdom forced British officials to adapt their own national identity into an imperial context, one that competed with the tendency toward ethnically-based citizenship that was becoming increasingly common across the globe.

What emerged from these attempts to create an imperial identity were areas of ambiguity regarding which Indians were British subjects, whether Indians should be treated exactly the same as other British subjects without any reference to the land from which they came, and how Indian social and professional ranks should be understood legally in the British setting. This chapter examines the ways in which these legal ambiguities surfaced in the encounter between Indians and institutions in the United Kingdom. It demonstrates the willingness of British institutions to accept Indians as 'British subjects', but it also highlights the confusion that officials felt regarding this status, especially as it applied to Indians in the United Kingdom. Perhaps most importantly, this chapter demonstrates the importance of class in determining Britishness at the legal level, for Britishness itself was partly a construct of class.

The concept of British subjecthood

At a time when the concept of citizenship was well evolved on the European continent and in the United States, it remained vague in the British Empire. This ambiguity resulted partly from the way in which Britain had acquired its Empire and partly from the inconsistency with which Britons regarded people of colour. The Empire was a patchwork quilt of territories with different forms of legal subordination to the United Kingdom. Like the metropole, the Empire had no precise moment of formation nor a formal constitution to embody the motives of such a moment. Rather it emerged as a disparate set of ad hoc acquisitions that reflected the varying history of British strategic priorities and the political weakness of indigenous governments at the times of their territories' colonisations over the previous three centuries. By 1890, therefore, the Empire embraced, among its many territories, a single self-governing 'dominion', Canada , which was a federation of earlier self-governing colonies; various partially self-governing settler colonies, such as those of Australia; crown colonies, such as Hong Kong, which had authoritarian governors; protectorates, such as Egypt, whose indigenous rulers served at the behest of the British Government; and India, which was run under an entirely separate cabinet office from the other colonies. Indeed, British administrators often referred to India as an empire, rather than a part of the larger British Empire, partly because the India Office and the 'Government of India' themselves controlled satellite princely states that amounted to about two-fifths of India's land area and a quarter of its population.

If the legal status of British territories was varied, so was the ethnic identity of their inhabitants. The British Empire embraced cultures that were radically different from one another, and which had, in some cases, no contact among themselves before the British arrived. Moreover, Britain was geographically remote from the rest of its empire, separated by thousands of miles of ocean. Such conditions raised problems of identification with the imperial metropole as early as the eighteenth century, when distance played no small role in the creation of the United States of America. The process, beginning with the Durham Report of 1839, of extending self-government to white-settler colonies, was designed to retain a global sense of British identity across the oceans by granting colonists a regional level of responsibility that reflected the imperial power of the electorate in the United Kingdom. This process was effective in slowing the development of separate national identities in these territories, whose inhabitants continued well into the twentieth century to regard themselves at some level as being British. The question remaining was whether this transoceanic concept of Britishness could extend to inhabitants of the Empire who were not descendants of British emigrés. From the perspective of white settlers in the dominions, the answer was clearly no, since their tenure of the land arose only from the expulsion of indigenous inhabitants. In other words, for British settlers in the Empire, the very attraction of Britishness was its ethnic and biological character that distinguished them from the indigenous population and justified their dominance of new territories. Thus the dominions early on developed draconian racially-based restrictions on immigration and denied people of colour many basic rights of citizenship.[3]

The same was not true, however, for the leaders of the British Empire. In spite of the important role of Asian and African 'otherness' in uniting the inhabitants of the British Isles under a single, albeit incomplete, sense of national identity, strategic priorities dictated a more open concept of Britishness in the imperial metropole.[4] The realities of imperial power belied any suggestion of common citizenship in the sense that it was developing in nineteenth-century Europe. British rulers knew that to allow democratisation in the tropical Empire, where cultural differences from the metropole were marked, would rapidly lead to independence. Nevertheless, as they acquired direct rule over an extensive multi-ethnic empire with large territories that would not serve as potential settlements, they encouraged the evolution of an imperial identity that would ensure the loyalty of this diverse population. Modern concepts of national consciousness and ethnically defined citizenship threatened this endeavour, since they encouraged divisions among British possessions and discouraged the development of imperial identity. The model that British imperial administrators encouraged instead was an older one of dynastic loyalty. Because Britain was a monarchy, this focus on a loyalty which transcended ethnicity was readily available. The concept of British subjecthood, in contrast to citizenship, was therefore very important for British rule. Whatever one's ethnicity, one could be a British subject by living in a territory over which the British monarch was sovereign.[5] The reality of equality was, of course, quite different from the theory. British authorities systematically denied Indians access to commissions in the Indian army, membership in the Indian civil service, equality before the law, and decision-making power in the Indian Government. Yet the theory was still important, because it provided a framework in which Indians could try as a group, through nationalist movements, and individually, as we shall examine here, to gain access to the privileges that their counterparts in Britain enjoyed.

In spite of the racial prejudice they encountered in the United Kingdom, Indians realised some tangible benefits from being able to claim British subjecthood. They could apply for British passports, allowing them to claim consular help if they encountered trouble while visiting the European continent or the United States. British subjecthood also entitled Indian men who met the property qualifications to vote in elections and hold public office in the United Kingdom. The British subjecthood of Indians, therefore, formed an important legal context for their encounter with institutions in the United Kingdom. It was a status that many Indians raised when seeking treatment equal to that of their British social counterparts.

Certificates of identity and social status

One way in which British institutions could establish Indians' status, both in terms of social rank and national allegiance, was through certificates of identity. The title of these documents was appropriate in many respects, since they certified, that is officially categorised, multiple levels of identity among Indians who obtained them. The provision of certificates of identity to Indians desiring them for travel to late Victorian and Edwardian Britain provides evidence of the complexity of institutional Britain's understanding of the differences and similarities between natives of the United Kingdom and visitors from India in the social context of the imperial metropole.

The little attention that these documents have received has treated them almost exclusively as instruments of control.[6] Certainly they served such purposes, since the India Office was thereby able to compile lists of Indians in the United Kingdom and better monitor their activities. Nevertheless, as John Torpey has noted, since 'possession of a passport ... constitutes *ipso facto* evidence of a legitimate claim on the resources and services of the embassies and consulates of the issuing state ... these documents cannot be regarded merely as a means of governmental control'.[7] This analysis also applies to certificates of identity, which until the First World War the British Government did not require for Indians, because, as Sir Louis Mallet, Permanent Undersecretary of State for India, 1874–83, had pointed out, 'restrictions on the departure of Natives from India, able to pay their passage to this country, would be regarded as an interference with the liberty of the Subject'.[8] Rather, British authorities encouraged Indian visitors to the United Kingdom to obtain these certificates in advance, in order to gain the full benefits of their status as British subjects. They highlighted the benefits in the Government of India's formal resolution on the subject in 1903 claiming that Indians 'who have proceeded to England, desire to obtain passports to enable them to travel to foreign countries in which the possession of a passport is necessary or desirable, and that difficulty often arises from a want of evidence to show that the applicant is a British subject and therefore entitled to a passport'.[9] That this statement reflected the actual beliefs of its authors is evident in internal India Office correspondence using similar language.[10]

Indians would, therefore, acquire certificates of identity, not because they were coerced into doing so, but because they would receive benefits for holding them. For Indians, therefore, certificates of identity were two-edged swords which allowed British authorities to trace their movements in the United Kingdom, but also provided them with *bona fides* of their proper status in British society in terms of both British subjecthood and class. In this sense, like the passports that they entitled a holder to acquire, certificates signified not only Jürgen Habermas's sexual metaphor of the state's 'penetration', but also Torpey's counterpart of its 'embrace', of individuals' private lives, that is 'the ways in which states bound – and in certain senses even "nurture" – the societies they hold in their clutches'.[11] The dual use of these certificates in no way lessened the importance of the state, because by using them and allowing them to determine their behaviour toward one another, Indian visitors and residents of the United Kingdom acknowledged their value for expressing the holder's social rank every bit as much as they did coinage for expressing financial value. Both the certificates and coinage were the product of government agencies, and both were valuable because they denoted the government's authority in their respective areas. Gérard Noiriel points out: 'It is often overlooked that legal registration, identification documents, and laws are what in the final analysis, determine the "identity" of immigrants.'[12] In applying for these certificates, therefore, individual Indians negotiated with British authorities the creation of social identities that would be understood and valued in the United Kingdom.

British authorities had two major reasons for encouraging Indians to acquire certificates of identity. One was political. Since the 1870s Indians had been visiting Britain in increasing numbers in order to acquire qualifications that would give them an edge over their competition back home and enable them to enter influential professions, such as the Indian Civil Service (ICS), that were normally available only to residents of the United Kingdom. By the 1890s the number of students residing at any given time in Britain was over three hundred. Many of them, at once disappointed by the unexpected poverty and racism of Britain and also radicalised by encounters with British students and faculty, took part in organisations that criticised Britain's governance of India. Even societies such as the National Indian Association, which boasted several India Office administrators on its membership list, served increasingly as a forum for Indians to voice their frustrations. It was in this context that Lord George Hamilton, the Secretary of State for India, informed the viceroy's council that 'it is in regard to young Indian students that the measures of inquiry and registry which I have suggested would be most advantageous'. One of his concerns was that 'Strenuous endeavours are being made in this country to interest young Indians in political discussions and public meetings of a very controversial and essentially party character.'[13] Even so, because Hamilton limited his formal opposition to political activity to Indians studying for ICS exams, he was, theoretically at least, asking no more of Indian students than he did of their British counterparts. Significantly, Viceroy Lord Curzon and his council did not devote much space to this issue in their reply, merely leaving it up to the Secretary of State 'to ensure that those who are studying for competitions for the public service are warned to dissociate themselves from politics'.[14] Furthermore, Government of India officials insisted that the 'system must be voluntary and therefore can only be expected to include a part of those who travel'.[15] British authorities, therefore, intended to use certificates of identity to monitor students bound for the ICS but not to prevent them from entering the United Kingdom.

The other reason for encouraging Indians to acquire certificates of identity was financial. From the enactment of the Poor Law in 1834 until the Second World War, British authorities pursued an emigrationist policy toward their own poor. That is, in order to lower the charges to the government of destitutes throwing themselves on the mercy of British workhouses, British authorities encouraged them to migrate to North America, Australia, and New Zealand. Concomitantly, the British Government discouraged immigration from the European continent which might further swell the number of people receiving state aid. The Aliens Restriction Act of 1836 required captains of ships arriving from foreign countries to declare to customs officials the name, social rank, occupation, and description of their passengers and crew.[16] Although it did not require a passport of foreigners, it did demand that they present one if they had it. This rather haphazard provision, which did not actually restrict immigration, remained largely unenforced until the Aliens Act of 1905, which required all aliens entering Britain to prove their identity.

Most Indians, however, were not aliens but 'British subjects'. Yet British law treated many of them as if they were the former. The Indian Emigration Acts of 1874 and 1883 discouraged Indian labourers from settling in the United Kingdom by requiring employers to provide for their return to India. This legislation, however, like the Coloured Seamen's Order of 1925, was clearly as much a matter of discrimination by class as race. Britain's policy toward immigration from India was therefore vastly different from that of the dominions. The latter had small white populations in large territories and suffered from a shortage of cheap labour. They therefore encouraged 'coolie immigration', only to discriminate against the immigrants by race, and stereotype their cultures on the basis of the narrow selection of classes that they had imported. Partly in order to reduce competition against British manual labourers, and partly to diminish the burden on British taxpayers for poor relief, late Victorian legislation severely limited the presence of Indian labourers in the United Kingdom by requiring employers to guarantee their return. As India Office administrators were well aware, if manual workers were allowed to enter Britain unrestricted, 'the U. K. would have to maintain an agent at each emigration port & incur other obligations, just like most of the colonies wh [*sic*] import Indian labour'.[17]

British law did not, however, prevent Indian professionals from remaining in Britain. Indeed, until 1902 it did not even cover artisans and entertainers. To restrict their entry into the United Kingdom officially would have been fraught with negative political consequences for British authorities, since it would have dispelled the legal fiction of equality before the law, which all British subjects were supposed to enjoy. Furthermore, the lack of any requirement that Indians, other than labourers, make arrangements for their return passages before travelling to Britain meant that even those who did not intend to settle in the United Kingdom might find themselves trapped there if they ran out of money. In such situations they were as likely to become charges on the poor rates as was any native of Britain. Yet British authorities could not agree on financial responsibility for the repatriation of Indians, whatever their class, with Poor Law guardians, the India Office, and the Foreign Office frequently bickering over who should bear the burden of an Indian subject's repatriation to the subcontinent. British practice therefore treated middle- and upper-class Indians effectively as more British than their labouring class compatriots.

Certificates of identity provided a compromise solution between the evolving exclusivity of acts restricting aliens and lower-class people of colour, and the illusion of legal equality for all British subjects above the rank of manual labourer. Rather than agree to repatriate destitute Indians, the solution that the India Office and the British Government of India arrived at was a policy similar to the British Government's toward foreigners: discourage them from coming in the first place. As Lord George Hamilton pointed out, during the process of issuing certificates of identification,

> measures could be taken in India regarding persons contemplating such visits to England, and reported to me. Inquiries could then be made in India as to the objects in view and the means of the travellers to carry out those objects. False impressions could be corrected, and timely advice given. If the advice should be ignored the responsibility would rest on the parties themselves, and it would be easy to dispose of any subsequent applications for aid which might be addressed to this Office.[18]

In order to achieve this end, however, the India Office transformed certificates from documents that simply attested to the holder's British subjecthood to those that provided the government's imprimatur on the bearer's social value. The certificates required identification not merely of the holder's 'subjecthood' but also of his or her social status – because, much like a loan officer determining whether an applicant is worth the risk, local authorities in India were to assess an applicant's ability to live in Britain on the basis of lineage, occupation, and wealth – in a word, class. Thus, certificates of identity became, in effect, passports that asserted an Indian's Britishness in the most practical terms, his (rarely her) right to reside in Britain, on the basis of class. Hamilton doubted that British authorities in India 'would find much difficulty in ascertaining the names, parentage, and position of most of the Indian students or others who are coming to England for a prolonged visit', and, although they did not 'consider it expedient to bring into prominence the requirement that the certificate should state the social and pecuniary position of the father', the viceroy and his council agreed to include it.[19]

Yet it was this feature of the certificates of identity that made them desirable to upwardly mobile Indians. Curzon saw little need to pressure Indians into acquiring certificates, because 'Natives of India have a well known predilection for certificates of any kind, and there should be little difficulty in inducing them to provide themselves with certificates of identity of the nature proposed, if suspicions are not aroused that they will be subject to espionage in consequence.'[20] Although this statement was a typical example of Curzon's ethno-centric condescension, it was partially true, albeit for reasons that he might not have understood. For centuries, many Indian kinship groups of humble origin had managed to influence their rulers' understandings of caste in ways that elevated their own social and political status under Mughal and then British rule. The invention of ethnic traditions and histories was often central to this process and was all the easier to accomplish during periods of political upheaval, regime change, and geographic mobility. We have already seen in Chapter 2 that recent scholarship has highlighted such cases most dramatically among the lordly castes. Bernard Cohn's description of the Imperial Assemblage of 1877 is but one of many instances in which Indians cooperated with British administrators in the 'invention of traditions' that simultaneously secured imperial sovereignty for Britain and social status for Indian princes. Yet this process also extended to the professions. Susan Bayly has noted that many of those who 'sought to stabilise their "caste" status by seeking service in the colonial revenue bureaucracies' were the descendants of 'incomers of humble origin who had only recently moved into the scribal specialisms'.[21]

Certificates of identity presented the ideal opportunity for Indians to continue in a centuries-old practice, the assertion of higher social status in potentially hostile political environments. British administrators were not ignorant of such calculations. Indeed, implicit in Hamilton's proposal regarding certificates of identity was the hope that they would better enable authorities to combat nationalist sentiments among India's educated elite through public recognition of their social status. Thus, immediately preceding his statement regarding Indian attendance of political meetings in the United Kingdom, Hamilton argued that with the information certificates provided: 'When the sons of

Indian nobles or high families visit England, it would be possible to obtain for them social and other attentions which might prove of great value if due notice of their plans and of their status had been given.'[22] Indeed, such advanced information was of great political importance to British authorities, since the extension of honours to Indian princes was central to Britain's attempts to maintain its power on the subcontinent by ruling in cooperation with India's aristocracy. Thus the India Office prevailed on British customs officers to speed Indian princes through entry formalities at British ports, and it organised receptions for princes who attended Queen Victoria's jubilees and Edward VII's coronation.[23]

For the most part, therefore, it was wealthy Indians who applied for certificates of identity. This pattern is evident in returns of certificates retained in the India Office Records. In the first quarter of 1900, for instance, thirty-five Indian men received certificates – surely only a small fraction of those actually travelling to Britain during those months. Of these recipients twenty-five were travelling abroad for study, twenty-two of them in Britain. Four recipients were attending the Paris exhibition, and two were travelling generally. In every case in which the recipient indicated his intention to travel beyond the British Empire, the local authority endorsed his request for a passport. Under the column headed 'Social and pecuniary status of father (or guardian)' all the entries indicated men who owned large estates, controlled sizeable businesses, or held high-ranking professional positions. Furthermore, Hindus were invariably listed as Brahmins or Kshatryas, the two highest *varna* of classical Hindu scriptures.[24] These patterns persisted. Government promotion of these certificates nearly doubled their use over the next decade but still hardly reflected the number of Indians, even professionals and students, travelling outside the subcontinent. Returns for the second quarter of 1908 show that out of sixty-six recipients, twenty-nine were travelling abroad for education, twenty-eight for business, twelve for health, and seven solely for pleasure. Caste listings for this sample were more specific than for that mentioned above, often identifying *jati* or *gotra* for Hindu recipients. For the most part, however, these ranks were still upper caste, and more than anything, the category of caste was used to identify the applicant's religion. Many of the certificates upon which the return was based added helpful comments on the recipient's class, such as 'belongs to a respectable family', 'is a respectable Hindu gentleman', and 'zamindar – Has landed property'.[25] Both the samples from 1900 and 1908, therefore, indicate that Indians who applied for a certificate of identity could expect it to establish or enhance their social rank.

If the certificate achieved this end, then it could be a valuable tool, not only for gaining access to high society, but also for receiving the tangible benefits that high social rank bestowed in a society primarily ordered according to class. For instance, the certificate of Bilash Chandra Das listed his father as a 'Hindu-Kayestha'.[26] Potential employers, faculty, and landlords who had access to the 1891 Indian census could have learned that the 'Káyasth' caste, numbering over two million, was the 'most important' of Group 5 ('Writers') of Class IX ('Professional'). Census Commissioner J. A. Baine's accompanying commentary, prepared at the India Office, suggested that the writing castes came from a combination of lower- and upper-caste ancestry, but being 'a naturally intelligent community have lost no time in taking advantage of their opportunities ... but have devoted a good deal of research and ingenuity to proving their right to Kshatria origin'.[27] If Britons unfamiliar with India did not see the census, the certificate came to Das's aid by informing the reader, under the heading 'Social and pecuniary status of the father (or guardian)' that the holder came from a 'Respectable family – having an annual income of Rs. 2,000/-'.[28] In Das's case the certificate served as a credential of his genteel status, which the India Office rewarded accordingly, for even though the India Office's policy was to reject indigent Indians' petitions for financial assistance, it arranged for a loan to pay his return journey when he ran out of funds.

Perhaps most important, by encouraging people in the United Kingdom to order Indians by class, certificates of identity reduced the tendency of Britons to treat all Indian visitors as 'coolies', a practice that was common in the dominions. This tendency explains why, for the most part, only wealthy Indians bothered to acquire them, and it points to an irony in the history of the certificates' uses before the First World War. The British Government encouraged the acquisition of certificates of identity in order to discourage India's lower classes from visiting the United Kingdom while manipulating and monitoring those of its middle and upper classes who did. However, Indians themselves transformed their primary purpose into statements of social rank that separated them from the mass of 'coolies' who inhabited the lower-class districts and docklands of Britain's major cities. A policy that began for the purposes of empowering British authorities, therefore, evolved rapidly into a practice that empowered Indians who complied with it. Nowhere is this tendency clearer than among businessmen and students, the middle classes of India. British institutions did not recognise the social status of these classes as easily as they did that of India's rural elite. Yet it was vital to the purposes of these Indians' presence in Britain that they did so. Long before the government encouraged Indians to acquire certificates, therefore, many travellers from the subcontinent had already requested and received them, in order to establish respectability as they attempted to launch businesses or acquire professional qualifications in England. The vital importance of such documents became apparent in the widely publicised trial of four Indian 'oculists' at London's Old Bailey in 1893.[29]

Professional identity and Indian culture: Indian oculists at the Old Bailey

'Heere Shah and his three companions, the Indian "oculists", are extremely fortunate men.' This was the verdict of a *Times* editorial on 31 October 1893 regarding the trial of four Muslim Punjabis at the Old Bailey for practising medicine and surgery on a patient's eyes without proper qualifications. It probably expressed the implicit dissatisfaction of many British readers, who had followed this trial over the previous week. For these men avoided conviction for fraud, not because the jury thought they had done no wrong, but because there was no law on the books to punish them for their apparent deceit. English law at the time made practitioners of medicine and surgery liable for criminal prosecution if their treatments caused death, but not if they merely caused injury, no matter how great it was. The common serjeant, the part-time judge serving the City of London, virtually guaranteed an acquittal when, in his summary, he pointed to this limitation in the law. Nevertheless, he shared the jury's frustration, which it expressed in the following rider to its decision: 'We very deeply deplore that there exists at present no criminal law to prevent persons with such gross ignorance as the defendants from practising medical surgery.'[30] Indeed, it was the absence of such a law that forced the government to seek a conviction for fraud, however tenuous the case.

Yet, although the verdict focused on medical malpractice and the law, the trial itself was a clash of cultures that showed how scientific advances occurred in the context of an empire defined by class and ethnicity. Seen from a social, rather than a purely legal perspective, the Indian oculists became the focus of a contest between classes over access to medical science. Their case also represents a little-examined aspect of imperial culture: the informal alliance of disadvantaged groups across ethnic boundaries in order to circumvent financial barriers to health care.

As we have seen, British authorities tended to regard some Indians, such as princes and professionals, with greater respect than others, such as sailors and unskilled workers, because they saw them fitting into social classes analogous to those in Britain. The British institutional response to the presence of oculists was something of an exception to this practice, because although the oculists continued to command respect among the wealthy in India, British polite society often viewed them as 'quacks'. The tension that resulted between culturally differing perceptions of respectability highlights the importance of class as a register for determining Britishness, in this case the right to reside in the United Kingdom versus treatment as a criminal.

It was the perception of the defendants as 'quacks' that the London and Counties Medical Protection Society, formed only the previous year,[31] sought to instill in the public when it brought the matter to the attention of the police. The prosecuting attorneys presented nine witnesses, all white and working class, who were dissatisfied with the treatment that they had received from the defendants. Five complained that the oculists' remedies had done nothing to improve their sight, and had caused pain and deterioration of their vision. Of one defendant, a witness declared, 'he has ruined me for life'. Also testifying for the prosecution were six expert witnesses, who had examined the patients. Five were Fellows, and one a Member, of the Royal College of Surgeons. All six had examined one or more of the patients. They interpreted the accounts of the witnesses in the context of medical science by diagnosing their conditions, explaining the treatments that British surgeons would prescribe, and pointing out the ways in which the defendants had erred.[32]

The surgeons criticised the defendants on several grounds. Foremost was the oculists' employment of poor equipment and sanitary procedures, which included their use of regular knives rather than surgical ones and their practice of cleaning them with their own spit. Particularly important to the British surgeons was the defendants' lack of an ophthalmoscope, which allowed examiners to view tissue inside the eye and became the most important tool in modern medicine for diagnosing diseases of the eye. The oculists also conducted their operations without anaesthetics. Another issue was the oculists' practice of relieving pressure in the eye socket by cutting flesh away from the area around the tear ducts. This, the surgeons pointed out, only temporarily alleviated the pain from inflammation, while it often led to infection and sometimes damaged the tear ducts. A further transgression was their use of cuts at the temples to promote bleeding that supposedly released poisons affecting the eye. Finally, the oculists treated cataracts by 'couching' them, that is pushing the cataracts out of the way, rather than removing them.[33]

Although the prosecution portrayed the oculist treatments as quackery, even its own expert witnesses admitted that they were similar to those performed by British surgeons of previous generations. Anaesthetics had been in common use for fifty years, but antiseptic procedures dated back no more than twenty. General use in Britain of the ophthalmoscope began in the late 1850s, around the same time that ophthalmologists abandoned the time-honoured operation of couching the cataract. Ironically, many of these changes had come about through the pioneering efforts of Indian army medics, both British and Indian, who confronted eye diseases more often than their counterparts in Britain. Therefore, although one may use the term 'modernisation' to describe late nineteenth-century advances in eye treatment, it would not be entirely accurate to describe it as an aspect of Westernisation. Furthermore, although Western ophthalmology had undergone radical changes over the previous forty years, not all the assumptions of an earlier age had disappeared. For instance, testifying for the prosecution, George Anderson Critchett, FRCS, conceded that 'inflammation of the eye might be relieved by letting blood from the temples, but might be done in a far less cruel manner [than the knife incisions of the defendants] and more successfully ... bleeding by leeches might relieve the inflammation – I should employ leeches'.[34]

This recommendation, which would sound ludicrous to later generations,[35] demonstrates how tenuous were the prosecutors' attempts to draw a clear line between the supposedly legitimate medicine of the British professions and the allegedly fraudulent medicine of the Indian defendants. While many of the criticisms that professionals levelled against alternative medicines were valid, the efficacy of medicine was not the only issue motivating their objections. Financial and class considerations also guided the medical profession's efforts. As an educated class they sought government support in the creation of a monopoly of medicine that would render any unlicenced practitioner outside the law. Such a monopoly ensured the medical profession the gentlemanly status that was the hallmark of success in Victorian Britain. Late nineteenth-century British doctors dressed as gentlemen, joined gentlemen's clubs, did not advertise their services, and were discreet in their discussion of fees. They cultivated this etiquette because, as one medical sociologist has observed, 'It is bad form for gentlemen to appear to be technicians or uncultivated, narrow specialists.'[36] By contrast, because the Indian oculists were not members of an established professional organisation, they had none of the privileges signifying class that members of the established medical profession enjoyed. Although they occasionally performed their services free of charge, the court records show that fees were a prominent issue in their discussions with their clients. Furthermore, the oculists were very concerned about public advertisement, which they performed through renting space in local newspapers, distributing handbills in their vicinity, and pressing their clients to sign testimonials whose precise wording they had prepared ahead of time. By 1893 the British medical profession had established themselves as gentlemen set off from all other medical practitioners, whom they often called 'quacks', but they had not persuaded the government to outlaw the practice of medicine outside their guilds. Rather the Medical Act of 1858 had merely given the imprimatur of respectability to the Colleges of Physicians, Surgeons, and Pharmacists, allowing them monopolies over the use of these titles and over government medical positions. Thus did Critchett declare in court, 'I prefer the term ophthalmic surgeon as applied to myself.'[37]

The defendants, however, had not claimed any of these titles. At home they used the Arabic term, *hakim*, which in the Indian context had come to mean a doctor who practised *unani* medicine, which tapped into the traditions of Islamic societies. This was in contrast, but not unrelated, to the practice of *ayurvedic* medicine, which arose in the context of Hindu culture. Both forms of medicine, however, bore marked resemblances to early modern European theories of disease, which treated the body holistically and sought to remove evil substances from it. Islamic medical knowledge had provided much of the foundation of early modern Western medical science and was still regarded highly among many in India. Indeed India continued to play a major role in modern science as a laboratory of conditions that were often more extreme than those of Western Europe. At the time of the trial, *ayurvedic* and *unani* practices were gaining new respect among Indians and even some Britons. The presence of Indian *hakim* in Britain was therefore more a feature of what Arnold Pacey has called a technological 'dialogue' between regions than it was an anomalous setback in the otherwise persistent diffusion of scientific knowledge from the West to the rest of the world.[38] Recognising the oculists' value in their traditional context, the British magistrate in India who issued the defendants' certificates of identity, translated *hakim* as 'eye doctor', thus apparently legitimising their practice in British society. In handbills and testimonials they distributed to advertise their services, the defendants described themselves as 'Indian oculists'.[39] By urging the police to charge the defendants with fraud, the London and Counties Medical Protection Society tried to replace the respectable English translations that the magistrate and the defendants had given of the term *hakim* with their own less respectable versions. The term 'quack' does not appear in the minutes of evidence, but the prosecutor implied it by using adjectives, such as 'fraudulent' and 'cruel', to describe the defendants' work.

It was around the objection to this appropriation of language that the defence's case centred. The defence presented four material witnesses who claimed to have benefited from the defendants' treatments. One testified that he had completely lost the sight in his left eye after surgeons at the Nottingham Infirmary had removed a cataract from it, but that the Indian oculists had restored the sight to his right eye through couching its cataract. The sole expert witness for the defence was Mahommed Yusef Khan, who held an MD from Dublin College and was a former surgeon for the Indian army. He portrayed the defendants as practitioners of traditional medicine, pointing out that although trained in modern techniques himself, he also used 'a great many of my Indian remedies'. The cross examination of Dr Khan brought about the most racially-charged moment of the trial, when the prosecution claimed that the witness had admitted that his reason for testifying on behalf of the defendants was 'that blood was thicker than water, and that I would stick to my own colour', an allegation that Khan denied.[40]

In his summation for the defence an attorney, whom the records identify only as Mr Jervis, argued that in initiating this prosecution the London and Counties Medical Protection Society was putting professional privilege above the needs of the poor. The only reason that his clients were on trial at all was because the 'College of Surgeons was always so jealous of its privileges that it could not endure anyone to think differently from what it did'. Referring to the humble backgrounds of his clients' patients, Jervis also argued that 'the patients had been to hospitals, but had not derived any benefit from the treatment they had received in those institutions, so they resorted to the Oriental knowledge of the Indians'. Indeed, through their use of this knowledge the oculists 'had conferred a benefit on the poor'. As for the medicine that his clients practised, Jervis portrayed it as a valid alternative to that of Britain's medical establishment. In doing so he spoke of India's medical culture in terms equivalent to Britain's. The defendants were entitled to call themselves Indian oculists, because they practised 'the art which was practised in India'. Pointing to the inadequacies of modern medicine in Britain, he asked the jury: 'Qualified persons made mistakes sometimes, and was it right that because the prisoners failed in some cases they should be charged?'[41]

In his summary of the case and instructions to the jury the common serjeant rejected this line of argument. Seeking to delegitimise the form of medicine the defendants practised, he declared that their 'methods were obsolete and barbarous and that they were incapable of diagnosing the diseases of the eye without an ophthalmoscope'. Dismissing the notion that the case was about privilege and class, he 'did not agree that the presence of these men was a benefit to the poorer classes in this country', and he declared that 'it was absurd to say that there was any jealousy on the part of the medical profession in respect of these men'. On the contrary he had 'thought it right to have all the medical evidence which had been given interpreted' to the defendants, so that if they continued 'to do what they had done in the past, they could never urge that they did not know that the representation they were making that they were skilled oculists was false, because they had heard the best medical experts in the land'. Rather than acknowledge that the case involved in any respect the dominance of a particular class or ethnic group, the judge insisted on an absolute interpretation of the value of modern medical science.[42]

The common serjeant's summation and the jury's rider to its verdict meant that, although the defence won its case, it lost its argument. The Indian oculists were acquitted on a point of law, not because they had established their legitimacy as practitioners of alternative medicine. Negative publicity projected the oculists' failure in court into a failure in business. Whatever the demand for alternative forms of ophthalmology existing among Britain's poor, the trial effectively ended the marketability of Indian techniques. Deprived of their livelihood, the oculists fell into destitution, and, along with a companion who had been practising in Norwich, became inmates of the Strangers' Home. Chamier promptly appealed to the India Office for financial support, pointing out that since the oculists were not seafarers, he had 'no way of getting rid of them, that is, of finding employment for them on their return journey', to India.[43]

A debate ensued in the India Office. All agreed that the oculists were 'quacks'. The question was how to treat them in relation to other paupers. The issue revolved around their morality, which in turn drew on varied perceptions of their respectability. Sir Gerald Fitzgerald, the political *aide-de-camp*, took a hard line, arguing that they were 'adventurers pure and simple', and that they could 'work in the Poor House just as well as hosts of others who are accommodated there'.[44] S. C. Bayley, the Political and Secret Department secretary, disagreed. Striking an attitude that combined cultural chauvinism and relativism, he declared: 'Of course they were quacks, but what is quackery in Europe is scientific practice in India.' Furthermore, he argued that to keep them in Britain was a waste of resources: 'They can not do poorhouse work, & they can on the other hand, if sent back to India earn their living there.'[45] Philip Hutchins, the Judicial and Public Department secretary, concurred on the latter point: 'In the poorhouse they can neither eat the food usually given, being Mussulmans, nor do the hard manual task ordinarily exacted from paupers.'[46] Neither Bayley nor Hutchins explained why the oculists could not work in the poor house. But their opinion may have derived from their own experience that *hakim* were regarded as skilled practitioners of a learned 'art' in their own country and that they were simply victims of a culture clash that resulted from their presence in England. For Secretary of State

Lord Kimberley, any aid forthcoming from the India Office hinged on the ethical behaviour of the defendants: 'Was the issue of the trial generally discreditable to the quacks, or were they bona fide quacks?'[47] In other words: did the trial indicate that the defendants were dishonest or merely ignorant? In the former case they would be morally guilty of fraud, but free on a technical point of the law. In the latter, they would, as a result of their cultural backgrounds, be innocent victims of their own ignorance. Godley, the Permanent Undersecretary, asked Ritchie, at this time a senior clerk, to investigate the charges against the oculists. Ritchie's conclusion appeared to confirm Bayley's relativist assertions: 'The prosecution is not reported to have alleged either that the men were deliberate impostors selling what they knew to be worthless; or that they did anything otherwise than in the exercise of their art as they understood it.'[48] Godley, however, refused to treat them purely as victims of a cultural misunderstanding. Reporting to Kimberley, he wrote:

> The answer to your question is that these so called oculists were *bona fide* quacks. But they came very near committing a crime, though they did not quite bring themselves within reach of the law. This being so, ought they to receive the exceptional favour (which is often refused to pauper natives against whom no fault can be alleged) of a *free* passage to India? I should say, certainly not . . . The *most* that I would do would be . . . to advance the money, £54.2.6, on their giving bonds to repay it on arriving in India.[49]

Kimberley concurred. Yet three days later Godley admitted that he was basing this compromise between the workhouse and a free passage on wishful thinking: 'Very possibly the bond may be forfeited, but we shall at least have avoided a bad precedent.'[50] Nevertheless, he authorised the loan, because 'it was desirable to get them away from the Asiatic Home'.[51]

Two reasons account for the India Office's departure from its established policy of not providing financial assistance to Indians in Britain. One was expedience, since the trial had highlighted the presence of potentially criminal Indians in the United Kingdom. The medical profession's attitude only strengthened the pressure on the India Office. To the public opinion that mattered in Britain, the India Office was responsible for clearing the streets of this class of Indians. Yet ironically, the inverse perception among a minority of Britain's elite also argued for the repatriation of the oculists, because those who recognised them as *hakim*, legitimate practitioners of medicine in their Indian cultural setting, also tended to regard them as hopelessly out of place in the social context of the United Kingdom. For officials such as Bayley, Hutchins, and Ritchie, who unlike Godley and Kimberley, had lived in

India, the trial and subsequent destitution of the oculists highlighted that some occupationally-defined Indian classes could not translate well into British society.

At the same time, however, those with Indian experience also accorded some respect to the oculists because they knew the social standing of *hakim* in India. Thus, perhaps, the insistence of Bayley and Hutchins that the oculists were not fit for the labour or diet of the workhouse. Since publicity regarding the trial made it unlikely that further Indian oculists would migrate to Britain, the compromise, to which Godley reluctantly agreed, might have set a precedent for the India Office's dealings with other members of the profession – if it had worked. Unfortunately, the former defendants left their ship as it was passing through the Suez Canal in late February, and did not attempt to repay the passage.[52] Thereafter, the India Office refused to repatriate oculists.[53]

In many respects this case reinforces much of the post-colonial argument regarding the use of knowledge to reinforce ethnic stereotypes and imperial dominance. The prosecution's attempts to use Khan's race to cast doubt on his testimony, and the common serjeant's insistence on the absolute superiority of Western science over the 'barbarous' practices of these defendants from the East are ample testimony to the chauvinist assumptions of the British justice system. Its declarations were immensely important, because as the dispenser of punishments and the arbiter of ethics, it served as the mouthpiece of official Britain. This criticism of the medical and legal establishments of the day does not mean that all medical knowledge was relative. Few people today would prefer to receive the oculists' treatments to those of modern ophthalmology, which is the successor of the medical practices that the establishment in this trial espoused. The point here is that, whatever the merits of the established medical science of that day, they were not the only, or possibly even the primary, reason that the Indian oculists were on trial. Professional privilege was at least as important.

Yet, in spite of the judge's and jury's condemnation of Indian medicine, the case revealed diversity in British attitudes toward Indians and their culture. The limitations of the law regarding injury, and the existence of a certificate describing the defendants' profession as 'eye doctor', weakened the prosecution's case. The defence could have chosen simply to highlight these facts and relied on a technical rather than a moral victory. It certainly pointed out the legal technicalities that ultimately exonerated its clients. But it also chose to mount a remarkable attack on the ethnic and class assumptions of Britain's medical establishment. Jervis's background, and even his first name, remain elusive, so it is impossible to tell what motivated such an argument. Perhaps, as a good defence attorney, he merely sought to recover his defendants' reputations, and therefore their livelihoods, as well as their freedom. Nevertheless, the mere fact that he raised the type of defence that he did is evidence of an alternative to assumptions of class and racial superiority among the elite.

Even more surprising is the division of opinion among India Office administrators. It is worth noting that neither Kimberley nor Godley, who adopted more jaded views of the oculists' behaviour, had actually visited India, whereas Bayley and Hutchins, who accorded some respect to the oculists on the basis of their social standing in India, had both served there for many years. Ritchie, who shared the views of the latter, had not served in India, but he was born and spent his early childhood there. These men knew from personal experience that *hakim* were not considered 'quacks' in their own country, although Fitzgerald, who also had experience of India, was the most hostile to the oculists. The compromise that Godley chose was based on the premise that, if the men really were physicians, they would be able to repay their passage upon their arrival in India. Yet the tone of Godley and Kimberley was much more suspicious and derisive of the oculists than was that of Bayley, Hutchins, and Ritchie. To a certain extent, the India Office revisited the salient argument of the trial: the legitimacy of the oculist's procedures in the context of their own culture. Like the jury at the Old Bailey, its administrators settled on a solution that minimised the oculists' potential suffering resulting from the culture clash of their presence in England, but delegitimised their occupation in British eyes. Thus the oculists avoided treatment as criminals, but by losing class status, they also lost the ability to reside in Britain which their certificates of identity had granted them. In effect the jury, and the India Office, had determined that the oculists were insufficiently British to live in Britain. In stripping them of their 'respectability' they also stripped them of their Britishness.

If the trial and repatriation of these oculists reveal the diversity of opinion among British officials, it also demonstrates the variety of legal and medical cultures within the Empire. The type of medicine that the oculists practised was so acceptable in India that a British magistrate there was willing, in an official document, to describe it as a 'profession'. In Britain, however, the colleges of medical practitioners, whose knowledge was based on modern scientific inquiry, had long since enlisted the government as an ally in their attempts to marginalise medicine practised outside their guilds. That medical cultures should differ so markedly across thousands of miles and between two such different societies is not surprising. That legal attitudes toward them should differ so markedly within the same empire demonstrates how decentralised were the efforts of Britain's elite to control the uses of knowledge in the imperial setting.

Equally striking is the number of English patients of humble economic circumstances who chose, out of hope and desperation, to trust their eyes to men who must have seemed utterly alien to them. Whether the medicine that these men practised was so foreign is a different matter, since it resembled methods that were commonplace in England a generation or two earlier. The wealth and influence of the British medical profession had gradually driven British practitioners of traditional medicine out of business, but the niche remained, to be filled by similar practitioners who continued to flourish in India's more permissive environment. In order to fill this niche, *The Times*, hardly known for its radical political opinion, went so far as to suggest that the government 'must do much more than at present in providing medical and surgical aid to the poor and even, in the end, take over the hospitals'.[54] The ultimate realisation of this suggestion owed nothing to the presence of Indian oculists, but *The Times* editors' mention of it in the context of this trial demonstrated the extent to which, in Britain, medicine was at once an issue of class, empire, and institutional authority.

The government encouraged Indians to acquire certificates of identity for political and financial reasons. But Indians were already applying for them for social and economic purposes, and the government assumed that they would do so. These facts are evidence enough that, even more than passports, certificates of identity demonstrated the British state's 'embrace' as much as its 'penetration' of the lives of its Indian subjects. The institutional approach to the status of Indians in the United Kingdom as British subjects revealed the ways in which the Empire influenced the development in Britain of nationalist concepts, such as citizenship. For it encouraged British officials to use the concept of imperial subjecthood in order to promote unity within the Empire. Therefore, whereas much of the rest of the Western world, and indeed many Asian countries, was embracing the concept of national identity, often ethnically based, the dilemma of dealing with a multi-ethnic empire discouraged so simple a definition of Britishness and encouraged the perpetuation of pre-nationalist forms of political allegiance which depended greatly on socio-economic status. The multiple uses of certificates of identity highlight the connection between allegiance and rank. Their use in the trial of the Punjabi oculists demonstrated their importance in the interplay of class, race, and the construction of knowledge in an imperial setting. Thus while all Indian subjects of the Queen might be British in theory, only those of 'respectable' class were welcome to reside in Britain. For Indians in the United Kingdom, therefore, class was an aspect of their identity that affected another very important one, their Britishness, in a very practical way.

Notes

1 A. Barriedale Keith (ed.), 'Proclamation by the Queen to the Princes, Chiefs, and the People of India, 1 November 1858', in *Speeches and Documents on Indian Policy, 1750–1921* (Oxford: Oxford University Press, 1922), 1:384.

2 *Ibid.*

3 For the exclusionist immigration policies of the dominions, see Sean Brawley, *The White Peril: Foreign Relations and Asian Immigration to Australasia and North America, 1919–78* (Sydney: UNSW Press, 1995). For scholarship on domestic aspects of discrimination against Asian Indians, see Norman Buchighnani and Doreen M. Indra, *Continuous Journey: A Social History of South Asians in Canada* (Toronto: McClelland and Stewart, 1988); S. Chandrasekhar, *From India to Canada: A Brief History of Immigration; Problems of Discrimination; Admission and Assimilation* (La Jolla, CA: Population Review, 1986); Robert A. Huttenback, *Racism and Empire: White Settlers and Colored Immigrants in the British Self-Governing Colonies, 1830–1910* (Ithaca: Cornell University Press, 1976); Joan M. Jensen, *Passage from India : Asian Indian Immigrants in North America* (New Haven: Yale University Press, 1988); and Peter W. Ward, *White Canada Forever: Popular Attitudes and Public Policy Toward Orientals in British Columbia* (Montreal: McGill-Queen's University Press, 1974).

4 For the role of difference in the creation of British national consciousness see Colley, 'Britishness and otherness'.

5 Rieko Karatani, *Defining British Citizenship: Empire, Commonwealth and Modern Britain* (London: Frank Cass, 2003), 39–62.

6 Lahiri, *Indians in Britain*, 5 and 71.

7 John Torpey, *The Invention of the Passport: Surveillance, Citizenship and the State* (Cambridge: Cambridge University Press, 2000), 160.

8 IOR L/PJ/6/158 No. 1283, Sir Louis Mallet, India Office Minute Paper, 'Treatment of Native Paupers in England', 24 January 1879. Lahiri claims that these certificates were mandatory (see *Indians in Britain*, 5 and 71), but the file she cites does not indicate that they were, and I have found no evidence to this effect elsewhere in the correspondence.

9 Quoted in 'Certificates of identity', *The Indian Magazine and Review*, 402 (June 1904): 166.

10 IOR L/PJ/6/647 No. 1972, R. Ritchie, minute, 19 August 1903, on India Office Public Department Reference Paper, 16 July 1903.

11 Torpey contrasts his concept of the state's 'embrace', with Habermas's of its 'penetration', in *Invention of the Passport*, 10–12.

12 Gérard Noiriel, *The French Melting Pot: Immigration, Citizenship, and National Identity*, trans. Geoffrey de Laforcade (Minneapolis: University of Minnesota Press, 1996), 45.

13 IOR L/PJ/6/483 No. 1231, Hamilton to Curzon, India Office Political Department No. 61, 9 June 1898.

14 IOR L/PJ/6/515 No. 1381, Curzon *et al.* to Hamilton, Government of India (hereafter GOI) Home Department No. 41, 6 July 1899.

15 S. W. Edgerley to the Secretary to the GOI Home Department, No. 5487, 30 September 1898, Enclosure No. 15 to Curzon *et al.* to Hamilton GOI Home Department No. 41.

16 Torpey, *Invention of the Passport*, 68–70.

17 IOR L/PJ/6/435 No. 2206, unsigned memorandum, 'Repatriation of Destitute Burmans', Jan. 1896.

18 Hamilton to Curzon, India Office Political Department No. 61, 1.

19 *Ibid.*, 2; and Curzon *et al.* to Hamilton, GOI Home Department No. 41, 2.

20 Curzon *et al.* to Hamilton, GOI Home Department No. 41, 2.

21 Bayly, *Caste, Society and Politics*, 71; see also 56–61; 'A spurious Rajput clan', in Dirk Kolff, *Naukar, Rajput and Sepoy: The Ethnohistory of the Military Labour Market in Hindustan, 1450–1850* (Cambridge and New York: Cambridge University

Press, 1990); Bernard S. Cohn, 'Representing authority in Victorian India', in Eric Hobsbawm and Terence Ranger (eds), *The Invention of Tradition* (Cambridge: Cambridge University Press, 1983), 165–210; and David Cannadine, *Ornamentalism: How the British Saw Their Empire* (Oxford: Oxford University Press, 2001), 41–57.

22 Hamilton to Curzon, India Office Political Department No. 61, 2.

23 IOR L/PS/18/D208, 'Memorandum enclosed in circular letter to Local Governments &c. from Deputy Secretary to Government of Indian in Foreign Department No. 1558 I. C., dated 28th June 1913 (India Foreign Department Proceedings, Internal, page 5, August 1913)'; and IOR L/PS/18/D122, 'List of Feudatory Chiefs and Nobles of India who are expected to be in England on the occasion of the celebration of the Jubilee of Her Majesty the Queen, Empress of India'.

24 IOR L/PJ/6/550 No. 1860, 'Return of certificates of identity granted to natives of India visiting England and other foreign countries for the quarter ending the 31st March 1900', enclosed in Government of India, Home Department, Public, No. 65 of 1900, H. J. McIntosh to Sir Arthur Godley, 20 September 1900.

25 IOR L/PJ/6/891 No. 3379, 'Return of certificates of identity granted to natives of India visiting England and other foreign countries for the quarter ending the 30th June 1908', enclosed in Government of India, Home Department, Public No. 57, H. A. Stuart to Arthur Godley, August 1908, 27. See also certificates attached for Mr Thakorlal, Keshan Balkrishna [Maulainkas?], and Chandhai Daya Ram.

26 IOR L/PJ/6/922 No. 440, Judicial and Public Department. Minute Paper, Certificate of Identity for Bilash Chandra Das, enclosed in 'Student sent by Calcutta Association to study in England and entitled to return passage asks for assistance', 4 February 1909.

27 J. A. Baines, *Census Commissioner For India: Report for 1891* (London: HMSO, 1893), 204.

28 Certificate of Identity for Bilash Chandra Das.

29 City of London Central Criminal Court, Sessions Papers, Minutes of Evidence [henceforth CCC Evidence], Vol. 118 (1892–93), Twelfth Session, 1424–5.

30 *The Times*, 31 October 1893, 9 and 13. The defendants were brothers ranging in age from twenty-five to thirty-six years old. Although Karim Baksh was the oldest and most experienced practitioner, Heere Shah, the third oldest, had the most contact with British patients, because he was the most fluent in English. The common serjeant is unidentified. The prosecuting attorneys were Charles Matthews, assisted by a Mr Bodkin, whose first name appears in neither *The Times* nor the records of London's Central Criminal Court. The records are similarly obscure regarding the four defence attorneys, whose last names were Jervis, Bovill Smith, Ball, and Warburton.

31 A brief history of this organisation is available at its website, which states that a major reason for its creation was 'an increasing number of unregistered and unqualified quacks'. See www.medicalprotection.org/medical/united_kingdom/About_Us/History/default.aspx (accessed 24 October 2005).

32 CCC Evidence, Vol. 118 (1892–93), Twelfth Session, 1370–1411. The instances of medical malpractice that the prosecutors cited in support of their case were the following: Sarah Ralph of Clapham Junction; James Russell, a retired gasfitter from Richmond; Alfred Parsons, a railway pointsman from Hammersmith; Evelyn Parsons, his daughter; William Turner, the six-year-old son of a stonemason; Eliza Marina Gillingham of Hammersmith; Mary Ann Bockett of Brixton; Mary Perry of Richmond; and Harry Allison, an inmate of Wandsworth Union. The minutes of evidence do not provide information regarding the professions of the women or their husbands, but *The Times* editorial describes them as 'chiefly among the working classes'. Where the minutes of evidence refer to the occupations of the patients, they are all working class. The expert medical witnesses, in order of appearance, were Charles Notting McNamara FRCS, consulting surgeon to the Royal Ophthalmic Hospital; Gustavus Partridge FRCS, surgeon to the Royal Westminster Ophthalmic Hospital; George Anderson Critchett, FRCS, Senior Ophthalmic Surgeon at St

Mary's Hospital; Edward Nettleship, FRCS, ophthalmic surgeon to St Thomas's Hospital and Moorfields Ophthalmic Hospital; John Bowering Lawford, FRCS, assistant surgeon to Moorfields Ophthalmic Hospital; and T. Britten Archer, MRCS, a private practitioner. The quote is from Mary Perry, 1389.

33 CCC Evidence, Vol. 118, 1391–1411. C. N. McNamara, one of the prosecution's expert witnesses, had served formerly as a 'professor of surgery in a school in Calcutta'. For developments in nineteenth-century British ophthalmology, see Frederick F. Cartwright, *The Development of Modern Surgery* (New York: Thomas Y. Crowell, 1967), 267–74; and George Gorin, *History of Ophthalmology* (Wilmington, DE: Publish or Perish, 1982), 71–80 and 170–84. See also Gorin, 22–27, for Middle Eastern and Indian advances in eye surgery, upon which the Indian oculists may have based some of their techniques.

34 CCC Evidence, Vol. 118, 1403. The instances of successful treatment that the defence attorneys cited in support of their case were the following: William Randall, a machine upper closer from Wellingborough; Thomas Whitehouse, an engine driver from Loughborough; William Albert Martin, son of a painter from Tottenham; and Hannah Reeve, a brushmaker from Norwich.

35 Nevertheless, leeches have recently regained respect as a medical tool. See Carol Rados, 'Beyond bloodletting: FDA gives leeches a medical makeover', *FDA Consumer Magazine*, 38:5 (September–October 2004): http://www.fda.gov/fdac/features/2004/504_leech.html (accessed 24 October 2005). The FDA is the United States Food and Drug Administration.

36 Edward Shorter, *Doctors and Their Patients: A Social History* (New Brunswick, NJ and London: Transaction Publishers, 1985), 106.

37 CCC Evidence, Vol. 118, 1406. For the history of surgery and the rise of the medical profession in Britain see Peter Bartrip, *Themselves Writ Large: The British Medical Association, 1832–1966* (London: BMJ Publishing Group, 1996); Anne Hardy, *Health and Medicine in Britain Since 1860* (New York: Palgrave, 2001); Joan Lane, *A Social History of Medicine: Health, Healing and Disease in England, 1750–1950* (London and New York: Routledge, 2001); Christopher Lawrence, *Medical Theory, Surgical Practice: Studies in the History of Surgery* (London and New York: Routledge, 1992); and Noel and José Parry, *The Rise of the Medical Profession: A Study of Collective Social Mobility* (London: Croom Helm, 1976)

38 Arnold Pacey, *Technology in World Civilizations: A Thousand-Year History* (Oxford: Oxford University Press, 1990). See also David Arnold, *Science, Technology and Medicine in Colonial India* (Cambridge: Cambridge University Press, 2000) in *The New Cambridge History of India*, Series 3, Vol. 5, 92.

39 CCC Evidence, Vol. 118, 1424.

40 *Ibid.*, 1424–5.

41 *The Times*, 30 October 1893, 12.

42 *The Times*, 31 October 1893, 13. Discussions of the appropriation of knowledge in the service of the imperial enterprise are too numerous to list here. For the uses of medicine in this context see David Arnold (ed.), *Imperial Medicine and Indigenous Societies* (Manchester: Manchester University Press, 1988); David Arnold, *Colonizing the Body: State Medicine and Epidemic Disease in Nineteenth-Century India* (Berkeley and Los Angeles: University of California Press, 1993); Mark Harrison, 'Was there an Oriental Renaissance in medicine? The evidence of the nineteenth-century medical press', in *Negotiating India*, 233–53; and Roy McLeod and Milton Lewis (eds), *Disease, Medicine, and Empire: Perspectives on Western Medicine and the Experience of European Expansion* (London and New York: Routledge, 1988).

43 IOR L/PJ/6/365 No. 77, F. E. A. Chamier to Philip Perceval Hutchins, 4 January 1894.

44 *Ibid.*, Fitzgerald to Campbell, 11 January 1894.

45 *Ibid.*, S. C. Bayley to P. Hutchins, n.d. (but certainly 11–13 January 1894).

46 *Ibid.*, Hutchins (unsigned), 'Question whether "the Indian oculists" sd. be sent back to India at the public expense', Judicial and Public Department Minute, 13? January 1894.

47 *Ibid.*, Kimberley to Godley, 16 January 1894.

48 *Ibid.*, R. W. T. Ritchie [signature illegible, but identity apparent from the context of the correspondence], n.d. [probably 18 or 19 January 1894].

49 *Ibid.*, Godley to Kimberley, 19 January 1894. Emphasis is Godley's.

50 *Ibid.*, Note by Godley, 23 January 1894.

51 *Ibid.*, Godley, marginal note, 25 January 1894, in 'Return to India at the public expense of the "Indian Oculists"', Judicial and Public Department Minute, 18 January 1894.

52 *Ibid.*, See letters by G. S. Purslock (?), Clan Line Steamers Limited, to Sir Philip Percy Hutchins, India Office, 23 February and 13 March 1894.

53 IOR L/PJ/6/958 No. 3122, 'Précis of Precedents relating to the Relief or Repatriation of Natives of India found destitute in England, 1887–1909', 2 September 1909, Case no. 1264/1895, 3.

54 *The Times*, 31 October 1893, 13.

CHAPTER SIX

Patterns of compassion: aiding Indians in need

On 12 June 1894 during question time in the House of Commons, R. J. D. Burnie, MP for Swansea, asked H. H. Fowler, the Undersecretary of State for India, why the India Office would not provide the funds to repatriate two Indian 'oculists' in his constituency who had fallen into destitution (as a result of negative publicity attending the trial mentioned in the previous chapter). Fowler replied that it was 'not the general practice of the Secretary of State in Council to defray out of the Revenues of India the passage to India of natives who, like these two oculists, have come to this country for purposes of their own; it is only for special and exceptional reasons that he does so'.[1] This answer was standard for the India Office from the 1880s to 1910. Yet as the answer suggested, faced with specific cases rather than a general rule, India Office administrators frequently departed from this policy, either at an official level as a government ministry or at the individual level as members of Britain's ruling class who had a special knowledge of or interest in India. In fact, the proportion of cases in which the India Office provided some sort of assistance was substantial, fully one-third (57 of 155) from 1889 to 1915.[2] In many cases the opinions of others, particularly the Honorary Secretary of the Strangers' Home, influenced administrators' attitudes. The India Office and the Strangers' Home worked in concert to relieve and repatriate Indians even as the former argued publicly that it was under no obligation to provide them with financial assistance.

Although the total number of destitute cases involved was small, they provide a window into two aspects of the Indian experience in Britain. One is the financial difficulty that Indians from many social backgrounds experienced, while trying to pursue their careers or educations, or simply subsist thousands of miles away from home. The cost of living in Britain, particularly in London, and the problem of relying on a flow of cash from families in India, drove many people of even moderate family income to the verge of ruin. The cases that came before the India Office, therefore, represented a broader cross-section of social strata than their immediate financial means would otherwise indicate. While few cases included the truly rich, neither did they include the most common classes of labouring Indians, ayahs and lascars, since provisions for the relief and repatriation of people working in these occupations already existed between the India Office on the one hand and the Ayahs' Home and Strangers' Home on the other. Nevertheless, the cases that did come before the India Office included businessmen, scholars, missionaries, entertainers, and unskilled labourers, to name but a few of the occupations represented. The variety of the social backgrounds of these applicants for aid presented administrators of the India Office and the Strangers' Home with the opportunity to aid applicants on the basis of their social rank.

This opportunity provides the other reason for the importance of these cases, in spite of their infrequency. For if they provide a window into the lives of Indians in Britain, they also open one into the minds and prejudices of the 'better sort' of Britons and Indians in the United Kingdom, who had the financial power to deliver them from a life on the streets of Britain's cities. As the case of the oculists shows, effective Britishness, that is the right to reside in Britain, relied greatly on acceptance into polite society. By contrast, many Indians discussed in the current chapter wanted to return to their homeland, simultaneously relieving British officials of their now unwanted presence on London's streets. Yet whether and how they returned still depended greatly on perceptions of their class status. The same was true for seeking assistance to remain in Britain.

The seventeenth-century philosopher, Thomas Hobbes, observed: 'Griefe for the calamity of another is pitty; and ariseth from the imagination that the like calamity may befall himselfe; and therefore is called also compassion.'[3] The records of cases pertaining to destitute Indians in Britain indicate that for India Office administrators compassion involved such a process of identification with the less fortunate. What these cases reveal is an ad hoc institutional approach to assistance, based largely on the personal prejudices of the administrators who reviewed them. These prejudices reveal the centrality of social rank in official decisions to provide aid. This awareness of such ranks depended on a variety of indicators, such as fluency in English, general literacy, appearance, demeanour, caste, household wealth, and family occupation. Moreover, for Britons and Indians, in their capacity as private citizens in the United Kingdom, individual acts of charity in such cases amounted to a form of *noblesse oblige* that reinforced their status as members of polite society. Many cases that did not receive official aid, therefore, did not go ignored.

The cases that provide the least evidence of motive are those for which the India Office denied assistance. Since denial of aid was in accordance with general policy, it is not surprising that no justification would be recorded in such cases. Of greater interest are the fifty-seven cases that the India Office assisted. Twenty received partial aid, and thirty-seven were repatriated, albeit usually via third-class accommodation. Almost all of these cases provide some indication why administrators chose to depart from their official policy. Twelve cases were clearly matters of expedience, for instance those examined at length in the previous chapter – the four Indian 'oculists', whom a jury acquitted of fraudulently practising medicine – and critics of the British Government whom the India Office could claim were mentally ill. Although they tell us much about the role of science, professions, and the law in Indian encounters with institutions in the United Kingdom, the behaviour of administrators in these situations was rather predictably one of self interest. It was compassion unmotivated by practical self-interest that revealed the most deeply-held, and often subconscious, assumptions of officials in the United Kingdom.

Class and caste: the treatment of upper-caste Hindus

We have already seen how the India experts who advised institutions in the United Kingdom sometimes conflated caste, class, and race as they applied it to Indian society. Such a conflation was hardly unique in its application to the Indian subcontinent, since the assumption that poverty was a manifestation of racial weakness was an important aspect of Social Darwinism and eugenics. Class and caste could therefore be seen as manifestations of racial hierarchy while simultaneously serving as alternatives to it. Although many upper-caste Indians lived in humble economic circumstances in their own country, authorities in Britain tended to regard them inherently as a respectable class. This was particularly the case with *brahmans*. The mystique surrounding *brahmans*, and the complex set of rules governing their interaction with the world around them, provided them in practice with a claim to special treatment.

Indeed upper-caste Hindus forced authorities to treat them exceptionally in even the most abject conditions. Of eight Indians reported in London area workhouses in 1886, three required special dietary considerations. Their refusal to eat the standard workhouse fare is hardly surprising, since in the London area the only protein it usually provided was in the form of meat and suet puddings, food that would be ritually polluting to most Hindus and, depending on its content, Muslims as well. Reports, such as 'The Hindoo gave a good deal of trouble as regards his food and would eat nothing but what he cooked himself',[4] mask what must have been very trying culture clashes in conditions where workhouse supervisors, unacquainted with or unsympathetic to Indian dietary restriction, reacted harshly to the refusal of their inmates to eat what was available. Only the threat of self-imposed starvation appears to have forced most of these workhouses to accommodate their Indian inmates' most basic needs.

Such accommodation occurred, not only in the workhouses, but also in the India Office and the Strangers' Home. Once an upper-caste Indian came to the attention of these institutions, their administrators could tap on their apparently extensive knowledge of India to judge the appropriate way to behave toward them. An example of this practice can be found in George Small's account of his attempt in 1886 to help a Punjabi plaintiff, Girwal Singh, to return to India. A former missionary to India and author of a Hindustani–English lexicon, Small may have been the most experienced orientalist to serve as the Strangers' Home missionary in the nineteenth century. In his 1887 annual report to the Home, he described how, with the help of an Indian lawyer in London, he persuaded Singh that it was impossible to appeal his land dispute in England. Regarding the plaintiff's return to Aden, where he was to meet up with family members, Small added: 'As he was a man of caste and without money, I managed to collect for him enough for his passage and food on the voyage.'[5]

This missionary did not indicate a similar concern in the next paragraph of his report when he described the plight of five circus entertainers, also from Punjab. These men, whom Small described as members of the 'Adventurers' Class', had sought their fortune in England by performing with a bear that they had brought from Kashmir. When their efforts to secure a booking with an agent failed, the Strangers' Home admitted them, and apparently the bear as well. Small helped to find accommodation for the entertainers, but the landlord evicted them 'after a fortnight, as a nuisance'. Thereafter, because they owed the Strangers' Home £15, it would not readmit them (probably in this case the decision was Honorary Secretary Fergusson's), and they 'would not go to the workhouse'. Small seems to have had an easier time finding accommodation for the bear, at 'the Zoological Gardens ... as a gratuitous boarder', than return passage for the entertainers. Two of them worked their passages home, and although the remaining three received 'comfortable berths ... in a fine steamer', Small does not state who paid for them.[6] The difference in treatment of the two cases is significant. Nowhere does Small suggest that the upper-caste landholder should have gone to the workhouse, a recourse which somebody, possibly Small himself, must have suggested to the circus entertainers.

Ultimately, Small and his acquaintances considered it acceptable for the circus entertainers to work their passages home, but not for the landholder. Occupationally-defined class, buttressed by caste, accounted for the difference.

In such situations, upper-caste Hindus could reinforce authorities' predilection to treat them in a privileged manner. This tendency was very apparent in the different treatment of two Punjabis who came to England to appeal rulings against them over land disputes in India's civil courts. Most litigation appeals resulted from British land development in Punjab. None of them was successful, because Indian civil cases could not be appealed beyond the Indian judicial system. The cases of Tari and Khemchund were, therefore, typical in that these ill-informed litigants ran out of money while pursuing fruitless petitions to the British monarch. What sets these two cases apart from others is that Strangers' Home and India Office administrators considered Tari and Khemchund's appeals simultaneously, and that the former was a Muslim, whereas the latter was an upper-caste Hindu.

Little is known about Tari, but Chamier, the Home's secretary, considered it appropriate for him to work his return passage as a coal trimmer. Indeed, Tari's case never really received India Office consideration, because Chamier insisted that he work his return passage. When Tari refused, Chamier evicted him from the Strangers' Home. Three days later the Muslim litigant returned 'very penitent', and Chamier secured him a job on a ship bound for India. The Honorary Secretary of the Strangers' Home was quite comfortable with this tough approach to Tari, because: 'He was just the man for a coal trimmer – a Mahomaden, strong & dirty.' Tari's appearance was an important issue: 'He was in a filthy state when he arrived & was made to take a warm bath.'[7] Since appearance was a sign of respectability and consequent treatment, Tari clearly qualified for the menial labour that he ultimately had to perform in order to return to India. Furthermore, as a Muslim, he did not emphasise an array of religiously-defined obstacles to such activity. Chamier saw no problem in making 'a distinction between Mussulmen & Hindus' regarding the application of aid.[8]

This distinction was obvious because the case of Khemchund was under consideration at the same time. In marked contrast to his insistence that Tari work his passage home, Chamier recommended that the India Office grant Khemchund a return ticket. The reason for this distinction was Khemchund's caste. Indeed in his letter outlining the case to the India Office, Chamier highlighted Khemchund's 'caste, Thakur of Shihapur, in Sind'. He was, therefore, either a *brahman* or a Rajput.[9] In the latter case, he would likely have claimed *kshaitrya* lineage. Indeed, through his own actions, Khemchund did his best to assert his upper-caste status. Chamier complained that the Strangers' Home could 'do nothing for him', because he 'cooks his own food and apparently has not yet lost his caste'. The Honorary Secretary concluded that his charge was unused to manual labour, because 'His family like the brahmins of Bengal live by the offerings of pious Hindus.'[10] Furthermore, Khemchund's attire (his box consisted of two dhotis) reinforced the aura of the ascetic that he projected. At the same time, he projected a sense of accessibility and education, because he spoke and wrote English 'fluently'. Chamier disdained this behaviour, describing his possessions as 'rubbish' and his mind as 'somewhat unhinged'. Nevertheless, he rejected the recommendation of Curzon Wyllie, then the Secretary of State's *aide-de-camp*, that Khemchund work his passage home, arguing instead that the India Office comply with the demands of caste that Khemchund presented, and sent him to 'state his case in person'.[11] The India Office agreed to pay for Khemchund's return passage, in spite of its recognition that 'the case is on all fours with that of the man Tari'.[12]

If Khemchund projected upper-caste asceticism, some of those who did not found British administrators making connections between caste and class for them, and in their favour. For instance, Ajoodhia Prashad Sharma ran out of money during a visit to attend the coronation of Edward VII. Not only was he of high birth and well educated, but he was engaged in a display of loyalty to the Empire. In his letter requesting assistance from the India Office he highlighted his profession, an 'English teacher', and loyal purpose, 'to see the Coronation of our Emperor'.[13] But it was Chamier who introduced him to W. Neville Sturt, the Assistant Secretary of the Judicial and Public Department, as 'a brahmin' who 'speaks English well', and was 'not a sea-faring man'.[14] Sturt immediately referred the matter to the Council of India with a recommendation to grant the return passage outright, not as a loan. His reason for such exceptional and generous treatment was blatantly based on caste and class: 'This is really as the letter states a "distressful" case. The man is a Brahmin gentleman of Lucknow, an English teacher in Calcutta, of a very different class from those who as a rule come here for assistance to return to India. It wd [*sic*] be a cruel thing to send him to the workhouse.' The only practical reason he provided for repatriating Sharma was the fact that 'he admits the folly he committed in coming to this country and says that he will tell all his friends on his return, to prevent them doing the like'.[15] Applications for repatriation usually encountered objections at every level, but in this instance the petition sailed through the Judicial and Public Committee and the Finance Committee of the Council of India without comment. Within two weeks of the petition the passage was paid. Furthermore, the India

Office arranged for an agent to meet Sharma at the Calcutta docks and provide him with a third-class ticket to Lucknow.[16]

Sharma's case was unusual in that it embodied so many features that were likely to elicit the sympathy of India Office administrators. Not only was the applicant for aid a *brahman*, but he fitted the classic image of what a *brahman* should do. In accordance with the Vedic description of *brahmans* as coming out of the mouth of the primeval being, or the *Bhagavad Gita*'s assertion that among the 'works of a Brahmin are ... vision and wisdom',[17] Sharma was a teacher, fulfilling traditional Hindu and British orientalist expectations of his *varna*. Caste and class thus combined to confirm his gentlemanly status. So did his demeanour. As Chamier observed, 'A. P. Sharma was a quiet, respectable man'.[18] If Sharma's Indianness fitted the stereotype of gentlemanly status as India Office administrators perceived it to exist in his society, the ways in which he had assimilated Western culture presented the perfect complement. As a teacher of English, he realised one of the central goals of Anglicising reformers of the early nineteenth century, and as a loyal subject of the British King-Emperor, who impoverished himself in order to pay him homage, Sharma was an exemplary imperial subject – Indian where appropriate, but British where it mattered. Clearly this destitute Indian was exceptional, but because of his station and loyalty rather than his need.

Another case that fitted the pattern of British expectations regarding caste behaviour was that of Rajaram Bhasker Panwalker, who arrived in England in 1900, in the company of Swami Nirir Kalpa, to preach Hindu philosophy. Seeking a warmer climate, the swami returned to India, leaving his disciple, Panwalker, who relied on funds from home, to carry on the work. While Panwalker was still in England, however, his father died, causing the funding to cease and ultimately forcing the disciple to seek lodging in the Strangers' Home. He left this refuge in the hope of making a living teaching Asian languages. When this effort drove him once again into destitution he received food and shelter from M. S. Kolasker, a roughly thirty-year-old student at Lincoln's Inn, who knew Wyllie, then the political *aide-de-camp* to the Secretary of State, and William Lee-Warner, then a member of the Council of India. Class immediately became an issue in ascertaining Kolasker's reliability, since in his letter referring the matter to Sturt, Wyllie described Kolasker as 'a man of respectable family in Bombay', adding 'he is known to Sir William Lee Warner, and is a dependable person'.[19] Up to this point Panwalker's caste does not appear in the correspondence. In the heading of his minute recommending assistance, however, Sturt describes Panwalker as 'a Karādā Brahmin'. He reiterates the applicant's occupation, 'to preach oriental philosophy to the Western world'.[20]

Although Kolasker and other law students had begun to raise a fund for Panwalker's repatriation, the Judicial and Public Committee of the Council of India recommended repatriation 'at govt [*sic*] expense'.[21]

The correspondence surrounding this case does not state explicitly the reason for the India Office's funding of Panwalker's repatriation. Yet the only distinguishing aspects of the case that set it apart from the majority of others that did not receive assistance were the applicant's caste, activity, and indirect personal connections with India Office administrators. In this case the petitioner's high caste and his practice of its classical occupation, the teaching of Hindu philosophy, created an aura of respectability around him that probably played a significant role in the India Office's decision to break with its normal policy. *Brahmans*, after all, were *supposed* to teach oriental philosophy. This activity fitted perfectly into the British elite's view of what one of their counterparts in India should do.

Sharma and Panwalker were both products of a society that appeared to many contemporary Britons to be vastly different from their own. Yet even though British and Indian scholarship of the period often highlighted these differences, it also acknowledged similarities. It was these similarities that became so important to Indians in Britain as they attempted to navigate the unfamiliar waters of the country's society. For in their effort to differentiate Indians from one another in ways that were meaningful to their compatriots, India Office administrators tried to translate caste rankings into British class equivalents. In doing so they applied the conventions of classical Hindu *varna*, even when at an intellectual level they believed them to be barely relevant to contemporary Indian society. In justification of his caste classifications in the 1901 Indian census, Risley claimed:

> The best evidence of the . . . remarkable vitality of caste at the present day, is to be found in the great number of petitions and memorials to which it gave rise, the bulk of which were submitted in English and emanated from the educated classes who are sometimes alleged to free themselves from the trammels of the caste system. If the principle on which the classification was based had not appealed to the usages and traditions of the great mass of Hindus, it is inconceivable that so many people should have taken the trouble and incurred substantial expenditure with the object of its application.[22]

At least in the British setting, one might respond that as long as the India Office acted as if castes had equivalent ranks in the British class system, then caste remained a highly relevant way for Indians to describe themselves. When it came to practical decisions about real people and advising others regarding the same, the India Office could apply rough analogies between Indian caste and British class without rejecting the supposed differences between the two.

Pandita Ramabai: reluctant brahman

Perhaps the most famous beneficiary of this bias toward *brahmans* was Pandita Ramabai (the subject of two recent biographical treatments by Antoinette Burton and Uma Chakravarti), even though she neither qualified at the time as destitute nor supported caste distinctions. Destitution was, however, in her family background. Her parents were well-educated Marathi *brahman*s, and her father had at one time owned rice and coconut plantations in Maharashtra. Partly because they were devout Hindus who invested too many of their financial resources in a temple, her parents lost their property shortly after her birth. Thereafter they earned a meager living wandering from village to village reading Puranic verses. This type of non-celibate mendicancy was a respectable form of poverty in India. Nevertheless, it ultimately led to her parents' death through starvation when she was sixteen. These experiences contributed to Ramabai's loss of belief in Hindu doctrines. Yet her parents left her and her brother with a legacy of respect for women acting in traditionally male roles that survived her apostasy. Her father had scandalised pundits by encouraging her mother to read or recite scripture publicly. Ramabai and her brother, therefore, became advocates of female emancipation through education and travelled around India spreading this message. They also rejected caste distinctions, which they regarded as a negative legacy of Hindu thought. After her brother died in early adulthood, Ramabai moved to Calcutta and, in 1881, demonstrated her convictions regarding caste by marrying a *shudra*. Within a year, however, he died of cholera, leaving her with a daughter.

Ramabai's sojourn in England began in 1883 when she travelled there to study medicine. This goal proved to be unattainable due to a hearing disability. In the meantime, however, inspired perhaps by the Anglican sisters of St Mary the Virgin in Wantage, who hosted her stay, she was baptised into the faith under the guidance of one of their number, Sister Geraldine, who was also a member of the Church Missionary Society. Ramabai had already become interested in Christianity before her marriage, but had hitherto refused baptism on the grounds that she could not accept the entirety of the faith's orthodoxy. It soon transpired that Ramabai's baptism had signified little change in her beliefs. Meanwhile, the sisters of Wantage suggested an alternative career for Ramabai, perhaps in their view more appropriate for her sex, and sent her to Cheltenham Ladies' College, which focused on training women as teachers. The next two years, however, became increasingly contentious for Ramabai as Sister Geraldine realised that the former's Christian faith, which questioned central doctrines such as the Trinity and the bodily resurrection of Christ, continued to be unorthodox. More sympathetic was Dorothea Beale, head of Cheltenham Ladies' College, where Ramabai was receiving her education. When in November 1885 Ramabai began to exhaust the funds she had collected from the publication of a book before her voyage to England, it was Beale who appealed to the India Office for the £100 necessary for the completion of her education.[23]

In spite of Ramabai's renunciation of caste and the unorthodox nature of her religious beliefs, her status as a *brahman* and a Christian figured prominently in Beale's correspondence with the India Office and in the latter's decision concerning assistance for her education. Also important was Ramabai's career as an advocate of female education in India. All three made her a sympathetic figure for Britain's elite. However, the ambiguous effect of her Christianity is the subject of a later discussion. The focus here is on the other two aspects of her identity as they concerned Beale and the India Office.

Although Ramabai had testified before the Indian Government's Commission on Education in 1882 and was becoming a person of some note among women's organisations in Britain and the United States, she was not well known to India Office administrators by the time of Beale's appeal to the Secretary of State three years later. Beale's introductory letter on the subject, therefore, contained descriptors of her social rank and background: 'a high-caste Brahmin lady' who 'is generally acknowledged to be one of the best Sanscrit [*sic*] scholars'.[24] As with Sharma and Panwalker, India Office administrators were impressed with her caste pedigree and scholarly credentials, which complemented each other so naturally in their view of Indian society. That she was a reformer bent on liberating Indian women from what most of Britain's elite regarded as oppression further helped her cause. In a minute highlighting Ramabai's caste in its title, Arthur F. Hobhouse, Assistant to the Secretary of the Judicial and Public Department, noted: 'The career of this Brahmin lady is very remarkable and, in the interests of female education in India, it is no doubt desirable that she should complete her English education.' Nevertheless, he acknowledged that there was 'no precedent for the grant of money to her out of the Indian Revenues'.[25]

But this was no ordinary petitioner. Nor were her supporters, among whom was Oxford University's renowned professor of Sanskrit, Max Müller. Within five days of its receipt at the India Office, the letter, with the accompanying minute, had reached Lord Randolph Churchill, the

Secretary of State. Quite uncharacteristically, Churchill intervened, informing Sir Gerald Fitzgerald, his *aide-de-camp*, through his Private Secretary that he wanted him 'to see if anything can be done, unofficially, in this case'.[26] Seeking money from a fund for female education in India, established by Lady Dufferin, the former viceroy's wife, Fitzgerald assured Beale that although the India Office's official reply to her petition was negative, it would find the money from a private source.[27] By this time, however, Ramabai was considering other options, particularly an invitation from Rachel Bodley, the dean of the Women's Medical College, Philadelphia, to attend the graduation ceremony of its first Indian student, and 'address audiences of ladies concerning the women of India'.[28] Because the assistance that Fitzgerald was arranging was conditional on Ramabai remaining in Britain until she had finished her course of study, she turned it down and, in February 1886, embarked for the United States.[29] Significantly in Ramabai's case, British officials encouraged an Indian to remain in the country, because her behaviour, goals, and ironically her caste interpreted through Britain's class hierarchy made her a more worthy member of British polite society than the masses of Britain's poor.

The fact that Ramabai opposed caste discrimination did not prevent her from becoming a beneficiary of it. Beale, who shared Ramabai's disdain for the caste system, nevertheless highlighted it to India Office administrators, probably knowing that it would add to the veneer of respectability that Ramabai's educational credentials had already established. Ultimately, Ramabai chose to extol the respectability of the upper castes in *The High Caste Hindu Woman*, which she published in 1887 in order to persuade American women to help educate upper-caste Indian women. She reminded her American audience (and no doubt, a British one too, since the book soon became available in England) that: 'Among the inhabitants of India, the high-caste people rank as the most intelligent; they have been a refined and cultivated race for more than two thousand years.'[30] In this case the education of upper-caste males legitimised their respectability. The book's central criticism of Indian society was that upper-caste females did not receive an education sufficient for them to participate in polite society as well. Like other upper-caste Hindus mentioned above, Ramabai had learned that when it came to earning the respect of British polite society, caste translated into class, even among those who criticised it officially. Ironically, in her encounter with British institutions, all the principle actors criticised the application of caste distinction. Yet all applied it to some extent in their decisions regarding whether or not to assist her. Of course, Ramabai's educational credentials were important too, as was her potential service to the British Empire through her attempts to reform Indian society in ways that British authorities would not dare since the Indian Rebellion. But her education merely buttressed the British officials' stereotyping according to caste. At an intellectual level, India Office administrators knew better than to believe such stereotypes. But they did not act as if they did.

Punjabi 'yeomen': destitution and land litigation

'What is to be done with these men?' bemoaned Sir William Lee-Warner, secretary of the Political and Secret Department, in a note to his superior, Sir Arthur Godley, in 1896. Drawing on their common cultural literacy in classical Greek he added, 'παθη μαθη [*pathe mathe* – learning by suffering] are I fear the only solution, such misery in London as will make a fruitless return bearable'.[31] Lee-Warner's use of this fatalistic concept from Aeschylus' *Agamemnon* indicates the frustration and perplexity that British authorities felt over the increasing number of Punjabi litigants arriving in England to appeal the decisions of civil courts in India against their claims to property. The reasons for such perplexity, however, arose from the unwillingness of British authorities to recognise the damage that imperial capitalism was exerting on India's agrarian communities. The economic analysis of contemporary British and Indian critics of imperialism, such as Hyndman and Naoroji, went largely ignored amid the self congratulation that accompanied late Victorian and Edwardian empire building. India Office and Strangers' Home correspondence on this issue posited only that Indian landholders, in almost childlike innocence, believed that the British monarch actually held the power of judicial review over their cases. Imran Ali, however, suggests two developments that combined to make Punjab in particular the scene of land disputes that left the losing side in such desperation as to travel to England in the hope of restitution.

One was the change in patterns of farming and land ownership that accompanied British occupation. Punjab was the last heavily-populated region of India to fall under British rule – in 1849. Yet some of the effects of occupation were more pronounced there than in many other parts of the subcontinent. In particular, the ambitious irrigation projects of the Crown Raj significantly altered the social as well as the physical landscape of the area, by opening up new lands in Western Punjab for agricultural development by the region's elite. This agrarian transformation encouraged internal migration and colonisation. From the very beginning, British authorities in India viewed these projects largely in terms of caste and class. In doing so, they did not hesitate to translate the former into the latter. For instance, in explaining its reasons for funding a massive irrigation project in the Lower Choab

Colony, near the confluence of the Ravi, Choab, and Jhelum Rivers, the Government stated as one of its aims:

> To colonise the area in question with well-to-do yeomen of the best class of agriculturists, who will cultivate their own holdings with the aid of their families and the usual menials, but as much as possible without the aid of tenants, and will constitute healthy agricultural communities of the best Punjab type.[32]

But in the eyes of British officials, Punjabi 'yeomen' came almost exclusively from a limited set of sub-castes, including Arains, Kambohs, Sainis, and Gujars. Most important among these 'agricultural castes' were Jats, who formed the largest group of landholding peasants in Punjab and cut across the three religious communities that dominated the region's population: Hindu, Muslim, and Sikh. By contrast, British officials regarded the 'landlord' castes, which drew their income mainly from rents, as consisting mainly of Qureshis, Rajputs, and Syeds.[33] To the extent that these castes fitted into the *varna* scheme of Hinduism (which for Muslims and Sikhs they did not), the Rajputs claimed *kshaitrya* origins, and the Jats, *vaishya*. Although British ethnographers of the period realised that such claims were largely invented traditions, in practice British officials (sometimes ethnographers themselves) treated these distinctions of occupation as if they were real, and made them more real by doing so. The effect was a tendency to grant smaller plots to the 'agricultural castes' and larger ones to the 'landlord castes' on the premise that the former would make their income directly from the produce of their land, and the latter from rent. Punjab would therefore form an idyllic agrarian economy of loyal and prosperous Henry Maine-style village communities, remodelled along English patterns of private ownership, but preserving the local caste hierarchy.

As with previous British land reforms, however, this one went awry. A familiar pattern, dating back to the Permanent Settlement of 1793, reasserted itself, with landholders, particularly the 'yeomen', defaulting on debts to capitalist proprietors, who in turn became absentee landlords. This process increasingly affected the established farming communities of Eastern Punjab as well. The Indian Government tried to rectify the problem with the Land Alienation Act of 1900, which established three forms of land grant: agricultural, landlord, and capitalist. The first two restricted the right of the landowner to sell his property only to members of castes whom the government had identified as agricultural. It therefore institutionalised the interpretation of caste as class in a very tangible way.

Added to the increased competition over land was famine, which in the 1890s arose from a combination of British reforms and crop failure. The story in Punjab was similar to that in Bengal early in the nineteenth century. The creation of a landlord–tenant model of agrarian society encouraged the shift from subsistence agriculture to the production of cash crops for export. Following the British model, the Government of India facilitated private property owners' enclosure of common lands, denying subsistence farmers access to them. The result was a reduction in supply and a rise in prices of the basic foodstuffs that supported the peasantry. The improved transport system, that British officials touted as their solution to famine, did little to alleviate the hunger of peasants who could not afford to pay the prices resulting from market forces with which the government was unwilling to interfere. The stakes over losing farming rights on pieces of property were, if anything, greater than they had been before British interference.[34]

Land disputes abounded in the wake of the social dislocations attending these developments. Driven by the prospect of destitution, families that lost their cases in Punjab's civil courts often threw their meager remaining resources into appeals. Familiar with the considerable propaganda that had accompanied Queen Victoria's assumption of the title, 'Empress of India', and unfamiliar with the true balance of power in Britain, some sent representatives of their families to England to appeal to the monarch. What they did not realise was that the highest court of appeal for Indian civil cases was in India, and that no court in the United Kingdom would hear them. Mathur points to the apparent inconsistency of such a fractured legal system, lacking a central court of appeal, with the 'narrative [in which] the monarch symbolized the top of a social order that brought all British and colonial subjects into a single hierarchy'.[35] Yet this system arose more out of the ad hoc nature of imperial acquisition than from any systematic policy of denying Indians a hearing in London. If, as Maya Jasanoff observes, 'Britain collected an Eastern Empire in India and beyond',[36] it also collected a bewildering array of legal jurisdictions. Like the legal arrangements that created these problems, British officials' responses to them were ad hoc. Nevertheless, such jurisdictional details would have been cold comfort to the many Indian litigants who exhausted their funds travelling to and staying in England, and then fell into destitution, unable to buy return passages even when they were willing to abandon their appeals.

It is in this context, of imperial dislocation and attempts to identify specific castes with corresponding relationships to the land, that the institutional response to the destitution of Punjabi litigants in England occurred. To the professionals employed in the India Office and running the Strangers' Home, property ownership was one of the surest signs of genteel status. For these administrators, rentier landlords formed the traditional governing class in spite of the industrial revolution and the collapse of land values in Britain. Lower down the social hierarchy, individual 'yeomen' farming families represented much that they regarded as good in rural England. And since rural England still formed the ideal society for much of Britain's elite, the 'yeoman' class represented the backbone of society, the ultimate achievement of the industrious commoner.

The presence of what British officials regarded as Indian equivalents of landlords and yeomen in destitution on the streets of London presented them with a considerable moral dilemma. On the one hand, they did not regard the workhouses as appropriate places for visitors of these classes. On the other hand, they were reluctant to set costly precedents by agreeing to repatriate them at the government's expense. The result was inconsistency. Many litigants remained on the street or in the workhouse, trapped in a foreign land and culture, but many received assistance, officially or privately, from British officials who were unwilling to see members of the landowning classes meet the fate of the lower orders.

Charles E. Bernard, secretary of the India Office's Revenue and Statistics Department, was most explicit in his desire to treat litigants exceptionally because of their class. In 1890, regarding a 'Sikh Jat and a Hindu landholder' both of whom had lost disputes over 'ancestral land', he wrote:

> It seems that the official way of repatriating these men is to send them to the workhouse as destitute mendicants, and that after keeping them sometime, the guardians will use their discretion about sending the men back to India at the cost of the Union. But the men are not mere beggars; and so long as they have a few rupees the house will not receive them as destitute persons. Moreover the men, tho [*sic*] in an ill strait here, are respectable yeomen in their own country, and the workhouse is hardly the place for them ... Sir Arthur Macpherson, having heard the details as now stated, desired me to put the facts before him, as in some cases the India Office has sanctioned passages.[37]

Bernard's attitude in this case, regarding men he had interviewed, seems to have affected his view of Punjabi litigants in general. The fact that these men were coming to England to appeal to the 'Queen-Empress', thereby implying their loyalty to her, only magnified their respectability in his mind. The following August, he argued on behalf of all of them:

> These men, so far as I have seen them, are respectable landholders who have been litigating their claims for years. They are mostly respectable yeomen or gentry in the Punjab. It is very hard on them to be sent to jail,

or to the workhouse, because from ignorance they have come home to get redress at the hands of the Queen-Empress.[38]

In fact, the India Office had repatriated several Punjabi litigants over the previous six years. Furthermore, Sir Gerald Fitzgerald, the political *aide-de-camp*, had dealt with some cases 'by private charity ... in former years'.[39] Indeed this private charity sometimes came from Fitzgerald himself. In 1891 he offered to pay privately for the repatriation of a litigant who had been arrested on the grounds of Balmoral Castle in Scotland, attempting to gain an audience with the Queen, but the man in question would not return until his appeal was heard.[40] This last instance illustrates a curious inverse of the usual situation with destitute Indians, and one that confounded British authorities: the refusal of some Punjabi litigants to accept return passages offered them until they received satisfaction regarding their appeals.[41]

Such favouritism toward Indian litigants who struck authorities as 'respectable' continued, in spite of the India Office's public assertions that it was not responsible for them. We have already seen the importance of class, caste, appearance, and linguistic ability in the case of Khemchund. Similar issues arose regarding Hidayat Ali Mohamed Nazir in 1907. Describing him as a 'zamindar', Chamier declared him to be 'too respectable to be allowed to drift into the Workhouse'.[42] Wyllie, the political *aide-de-camp*, seconded this assessment, because the plaintiff 'describes himself as a Siyad & evidently belongs to a respectable class of zamindars'. It is worth noting that Syed was a 'caste' by now officially recognised as 'landowner' in the Land Alienation Act, 1900, and it was also the proud lineage to which Syed Husain Bilgrami, the new Indian member of the Judicial and Public Committee of the Council of India, belonged. This information, which Ali had himself provided, complemented his 'delicate' appearance, which led Wyllie to 'doubt if he wd [*sic*] stand rough work on board ship'.[43] After Wyllie verified Ali's account, Bilgrami recommended repatriation at India Office expense 'in view of the fact that cases of this kind are not now frequent, & that Hidayat is a man of respectable family'.[44] Respectable indeed, since it was the same clan to which the writer belonged! Ali received his return passage courtesy of the India Office.

By 1907 cases of destitute Punjabi litigants in Britain were rare. The Land Alienation Act and the end of the famine of the 1890s had helped to minimise the dislocation attending British land reforms. Furthermore, word circulated in India that there was no point in travelling to England to appeal civil suits. The result was that British authorities no longer faced the dilemma of how to deal with a class of destitutes whom officials of the Raj had defined as gentry.

That these cases presented authorities with a dilemma and occasionally received exceptional treatment is testament to the importance of social hierarchy in the application of assistance. The judgements behind these decisions revolved around qualities that often determined class status in Britain, such as current or former landowning status, and personal appearance and behaviour. But they also involved an interpretation of caste and clan membership in Punjab into class equivalents in Britain, for it was this aspect of Indian society that provided British authorities with that other key to determining social status in a British context: family antecedents. Even in the case of landownership, one of the most tangible signs of wealth, the complexities of Indian society required interpretation in order to render them into intelligible British equivalents. In some cases, such as Hidayat Ali's, the petitioner himself provided the necessary information, helpfully encouraging authorities to regard him as part of 'respectable' society in their own terms as well as his.

Entertainers: respectable and popular

Nowhere was the application of social and cultural hierarchy more apparent in the treatment of South Asians than when it came to entertainers, because more than most other petitioners, their fate caught the public eye. Two cases in particular highlight the contrast in the institutional behaviour toward Indians in need. The first, involving seven Burmese entertainers, is a fascinating study in itself of the operation of charity in Victorian England, because it highlights the way in which destitute Indians, as objects of paternal charity, could reinforce the imperial social hierarchy, highlighting the upper-class status of Britain's and India's elite alike. Two Indian agents, identified only by their surnames, Fowle and Fairlie, signed a contract with a troupe of twenty-two Burmese circus performers to take them on a tour of Britain and, in accordance with the Indian Emigration Act of 1873, return them to Burma. In the summer of 1896 they took part in a command performance before Queen Victoria at Windsor Castle. They also performed at the Crystal Palace. After the end of the troupe's engagement there, Fowle and Fairlie returned fifteen of the performers to Burma. Of the remainder, three were men and four women. The men accompanied Fairlie on a tour of Europe, and the women performed in Britain's provincial cities. In the autumn, however, Fowle disappeared to the European continent and Fairlie approached the British consulate in Hamburg, declaring that he was broke and did not have the money to send the three men accompanying him back. The Foreign Office repatriated the Burmese men to Britain rather than Burma. In the meantime,

Fowle's disappearance left the four women penniless. Fortunately for the men, a middle-class Englishwoman who had heard of their situation gave them shelter in her London home. The women ended up in St Pancras Workhouse, where the guardians discovered the pointlessness of bringing a lawsuit on their inmates' behalf against the two agents who no longer had the means to pay. The India Office refused to pay for their return, citing its policy regarding repatriation.[45]

By late November the plight of these entertainers had come to the attention of Maxwell Laurie, who was a member of the Indian Civil Service stationed in Burma but currently on leave in England. He wrote letters to the editor of *The Times*, in which he portrayed the India Office in a hardly more flattering light than he did Fairlie and Fowle. In a printed, open letter to the India Office, Laurie argued that 'the India Office stands in Consular relation to these men, and should have undertaken their case'.[46] His portrayal of the social standing of these entertainers was, however, contradictory. On the one hand, he portrayed the women as worthy of assistance by building up their respectability: 'It cannot be charged against these women that they are in any way of disreputable character. They are, in their own country, small shopkeepers, cigar makers, &c., and they have relations who occupy responsible subordinate positions under the British Government.' On the other hand, he tried to elicit sympathy for them by stressing their vulnerability in a condescending manner: 'For all practical purposes these Burmans are, outside of their own country, mere children, and it is impossible to exaggerate their helplessness.'[47]

Hutchins, the Judicial and Public Department secretary, took a jaded view of their class background. In a letter to the Lieutenant Governor of Burma the following April he referred repeatedly to the Burmese entertainers that Fairlie employed as 'artists', but always surrounding the word with quotation marks. As for the Burmese entertainers' account of their treatment, Hutchins noted condescendingly, 'Of course we have only ex parte statements and these were probably exaggerated, but making large allowances for over colouring and Asiatic imagination, Fairlie or those connected with him seem to have been guilty of such acts.'[48] In this instance Hutchins' racial stereotyping, which he expressed rarely, if ever, so overtly elsewhere, complemented his low estimation of the Burmese entertainers' occupation, which he denigrated on the grounds of class-based cultural preference.

Nevertheless, in the proper class context, Hutchins was willing to help as a private citizen. Frustrated by what he regarded as the India Office's obstinacy, Laurie and his brother, Werner, solicited private donations to pay for the Burmese performers' return passage. Among these overtures was a confidential one to the very India Office administrators who had refused official aid. The Laurie brothers estimated a cost of £87 to repatriate the Burmese entertainers. They received £183 6s. in donations. This sum enabled them to recoup the victims' earlier losses in addition to repatriating them with a balance of £34 6s. 9d. Of equal interest to the size of the response was the identity of the contributors. Hutchins and Alfred Lyall gave one pound each. Bernard, whose interoffice correspondence shows that he found the plight of destitute Indians more troubling than did many of his colleagues, contributed five pounds. Among prominent Indians in British society, Naoroji gave two pounds and Queen Victoria's *'munshi'*, Abdul Karim, gave five. Even General Lord 'Bobs' Roberts, the conqueror of Afghanistan, donated a pound. Perhaps most notable, but known only to a few of the Laurie brothers' acquaintances, was Queen Victoria's anonymous contribution of eight pounds.[49] Werner Laurie let Hutchins know of 'how shocked she was at the way they [the Burmese entertainers] had been treated' and added, 'I feel confident that she would use her influence to veto the proposal [to bring any other entertainers over under similar circumstances] should it not come within the range of the India Office to do so'.[50] To this implicit criticism of the India Office, Hutchins replied that he would ask the Lieutenant Governor of Burma to 'to use some pressure against Mr. Fairlie', who had now returned to Burma. Added Hutchins, 'I do not think that the interposition of Her Majesty herself could do more.'[51]

The Laurie brothers' correspondence with Hutchins indicates that the latter may have donated his pound to the relief fund in order to diminish the opprobrium they were casting on him in his role as secretary of the Judicial and Public Department. Nevertheless, more was going on here than the mere shaming of a government official. The contributors mentioned above represent a pattern of giving that confirmed one's status in polite society through charity to the lower orders. Where Hutchins, Lyall, and, to a lesser extent, Bernard were reluctant to commit government resources to assist people of low birth, they were willing to give of their own resources. Similarly as leaders of the Indian community in Britain, Naoroji and Karim reinforced their status through generosity to their inferiors. That, according to the standards of late Victorian society, the Burmese entertainers were the social inferiors of these benefactors cannot be in doubt, in spite of Maxwell Laurie's attempts to diminish their distance in class. Hutchins stated as much with his disapproving quotation marks around his description of their profession, and he probably attributed racial stereotypes to them more easily as a result. The Burmese entertainers could, therefore, receive assistance, but only as objects of charity, not as deserving recipients of official assistance. Ad hoc private subscriptions did nothing to solve the systemic problem of the mistreatment of British Indian subjects in the United Kingdom. They merely softened the more grievous repercussions of British authorities' failure to address the problem.

Not all entertainers visiting Britain from the Indian Empire received treatment in the context of such class condescension. Two who did not were J. Dorasami and his secretary, P. A. Rajia. At first glance the story of these two men appears to be similar to that of the Burmese entertainers. Both were Madrasis, hired by an American talent recruiter, Stapleton Boyne, to perform in Britain. They arrived in London in June 1906, where Dorasami performed on the violin. Like the Burmese entertainers he was treated as an exotic and even primitive object. A leaflet advertising his performances described him as 'a sensational novelty', and *The Standard* referred to his posture, which involved holding the violin upright between his knees, as 'the prehistoric way'.[52] The *Daily Express* announced that in performance 'he imparted an Eastern dreaminess', and *The Tribune* asserted that 'his manner has the true Oriental dignity'.[53] Edwardian fascination with this exotic exponent of classical music (whether it was Western, Indian, or a combination of the two is unclear) was not, however, sufficient to prevent Dorasami and Rajia from falling into destitution, when their agent deserted them, much as Fairlie and Fowle had abandoned the Burmese performers.

Similarities between the two cases end, however, with their descent into poverty. For one thing, these two entertainers were literate, at least one of them in English. It was Rajia who first appealed for repatriation in a letter to the India Office, pointing out that he was 'an employee of His Majesty's Government in Madras'.[54] He did not, however, mention his caste or Dorasami's, although an excerpt from *The Standard*, in a press notice he included with his appeal for help, described him as 'high caste'.[55] After Rajia's first contact with the India Office, Dorasami secured a further engagement to perform, one that he expected would 'keep them going for the winter'.[56] This engagement soon failed, however, and by late October, both Dorasami and Rajia were once again appealing to the India Office for help in returning to India. Initially, one unidentified India Office administrator had suggested that the two men could earn sufficient funds to finance their own return, since Dorasami had a skill with which he could hope to earn money in the future, and because Rajia 'was in Government employment he could scarcely be called destitute'.[57] Rajia, however, protested that as a clerk making Rs. 20 per month, he had no funds to draw on, and that Dorasami could only earn the money to pay for his return once he had reached India. Wyllie recommended that the India Office pay their passage, because 'Dorasami is a very respectable delicate looking man, scarcely capable of acting as a coal trimmer or doing other rough work on board ship. Rajia is stronger, but it wd. [*sic*] be difficult to find employment on a vessel for him also.'[58] In support of Wyllie, C. J. Lyall recognised that the India Office's policy of denying such cases 'was clear', but he urged: 'This case has features which make it one of exceptional hardship – the treatment of Dorasami by Boyne and the agents, his refinement, and his inability to work his passage out.'[59] The Council of India approved a grant for the violinist and his secretary, only to receive notice that Dorasami was embarking on another concert tour and would not need the money.

While Dorasami and Rajia were in considerable financial trouble, they were no more destitute than hundreds of other Indians to whom the India Office had refused aid. They were certainly no worse off than the Burmese entertainers discussed above. Why then, were India Office administrators unwilling to sanction official assistance to the Burmese performers, but willing to do so for Dorasami and his secretary? India Office correspondence suggests a number of reasons. First, Dorasami was performing classical music – the type of entertainment most respected in British polite society. Although the Burmese entertainers performed before Queen Victoria, the nature of their art was clearly popular and lower-class in its appeal. Second, Dorasami was 'high-caste', an issue which India Office administrators did not discuss at the time, but one which figured prominently in the India Office summary of the case compiled less than three years later.[60] To India Office administrators, Dorasami's artistic pursuit would not have seemed out of place with the traditional calling of the *brahman* caste, some of whose members were music teachers. In any case, Wyllie and Lyall considered him too 'respectable' to work his passage back, and were therefore willing to have the India Office pay for his return.

Comparing the cases of the violinist and the Burmese entertainers, however, does not present a clear issue of sympathy for the former and indifference to the latter, because some India Office administrators gave of their own income to fund the Burmese performers even when they were unwilling to help them out of India Office funds. In other words, they were effectively paying out of their own pockets to avoid breaking a precedent which, as this chapter shows, they broke in a third of the cases they encountered anyway. A couple of possibilities account for this behaviour. One arises from class distinction that treated it as fitting for the India Office to assist 'respectable' people from its own funds, while designating the lower classes as proper objects of private charity. The other was embarrassment that negative publicity caused the government. In either case, the India Office avoided creating any entitlement to assistance by discreetly helping those they deemed to be respectable entertainers as exceptions to public policy while privately helping performers who clearly were not members of polite society. As objects of charity, each group had its role to play in the imperial class hierarchy.

Religion

So far this chapter has focused on caste and class, often indistinguishably intertwined, as reasons for receiving emergency aid from institutions in the United Kingdom. Another identifier of social status implicit in these decisions was religion. Inasmuch as British authorities thought that caste membership carried with it cultural traits, then religion was a matter of social hierarchy. In the India Office's treatment of destitute Indians, however, religious discrimination was far from being simply a matter of Christian rulers favouring their fellow believers over rival faiths. Rather religion's role in India Office decisions was contingent on other aspects of hierarchical status such as caste or clan, and profession. It was also dependent on the political context in which it operated, particularly its relationship to an Indian's perceived loyalty to the British Empire.

Nowhere would that loyalty appear to have been more secure than among Indian Christians. Certainly for missionary organisations a petitioner's Christianity merited special consideration, and occasionally an Indian seeking financial aid or a return passage highlighted his or her membership of the church. In 1886, for instance, Abdul Khan, a Bengali who, according to George Small, 'professed to have renounced Islamism and embraced Christianity', came to the Strangers' Home. Within 'a few weeks' some of Small's 'Christian friends in London' had assumed responsibility for the convert's welfare.[61]

Nevertheless, Christian faith rarely weighed heavily in India Office decisions. When it favoured an appellant for aid, it usually did so through outside forces that then exerted pressure on the government ministry. In June 1882, for instance, Jawan Singh appealed for a return passage to India only to receive the India Office's 'usual [negative] answer in connexion with passages to India for Natives'.[62] His response was to address his next letter to the Queen and include two testimonials from missionaries in India, one attesting that he had been 'a pupil of the Umbala [*sic*] city mission school and baptized by me', and the other certifying that he had 'been teaching the Gospels and Catechisms in the mission High School' in Ambala. The first letter added: 'His conduct as a Christian has been good & his attendance at church regular. He seems to be anxious to hear more of the Word & I trust that he is a true Christian & will be able to do much for Christ.'[63] In his own letter, however, Singh did not mention his religious affiliation, but chose instead to emphasise his status as 'a jagirdar' (holder of a hereditary land grant) and his pursuit of an education in England.[64] It is uncertain whether the Queen saw this letter, since even her Private Secretary left no note in the correspondence. The only indication that she may have is the fact that, quite unusually in cases of destitutes, the Secretary of State himself wrote about Singh to the Indian Government. Moreover, upon re-examining the case, Fitzgerald decided to recommend a loan for the return passage, arguing that 'compliance is desirable, to get rid of the man'.[65] Most notably, there is no evidence of discussion of Singh's social status, whether by class or religion, among India Office administrators. It is therefore unlikely that either weighed heavily in the decisions of the India Office. But they may have with the Queen. Victoria was very sympathetic to Indians who had converted to Christianity, as was apparent in her relations with the Maharaja Duleep Singh and Princess Gourama of Coorg. The Queen was apt to let her displeasure with the India Office show through the comments of her advisers, as was the case fourteen years later with the Burmese entertainers. The fate of Jiwan Singh, therefore, may indicate the Queen's high regard for Indian Christians more than it does the India Office's.

Of the three other cases of Christians receiving India Office aid, two had other circumstances that might have elicited official sympathy. For instance, in 1902 Anukeram, a sixteen-year-old boy from Madras, received partial aid to maintain him until he secured light work (which he was willing to do) on a return passage. Chamier mentioned the boy's religion in passing, but in recommending assistance no India Office administrator did. Rather Horace Walpole, the Assistant Undersecretary of State, simply described him as a 'lad . . . of respectable birth & good education'. Walpole also mentioned 'his grandfather's loyalty' during the Indian Rebellion, an issue which Anukeram himself had raised and Chamier had duly passed on.[66] It was probably these last two issues, rather than Anukeram's religion, that moved Walpole to recommend assistance. Similarly, Pandita Ramabai's request for assistance, discussed at length earlier, did not hinge on her baptism as a Christian, although her British patrons, both of whom were women actively involved in the church, certainly highlighted her conversion. On the contrary, Arthur Macpherson argued: 'The fact that this lady has embraced Xtianity since coming to England rather increases the difficulty of giving her a Govt. grant.'[67] Ever conscious of the role that supposed Christian indifference to Hindu and Muslim dietary restrictions played in the origins of the Indian Rebellion, India Office administrators were reluctant to open themselves to accusations of proselytising or religious favouritism.

Perhaps the only case where an Indian's Christianity worked in his favour was that of Pandit Ram Gopal, an agricultural student and son of a judge in Punjab. In 1909 after Gopal had nearly completed his course of study in agriculture at the University of Reading, his father stopped his funds, because Pandit Ram had converted from Hinduism to Christianity while in England. The son's request was not, however, for funds, but for the India Office to pressure his father to continue sending his allowance of £20 per month. Wyllie agreed and the India Office contacted the father. In the meantime, however, C. J. Lyall suggested providing him with a grant of £70 to cover his return passage and living expenses until the voyage. No doubt sympathy over the son's persecution on behalf of Christianity was an issue. But so was the son's parentage. Many Indian students in Britain fell into destitution because their allowances ceased, but few received the extraordinary consideration that Gopal did.[68]

The effect of an Indian's Christianity on the behaviour of British authorities toward his or her assistance was, therefore, mixed. Christian missionaries overseas probably regarded Indian Christians as a group deserving special, favourable consideration. But India Office administrators, who were in the best position to lend practical aid, were much more ambivalent. Sometimes an Indian's Christian beliefs helped his or her case, as with Gopal. Sometimes they hurt it, as with Ramabai. Most often though, India Office administrators simply ignored the Christianity of Indian applicants for aid, focusing instead on parentage and education.

The same was true to a great extent concerning Hindu applicants, who were far more numerous than Christians. British authorities, however, could not approach Hinduism without dividing it according to caste, a hierarchy which, as we have seen, they translated easily if overly simplistically into British class equivalents. Since Hinduism was more a religion of practice than doctrine, caste lent itself to such an approach on the part of British authorities. However, when doctrinal belief was an important aspect of a Hindu's profession, British administrators treated petitioners favourably. Panwalker's case, examined above, was perhaps the best example of such favouritism. Yet caste, and consequentially class, were inextricable from such religious considerations. Panwalker was not merely a devout Hindu, he was a *brahman* and a philosophy teacher. The combination of these last two aspects of his profile made him appear respectable to India Office administrators. Thus, in this case, what British authorities might have regarded as missionary activity on behalf of a foreign religion, they identified instead as intellectual pursuit in keeping with high social status.

If caste and class considerations accounted for positive attitudes toward some Hindus of high social standing, nationalist activity explained hostility to others. An 1898 intelligence report, commissioned by Lee-Warner, attempted to list all middle-class Indians currently in Britain along with their reasons for being there. More importantly for British authorities, it assessed these Indians' loyalty to the British Government, commenting on their attendance at dissident meetings and affiliations with nationalist organisations. In this case, professional training and education, normally signs of respectability, brought Indians under suspicion, because British authorities feared, correctly as it turned out, that professional Indians training and living in Britain might present a serious threat to British governance of the subcontinent.[69] The important point regarding British authorities' attitudes toward Indian nationalism, however, is that a dissident's Hinduism was not an important feature of their concern. For instance, Swami Vivekananda was perhaps the most famous Hindu missionary to visit the United Kingdom in the 1890s and was unusual among Hindu thinkers in his active attempt to convert Christians to a belief in Indian philosophical teachings. Yet the India Office report mentioned him only as a 'theosophical lecturer', and passed no further comment on him. Furthermore, the report mentioned Parsi, Sikh, and Muslim members of the British Committee of the INC. Even in British eyes, therefore, the INC appeared to transcend any particularly religious affiliation. As a result, not only did British authorities not perceive Hindu practice as an inevitable challenge to British rule; they hardly ever treated it as pertinent to nationalist dissent.

The attitudes of British authorities toward Islam were quite different, if equally ambivalent. On the one hand, some Muslim members of India's elite, such as Indian Council Member Syed Hussain Bilgrami, offered the potential for creating a pro-British balance to the Indian National Congress. Furthermore, many Muslims came from 'martial races' that British administrators respected as 'virile'. (Of course, so did some Hindus, particularly the Rajputs.) In addition, as evident in Challis's response to the recipients of his mission, theologically liberal Christians sometimes found the unitarianism of Islam appealing. On the other hand, because of its missionary zeal and its strong sense of *umma* (worldwide community) the presence of Islam in Britain presented a much greater challenge to British rule in India than did the visits of Hindu proselytisers such as Vivekananda. In one case this challenge guided the India Office's policy toward aiding a destitute Burmese couple.

During the 1890s India Office administrators grew particularly hostile to the leadership of the Liverpool mosque, whose activities lent decidedly political overtones to its decision to aid a Muslim missionary couple stranded in England. The founder of the mosque was William

Henry Quilliam, a British solicitor raised in a Methodist household. After spending three months in Morocco in 1882 and studying Arabic over the next five years, he converted to Islam and adopted the first name Abdullah. Shortly after this decision, made in 1887, he founded the Liverpool Mosque and Muslim Institute using his personal funds. It was not long, however, before the institute became a focus of international interest and divided loyalties. Quilliam's conversion soon grabbed the attention of the Ottoman Sultan, who invited him to visit Turkey in 1890 and four years later conferred on him the title 'Sheikh-ul-Islam of the British Isles'. Quilliam subsequently served as the Ottoman consul in Liverpool, and his son, who also converted to Islam, was for a time the Sultan's *aide-de-camp*. Funding for the institute poured in from the Muslim world, and included a substantial gift from the crown prince of Afghanistan. Particularly disturbing to British authorities were the political implications of speeches at the meetings of this institute and its counterpart in London. Lee-Warner's report warned: 'The supreme authority of the [Ottoman] Sultan as Caliph, and measureless laudation of the diplomatic ability and good qualities of [Sultan] Abdul Hamid II form the staple of the speakers at all their meetings.' As a result, the report questioned 'whether the Moslem considers his prime allegiance due to his Queen or to his Caliph'.[70]

Into this political fray in November 1895 entered Mustafa Khalil and his wife, responding to a call they had read in Rangoon from the Liverpool Institute's weekly, *The Crescent*, for more missionaries to spread Islam across the British Isles. Quilliam paid Khalil a guinea a week to give lectures at the institute. Khalil, who was fluent in several languages, also tutored Quilliam's children in French. Early in 1897 he resettled in Manchester and served as the imam for the community of Muslim merchants in the area. Hutchins asserted that the reason for the move was Khalil's realisation that Quilliam was a fraud, a theme he emphasised in the rest of his report on the Liverpool Institute. But such an assertion served the India Office's political agenda so conveniently that, in the absence of other information, it is impossible to determine how accurate it was. Whatever his reasons for arriving in Manchester, however, Khalil remained there only a year, because his community was temporary, and as the merchants he had befriended gradually dispersed to other parts of the world, so went their financial support for his service. By 1898 he and his wife were in London in what Lee-Warner called 'extreme destitution'.[71]

At this point two forms of prejudice came into play: one class and the other political. Lee-Warner described the Khalils in sympathetic terms. However mistaken his venture, by heeding the call to proselytise in England, Mustafa had 'followed the precepts of his religion in resolving to work in the cause'. Furthermore, Mustafa's education rendered him unsuitable to work his way back to Burma: 'He has always followed literary pursuits, and never undertook manual work.' As if to confirm this missionary couple's respectability, their domestic life was above reproach:

> The room in which they live is squalid, but not dirty. The woman has a nice clean Burmese face, her hair is neatly done up, and her dress & manner are in pleasing contrast with her surroundings. The man's hands show no signs of work, while the lady stitches diligently.[72]

As he often did with destitutes, Fitzgerald adopted a hard line. But this time his hostility to the Khalils' mission inspired his declaration that 'Anybody likely to be engaged by the Moslem Institute at Liverpool is better in an English workhouse than in Rangoon.'[73] To this, however, Lee-Warner reiterated the justice of Mustafa Khalil's cause: 'No doubt Mustapha hoped to better himself by joining Quilliam, but the religious motive for which he takes credit also existed, and may very well have been the stronger.' Furthermore, Lee-Warner argued, there was a practical reason to return Khalil and his wife: 'Though it would not be judicious to countenance in any way the apostles of the doctrine of the Khalifate, a kindness shown to a destitute & unimportant follower can hardly do harm . . . On the other hand, he may do some good by witnessing against Quilliam.'[74] Impressed with this argument, the Council of India's Judicial and Public Committee dropped any objection to the couple's repatriation at public expense, and the Khalils returned to Rangoon, courtesy of the India Office.[75]

Ironically, Khalil managed to make the India Office's hostility to the Liverpool Muslim Institute work in his favour, by promising to discourage other believers from attempting a similar mission. The Khalils' class, identified by education, demeanour, and appearance, also earned the grudging respect of the influential secretary of the Political and Secret Department on an issue that, because it involved dissent, pertained to him. For Lee-Warner, Mustafa Khalil was acting as a devout Muslim should. That this associated him with disloyal subjects of the Queen was a matter of concern. But once Lee-Warner satisfied himself that Khalil himself harboured no ill will to the British Empire, he was willing to consider him sympathetically and, in the face of objections, find a practical reason for repatriation that his colleagues could support.

As with so many other cases of destitution to come before the India Office, the decision to repatriate the Khalils was complex. It involved considerations of class and loyalty. Inasmuch as it involved religion, Mustafa's behaviour and sincerity became central features. Like

Panwalker, Khalil was living up to the expectations of India Office administrators concerning the appropriate actions of a devout Muslim. Inasmuch as he fulfilled this role as the learned *maulvi*, and exhibited the proper context of harmonious domesticity, he and his wife earned the respect of some India Office administrators. If, however, they had participated in potentially seditious activities, as the India Office considered Quilliam to have done, then they would have sacrificed the perception of respectability necessary for them to be treated as members of polite society. Lee-Warner's assessment of Quilliam's character was scathing. He considered Quilliam to be 'a fraud' whom Muslims from India should 'expose' once they knew 'he was not a real Moslem'.[76] Of course, Lee-Warner may have considered Quilliam a fraud, in part, because he was English. In any case, the Political and Secret secretary did not regard the Khalils as seditious. For his colleagues, the political benefit of repatriating the couple may have been more important, but the couple's adherence to expectations, and the respectability of their actions and education did not hurt their petition.

It appears then that adherence to any religion added to an Indian's respectability in the perceptions of India Office administrators, so long as doing so did not cast doubt on the adherent's loyalty to the British Empire. Unfortunately, because of its concept of a united, worldwide political community led by a single caliph, Islam tended to fall under the suspicion of disloyalty more readily than Hinduism. Christianity, however, was a special case. Missionaries and the monarch may have considered it an asset among Indians, but India Office administrators considered it more of a political liability in terms of granting aid. Ironically, in the political climate of late Victorian and Edwardian Britain, it was safer and more useful for a Christian India Office administrator to aid a potentially seditious Muslim than an obviously loyal Christian.

Institutional administrators' decisions to show compassion toward needy Indians in Britain were ad hoc and drew on their most basic assumptions about the structure of society. One of these assumptions was that gentlemen should not be expected to perform menial labour, whether in a workhouse or on a steamship. In order to determine who held gentlemanly status, British officials translated Indian social ranks into British equivalents. Much of this process involved interpreting the meaning of caste and clan by occupation. Thus British institutions tended to treat litigants from the so-called 'agricultural' sub-castes of Punjab as 'yeomen', and *brahmans* as scholars, philosophers, or practitioners of high art. Equally important were the efforts of Indians to influence the interpretation of their ranks. Punjabi litigants testifying to their position as 'landholders' (i.e. *zamindars*) would immediately declare their gentlemanly status in British eyes, even if their families were in practice workers of the land themselves. Even more pronounced was the mystique surrounding the *brahman* caste that its members developed through exclusionary practices and taboos, particularly concerning diet and labour. The refusal of *brahmans* in workhouses to eat or work forced British authorities to treat them with special consideration unless they were willing to see them die. That such behaviour reinforced orientalist assumptions about Indian society only enhanced the tendency of British officials to give *brahmans* preferential treatment. Such treatment extended to Indian guests, such as Ramabai, who rejected the caste structure but nevertheless benefited from its existence.

The effect of translating Indian castes occupationally into British classes also impacted the behaviour of authorities toward Indians according to the religious communities to which they belonged. British officials ranked Hindus according to caste. Moreover, they treated Hindu religious leaders as the near equivalent of British scholars and philosophers, and not as threats to the British Empire. By contrast, British officials regarded caste as less a matter of religion among Indian Muslims than among Hindus, because Islamic religious texts made no provision for it whereas Hindu ones did. Although British officials often treated Muslim religious leaders with respect, however, they suspected them of disloyalty in a way that they did not suspect Hindu religious leaders visiting Britain. The reason was the Islamic *umma*'s extension beyond the British Empire. Most importantly, the claims of many Muslims in Britain of religious loyalty to the Ottoman Sultan made their allegiance to the British Crown suspect. Christian Indians presented no such problem, since their religion made them better candidates for British polite society than did Islam, and they certainly elicited the sympathy of many British officials. Yet Christians presented the opposite problem, because the British Government wanted to avoid creating the impression that it had a religious agenda in India.

Of equal importance to the motives behind decisions to aid Indians in Britain was the use to which such aid was put in establishing the social rank of the donor. Britain's elite, particularly those who identified themselves as a having a special interest in India, were often willing to give from their personal funds to causes that they would not fund institutionally. The presence of needy Indians in the United Kingdom also provided opportunities for Indians living there to do the same. Notable Indians living in Britain could, therefore, reinforce their claims to gentlemanly status through acts of *noblesse oblige* toward charitable institutions, such as the Strangers' Home, or ad hoc cases of need, such as the Burmese entertainers. Such patterns of compassion reinforced the impression of an imperial hierarchy, embracing diverse ethnic groups, but run by a group of elites, both British and Indian, who behaved similarly to one another in their treatment of the lower orders.

Notes

1 Great Britain, Parliament, House of Commons *Parliamentary Debates*, Fourth Series, Vol. 25 (12 June 1894): 928.
2 This figure is compiled from a close reading of individual case summaries in, 'Précis of Precedents' and IOR L/PJ/6/1083 No. 1499 'Supplement No. 2 to Précis of precedents relating to the relief or repatriation of natives of India in distressed circumstances in England (in continuation of J. and P. 3122/1909)', originally dated May 1911, but supplemented on further pages up to 1915.
3 Thomas Hobbes, *Leviathan*, Part 1, Ch. 6 (London: J. M. Dent and Sons, 1914), 28.
4 IOR L/PJ/6/209 No. 1399, 'Return showing number of East and West Indian and foreign seamen relieved in the metropolis during the year ended Michaelmas 1886', handwritten copy enclosed in J&P Deptartment minute paper, 'Pauper natives of India and other countries relieved by certain workhouses in 1886', 6 August 1887. For a description of workhouse diets see M. A. Crowther, *The Workhouse System, 1834–1929: The History of an English Social Institution* (Athens, GA: University of Georgia Press, 1982), 213–21.
5 PRO MT 9/362 M.1067/1890, Board of Trade's refusal to grant a licence to the Strangers' Home, Correspondence, George Small, 'The missionary's report', in Strangers' Home, *Annual Report for 1886*, 13.
6 *Ibid.*
7 IOR L/PJ/6/682 No. 1431, Chamier to Wyllie, 27 May 1904.
8 *Ibid.*
9 IOR L/PJ/6/682 No. 1431, Chamier to the Undersecretary of State for India, 17 May 1904. See Henry Yule and A. C. Burnett, *Hobson-Jobson: a glossary of colloquial Anglo-Indian words and phrases, and of kindred terms, etymological, historical, geographical and discursive*, 2nd edn (London: Murray, 1903), which describes *thakur* as 'a term of respect, Lord, Master, &c., but with a variety of specific applications, of which the most familiar is as the style of Rajput nobles'. This dictionary also states that 'in Bengal it is the name of a Brahman family, which its members have Anglicised as *Tagore*' (915). Since Khemchund came from Sind, the former meaning is far more likely. However, Chamier's comparison of the petitioner's family to 'the brahmins of Bengal' might indicate that he was a *brahman*.
10 Chamier to the Undersecretary of State for India, 17 May 1904.
11 IOR L/PJ/6/682 No. 1431, Chamier to Sir Charles Lyall, 20 May 1904, and Chamier to Wyllie, 27 May 1904.
12 *Ibid.*, 'Case of the man Khemchund Thakur: A native of India', 24 May 1904. The final approval is noted in a draft telegram attached and dated 8 June.
13 IOR L/PJ/6/613 No. 1944, Ajoodhia Prashad Sharma of Lucknow to the Under Secretary of State for India, n.d. [September 1902].
14 *Ibid.*, Chamier to W. N. Sturt, 11 September 1902.
15 *Ibid.*, Sturt, Note in J&P minute paper, 'Ajoodhia Prashad Sharma, destitute native of India: Brahmin of Lucknow asks to be repatriated', 11 September 1902.
16 IOR L/PJ/6/613 No. 1944, Chamier to the Under Secretary of State for India, 15 October 1902; Chamier to Wyllie, 20 October 1902, and Wyllie's note to Sturt, Political and Secret Department Reference Paper, 21 October 1902. The last indicates Wyllie's approval of the ticket to Lucknow, although it does not confirm that the India Office paid for it.
17 *Rig Veda* 10.90:12, and *Bhagavad Gita* 18:42 (trans. Juan Mascaró).
18 Chamier to Wyllie, 20 October 1902.

19 IOR L/PJ/6/645 No. 1872, W. H. C. Wyllie to Sturt, 3 September 1903.
20 *Ibid.*, Judicial and Public Department Minute Paper, Sturt [initialed], 'Case of Rajaram Bhasker Panwalker: A Karādā Brahmin now destitute and seeking repatriation', 16 September 1903.
21 Marginal note in *ibid.*
22 Risley, *People of India*, 112.
23 Ramabai has received considerable attention from scholars, although Beale's appeal to the India Office on her behalf has not. Her most recent full biography is Uma Chakravarti's *Rewriting History: The Life and Times of Pandita Ramabai* (New Delhi: Kali for Women, 1998). Burton focuses on her activities up to 1886 in *At the Heart of the Empire*, 72–109.
24 IOR L/PJ/6/165 No. 2167, Dorothea Beale to Lord Randolph Churchill, 17 November 1885.
25 *Ibid.*, Judicial and Public Department Minute,'Ramabhai, a Brahmin lady, application for a pecuniary grant', note by Arthur F. Hobhouse [unsigned], 19 November 1885.
26 *Ibid.*, A. W. M. (probably Adolphus W. Moore) to Fitzgerald, marginal note, 26 November 1885, in Hobhouse, Minute. For mention of Ramabai's supporters, see unsigned note to Churchill, 24 November 1885, in *ibid.*
27 *Ibid.*, draft letter to Beale, 3 December 1885.
28 Pandita Ramabai, *The Letters and Correspondence of Pandita Ramabai*, ed. A. B. Shah (Bombay: Maharashtra State Board of Literature and Culture, 1977), No. 93.
29 Ramabai, *Letters and Correspondence*, Nos 94 and 95. In the latter Ramabai mentions Fitzgerald by name.
30 Pandita Ramabai, *The High-Caste Hindu Woman*, 2nd edn (Philadelphia: Jason B. Rogers Printing Co., 1888), 108.
31 IOR L/PJ/6/413 No. 104, W. Lee-Warner to Sir Arthur Godley, n. d. [January 1896]. Lee-Warner's marginal note provides a fuller quote indicating that this expression comes from Aeschylus, *Agamemnon*, lines 176–8, which translate: 'Zeus, who leadeth mortals the way of understanding, Zeus, who hath stablished as a fixed ordinance that "wisdom cometh by suffering"': Herbert Weir Smyth, Loeb Edition 1926, 1999 reprint.
32 From the *Chenab Colony Gazetteer* (1904), quoted in Imran Ali, *The Punjab Under Imperialism, 1885–1947* (Princeton: Princeton University Press, 1988), 13.
33 Ali, *Punjab Under Imperialism*, 64 and 72.
34 Davis, *Late Victorian Holocausts*, 141–52.
35 Mathur, 'Living ethnological exhibits', 515.
36 Maya Jasanoff, *Edge of Empire: Lives, Culture and Conquest in the East, 1750–1850* (New York: Alfred A. Knopf, 2005), 10.
37 IOR L/PJ/6/270 No. 205, Statistics and Commerce Department reference paper, note by C. E. Bernard, 7 February 1890.
38 IOR L/PJ/6/281 No. 1270, Public Department reference paper, note by Bernard, 1 August 1890.
39 *Ibid.*, Political and Secret Department reference paper, note by W. G. S. V. Fitzgerald, 26 July 1890.
40 IOR L/PJ/6/296 No. 278, Political and Secret Department reference paper, note by Fitzgerald, 13 February 1891.
41 IOR L/PJ/6/281 No. 1270, A. G. Macpherson to Sir Gerald Fitzgerald, 24 July 1890.
42 IOR L/PJ/6/838 No. 4092, Chamier to the Undersecretary of State for India, 26 November 1907.
43 *Ibid.*, Judicial and Public Department reference paper, note by W. H. Curzon Wyllie, 2 December 1907.
44 *Ibid.*, Wyllie [unsigned], 'Question of repatriating Hidayat Ali, the son of a zemindar [*sic*] of Punjab, who has come to this country to appeal against a decision of the Punjab Courts', n. d. [probably 12 December 1907].
45 This account is based on Maxwell Laurie's in IOR L/PJ/6/435 No. 1206, confidential memo to the India Office, 27 November 1896.
46 *Ibid.*

47 *Ibid*.
48 IOR L/PJ/6/444 No. 682, Hutchins to Frederick Fryer, 10 April 1897.
49 *Ibid*., 'Subscribers to the Burmans' relief fund', enclosed in 'Burmans' relief fund', notice by T. Werner Laurie and Maxwell Laurie, 10 April 1897.
50 *Ibid*., Werner Laurie to Hutchins, 9 April 1897.
51 *Ibid*., Hutchins to Werner Laurie, 10 April 1897.
52 IOR L/PJ/6/778 No. 3240, caption under Dorasami's photograph and excerpt from *The Standard* in *Press Notices: Dorasami – East Indian Violinist*, enclosed in P. A. Rajia to the Undersecretary to the Indian Government, 27 September 1906. The summary of the circumstances under which Dorasami and Rajia fell into destitution is based on Rajia's letter and subsequent correspondence in the same file. The India Office confirmed Rajia's account by contacting Boyne's solicitor.
53 *Ibid*., *Press Notices*, excerpts.
54 *Ibid*., Rajia to Undersecretary, 27 September 1906.
55 *Ibid*., *Press Notices*, excerpt from *The Standard*.
56 *Ibid*., Judicial and Public Department reference paper, note by Wyllie on conversation with Rajia, 8 October 1906.
57 *Ibid*., unsigned note on India Office letterhead, 29 September 1906.
58 *Ibid*., Judicial and Public Department reference paper note by Wyllie, 29 October 1906. For Rajia's response to the India Office administrator's queries about his and Dorasami's financial capabilities, see unsigned note 29 October 1906.
59 *Ibid*., Judicial and Public Department minute paper,'Case of Dorasami and Rajia, destitute natives of India', 6 November 1906, note by Charles Lyall [unsigned], n. d.
60 'Précis of Precedents', 12, Case no. 3240/06.
61 Small, 'The missionary's report', 14.
62 IOR L/PJ/6/76 No. 1065, Public Department minute, 'Request for a passage to India – to be repaid after arrival there', 22 June 1882, and Jiwan Singh to India Office 'Respected Sir', n. d. [June 1882].
63 IOR L/PJ/6/80 No. 1452, G. S. Berger, testimonials (copy), 1 April 1879, and A. P. Kelso, testimonial, 21 January 1881, attached to J. Singh to Her Gracious Majesty, n. d. [June 1882].
64 J. Singh to Her Gracious Majesty.
65 For Fitzgerald's opinion see IOR L/PJ/6/80 No. 1452, Arthur Hobhouse [unsigned], 'Request for £19 5[s.] for passage back to India, to be repaid in that country', 29 August 1882. For the Secretary of State's letter, see *ibid*., Hartington to Ripon, draft letter, 2 November 1882, in Judicial and Public Department memorandum, 'Case of Jiwan Singh, a native of India, to whom £32.5.0 has been advanced for passage to India, re.: as to recovery of the amount in India'.
66 IOR L/PJ/6/613 No. 2011, Judicial and Public Department minute paper, Horace Walpole, 'Anukeram, of Madras, a destitute young native', 17 September 1902, and Chamier, extract from diary, 16 September 1902.
67 IOR L/PJ/6/165 No. 2167, 'Ramabhai, a Brahmin lady', note by Macpherson.
68 IOR L/PJ/6/922 No. 582. Judicial and Public Department Minute Paper, 'Application for Pandit Ram Gopal for assistance to enable him to return to India', 16 July 1909.
69 IOR L/PJ/6/363 No. 1875a, 'Indians in England', unsigned intelligence report attached to Secret Department minute paper, Lee-Warner, 'The position of young Indians sent to England for education', 29 March 1898, fos. 813–98. The reference to Vivekananda is on fo. 898.
70 *Ibid*., fo. 915. The summary of Quilliam's career and the foundation of the Liverpool Mosque and Muslim Institute draws on G. Beckerlegge, 'Followers of "Mohammed, Kalee and Dada Nanuk": The presence of Islam and South Asian religions in Victorian Britain', in *Religion in Victorian Britain*, Vol. 5, *Culture and Empire* (Manchester: Manchester University Press, 1997), 246–8.
71 IOR L/PJ/6/470 No. 172, Lee-Warner [unsigned], 'Mustapha Khalil of Rangoon', 17 February 1898, attached to Judicial and Public Department minute, 'Petition of Mustapha Khalil: Begs for assistance', 26 January 1898. For the authorship of that report, see A. C. Lyall's [initialled] marginal note, n. d. [March 1898], on the minute paper.

72 *Ibid*.
73 IOR L/PJ/6/470 No. 172, Fitzgerald, note, n. d. [probably between 17 and 25 February 1898], on interoffice memorandum, referred to the Political A. D. C., 31 January 1898.
74 Lee-Warner [unsigned], 'Mustapha Khalil of Rangoon'.
75 Unsigned marginal note, 3 March 1898, in 'Petition of Mustapha Khalil'.
76 Lee-Warner, 'Mustapha Khalil of Rangoon'; and 'Indians in England', 921.

CHAPTER SEVEN

Scholarships and the civilising mission

No segment of the Indian population residing in Britain between 1858 and 1914 has received more attention than students. Since students were generally literate and articulate, they left memoirs, diaries, and letters that witness to their experiences more directly than the letters and memoranda of British officials encountering Burmese acrobats or Punjabi oculists. Furthermore, some of twentieth-century India's most prominent political figures, such as Muhammad Ali Jinnah, Mohandas Gandhi, and Jawaharlal Nehru, received education in England. Little wonder that historians have focused on this group to provide a voice for Indians in Britain. Tapping on post-colonial methods of analysis, they have highlighted the contemptuous stereotype of the 'babu', a would-be intellectual trying in vain to 'ape' the middle-class English gentleman. As a result, these scholars argue, even when Indians tried to assimilate into British society, racial prejudice prevented them from doing so. This book has shown many instances of British authorities favouring Indians who behaved according to the stereotype of their social rank and ethnicity – so long, that is, as their proclamation of ethnic identity did not involve a challenge to Britain's rule over India or to the dominance of certain institutions, such as the medical profession, within the United Kingdom. However, a persistent theme of recent scholarship is that Indian attempts to behave in a middle-class manner brought on even greater opprobrium than their willingness to fit into the role of Indians that British society prescribed for them.[1]

While this observation is valid in some instances, it would be inaccurate to regard class status as more of a liability than an asset in Indian interactions with British institutions. These considerations operated in the otherwise often racist environment of British education. There is no doubt that Indian students suffered racial discrimination. The examples are numerous and well-documented in recent scholarship. But the ways in which race interacted with class and simple political expedience were complex.

This chapter and the next one take a further look at this issue and offer different models for interpreting these encounters. This chapter analyses the motives that caused institutions in the United Kingdom initially to encourage Indians to study in Britain. Although they formed part of a culturally chauvinist imperial mission, these motives were firmly grounded in the assumptions and discourse of class hierarchy, to which India's elite readily responded. They also tapped into racially inclusive concepts of imperial subjecthood which claimed to extend Britishness to people of colour. Moreover, educational administrators in Britain approved of and even encouraged cultural diversity within assimilation. That this complex approach often clashed with the racial application of access to power led ultimately to serious misunderstandings and recrimination no less among Britons and Indians at the time than scholars today.

Indian motives

The migration of Indian students to Britain occurred independently of administrative fiat. Since it has been the subject of considerable analysis elsewhere, a brief summary of Indian motives is sufficient. Two important themes are worth highlighting, however, because they explain much of the interaction between British institutions and students studying or preparing to study in the United Kingdom.

First, the (usually temporary) migration of students to Britain was mainly a result of the unequal relationship in power between the two countries. What began as a bare trickle of Indian students to British universities in 1843 swelled to 100 in 1880, 336 by 1900, and between 1700 and 1800 in 1913.[2] These students came, in most cases, to gain an advantage over their competition in India or to circumvent British institutional obstacles to their advancement in the Indian Government. In the first instance, Britain's position at the pinnacle of empire ensured that, even among Indians, its academic degrees or professional qualifications carried considerably more prestige than their counterparts in India. British regulations, however, barred those who could not travel to England from entering some of the professions that carried the greatest influence in the Indian Government. Not until 1922 could one take the exam for entering the Indian Civil Service in India. Similarly, British Indian courts reserved the prestigious title of advocate for candidates who had received a call to the English Bar, a process that required passing the Bar exam in London and attending dinners at one of the Inns of Court over a period of three years. Few Indians, therefore, could aspire to hold important administrative posts or to argue cases before India's courts. In the latter instance the vast majority of Indian law students had to content themselves with being *vakils*, who could not lead the defence or prosecution of criminal cases on their own. This remained the case throughout the Victorian and Edwardian periods in spite of the opinion of a senior Indian jurist in England that 'It is well-known that the Bar examinations are not as difficult as those for legal degrees in India and this is exactly the reason why so many Indian youths come here.'[3]

Second, although the Indian student migration to Britain fuelled opposition to British rule, decisions to study in Britain were personal and individual, rather than political and communal.[4] Indian students initially sought advancement within the imperial system. It was this system's thwarting of their individual careers that caused them to group together and challenge the legitimacy of British rule. Central to the tension that this created was a sense that British authorities in India were violating the acceptable discourse of British imperial society – the discourse of class.

Class, education, and the civilising mission

> It is impossible for us, with our limited means, to attempt to educate the body of the people. We must at present do our best to form a class who may be interpreters between us and the millions whom we govern; a class of persons, Indian in blood and colour, but English in taste, in opinions, in morals, and in intellect.[5]

These famous lines, from a minute which Thomas Babington Macaulay penned only eight years before the arrival of the first Indians to study in Britain, sum up the primary motive for educating Indians according to British models, in this case using English rather than Asian languages. Almost every textbook on Indian history quotes Macaulay's minute as an example of imperial arrogance. It does, after all, contain the infamous opinion that 'a single shelf of a good European library was worth the whole native literature of India and Arabia'.[6] Yet, in spite of his cultural chauvinism, Macaulay was no biological determinist. Accusing 'the advocates of Oriental learning' of 'insinuat[ing]' that 'no native of this country can possibly attain more than a mere smattering of English', he retorted: 'There are in this very town [Calcutta] natives who are quite competent to discuss political or scientific questions with fluency and precision in the English language. I have heard ... gentlemen with a liberality and intelligence which would do credit to any member of the Committee of Public Instruction.'[7] Macaulay's minute, therefore, serves as an excellent declaration of an educational policy intended to incorporate Indians into British culture.

Yet, since this document signalled a shift in policy toward India that was to receive lip service for a century to come, it is worth examining two of its other features, which have received less attention. One is class. Macaulay wrote approvingly of Russia's French-speaking elite, which had brought it into the family of European nations. He clearly believed that the majority of people in all cultures relied on men of letters like himself to advance the society as a whole. India had the social material out of which such an intellectual class could be formed, and it was Britain's duty to encourage this process. Moreover, Britain's occupation of India was part of a global civilising process that had been taking place for millennia. 'History', according to Macaulay, 'furnishes several analogous cases' to what he proposed for the India of his day. Indeed, one was England, which itself would have remained mired in ignorance had it not been for the European Renaissance, which focused on the writings of ancient Greece and Rome: 'Had our ancestors ... neglected the language of Cicero and Tacitus; had they confined their attention to the old dialects of our own island ... would England have been what she now is?'[8] It is worth noting that all on the committee that he was addressing would have appreciated that the Renaissance was an intellectual movement of the elite and would have taken it as a given that all such movements required the guiding hand of the educated classes.

The discourse of class is so deeply embedded in Macaulay's rationale that, for historians of Britain, it may appear to require no comment. It serves, however, as a significant corrective to decades of scholarship portraying British administrators and scholars as imperialists who constantly sought to justify their rule by emphasising the unbridgeable differences between British civilisation and non-Western cultures. In this case, even amid a statement dripping with condescension toward Indian society and justification of Britain's governance of it, Macaulay recognised the differences as existing within a context that he described as 'analogous' to the past of Britain itself. This analogy, like those that Alfred Lyall and Henry Maine described forty to fifty years later, was between contemporary India and Britain in the past. As such, it could be seen to fit well with post-colonial scholarship's portrayal of British authorities regarding India as hopelessly mired in the past. It could, but for Macaulay's confident belief that India would borrow Western civilisation from Britain, as Britain had from Rome. This belief, in the potential for Western education to bring about social improvement, was central to late nineteenth-century efforts to encourage Indians to come to England. Yet at its heart the premise of social improvement was built around assumptions of class superiority, which, in the minds of British reformers and administrators, applied to India as readily as they did to Britain.

The other feature of Macaulay's minute that receives little attention is its implicit tolerance of certain levels of cultural diversity. This assertion may seem ironic and even counter-intuitive, considering the normal treatment of this passage in textbooks. But the historical thrust of Macaulay's argument demands it, and almost all British efforts to educate Indians in their own image bore a certain tolerance of at least superficial cultural diversity. Implicit in Macaulay's argument was a dialectic: just as the Renaissance civilised the British without making them into Greeks or Romans and the Enlightenment civilised Russians without making them French, so a similar process could be expected to occur in the Anglicisation of India's elite. This elite might become 'English in taste, in opinions, in morals, and in intellect', but it must mediate this way of life through its own culture. Thus Macaulay leaves it to this 'class ... to refine the vernacular dialects of the country, to enrich those dialects with terms of science borrowed from the Western nomenclature, and to render them by degrees fit vehicles for conveying knowledge to the great mass of the population'.[9] For Macaulay then, not only the elite, but the vernaculars themselves, which he so disparaged earlier in his minute, might, with a heavy infusion of Western culture, rise to the level of respectability, much as English did centuries earlier.

From its very inception, therefore, the effort to educate Indians according to British models involved perceptions of difference within a context of similarity. Like all pre-industrial societies, India possessed agrarian-based classes. British reformers believed that, in many respects, these classes bore more similarity to their British equivalents of the recent past than they did to one another in their own society. This was the first level of similarity. Within this context, however, were differences between Britain and India, particularly in terms of food, religion, law, and technology. These institutions, like the classes that they upheld, were expected to change under British tutelage.

Other aspects of Indian society, however, need not change. Language, dress, and even religious customs need adapt only to the extent that the civilising mission required. Certainly, this tolerance of ethnic diversity resulted in part from political considerations. Too great a level of interference in Indian customs had helped to spark the Indian Rebellion. Nevertheless, this tolerance also drew on deeper assumptions about ethnicity and empire. In a 'United Kingdom' of cultures to which contemporaries assigned inherent characteristics, few thought it possible or desirable to erase all the features of past ethnicity. Thus, just as the Scots and the Welsh might preserve token aspects of their distinctive cultures while adhering in practice to norms of behaviour defined in south-eastern England, so might Indians do the same. The extent to which such behaviour reinforced or challenged imperial hegemony will be discussed at greater length in the next chapter.

Macaulay's minute was about education in India, but a generation later, after the bloodiest war in the history of the British Raj, Pratt Hodgson, a former British member of the Indian Civil Service proposed to create, within this elite, a select group of Indians who would witness British culture more directly by receiving higher education in the United Kingdom.[10] Hodgson pointed to an inconsistency in British rule. On the one hand, the British East India Company had encouraged the development of an upper-middle class of Indians educated in British schools in India. On the other, the Company had increasingly reserved its administrative positions exclusively for British candidates. 'It is obvious,' Hodgson warned, 'that unless we intended to associate the natives with us in the administration of their country to a far greater extent than we have yet done, our educational institutions must be regarded as a most dangerous mistake.'[11] Hodgson treated Britain's civilising mission seriously. Britain had not 'cribbed, cabined, and confined the national [Indian] mind after the fashion of an Austrian or Papal Government'. Rather 'our sense of duty to the people of India – of the sacred trust we have to discharge towards them, has prevented us from following any such course'.[12] But 'without a larger share in the administration of their country, the natives of India never can become fit for self-government'.[13] It was to this end that the author wanted British authorities to encourage India's elite to send its sons to Britain for their education. To receive British-style instruction in India was not good enough, because such 'education in India is merely the education of the lecture room, and what I want is the education of English life out of the lecture room'.[14]

As loaded with cultural chauvinism as Hodgson's remarks were, they did not preclude Indians from equality with their British rulers on biological grounds. Far from it – Hodgson's entire treatise assumed that it required only a small group of India's elite to adapt to British culture in order to initiate a cascade effect that would lift the entire subcontinent up both culturally and materially. This 'mental aristocracy',[15] as he described it, need amount to only 'four or five natives', who having 'had the advantage of three years of such education and such influences . . . would give a valuable impetus to native society'.[16] In making these assertions Hodgson certainly denigrated Indian culture as different and inferior. At the same time, however, he treated India's elite in terms analogous to Britain's. Even if we take Hodgson at his word, the scheme was highly elitist. For it assumed that a handful of Anglicised middle- to upper-class Indians could remould a society, which according to its author's estimation, amounted to 'a corrupt and decaying civilisation'.

This stunning confidence in the ability of the educated elite to herd the labouring classes like sheep toward a national destiny was commonplace in Victorian England. It lay at the heart of the National Indian Association's *raison d'être* and the efforts of numerous charitable organisations to improve the lot of Britain's Indian subjects. It combined ethnic and class elitism, because it was not enough that Indians should behave as Britons – they had to behave as upper-middle-class Britons, the true mark of Britishness in the cultural sense. Thus the goals of the National Indian Association referred in general terms to 'promot[ing] friendly intercourse between English people and the people of India' and '[a]ffording information and advice to Indians in England'. But its one guinea annual membership fee (ten shillings for students) for 1893 restricted its concept of 'people', whether Indian or English, to a small portion of British and Indian society. Moreover, in order to avail themselves of one of the NIA's most important services, introduction to British polite society, students visiting the United Kingdom had to present, among other credentials, 'a voucher for respectability of the family'.[17] Basic recognition came with mention in the occasional lists in the *JNIA* and its successors of 'Indian Gentlemen in the West', which included only a small fraction of the actual number of Indians in the country.[18] In this context its goals of '[s]electing English and Indian teachers for families and schools ... [s]uperintending the education of young Indian students in England', and '[a]ffording information and advice to Indians in England' fitted well into the class-based model of *mission civilisatrice* that Macaulay and Hodgson enunciated earlier.[19]

Therefore, in marked contrast to the racial separation that characterised much of the relationship between British authorities and India's elite after 1858, policy toward the education of Indians in Britain continued to develop under the pre-Rebellion assumptions of Britain's civilising mission. As late as 1907 British academics testifying before a parliamentary committee argued that many of the obstacles facing Indian students resulted from their population not being sufficiently representative of the elite. For instance, W. A. Raleigh, an English literature professor at Oxford, argued: 'The difference in habits, manners, and intelligence, between Sir Syed Ahmed's grandson and the baser sort of Indian student is not less than the difference between the Duke of Devonshire and a street loafer.' On the basis of this belief he advocated that 'it would be well to keep out of England all who do not by their birth, relationships, or abilities command the respect of the people at home'. Failure to do so would jeopardise the imperial mission and the Empire itself. 'The *prestige* of a residence in England is enormous; when it is gained by a vulgar and self-seeking youth, he does no end of harm on his return to India, and awakens resentment towards our rule among the better sort of his own people.'[20] Similarly E. J. Trevelyan, a reader in law at All Souls College, Oxford, argued for restricting the admission of Indians into the university to those 'who had been educated at an English school', had 'taken a degree with honours in India', or were 'men of high social position'.[21]

Reinforcing this belief were the forms that all students, whether British or Indian, had to complete in order to attend universities. St John's College, Cambridge, for instance, required the applicants to write in the 'Father's rank or calling', and Oxford University's matriculation forms asked for the father's 'description'. Indian students typically responded in either institution by filling in titles such as '*zamindar*', 'landholder', or 'gentleman', thus showing their awareness of the importance of class in the selection process.[22] Indeed, their willingness to supply English translations of Indian terms, such as '*zamindar*', is *prima facie* evidence of their desire to secure their social status in the British class system and take control of a process which would inevitably assign them a rank. Moreover, from the perspective of Cambridge University dons, accepting Indian students into their colleges complemented their own mission to India at St Stephen's College, Delhi.[23]

It is commonplace in modern scholarship on Indian history to describe a shift from cultural chauvinism to biological determinism during the nineteenth century. Regarding British attitudes toward Indians, political events provide ample evidence of this trend. The rise of a military recruitment policy based on 'martial races' and the refusal to allow Indian judges to try Europeans were merely the most notorious of many acts of official racism under the late Victorian Raj. Yet the civilising mission of social improvement continued to permeate official attitudes toward Indians in Britain itself. Of course, social praxis was markedly different from reformists' theories, but it was the latter rather than the former that continued to serve as the acceptable discourse within polite society, particularly among educators. As long as it did, Indian students and British reformers could attempt to hold the imperial system to this rhetoric, as we shall see that they did.

The ICS and the creation of government scholarships

If reformists' theories could become political practice, then there was no more obvious method than in the preparation of Indian candidates for the Indian Civil Service. To include Indians in the civilising mission fitted admirably the elitist notions of the reformist agenda. Since the connection between education and ICS recruitment was so important to the future of British rule in India, it drew the attention of the highest officials, most of whom were independently wealthy and had public school educations. These men regarded middle-class professionals as valuable functionaries in the Imperial Government, but not fit to lead. They considered the book learning of professions less important than experience gained through the camaraderie and discipline of life in public schools. While many officials accepted or even advocated the participation of Indians in the ICS, they strove for a service run by the elite, whether British or Indian.

In practice, however, too few Britons, particularly those already governing India, truly regarded such power sharing among the British and Indian elites as in their personal best interest. A guild mentality that manifested itself in class cronyism in its British setting did so as racial cronyism in its Indian setting. By discriminating against Indians because of their race, British authorities in India undermined the main institutional reason for encouraging Indians to study in the United Kingdom and accommodating their cultural requirements once they were there. In this case class discrimination became the basis of racial discrimination as Britain's elite increasingly racialised their disdain for particular classes in India by attributing essential negative qualities to them.

The replacement in 1853 of appointment by patronage with competition through examination promised to provide upper-middle-class Indians with access to prestigious government jobs. The catch, however, was that the exams took place only in England, thus requiring Indian competitors to pay for the round-trip passage to Britain without any assurance of success. To allow simultaneous exams in India would have exposed British candidates to intense competition from Indian counterparts. Instead, in 1867, the Conservative Secretary of State, Sir Stafford Northcote, created nine competitive scholarships to enable Indians to study at British universities for the exams.

These reforms arose from elitist assumptions common in the mid-nineteenth century. The landed classes, being intellectual, were better suited to high administrative posts than the middle classes, who were more mechanically oriented. While restricting the administration of Britain and its empire to the more capable landed class, these reforms would improve this class's youth by steering them away from jobs less worthy of their social rank.[24] Such elitism was even more important in the ICS than in the British civil service, because on the prestige of the former rested the security of British rule. Moreover, much of Britain's elite believed that upper-middle to upper-class civil servants were more likely to be less racist than the middle-class candidates who, according to Charles Edward Trevelyan, had been 'brought to the front from obscure corners of society'.[25] This latter group was hardly the type that would civilise India. Theory, however, soon confronted reality. Efforts to make the ICS exam objective, with precise values for answers, unintentionally rewarded 'cramming' rather than culture and the liberal arts. Between 1858 and 1897 open examination recruited about 1600 officers into the ICS. Of this group 12 to 13 per cent were sons of farmers and lesser gentry; 21 per cent, of businessmen; and almost all the rest, of professionals.[26]

Significantly, Britain's elite treated the last two of these British classes with the same disdain that they did most Indians studying in the United Kingdom. By the mid-1860s top British officials were caricaturing recruits who were sons of professionals and businessmen as overly-ambitious philistines who were too racist in outlook to keep the peace among the Indians they ruled. Early in his ICS career Alfred Lyall described many such colleagues as:

> too like clever office men at home, very good at writing precis and accurate in their legal functions, but without sympathy for the semi-barbarous natives whom they govern, and only liking the respectable educated native, who to me is a bore. Also they are wanting in the sentiment of good fellowship and are all jostling each other to get on.[27]

Similarly, in his widely read book, *The Competition Wallah*, G. O. Trevelyan observed: 'It is impossible to believe that any class of Englishmen are deficient in natural courage; but the familiarity with arms and horses can only be acquired by men constantly exercised in field sports; and to field sports the new civilians are not addicted as a class.'[28] These remarks came close to identifying the new British ICS officer with the 'babu' stereotype that came to mark so many Indians studying in Britain. The latter were not 'semi-barbarous' but simply 'a bore'. Although the former had courage, which perhaps the 'babu' lacked, he nevertheless shared the 'babu's' distaste for 'manly' field sports that developed the camaraderie and self-confidence necessary to rule an empire. Many British ICS candidates, therefore, supposedly suffered from the same obsession with qualifications and lack of social skills that Indian students did.

For G. O. Trevelyan this class-based elitism was the basis of his own, similar racial biases. Arguing in 1868 against a renewed effort to institute simultaneous examinations, he proclaimed that:

> if 5 per cent of the English competition wallahs are found wanting in the vigorous and manly virtues, indispensable to the members of a ruling

> caste, what will be the percentage among the Hindoo competition wallahs? Why, many times as great ... because nine Englishmen out of ten are born to rule, and 99 out of 100 Hindoos are born to be governed, because we are manly and they are effeminate.[29]

Even Trevelyan must have regarded his figures as rhetorical hyperbole, since he disparaged far more than five per cent of British recruits. He based his feminisation of lower races on his feminisation of lower classes. Not having the benefit of British gentlemanly education, the former were even less likely to be fit to rule.

Such thinking created the context for Northcote's decision to forego simultaneous exams and create government scholarships for Indians to study in Britain. Since a public school and Oxbridge education was the surest way to achieve the stature necessary to rule an empire, only the scholarship system would ensure that Indian candidates were fit for the ICS. Furthermore, the additional financial burdens that Indians living in Britain would inevitably encounter would ensure that they came from privileged backgrounds. Sir Herbert Edwards, the former ICS officer who lobbied the most for the creation of the scholarships, argued that they were necessary to 'form an enlightened and unprejudiced class, exercising a great and beneficial influence in native society, and constitute a link between the masses of the people and the rulers'.[30] In order to ensure that the right type of Indian received Britain's most prestigious form of education, only three of the nine scholarships were by competition. The remainder were by nomination. Ten years after the Indian Rebellion, this adaptation of Macaulay's vision lived on.

In fact, as Sinha has noted, much of the official opposition to 'babus' bore class as well as racial overtones.[31] The post-Rebellion policy of allying with India's aristocracy provided a practical incentive to restrict admissions to upper-class Indians. The problem was that in reality the service attracted the same type of rising professionals in India that it did in Britain. The role of race was first, to imply that middle-class British officers were unsuitable recruits for the ICS, and second, to identify as part of the ungentlemanly professional class any Indian who did not seem to fit the gentlemanly stereotype to which senior British officials belonged. For many British officials, the behaviour of Indians studying in Britain fitted and reinforced this class-based stereotype of the ungentlemanly, self-advancing aspirant to the professions, who would better have remained an artisan or an office clerk. As Lahiri points out, the frequent poverty of Indian students, due to the circumstances of geography, augmented this negative perception by curtailing their ability to take part in high society.[32] This antiquated notion of gentlemanly status, already under considerable middle-class pressure by the mid-nineteenth century, helps to explain why so many Indian applicants for admission to Oxford University or St John's College, Cambridge, described themselves as sons of *zamindar*s, whom British officials still treated as India's landed class.

It was, ironically, in order to ensure that elite Indians staffed the ICS that Prime Minister Gladstone's Secretary of State for India, the Duke of Argyll, suspended government scholarships just one year after they had become available. The reasons show how intertwined were concepts of race, class, and morality among the landed elite who still dominated the Imperial Government. They also reveal the projection of domestic political considerations into an analogous imperial framework. Arguing that 'mere intellectual acuteness is no indication of ruling power', Argyll pushed through Parliament a bill replacing the scholarships with a policy enabling the Indian Government to appoint Indians to the ICS without requiring them to pass exams. Argyll explained the reasons in terms of the 'martial races' concepts popular at the time:

> In vigour, courage, and in administrative ability some of the races of India most backward in education are well known to be superior to other races, which, intellectually, are much more advanced. In a competitive examination the chances of a Bengalee would probably be superior to the chances of a Pathan or a Sikh. It would, nevertheless, be a dangerous experiment to place a successful student from the Colleges of Calcutta in command over any of the martial tribes of India.[33]

This racial discourse, however, included social distinctions analogous to the pre-industrial British class system that Argyll wanted to perpetuate, for the subject was not the recruitment of the army rank and file, to which 'martial races' preferences normally applied. Rather it was the appointment of leaders from the indigenous communities of the subcontinent. Underlying Argyll's remarks was the assumption that any candidate would be drawn from the already educated classes. His comments, therefore, compared Indian elites across different ethnic groups. In doing so, however, Argyll compared geographically specific groups that he stereotyped alternately as urban business and professional (Bengali) and rural landed elite (Pathan or Sikh). Neither stereotype reflected, in its entirety, the social reality of its respective ethnic group or groups. Most Bengalis of the period, for instance, lived in rural communities. Nevertheless, this reality does not alter the fact that Argyll was preferring what he and many others *believed* to be a rural elite over an urban one. Excluding graduates of the College of Calcutta and appointing the supposedly 'superior' races amounted to rejecting urban professionals in favour of a landed elite, in other words people more like the Duke of Argyll. The latter 'races' had, not coincidentally, supported the East India Company during the Indian Rebellion. It was these groups that British authorities wanted to speak for India, since they were less likely than the middle classes to agitate for democratic institutions, which would inevitably undermine British control.[34] This political concern dovetailed nicely with the disdain of the landed elite in Britain for the lower-middle classes of their own country. It also complemented the efforts of the landed elite of northern India to invent their own traditions in the mould of either the Turkic Islamic or *kshaitrya* Hindu warrior codes. The result was a conscious effort to elevate the status of Indian princes as natural rulers, while delegitimising the claims to leadership of Calcutta's urban elite.

Nomination was not an attempt to limit the number of Indians serving in the ICS. As B. B. Misra notes: 'The discontinuance of the scheme of scholarships was not designed to shut out Indians from the competitive examination.'[35] Rather it was an effort to ensure that the right type of Indians entered the service. Argyll raised this issue more explicitly by arguing that competitive exams would raise 'serious difficulties' due to 'the circumstances of rank and caste'.[36] Ten years later, the conservative viceroy, Lord Lytton, made the point clearer when he objected to the requirement that Indians nominated for the ICS have experience in subordinate posts in which Indians commonly served. The problem, he declared, was that it excluded 'all untried persons; or, in other words, the very men whom, from a political point of view, it is our object to attract to our service'.[37]

As if to underscore their agreement with Argyll's theory of leadership, British-Indian officials spurned some of the earliest candidates to pass the exam. In what became an infamous episode for India's professional classes, Sripad Babaji Thakur and Surendranath Banerjea, who passed the ICS exams in 1869, were denied appointments on the grounds that they had lied about their ages on their applications. The error may have occurred because *brahmans* calculated their age from conception whereas Europeans calculated it from birth. The decision against the two was reversed, but Banerjea was subsequently relieved of his administrative post on a dubious corruption charge.[38]

Since so many Indian professionals were angry over the treatment of these two students in Britain, it is not surprising that they regarded as racist Lord Salisbury's decision in 1879 to reduce from twenty-one to nineteen the maximum age at which candidates could sit for the ICS exam. The common assumption was that narrowing the window of opportunity to enter the service to three years (seventeen to nineteen) was a cynical attempt to make it almost impossible for Indians to pass the exam. Indeed, Viceroy Lord Ripon's legal aide, C.P. Ilbert, complained that Viceroy Lord Lytton supported the measure for this very reason.[39] Yet Salisbury was probably more intent on discriminating against middle-class Britons than Indians, although he certainly did not mind excluding the latter. The purpose behind the new regulation was to recruit directly from the public schools rather than the universities. Since a significant minority of British university students had not attended public schools, this policy effectively barred them from competing in the exams.[40] Combined with the absence of simultaneous exams in Britain and India, however, it virtually assured that the only Indians to compete for these exams would have attended public schools in Britain, thus transforming them into members of an extremely small and thoroughly Anglicised elite. Race could be present in the calculations of British administrators without exerting a dominant role, particularly if a more immediate and threatening 'Other' was present in the form of Britain's own middle class.

Class, however, was a divisive issue in British politics as the Liberal party wooed the very middle-class professionals whom the Conservatives disdained. Just as the Liberal Duke of Argyll and Conservatives such as Salisbury and Lytton extended their rural elitism from Britain to India, so did the reformist Liberal viceroy, Lord Ripon, apply his belief in the power of the middle class to the Indian scene. To a sceptical Council of India, Ripon argued that the 'danger to our rule is much more likely to arise from a failure to afford openings for public employment of one kind or another to the men whom we are turning in large numbers from our Higher Schools, Colleges and Universities than from our not paying especial attention to the exclusive claims of wealth and birth'.[41] The council, however, based their resistance on a different fear for the Empire, that 'at least half the service would be Bengali'.[42] Ripon's desire to restore the maximum age for taking the ICS examination to twenty-two complemented his attempts to encouraged Westernised middle-class Indians to assume greater responsibility in governing India with British authorities. The success in 1883 of Anglo-Indian opposition to the Ilbert Bill may have encouraged a re-examination of scholarships. The bill would have allowed Indian judges to preside over trials of British defendants. The outcry from Europeans residing in India led to the bill's failure, and also to the creation two years later of the Indian National Congress as a counterweight to this lobby.

In this political context, scholarships indicated in a small way the government's intent to treat India's middle class as a partner in the civilising mission. Significantly, the Indian Government chose not to pursue a path that might have made the scholarships less challenging to British ICS candidates. This opportunity had arisen when Oxford Sanskrit Professor Monier-Williams renewed the discussion about scholarships in 1884 in a letter to Lord Kimberley, the Liberal Government's Secretary of State for India. Monier-Williams's proposal placed himself at the centre of the project, because it called for Indian Government funding for an Indian scholar to study Sanskrit at the Indian Institute at Oxford, which he himself directed. Such an award need not have had any explicit connection with appointment to the ICS. Yet Kimberley rejected this option in favour of allowing recipients of the scholarship to attend any British university and creating a '[p]reference in awarding the scholarships to be given to Statutory Civil Servants who are desirous of passing a probationary period in England'.[43] Ripon and his council modified the proposal arguing: 'Instead of selecting the scholars from among the probationers, we would select probationers from among the scholars',[44] who would be Indian university graduates competing in open examinations.

This proposal, however, ran into opposition from Lord Randolph Churchill, the new Conservative Secretary of State. An arch imperialist, Churchill feared that, in the words of the viceroy's council, 'if it [the proposal] were adopted, selection for a scholarship would practically amount (and would, by the class most interested, be certainly considered to amount) to appointment to the Statutory Civil Service'.[45] Such a policy would have practically stripped British authorities in India of the ability to decide which Indians they preferred as colleagues. Viceroy Lord Dufferin and his council immediately caved in to these objections and agreed to have the scholarships be appointments for Statutory Civil Service probationers. In 1886 the Indian Government created two three-year scholarships of £200 per annum to be awarded each year to Indians studying at British universities. The award also paid for passage between India and Britain. In doing so the Indian Government confirmed the class priorities of earlier reformers. British officials clearly intended the scholarships to assist wealthy Indians. Responding to news of Indian scholars who had run out of money during summer terms, the Indian Government's Home Department observed that 'while the scholarship allowance of £200 a year is sufficient to cover the necessary expenses of college life at Oxford or Cambridge, it is very desirable, if not absolutely necessary, that the scholars should have some small private resources of their own to enable them to meet expenses in the vacation and other general expenses which are scarcely avoidable'.[46]

In 1888, however, the Government of India followed this initiative with ICS reforms that threatened to close the service's upper echelons to the very upper-middle-class candidates for whom Ripon had created the scholarships. Significantly, although the previous round of ICS reforms had been the product of a parliamentary committee in London, these more overtly racist ones emanated from an Indian Government commission that kept decisions on the matter in-house among the Anglo-Indian elite living in India. The Public Service Commission reorganised the ICS's 'covenanted' and 'uncovenanted' services into an 'Imperial Service' recruited in Britain through the ICS exams, a 'Provincial Service' recruited in India to serve in provincial governments, and a 'Subordinate Service'. Since many senior positions in the covenanted service now passed to the Provincial one, the commission touted the new arrangement as making many upper-level posts more accessible to Indians, who two years earlier had staffed only twelve of approximately nine hundred covenanted posts.[47] However, although the first two services were now to be theoretically equal, the positions in the Provincial Service commanded much lower salaries than those in the Imperial. Moreover, as Sinha points out, the new arrangement made Indian participation in the governance of the Raj as a whole less likely, since local recruits, who Indian candidates were by far the more likely to be, had to serve in provincial rather than all-India posts. Finally, because of its lower salaries and limited access to decision-making, the Provincial Service in practice held a lower level of prestige in the eyes of Indian candidates and British administrators. In fact this reform actually made it harder for Indians residing in the United Kingdom to enter the new Imperial Service, because civil service commissioners tended to argue that since higher positions were now available in the Provincial Service, which Indians normally staffed, they were under less of an obligation to appoint Indians to the Imperial Service.[48] The handful of scholarships available to Indians wishing to study in Britain, therefore, increased in importance. Before the First World War, Indians passing ICS competitive exams remained in the single digits and averaged less than a tenth of the total number of British officers admitted. Yet ICS posts carried such symbolic importance that although few in number, they became an issue of intense debate at the highest levels of government.

This focus on a small number of awards for a small group of Indians is understandable in the context of the class consciousness that characterised Britain's elite. When British authorities reformed the Indian Civil Service in the 1850s they regarded it, like its counterpart in Britain, as the proper preserve of the gentlemanly class. In doing so they incorporated Macaulay's vision of a Westernised Indian elite who would serve as mediators between Britain's elite and the masses of India. Government scholarships for Indians to study at British universities were a logical result of this mindset. But this elitist notion of the civilising mission encountered two major obstacles. One was the reluctance in practice of British administrators of the Raj to yield much power to members of the indigenous population, no matter how high their social standing. The other was the tendency of ICS positions, and scholarships to train for them, to appeal more to the income-earning, urban professional classes, whether British or Indian, than to the rural landed elite of either country.

Although British authorities discriminated against Indians in hiring them for ICS posts, their hostility to Indian candidates was a combination of race and class prejudice. To many reformers in Britain the biggest problem with Indian candidates for the ICS was not so much that they were Indian as that they were the wrong class of Indians – not from a class that they considered analogous to the ruling class of the United Kingdom. Certainly, the systemic effect of holding exams in Britain for the most important administrative positions in India was to deny Indians access to power. But the sense of otherness that such discrimination projected was in terms of both race and class, and the level at which it was one or the other depended greatly on whether or not the British official involved was responding to pressure from the ICS's British membership.

The Gilchrist Scholarships

The government was not the sole source of scholarships for Indians wishing to study in the United Kingdom. Private endowments also provided such opportunities. These bequests perpetuated the elitism inherent in the attitudes of British and Indian reformers alike, but they sometimes exposed the hypocrisy of British authorities who encouraged Indians to study in England for positions in which they then refused to employ them. Meanwhile, however, private organisations limited Indian advancement by class, even as they provided opportunities for them. This was the case with the Gilchrist Trust, the bequest of John Borthwick Gilchrist (1759–1841), who began his career in Bengal as an East India Company surgeon but soon became an expert in Hindustani and spent much of his life teaching the language in London and Edinburgh. He bequeathed much of his fortune to a trust, which after the death of his widow and a subsequent legal challenge from other descendants, became available 'for the benefit, advancement and propagation of education and learning in every part of the world'.[49] In 1868 the trustees approached the India Office to establish two scholarships to be awarded annually to Indians for three years of study in the United Kingdom. Building on Macaulay's vision, the purpose of these awards was for 'the assistance of deserving Natives of India, who having already profited by the opportunities afforded to them in the Educational Institutions there open to them may be desirous of prosecuting a course of Academical Study in this country, either in Arts, Laws, Science, or Medicine'.[50]

But the trustees expected these 'deserving Natives' to have profited from the opportunities of birth as well as education, and they assumed that only Indians of high social birth and financial means should be eligible for the award. From the very start the trustees insisted that: 'Every Candidate must furnish proof satisfactory to the Local Authorities, that in regard to personal character and social position he is qualified to be admitted to competition for a Scholarship.'[51] Furthermore, the Gilchrist trustees expected their scholars to have money. When the India Office suggested that the trustees raise the amount of the Gilchrist award from £100 to £200 by reducing the number given annually from two to one, the trustees refused to change the amount. In spite of the trustees' determination on this point, the India Office was enthusiastic enough about the programme to agree to pay for the students' passages to and from England. Nevertheless, the India Office's participation did not prevent Gilchrist scholars from running into financial trouble. In 1881 one of them asked the India Office to supplement his stipend, claiming that it was insufficient to support him. Since that same year a writer for the *JNIA* estimated living expenses for the academic year at Balliol College, Oxford, to be £185 5s. 6d., the Gilchrist scholar's complaint was certainly plausible. Rather than increase the award, however, the Gilchrist trustees argued that: 'the words "qualified by social position" were intended to prevent the award of the Scholarship from being made to candidates not possessed of . . . additional income'.[52]

Nevertheless, the Gilchrist trustees soon realised that their project was foundering, because it did not provide enough money to defray the costs of living in Britain and because it required a knowledge of Latin in order to receive the award. When setting up the award, the India Office had encouraged the Gilchrist trustees to substitute Sanskrit for Latin in their exam. This suggestion the trustees had also rejected.[53] The lack of suitable candidates forced benefactors and the government to make the awards more generous, albeit fewer. In response to the lack of quality candidates for their awards, the Gilchrist trustees, starting in 1884, limited the number of new awards to one a year and raised the annual stipend to £150. In 1890 they raised this figure to £200.

An interesting indication of the elitism inherent in scholarships is the restrictions that institutions placed upon their use. A sharp distinction existed between awards available only for study in the liberal arts programmes and elite professions and those earmarked for technical education, with the former clearly having pride of place over the latter. Gilchrist scholars could study only at University College, London, or the University of Edinburgh, and the curriculum had to be in 'either the Arts, Laws, Science, or Medicine'.[54] When some award recipients shifted the emphasis of their study from theoretical science to medicine, the Gilchrist Trustees tightened the terms of the grant declaring 'that their object in framing the new regulations, was to encourage scientific study, and not to provide opportunities for medical graduates to obtain additional professional qualifications'.[55] These distinctions fitted well with those that the government practised. Although Indian Government Scholarships were for attendance at any British university,[56] they were distinct from Indian Government technical scholarships, which, during the Edwardian period, were for only £150 per annum, rather than the £200 allotted to university scholars at the time. The rationale may have been that maintaining oneself in the gentlemanly status expected at the universities required more money than did apprenticeship with a manufacturing firm. But technical students required, if anything, more money than their university counterparts, because they had to pay additional premiums to private firms willing to take them on.[57] Moreover scholarships were available only for higher education, a practice that reflected the Raj's priorities in India itself. An 1881 confidential memorandum called for a review of educational expenditure in India in order to respond to charges that 'the bulk of educational grants in India is spent on higher education, to the neglect of education for the masses, that one fourth of the whole grant is spent on government colleges and higher schools, attended chiefly by the richer classes'.[58] Such policies fitted Macaulay's vision of an Indian elite mediating between British administrators and indigenous masses.

The interaction of the India Office and the Gilchrist Trust indicates how closely private charities had to cooperate with the government in order to realise their goals for Indians. As did the Strangers' Home in housing destitutes, the Gilchrist Trust became a semi-official partner with the India Office in the allocation of scholarships. The trustees' upward adjustment of the grant award stipend in 1890 accompanied a more sweeping change of the Trust's administration of the scholarships. Hitherto, candidates in each of the three presidencies, the largest administrative divisions of British India, had competed for the awards. Now with competition for government scholarships rotating among Indian universities, the Gilchrist trustees decided to have theirs rotate among universities in years when they were ineligible for government-scholarship competitions.[59] Moreover, close cooperation occasionally led to social interaction between Gilchrist trustees and India Office administrators. For instance, in 1886 the Trust's president, Sir Ughtred J. Kay-Shuttleworth, invited the secretary of the India Office's Judicial and Public Department to join him for a week of grouse shooting.[60]

Nevertheless, the close cooperation between the Gilchrist Trust and the India Office was short lived and collapsed over the principles underlying the civilising mission. The cause for complaint occurred in the wake of the 1888 reorganisation of the ICS. Theoretically, the Imperial Service remained open to any candidate who had the necessary qualifications and passed the ICS exams in England. In practice, however, the Indian Government often assigned Indians to the Provincial Service, even if they had received their training in Britain.[61] Not surprisingly, when in 1892 two successful Gilchrist scholars completed their education only to find themselves relegated to the Provincial Service, they protested. Both claimed they were victims of racial discrimination. One, B. N. Mallik, even received a letter from the Private Secretary to the Governor of Bengal, declaring that 'the Superior Educational Service, as it is now called, will be closed to the natives of India and reduced in numbers and confined to Europeans appointed by the Secretary of State and sent out from England'. Mallik who had 'distinguished himself' at the Universities of London and Cambridge, refused the offer of a 'very inferior' position in the Provincial Educational Service. The Gilchrist trustees regarded this policy as undermining the central mission of their scholarships, declaring to the India Office that 'if natives are to be excluded from the higher branches of the Service, it seems worse than useless to bring them over to England by means of Scholarships, and give them, at great expense, the training of Europeans; such a training as fits them for the higher posts from which thay [*sic*] are afterwards excluded upon racial grounds'.[62]

In response to this charge, the India Office dissembled. Charles E. Bernard, the secretary of the India Office's Revenue and Statistics Department, claimed that the Private Secretary's assertion 'went beyond the facts', but the Educational Committee of the India Office's Judicial and Public Department defended the bifurcation of the special services as beneficial to Indians. Significantly, however, the committee did not respond to the assertion that Indians were in fact barred from posts in the Superior Educational Service. Rather, by focusing on opportunities in the Provincial Service, it implied that they could not hold posts in the Superior Service.[63] These responses did not impress the trustees. Citing Queen Victoria's 1858 proclamation, they issued an 'appeal to the Secretary of State for India to withhold his assent from any proposals which will make native blood a bar to entrance into any part of the Service of the British Empire'.[64]

This issue, however, was not going to disappear unless government practice changed. At their meeting of 19 March 1896 the Gilchrist trustees read a letter from Mallik, declaring that he had still not received satisfaction from the Indian Government. Citing the high cost of the scholarships and previous complaints of Gilchrist scholars excluded from the ICS on racial grounds, the trustees suspended the scholarships 'until it appears that natives of India who have obtained a University training in England, and possess the necessary education qualifications, are eligible for all posts equally with Europeans'.[65] Six years after ending the scholarships for study in Britain, the Gilchrist trustees created new grants for the higher education of Indian women in India. This time, however, they worked through the National Indian Association rather than the India Office.[66]

The history of the Gilchrist scholarships from 1866 to 1896 highlights the motives and contradictions in British policy toward Indians studying in the United Kingdom. On the one hand, British officials supported the civilising mission which they used so frequently to justify their occupation of the subcontinent. On the other, Indians who did so often encountered official resistance to their placement in these influential posts. One of the reasons underlying this inconsistency was doubtless the greater fear of British administrators already in the service that the presence of Indians in their ranks would undermine their authority and threaten their careers. The racism born of this fear would explain the willingness of government officials and benefactors in Britain, even those who opposed scholarships for Indians in the United Kingdom, to encourage Indians to train for upper-echelon ICS positions when British authorities in India appeared to discourage it. Caught between the racially defined fears of the Indian Government and the social improving aspirations of some British politicians and benefactors, the India Office tended to make excuses for the Indian Government in its dealings with Britons at home. It is perhaps for this reason that the India Office destroyed some of the key correspondence surrounding the termination of these scholarships.[67]

The Gilchrist Trust did not operate under this type of constraint. Its founder and trustees pursued a much more consistent vision of the civilising mission, one which they addressed in an elitist manner in the spirit of Macaulay. It was this mission which led to the creation of scholarships to bring Indians over to Britain, ostensibly to train for careers in the upper echelons of the ICS. Like the creators of the government scholarships, the Gilchrist trustees sought out India's gentlemanly class to be recipients of their largesse. Their insistence on perpetuating two £100 scholarships in the face of the declining interest and quality of candidates indicates the importance to them of recruiting Indians from wealthy families. Yet in two important respects the trustees exhibited a far more open and inclusive attitude to the education of India's elite than did most government officials. In 1890 they opened the scholarships to female applicants, and in 1893 and 1896 they protested discrimination in the employment of Indian scholars on the basis of race. Objection to this second issue was so fundamental that it led directly to the cancellation of the scholarships for Indians to study in Britain. Believing in the rhetoric of enlightened imperialism, the Gilchrist trustees broke their partnership with the government when they discovered that the latter was more interested in maintaining power than bequeathing it.

Perhaps most significant, however, is the discourse that the Gilchrist Trust and the India Office used to describe the crisis that ended their partnership in the 1890s. When the Gilchrist trustees accused the Indian Government of discriminating against their scholars on 'racial grounds', India Office administrators did not justify race as a valid reason for disqualifying a candidate for the Superior Educational Service. Rather they protested that the Indian Government's actions were either erroneous, unrelated to race, or designed to give Indians greater responsibility in the governance of their country. This response is markedly different from the franker racial bias of the Private Secretary to the Governor of Bengal, who informed Mallik simply that the posts he desired were 'closed to Natives of India'. It also contrasts markedly with the Gilchrist trustees' behaviour toward the social class of candidates, who were to be 'qualified by social position'. In late Victorian England there was nothing wrong with discriminating against candidates for scholarships or the civil service on the basis of their social class. Race, however, was a different matter. Already, in the polite society of the imperial metropole, few admitted openly to outright racism regarding employment and educational opportunities. That such racism existed caused a rift between a government office charged with pursuing the civilising mission and a private organisation whose members actually believed in it.

Yet the very class elitism that the Gilchrist trustees supported, in apparent opposition to the Indian Government's overt racism, itself thwarted the civilising mission that the trustees pursued. For in the context of an imperial economy, in which the rupee–sterling exchange rate was so unfavourable to Indians even of the upper-middle class, the social improving project of the Gilchrist trustees was foundering before the government's racist policies came to their attention. Although the trustees never realised it, the Gilchrist awards demonstrated the inherent flaws in the elitist civilising mission as fully as they did the hypocrisy of the British Raj. Even when philanthropists sought to give Indians an advantage within the imperial system, the class-structured nature of that system combined with the disparities of economic and political power between Britain and India to make it exceedingly more difficult for Indians than Britons to attain influential positions in

India's bureaucracy. What began as intentional class discrimination, therefore, led to racial discrimination, however unintentionally.

Educating women

The Gilchrist Trust's cooperation with the National Indian Association in creating scholarships for Indian women was part of a larger emphasis on female education among reformers. The number of women coming to Britain to receive their education was, however, only a small fraction of the total number of Indian students visiting the imperial metropole. The reasons were numerous. For one, British women were themselves only beginning to make inroads into higher education. It was an unusually bold Indian family that would willingly let its daughter travel thousands of miles to live, virtually unchaperoned, in Britain. Moreover, one of the few socially acceptable careers for a Victorian lady was teaching children or other women. Such a career hardly seemed to require the socialisation process of life in Britain. Nor did it demand rigorous technical education. Yet, as we have seen, so dim was the British view of female learning in India that many British reformers considered it desirable to train Indian women in Britain to become pioneers of women's education in India. The forms of education for Indian women in Britain that authorities supported, and those that they opposed, reveal the extent to which the civilising mission was defined by gender as well as class.

Nowhere was this definition clearer than when authorities chose to deny women opportunities available to men. It was, perhaps, inevitable that Indian women would seek the same scholarships that Indian men did. It is a sign of how far some Indian women were willing to break with cultural norms that the first attempt occurred in 1886, the first year that the Indian Government made scholarships available after a thirteen-year hiatus. The applicant was Cornelia Sorabji, who would in 1919 become India's first female barrister. The government's response was to rule women ineligible because 'These Govt. [*sic*] scholarships are in no way suitable for Women, – and would have to be entirely remodelled if women were made eligible.'[68]

Why they were unsuitable and how they would have to be remodelled was unclear. But perhaps Secretary of State Lord Randolph Churchill, this statement's author, regarded the scholarships as inappropriate because they were designed to prepare Indians to hold professional positions back home. Late Victorian polite society held such a goal to be unsuitable for Indian women, as it did for their British sisters. This restriction, however, did not preclude any perception of a need to educate socially respectable Indian women in Britain. Rather it restricted the type of training that they received to the sphere considered appropriate for their British counterparts. By contrast, four years later the Gilchrist Trustees, who, as we have seen, were having trouble persuading good candidates to compete for their award, opened it up 'to Women upon exactly the same conditions as to Men'.[69] This decision was in keeping not only with their commitment to female education, but also with their more liberal outlook toward the benefits of social improvement.

In fact, the education of Indian women was a major goal of British reformers' civilising mission, because it was in the behaviour and treatment of women that the elite societies of Britain and India seemed to differ the most. 'The education and improvement of women' in India was one of the four central 'wants' that the founders of the NIA identified, and they devoted many of their events and much space in their journal to this end.[70] It was the rare British intellectual, such as Oxford don Oscar Browning, who regarded purdah as a legitimate Indian equivalent of ladylike behaviour in Britain. He declared wistfully, that 'so long as women are regarded as refining influences in the world, so long as men have to learn what is becoming from the other sex, so long, I hope, will the veil of seclusion be only gradually lifted from the Indian Zenana'.[71] Even some Indian women visiting Britain provided similar positive assessments of the purdah system. Writing for the *Evening Chronicle* Mersha Chinappa, a classical scholar seeking further training in England, declared of the typical married woman in rural India: 'Is she contented? Yes, supremely so.'[72] Since this woman of an urban professional class – she was the daughter of the manager of Mysore's educational department – presumed to speak on behalf of the agrarian classes, her account bore the same condescending tone as that of her British counterparts describing the joys of village life in England.

Yet many Indian 'ladies' visiting Britain were quick to condemn the condition of India's elite women for not meeting the expectations of Victorian womanhood. Typically, the complaint was that these women did not live in a manner sufficiently elite. Writing in the *IMR*, Mary Bhore, a girls' school administrator in Poona who had recently studied in England, argued that the condition of 'English ladies' was superior to that of their Indian counterparts, because:

> English ladies, if they have several servants, do not occupy themselves, as we do, in personally superintending the cooking and domestic work ... Time is too valuable for ladies and servants to be doing the work the latter can do alone.[73]

And if English ladies' time was too valuable to clean and cook, to what better use did they put it? Why, needlework for their elaborate clothes and correspondence with distant family members, of course! The latter activity made them valuable helpmates of their husbands, who, 'having their own business or interests, family letters seem to be left chiefly to the ladies'.[74] In fairness, Bhore also noted that 'the women of a[n English] family, girls included, generally had some book of the hour to read, and so all were quite in touch with the literary, political, and general events of the day'.[75] This remark hinted at the political implications of female education that were already apparent in Britain. Yet there can be little doubt that for most reformers, the primary goal of educating the female elite of India was for them to serve as a cohort of supporters for their men.

At the same time, however, the education of elite Indian women was a matter of national pride in the struggle to attain the respect of the British. As one (probably white male) contributor to the *Madras Atheneum* noted: 'We do not so often mentally contrast the wife of a labouring man out here with the wife of a labourer at home, but we draw mental comparisons between such a poor native woman and our highly educated acquaintances of the fair sex at home.' The barrier, according to this writer, preventing greater British respect for elite Indian women was education: 'It is true that Hindu ladies are not so forward in intellect as their European sisters.' But there was reason for optimism since '[o]ur leading Hindus are day by day becoming aware of this one great defect in their daughters and wives, and are remedying this defect rapidly'.[76]

In this spirit, British institutions encouraged a small number of Indian women to pursue their education in the United Kingdom. Arguing in 1867 for the creation of teaching academies for women in India, Dadabhai Naoroji set out the main reason that would be used over the coming half century for educating Indian women in Britain: 'The exertions of the friends of female education have, however, for some time past come to a standstill and further progress is checked simply because properly qualified female teachers cannot be obtained in India.'[77] Similarly the President of the Bethune School for girls in Calcutta regarded as the primary purpose of educating his charges 'to make them good wives and good mothers', and hoped to persuade 'a number of respectable and educated native ladies' to play a leading role in this effort.[78] The impulse to educate women, therefore, was steeped in gendered stereotypes. Yet it was similar to that behind the education of men in its focus on India's elite (this time female) as the necessary conduit of its efforts.

The India Office rejected this proposal out of a post-1858 concern that interfering in the lives of elite women would raise opposition among the very elite males whom they sought to coopt in imperial rule. But it accorded great respect to Indian women of high social standing seeking to educate themselves in Britain in order help their sisters at home. Such respect was apparent in 1879, when the India Office made an exception to its rule of refusing aid to Indians in Britain. Responding to an appeal from William Butler, canon of Wantage, it provided £85 15s. 9d. to make up the balance of £300 that would allow two Indian women to complete their training as educators and return to India. These women, Pheroze and Mary Sorabji, had already passed the examination for Acting Teachers in 1877, but had decided to remain in England in order to 'enter a higher examination', which by the canon's own admission, 'was not necessary, nor indeed is ordinarily permitted to those who have passed the first examination'. Nevertheless he advocated, and the India Office provided, the extra grant because Butler 'wished them to gain all possible credit before entering on their Indian work'.[79] The India Office's unofficial offer of assistance to Pandita Ramabai seven years later, discussed earlier, is further evidence of its interest in the education of elite Indian women. In this case, however, it may also have been a sign of favouritism toward Christians, which the Sorabjis probably were.

Some women, however, came to Britain not in order to teach Indian girls to become Victorian ladies, but to enter professions themselves. Toward these social pioneers, British institutions were nearly as restrictive as the practice of purdah that they criticised. Most notable was Cornelia Sorabji, who after being disqualified for a government scholarship to Britain because of her gender, received a 'substitute scholarship' to Oxford University in 1889. Yet Oxford did not grant women degrees until 1923, so although Sorabji passed the university's examination in law in 1892 she did not receive her degree until the later date. As with other Indian women studying in Britain, therefore, British institutions treated Sorabji as an Indian certainly, but more so as a woman, with all the attendant stereotypes and restrictions of the age.

The policies of British institutions were, on the whole, consistent toward women coming from India to study in the United Kingdom. Administrators saw the education of women as essential to the civilising mission, because it would equip them to be guardians of the domestic sphere. In order to educate the educators of women, the NIA encouraged a small group of elite Indian women to study in Britain when this level of training was unavailable in India. The India Office cooperated with these efforts but excluded women from government scholarships, because these grants were earmarked for potential civil servants, roles that it considered appropriate only for men. NIA and

India Office policies were therefore consistent with each other in pursuing the goal of replicating late Victorian society in an Indian context. The Gilchrist trustees and authorities at Oxford University, however, pushed the boundaries of this policy with their willingness to provide scholarships for Indian women to attend British universities and train in professions normally reserved for men. In doing so they signalled that the civilising mission's goals might evolve even as the position of women in British society did.

Technical scholarships and apprenticeships in Britain

If professional considerations made many members of India's elite seek law and liberal arts degrees in Britain, wealth induced others to study business and technology there. These students presented less of a threat to the Raj than did those pursuing liberal arts degrees, because government employment was not the only obvious goal of their education. The business community and trade unions, however, objected to the potential competition of Indians in the private sector. The resulting clash between British businesses and workers on the one hand, and educational and governing institutions on the other, reflected a class conflict over imperial priorities and mission.

'It is a new and very satisfactory feature in the social progress of India that Natives are desirous of superior training in industrial arts', observed the *JNIA* in 1872. British authorities came to share this view, partly because the Indian pursuit of wealth did not directly threaten the power structure or career interests embodied in the Raj, and partly because the promotion of technical education among Indians helped to counter the nationalist argument that Britain occupied India solely to exploit it economically. Technical education, therefore, fitted the concept of the civilising mission and, given Victorian polite society's glorification of the rural, appeared well suited to ambitious professionals who might otherwise have sought positions in the government. Such considerations help to explain why in 1903 the Indian Government created scholarships for Indians 'studying in Great Britain or other Western countries'.[80] These awards covered all technical fields apart from law, medicine, forestry, and veterinary science. As Hamilton pointed out, there was 'no lack of Indian students who, without the inducement of a scholarship, visit this country in order to study the first two of these subjects'.[81]

Alert to the potential financial benefits for their own institutions and the Empire generally, some British technical colleges joined the government in encouraging Indian students to enroll in their courses. Perhaps most notable was the Yorkshire College in Leeds. After touring several

English technical and engineering schools, T. W. Holderness, the secretary of the India Office Revenue and Statistics Department, declared in 1901 that the Yorkshire College 'impressed me more than any other College which I visited'.[82] I. V. Bodington, the College's principal, was happy to exploit this favourable opinion by encouraging the India Office to send Indian students his way. What appeared to be an opportunity for British technical schools, however, loomed as a threat for managers and employees in British industries, who feared the loss of profit and jobs to Indian competitors. By 1905 the *IMR* warned that 'Indian students who come to England with the purpose of obtaining technical training are often discouraged by finding that it is extremely difficult to gain admission into manufactories here'.[83]

British institutions' continuing enthusiasm for Indians seeking education in the United Kingdom is worth noting, because it is in apparent contradiction to Lahiri's emphasis on government efforts to discourage Indian visits to Edwardian Britain.[84] This contradiction is, however, reconcilable. British institutions did not want to prevent *all* Indians from visiting Britain. Rather they wanted to discourage only those who might become a threat to their political and economic interests. Particularly regarding economic interests, different institutions perceived these threats differently. The most visible and organised forms of Indian nationalism were arising among the urban middle class, whose members were increasingly competing for jobs held by Britain's middle class. This class, therefore, presented a clear threat to the economic interests of Britons working, or hoping to work, for the Indian Government. For Britain's business sector, however, the threat was from Indian businesses. British unions, which were very powerful at the time, were suspicious of any technology transfers that might erode employment in the United Kingdom. Contemporary Indian nationalists based much of their critique of imperialism on the assumption that one country, such as Britain, could modernise only at the expense of another, such as India. The *Svadeshi* Movement (in which Indians bought only goods manufactured in India) thrived on this premise. It is hardly surprising then that workers of Edwardian Britain were hostile to educated Indians training in their factories. Such fears presented serious obstacles to Indians training in technical subjects.

Subscribers to the *IMR* were already acquainted with obstacles faced by Indian technical students in the United Kingdom through the account of Nikanth B. Wagle, who arrived in England in 1899 to study glass making. Repeated attempts to gain practical experience through employment at a glass works failed, because employers feared that to divulge such information to an Indian would lead to the rise of the same industries in India and thus increase the competition that British firms would face in the Indian market. It mattered little that India imported from the continent of Europe, rather than the United Kingdom, almost all of the type of glass (for scientific instruments) that Wagle wanted to make. For as Wagle discovered when Sir George Birdwood secured him a position in a glass works owned by a friend, the factory workers believed his presence would ultimately lead to the loss of their jobs. Within half an hour of his joining the friend's employees at a furnace, thirty workers walked off the job. A discussion with the foreman, however, revealed that the workers were as much offended by Wagle's class as his race 'for we don't strike just for you, but we hate all gents just the same'.[85] Claiming that 'he was a mere slave in the hands of the workmen', the proprietor let Wagle go. The Indian next found employment at the Blackfriars Glass Works with the aid of the owner's daughter, who managed the factory. Within a few days, however, representatives of the local union asked the owner to explain why a 'foreign gentleman was learning the trade in his factory'.[86] Ensuing discussions were unsuccessful and the union threatened to strike unless Wagle was dismissed. The owner, however, stubbornly defended his Indian apprentice and the union did not follow through with its threat.

As Wagle got used to working in the factory he befriended workers by adopting their culture. His account of this process reveals that, for him at least, the cultural differences between the British managerial and working classes were greater than those between British and Indian members of the managerial class. Much as an orientalist scholar might purport to bridge the gap between Indians and Englishmen by describing the former to the latter in terms that tended to objectify Indians, so Wagle informed his middle- to upper-class audience of Indian expatriates and British Indophiles of the curious behaviour of London's lower orders:

> When you meet them, never take your hat off your head, for that is gentlemanly, and therefore bad form. Only touch it. Never address them as Mr. but 'how do you do, old chap?' or 'Hallo! Jack or Jim,' whatever may come to you first. And when you meet them, do not forget to shake hands with them, in whatever condition their hands may be – dirty, or worse! Never be moody and grave, but always singing and jolly. Never call yourself unlucky or unfortunate, for that lowers you in their eyes instantly. Whenever you meet any of them, or when they go home, catch occasionally an opportunity to go as far as the man's house, and shake hands with his 'missus,' or 'missie,' and pick up the baby if there is one, and say, 'How nice; exactly like the mother!' It does not matter if it is so or not![87]

In fact, the tone of Wagle's account, which alternates between condescension toward the working class and praise for its simple virtues, is remarkably reminiscent of Salter's description of the inner-city Indians whom he proselytised.

Wagle's success was remarkable because it was so rare. Nearly a decade later, T. W. Arnold, the India Office's Educational Adviser to Indian Students in Britain, complained:

> From the Board of Education I can obtain the best expert advice as to courses of technical & industrial *study* ... But the matter of *practical training* is more difficult. English manufacturers refuse to take Indians as apprentices, on the ground that they do not wish their trade secrets to come into the possession of foreigners and possible rivals, & English workmen are also unwilling to work with Indians.[88]

Whatever official views on the British subjecthood of Indians, the commercial sector regarded them as 'foreigners'. This was a problem for which Arnold knew 'no remedy'. It was, however, one that concerned the India Office, because it had the potential to fan the fires of nationalist dissent by simultaneously angering Indian students and encouraging them to train outside the British Empire. The ramifications for the British Raj were obvious, and William Coldstream questioned 'whether it is politically wise to allow students from India, seking [*sic*] technical and industrial education to go in large numbers to America or any other foreign country'.[89] Indeed, at the time, Sikh students at Stanford University, through their Hindustani Ghadr movement, were advocating the overthrow of the Raj.

Other countries' companies and colleges seemed happy to receive Indians, since (scientific glass wares apart) they rarely had access to the Indian market anyway. In 1908 nine universities and colleges in the United States offered a total of over twenty tuition remission scholarships to Indian students. Working with them was the Association for the Advancement of Scientific and Industrial Education of Indians, a Calcutta-based organisation sponsored by prominent Indians and Britons, some of them holding government offices. The Association helped place Indian technical students in Western universities and businesses. It also provided loans to help these students set up industries on their return. It received the support of Viceroy Lord Minto, who, anxious to undercut *svadeshi* protesters, pointed to India's imperial role as a cash crop economy as evidence of the injustice of British rule.[90]

Contradictions toward Indian technical students existed not only among institutions but within them, most notably the India Office. Theodore Morison, a Council of India member, noted 'that when foreign Governments place orders with English engineering firms they frequently request; after the contract has been signed, the firm to take on some of their young men', and asked 'why India should experience difficulties which China for instance has not had to encounter'.[91] But when Secretary of State John Morley suggested to his Stores Department that it should only do business with firms that were willing to employ Indian students, the department's director-general, W. G. Butler, retorted that if the policy were implemented, he would not sign the letters informing the India Office's contractors.[92] Amid a growing chorus of objections, the India Office dropped the idea.

Discrimination against Indian technical students, however, did not stop at Britain's shores. The Indian Government, which inaugurated and maintained so many of the subcontinent's major engineering projects, was reluctant to hire Indians trained in Britain. As one observer put it regarding engineering companies working in India: 'My clients argue perhaps fairly that when India indents on England for men it expects Englishmen.' But Indians trained in India were no more likely to secure employment on Indian projects, because 'the claims of Anglo-Indian Officers of one kind or another leave, when satisfied, very little for the Eurasian or Indian even if employers would accept them'.[93]

As was the case regarding the Gilchrist scholarships, official discrimination in employment quickly raised objections from Indian students, particularly those who had received scholarships to study in England. Concerned over this apparent violation of the imperial mission's liberal ideals, Morley wrote to Minto listing five government scholars, of whom only one had received an Indian Government appointment after completing his study in Britain. At the same time the new Indian members of the Council of India were seconding the students' objections. Yet the India Office ignored the suggestion of K. G. Gupta, the newly appointed Hindu member, that it should reserve for Indian technical scholars some of the superior appointments that it, as opposed to the Indian Government, controlled. Morley concluded that the India Office needed to make clear to Indian students that receipt of a government scholarship was not a guarantee of government employment. Syed Husain Bilgrami seconded Gupta's proposal in theory, but took the teeth out of it by insisting that the India Office should not appoint any Indian scholar 'without first consulting Indian authorities as to the eligibility of the candidate on other than pure academic grounds'.[94] Both Bilgrami and Morley questioned the wisdom of the Indian Government providing technical scholarships to Britain if employment for their recipients was so scarce. In what must have surely appeared to be an understatement, the latter suggested that 'the expenditure involved in the grant of these scholarships may prove to be unprofitable'.[95]

British efforts to attract Indians to the United Kingdom for higher education followed the logic that Macaulay had set out in 1835. This logic did not arise from biological racism. Rather it was part of an ethic of social improvement that Britain's elite also applied to its own lower classes. This approach varied according to the institutions that applied it. In the opinion of Members of Parliament and civil servants in the India Office, the administration of the Empire properly belonged in the hands of the aristocracy and gentry. The ideal education for men of this class was in the British public schools, where character on the playing field was more important than knowledge in the classroom. This attitude complemented the priorities of India's British rulers after the Indian Rebellion, who preferred to govern with the cooperation of India's rural elite rather than the increasingly important urban professional class. But, like its British counterpart, this elite showed little interest in bureaucratic government service. This apathy left the designers of the new ICS facing the prospect of an Indian Empire administered by lower-middle-class 'competition-wallahs', whether British or Indian, whom they regarded as inferior for the positions that they sought. Thus successive secretaries of state tinkered with the ages for admission into the ICS and the content of ICS exams, sometimes inadvertently giving the impression that their policies were aimed at Indians specifically when they were in fact aimed primarily at Britain's lower-middle class.

If preventing this class of Britons from entering the ICS was the primary goal of these rulers, it failed. In spite of the obstacles erected in their path, lower-middle-class Britons could compete for ICS positions, because, unlike their Indian counterparts, they did not have to travel a quarter of the way around the world in order to do so. British authorities' refusal to hold exams in India remained the most serious obstacle to enabling all educated men to compete for these positions. Indeed, this geographic obstacle, which arose in part from the application of class prejudice to Indian society, gradually heightened the racial discrimination surrounding appointments to the ICS. For the presence of British self-made professionals in the ICS did not ease the ability of their Indian counterparts to enter. On the contrary, these British ICS agents lobbied more than ever to prevent competition from their Indian peers. Thus what began in many respects as a matter of class discrimination in both Britain and India evolved into an issue of race discrimination between Britons and Indians of similar social rank. The result, in 1888, was a new three-tiered civil service that, if anything, was more likely to discriminate against Indians than the one it replaced.

Ironically, it was not until the mid-1880s, when the basis of racial discrimination in the Raj had solidified, that Britain's governing elite encouraged Indians through scholarships to study at British universities with the intention of applying their skills in Indian public service. This policy, based very much on Macaulay's culturally and socially elitist, but racially inclusive, notions of imperial governance, may have made sense in London – but it ran into a wall of resistance in India, because it impinged on the privileges of middle-class Europeans, who constituted an exalted caste in the Indian context by virtue of their ethnic origin. The tendency of India Office administrators was to shrug off such discrimination as inevitable, whether they approved of it or not. The same, however, was not the case with the Gilchrist trustees, who had pioneered the practice of providing scholarships for Indians to study in Britain. When they confronted the insincerity of British claims to rule in partnership with India's elite, they abandoned their project in a tone of acrimony, turning their attention instead to cooperation with the NIA, whose members frequently criticised Britain's governance of India.

Other scholarships and educational aid, aimed at technical students and women, did not cause the same level of controversy as the original government and Gilchrist scholarships did, because they did not so directly test the shared governance that British rulers claimed to support in their civilising imperial mission. Least threatening of all was the education of women, so long as it conformed to Victorian polite society's expectations of womanhood. Disagreement occurred, however, when Indian women attempted to transgress the boundaries of this conformity, as Churchill's response to university scholarships for Indian women demonstrates. In this regard Indian women were no different from British counterparts who challenged restrictions to their personal development. They were simply more remarkable, given the foreign setting in which they made such challenges.

For technical students the most consistent obstacle was not the government, unless, of course, the student's goal was to enter a technical branch of the ICS. Rather hostility arose in the business community, and particularly among members of Britain's industrial working class. This hostility manifested itself not only through racism but also through class antipathy, which middle-class Indians could only rarely overcome. Faced with this situation, many, though not all, India Office administrators sympathised with Indian students. Yet as with discrimination in ICS appointments, these officials tended ultimately to resign themselves to the existence of racial discrimination and did not systematically attack the practice directly.

Nevertheless, the reluctance of India Office administrators, social reformers, and politicians to endorse openly such racially based discrimination in education and employment is significant. The India Office shied away from remarks of officials in India who openly supported a racially bifurcated ICS, and when the Gilchrist trustees determined that race was an obstacle to employment, they withdrew funding for the education of Indians in Britain. Moreover, India Office officials were quick to identify the behaviour of British workers as racist, and declare such behaviour unacceptable. Given their equivocation on ICS recruitment, this response was no doubt hypocritical. Yet it highlights the centrality of class in the official discourse, and the similar unacceptability of race. This tendency in official rhetoric continued to the eve of the First World War, in spite of the *svadeshi* protests following the partition of Bengal. Indeed, the *svadeshi* movement and more general accusations of British economic exploitation made the India Office more willing during the Edwardian than the late Victorian period to educate Indian technical students in Britain and pressure British firms to cooperate with apprenticeships.

Policies regarding scholarships, however, were not the only measure of institutional response to the presence of Indian students in Britain. If scholarships, and higher education more generally, were to apply Macaulay's vision for Indians in a British setting, then the behaviour of British institutions toward these students while they were studying was also important. This behaviour is the topic of the next chapter.

Notes

1 See, for instance, Lahiri, *Indians in Britain*, 92–5 and Metcalf, *Ideologies of the Raj*, 165–7.
2 Lahiri, *Indians in Britain*, 5.
3 Bhugwandiu Dubé, Barrister-at-Law, Reader, Indian Central College Law School, Allahabad, to Secretary of State for India, 20 October 1908, IOR L/PJ/6/901 No. 3923.
4 Nicole Herz, 'It's personal before it's political: Ambition and angst in the lives of Indian Civil Servants, 1880–1950', *Essays in History*, 40 (1998): 1.
5 Thomas Babington Macaulay, 'Minute Recorded in the General Department', 2 February 1835, in Lynn Zastoupil and Martin Moir (eds), *The Great Indian Education Debate: Documents Relating to the Orientalist-Anglicist Controversy, 1781–1843* (London: Curzon Press, 1999): 171.
6 *Ibid.*, 165.
7 *Ibid.*, 170–1.
8 *Ibid.*, 167.
9 *Ibid.*, 171.
10 Pratt Hodgson, *University Education in England for Natives of India: Considered with a View to Qualify Them for the Learned Professions or the Public Service; and to Create a Class Who Shall Mediate Between the Indian People and Their English Rulers* (London: James Ridgway, 1860), 21.
11 *Ibid.*, 5.
12 *Ibid.*, 6.
13 *Ibid.*, 8.
14 *Ibid.*, 21.
15 *Ibid.*, 23.
16 *Ibid.*, 26.
17 'Indian visitors to England', *JNIA*, 94 (October 1878): 425.
18 See, for instance, *IMR*, 278 (February 1894): 75–84.

19 'The National Indian Association', *IMR*, 272 (August 1893): v.
20 'Written statement by Professor W. [A.] Raleigh, Professor of English literature at Oxford University', 7 May 1907, *Report and Minutes of the Committee Appointed by the Secretary of State for India to Inquire into the Position of Indian Students in the United Kingdom* (London: Eyre and Spottiswoode, 1907 – hereafter *CIS*), 233.
21 'Evidence of Dr. E. J. Trevelyan, All Souls College, Oxford, Reader in Indian Law', 23 May 1907, in *ibid.*, 237.
22 These examples are taken from parents' registration forms St John's College Archives, Cambridge, TU 11.4, 11.7, 11.11, and 11.12, and Oxford University Archives, Bodleian Library, Oxford UR/1/1/39, UR/1/1/38, and UR/1/1/41. I am grateful to Malcolm Underwood, St John's College archivist, for his assistance.
23 St John's College Archives, C. L. F. Stafford to Ward, 17 October 1894, TU 10.9.360. For the history of the Cambridge Mission to Delhi and the foundation of St Stephen's College, see www.ststephens.edu (accessed 31 January 2005).
24 J. M. Compton, 'Open competition and the Indian Civil Service, 1854–1876', *English Historical Review*, 83:327 (April 1968): 266.
25 Quoted in Compton, 'Open competition', 269.
26 C. J. Dewey, 'The education of a ruling caste: The Indian Civil Service in the era of competitive examination', *English Historical Review*, 88:347 (1973): 283.
27 Quoted in Compton, 'Open competition', 272.
28 G. O. Trevelyan, *The Competition Wallah* (London: Macmillan, 1866), 9.
29 Quoted in J. M. Compton, 'Indians and the Indian Civil Service, 1853–1879: A study in national agitation and imperial embarrassment', *Journal of the Royal Asiatic Society of Great Britain and Ireland*, 3/4 (1967): 102.
30 Quoted in IOR L/PJ/2/36 No. 1547, Dadabhai Naoroji to Mountstuart E. Grant Duff, Esq., MP, Undersecretary of State for India, 3 March 1870.
31 Sinha, *Colonial Masculinity*, 103–5.
32 Lahiri, *Indians in Britain*, 65.
33 Quoted in B. B. Misra, *The Bureaucracy in India: An Historical Analysis of Development up to 1947* (Delhi: Oxford University Press, 1977), 110.
34 See David Omissi, '"Martial Races": Ethnicity and security in Colonial India, 1858–1939', *War and Society*, 9:1 (1991), 1–27; and Douglas M. Peers, '"The habitual nobility of being": British officers and the social construction of the Bengal army in the early nineteenth century', *Modern Asian Studies*, 25:3 (1991): 545–69.
35 Misra, *Bureaucracy in India*, 111.
36 Quoted in Misra, *Bureaucracy in India*, 110.
37 Quoted in Misra, *Bureaucracy in India*, 124.
38 Less than eighteen months after taking his first appointment, Banerjea was censured for abusing his judicial powers. This charge ultimately led to his dismissal, after which he became a leading nationalist calling for greater self-government. The first Indian to pass the competitive ICS exams was Satyendranath Tagore, who was not a Government Scholar. He received an appointment.
39 Quoted in Sinha, *Colonial Masculinity*, 114.
40 Anthony Kirk-Greene, *Britain's Imperial Administrators, 1858–1966* (New York: St Martin's Press, 2000), 92; and Compton, 'Indians and the Indian Civil Service', 109.
41 Quoted in Misra, *Bureaucracy in India*, 129.
42 Steuart Bayley, quoted in Misra, *The Bureaucracy in India*, 132.
43 IOR L/PJ/6/158 No. 1329, GOI Home Department, Education Division memorandum No. 4, Dufferin *et al.* to Lord Randolph Churchill, 4 July 1885, 2.
44 Quoted in *ibid.*
45 *Ibid.*, 3.
46 IOR L/PJ/6/199 No. 606, 'Resolution' in A. P. MacDonnell, 'Extract from the Proceedings of the Government of India in the Home Department (Education)', 11 March 1887.
47 See Sinha, *Colonial Masculinity*, 104.
48 *Ibid.*, 100–1; and Misra, *Bureaucracy in India*, 147–51.
49 London, University College Library Special Collections (hereafter UCL) GIL 3/3,

Codicil to 'Will of Dr. John Borthwick Gilchrist', 9, in William Braikenridge and Sons, 'Appendix to the case of the respondents: Charles Holland, M.D., Sir John Bowring. Knt., and Robert Verity, surviving trustees under the will of the testator, John Borthwick Gilchrist, LL.D., and also of the respondents, Mary Anne Pépé, Widow, George Linley and Violet his wife, and Elizabeth Harris widow' (London: Thomas Toovey, 1858?). For details of Gilchrist's career see UCL GIL7/5, *The Gilchrist Educational Trust: Pioneering Work in Education, 1865–1930* (Cambridge: Cambridge University Press, 1930). I am grateful to University College, London and the Gilchrist Educational Trust for permission use the Trust's papers.

50 IOR L/PJ/2/36 No. 36, William B. Carpenter, Secretary, Gilchrist Educational Trust, to Lord Cranborne, Secretary of State for India, 12 November 1866. John Borthman Gilchrist (1759–1841), the trust's founder, served as a surgeon in India and later as Professor of Hindustani in London. See 'The Gilchrist Trust', *JNIA*, 127 (July 1881): 425–6.

51 IOR L/PJ/2/36 No. 36, 'Conditions for scholarships to be instituted by the Gilchrist Educational Trust for the benefit of natives of India', n. d., attached to letter from Carpenter to Merivale, Gilchrist Educational Trust, 9 April 1867.

52 IOR L/PJ/6/28 No. 1751, William B. Carpenter to Sir Louis Mallet, 7 December 1880. For cost of living estimates at Balliol, see G. Sutherland Edwards, 'A student's expenses at the University of Oxford', *JNIA*, 121 (January 1881): 6–13. This amount did not include one-time start-up and termination expenses totaling £63 8s.

53 IOR L/PJ/2/36 No. 36, William Carpenter to J. Cosmo Melville, Assistant Undersecretary of State for India, 5 December 1867.

54 *Ibid.*, Carpenter to Lord Cranborne, 12 November 1866.

55 IOR L/PJ/6/317 No. 557, R. D. Roberts to Viscount Cross, Secretary of State for India, 29 March 1892.

56 IOR L/PJ/6/172 No. 439, GOI Home Department memorandum No. 2, C. P. Ilbert *et al.* to Earl of Kimberley, 2 March 1886; and IOR L/PJ/6/158 No. 1329 GOI, Home Department memorandum No. 4 of 1885, Dufferin *et al.* to Lord Randolph Churchill, 4 July 1885.

57 L/PJ/6/1100 No. 2650, 'Rules for Indian Government technical scholars in England' (1911), and 'Rules for Indian Government scholars in England' (1911); and 'Industrial training in England for Indian students', *IMR*, 411 (March 1905): 75. Government Sanskrit and Arabic scholars, however, also received only £150 per annum. See IOR L/PJ/6/1100 No. 2650, 'Rules for Indian Government Sanskrit and Arabic scholars in Europe' (1911).

58 IOR L/PJ/6/43 No. 970, Arthur Howell, Confidential memorandum, 25 June 1881.

59 IOR L/PJ/6/280 No. 1167, 'Rules and conditions relating to scholarships instituted by the Gilchrist Education Trust for the benefit of Natives of India', attached to R. D. Roberts, Secretary, to Undersecretary of State for India, 7 July 1890.

60 IOR MSS Eur C 342, Ritchie Collection, Miscellaneous Papers, Kay-Shuttleworth to Ritchie, 13 August 1886.

61 Misra, *Bureaucracy in India*, 151–7.

62 IOR L/PJ/6/340 No. 305, R. D. Roberts to the Rt. Hon. The Earl of Kimberley, 9 December 1892. The Private Secretary's letter is quoted in the correspondence.

63 *Ibid.*, reference paper 2032/1892, note by C. E. Bernard, 13 December 1892; and IOR L/PJ/6/340 No. 305, Public (Educational) Department minute paper, 'Draft proposed by Committee in substitution for original draft', 1 February 1893.

64 IOR L/PJ/6/340 No. 305, R. D. Roberts to Undersecretary of State for India, 18 February 1893. For the committee deliberations behind this letter see UCL GIL 1/3/19, Gilchrist Educational Trust, Minutes of the Meetings of Trustees, 5 December 1892, 15.

65 UCL GIL 1/3/23, Gilchrist Minutes, 19 March 1896, 4.

66 For the announcement of the new scholarships for women in India, see 'Gilchrist Scholarships', *IMR*, 381 (September 1902): 249. For details of the scholarship programme and the trustees' approval of it, see UCL GIL 1/3/9, Gilchrist Minutes, 5 March 1902, 5–6.

67 The destroyed correspondence is listed in IOR Z/L/PJ/6/17, Judicial and Public Department Register & Index, 1896. The first item is a response to the Gilchrist trustees' inquiry of April 1896. The second is a memorandum and comment sheet entitled 'Withdrawal of Gilchrist Scholarship from India after the present year'. The dates indicate that it contained a discussion of the letter terminating the scholarships.

68 IOR L/PJ/6/260 No. 1430, Minute paper, note by MacPherson, 'House of Commons – Question of Sir John Kennaway for Thursday Augt 22', n. d. 1889.

69 Gilchrist Educational Trust, 'Rules and conditions relating to scholarships'.

70 See preface to *JNIA*, 1 (January 1871).

71 Oscar Browning, *Impressions of Indian Travel* (London: Hodder and Stoughton, 1903), 227.

72 'Hindu ladies in Manchester: What zenana life is like', *IMR*, 417 (September 1905): 243.

73 'Some impressions of England', *IMR*, 35 (November 1900): 287.

74 *Ibid.*

75 *Ibid.*, 287–8.

76 'Hindu ladies', *JNIA*, 30 (June 1873): 357–8.

77 IOR L/PJ//2/37, Dadabhai Naoroji to the Secretary of State for India, 1 August 1867, enclosed in Education Department Minute Paper No. 50, 'Proposed schools for training female native teachers'.

78 *Ibid.*, W. S. Seton Karr to W. S. Atkinson, director of Public Instruction, 15 February 1867.

79 IOR L/PJ/2/38, William Butler to the Undersecretary of State for India, 5 February 1879, enclosed in Educational Department minute paper 5/101, 'Two young ladies sent to England to qualify themselves as mistresses of the Guzerat Female Training School'.

80 IOR L/PJ/6/633 No. 811, Public Memorandum No. 65, Hamilton to Curzon, 'Proposed technical scholarships for natives of India studying in Great Britain or other Western countries', 29 May 1903.

81 *Ibid.*

82 IOR L/PJ/6/583 No. 1987, Public Department minute, 4 November 1901, note by T. W. Holderness, 7 November 1901. See also Bodington's letter of 4 November 1901, attached.

83 'Industrial training in England for Indian students', *IMR*, 411 (March 1905): 75.

84 Lahiri, *Indians in Britain*, 116–17.

85 N. B. Wagle, 'Experiences of English factory life', a paper read on 17 December at the Imperial Institute, before the NIA, and published in *IMR*, 361 (January 1901): 13.

86 *Ibid.*, 19.

87 *Ibid.*, 21.

88 IOR L/PJ/6/947 No. 2390, reference paper, 30 July 1909, note by T. W. Arnold, 3 July 1909.

89 *Ibid.*, W. Coldstream to the Undersecretary of State for India, 30 June 1909.

90 IOR L/PJ/6/922 No. 440, *Report of the Association for the Advancement of Scientific and Industrial Education of Indians*, 1908, enclosed in Judicial and Public Department Minute Paper, 'Student sent by Calcutta Association to study in England and entitled to return passage asks for assistance', February 1909, 4 and 41. For information on American university tuition-remission scholarships, see IOR L/PJ/6/947 No. 2390, 'Extract from the Furman College Monthly, October 1908, Page 268', Appendix I to W. Coldstream, KCSI (retired), to the Undersecretary of State for India, 30 June 1909.

91 IOR L/PJ/6/998 No. 1115, note by Theodore Morison, Council of India, n.d., attached to Lord Morley (unsigned), Minute Paper, 'Facilities for Indian students to acquire practical experience under India Office contractors', 1(?) May 1910.

92 IOR L/PJ/6/998 No. 1115, W. G. Butler, Director-General, Stores Department, Reference Paper, 8 April 1910.

93 *Ibid.*, A. M. K. (or R?), typewritten letter to Director General (of Stores?), 17

December 1909, attached to Butler, 8 April 1910.

94 IOR L/PJ/6/958 No. 3136, Public No. 138, Morley of Blackburn to His Excellency the Right Honourable the Governor General of India in Council, 'Question of employment on their return to India of holders of Indian technical scholarships', 8 October 1909; Judicial and Public Department minute, K. G. Gupta, 'Employment of govt. technical scholars on their return to India: The case of Mr. Asok Bose & others', 15 September 1909, attached to above; and note by Syed Husain Bilgrami, 16 September 1909, attached to Gupta's minute.

95 *Ibid.*, Morley to Minto, 8 October 1909.

CHAPTER EIGHT

Assimilation and ostracism in education

The last chapter showed how many British institutions, far from discouraging students from visiting the United Kingdom, actively encouraged them to study there in order to spread Western civilisation to India. This chapter investigates the role of institutions in setting the climate of accommodation or prejudice in which Indian students lived during their stay in Britain. Its focus is not so much the type of discrimination that occurred, a topic that has already been the subject of considerable analysis. Rather the emphasis here is on the reaction of institutions in Britain to discrimination, either from British students or from the Indian Government. Many British institutions sought to accommodate the cultural requirements of their Indian students in ways that were far in advance of official practices in other white-dominated English-speaking countries of the period. This accommodation took place, however, in the context of a society in which racial bigotry was widespread. No matter how tolerant these institutions were in their own policies, their reactions to such bigotry and the extent to which they opposed it or acquiesced in it, were determined by their primary mission. Even within these institutions the reactions of key officials varied, ranging from protests regarding racist policies and behaviour to acquiescence or even complicity in their development. These reactions displayed a tension between class and racial constructions of a British imperial identity. Nevertheless, at the official level British administrators attempted, albeit with only partial success, to use the register of class in their dealings with Indians.

Accommodating Indian culture

> There is one beauty of the moon, another beauty of the stars, another beauty of the sun, yet each is beauteous, though their glory may vary. We

> are too narrow in our notions if we think no woman can be perfect unless she conform to the usages, the language, and the whole appearance and demeanour of our own women-folk.[1]

This poetic allusion to the behaviour and appearance of women around the world embodies the problems surrounding any analysis of statements from the Victorian and Edwardian eras appearing to point toward tolerance of cultural diversity. This passage, which appeared in an 1873 issue of the *JNIA*, was authored by an anonymous man (probably British) serving in the Madras presidency. Its praise of women exhibits a form that objectifies women as a sex. Furthermore, its celebration of difference is 'orientalist' inasmuch as it encourages Indian women to behave as exhibits in what Bernard Cohn has described as a 'living museum'.[2] On the other hand, the passage argues against the notion that Indian women should behave like British women, a position popular at the time. How then should we judge apparent cases of accommodation of cultural diversity in British educational settings? One line of scholarship argues that it matters little what British administrators thought they were doing if the effect was to marginalise and tokenise Indians in their midst, turning them into cultural exhibits of the undying differences separating supposedly superior Britons from inferior subject races. Even if one dismisses the importance of British opinions and concentrates solely on their effects, however, analyses that identify the tolerance of culture solely as the internalisation of subjugation are problematic when applied to the behaviour of Indian students in the United Kingdom.

Among the objections to this approach is the fact that such tolerance often resulted from Indian protests at attempts to assimilate them more fully into the culture of Victorian polite society. When Queen Victoria requested that the Indian women she received wear 'oriental costume', we do not know whether they would have wanted to do so anyway. The *JNIA* portrayed the request as a reason for Indians to rejoice, because 'much of the success among Indian women will depend on not denationalising them'.[3] Furthermore, some female Indian students, such as Cornelia Sorabji, chose to wear saris in Britain as a sign of their ethnic identity, even though they had worn Western clothing in India.[4] The receptions in Victoria's drawing room, therefore, may be indicative of two apparently contradictory modes of thinking actually complementing and reinforcing each other. On the one hand, there is considerable evidence from the Queen's own diaries to suggest that she favoured Indians wearing their native attire in order to present her court as a microcosm of the different nations over which she reigned. On the other hand, women attending her court may have been happy to display cultural emblems of which they were proud. Both motivations could operate in the same space and time without undermining the other.

Such ambiguity in motivation is less apparent in the concessions that educational institutions made to Indians. In these cases, there is little to suggest that accommodations of cultural difference were anything other than responses to initiatives from Indian students unwilling or unable to conform fully to British culture. The most intractable situations were religious. Hindu and Muslim students could, with some difficulty and sacrifice, negotiate the dietary minefield of British cuisine. Dress codes, however, were a potentially more explosive issue for Sikh men. Even today the requirement, enshrined in three-century-old religious law, that Sikh males must not cut their hair, clashes with private and government regulations outside India. Not surprisingly, as the number of Sikhs studying abroad rose, so did the number of potential conflicts over this requirement. Such conflicts around the Empire caused the Sikh Educational Conference, meeting in Gujranwalla in April 1908, to pass a resolution calling for greater institutional tolerance. Yet official correspondence indicates that British institutions had, for the most part, been accommodating the Sikh dress code for over a generation. For example, in Britain university students wore mortar boards at their graduation ceremonies, medical orderlies in the military wore helmets, and law students wore wigs when called to the Bar. In almost all such cases the institutional response was to grant exceptions to Sikhs on an individual basis in response to their petitions for exemptions.

Nevertheless, the India Office treated the Gujranwalla resolution seriously, in part because of the dissension such regulations might cause among Sikhs within India. Before agreeing to the initial creation of government scholarships in 1868, the India Office had sought assurance that 'both at Oxford and Cambridge, Natives of India may take degrees without any interference by the University with their religious usages and customs'.[5] Now it requested and received similar commitments from the benchers of the Inns of Court. The cause of the resolution appears to have been an exception to the normally tolerant practice, since the under-treasurer of Gray's Inn protested that 'many Sikh students at Gray's Inn have elected to wear their turbans during the ceremony of the Call to the Bar, and no difficulty has ever been placed in their way'.[6]

Such exemptions were typical of institutional responses to petitions from Indians based on their Indianness. Rather than create formal policies of tolerance, institutions tended to grant individual exemptions in ad hoc cases as they arose. The Black Books of Lincoln's Inn, the best preserved and organised of the Inns of Court records, chronicle numerous examples of the benchers granting such exemptions. Sometimes the petitioners' requests confirmed contemporary scientific understandings of the physical basis of racial difference. Such was the case of K.V. R. Swami, who in 1910 sought exemption from his last two terms of residence, because he had been suffering from chronic bronchitis: 'Unfortunately I do not find any permanent relief from the malady on account of the changeable and damp climate of this country as I lived all my life in the dry climate of India.'[7] Other cases were simply acts of compassion in response to unexpected hardship. For instance, in 1906 the benchers exempted Divijendra Nath Basu from two terms of residence so that he could return to India to settle the estate of his recently deceased father.[8]

A frequent petition that the benchers almost always looked upon favourably was for a change in a candidate's name as recorded officially in the Inn's membership roll. Often these changes were a result of the initial confusion over what constituted a title, given name, or surname. Mistakes of this sort, if left unaltered, could have serious repercussions on a barrister's career in India. For instance, when applying for admission to Lincoln's Inn, Balwant Singh, a Sikh student, learned that most barristers posted only their surnames in full and placed the initials of their given names before them. Singh, however, did not have two given names, so, misunderstanding the British practice, he enrolled at Lincoln's Inn under the name Balwant Singh Garwal. (His correspondence does not explain why he used 'Garwal', but it may have been the name of his home town.) Later he realised that this decision would force him to use Garwal as his surname while practising law in India, a situation which he feared 'would prove disadvantagious [*sic*] to me'. Perhaps most important was the name's affront to Singh's sense of Sikh national identity, because 'It is my national custom to be called Mr. Singh because we the Sikhs are always called by the names of Singhs. For this reason also I want to be called Mr. Singh rather than Mr. Garwal.'[9] In this case the tendency of British officials to stereotype cultural practices may have helped Singh, because far from expecting him to assimilate British nomenclature, the benchers understood the perspective of someone from a culture other than their own. Although there is no record of the reasoning behind their decision, it would have made perfect sense to a late Victorian barrister to let a Sikh use the name Singh. After all, that was what Sikhs were supposed to do.

Another area of cultural concession revisited the Orientalist–Anglicist debate of the early nineteenth century. One of the central issues in that debate was whether the languages of instruction should be Asian or European. The Anglicists advocated the creation of an educational system for India's elite that duplicated as closely as possible its British counterpart. Thus the language of instruction would be English, and the languages to learn would be Latin and Greek. Although the Anglicists apparently won the argument in the 1830s, Indian educational reformers of the nineteenth century never abandoned Sanskrit, Arabic, and Persian, the languages of India's pre-British institutions. Aligarh University, founded by Sir Syed Ahmad Khan, offered these languages, as did Elphinstone College in Bombay. In an ironic reversal of what Macaulay had envisaged, the presence of Indian students in the United Kingdom caused British institutions of higher education to allow Indians to substitute ancient Asian languages for Latin and Greek, and thereby further encouraged the development of these languages as subjects of study in Britain.

The very linguistic research that contributed to much nineteenth-century racial theory encouraged the administrators of these institutions to regard Sanskrit, Arabic, and Persian as 'classical languages', and, therefore, Asian equivalents of Latin and Greek. Geographically distant from the practical implications of debates over Indian education, European scholars continued to expand the system of comparative linguistics pioneered by Sir William Jones in the late eighteenth century. The prominence of such scholarship in Germany forced England's premier universities to revisit the study of classical Asian languages. Before 1858 Haileybury College, the East India Company's academy for training its civil servants, taught Sanskrit in order to equip its agents to understand and apply Indian law. Not until 1832 was Sanskrit taught primarily as an academic subject at a British university. That year H. H. Wilson, a company official, became Oxford University's first Boden Professor of Sanskrit.[10] His successor, Monier Monier-Williams, founded the Indian Institute at Oxford in 1884.

What caused British universities and the Inns of Court to allow Indians to substitute Sanskrit for Latin or Greek, however, was not pressure from British Sanskrit scholars, but the obstacle that Latin and Greek requirements posed for Indians pursuing higher education in Britain. These difficulties threatened to undermine the civilising mission behind Indian study in Britain. For instance, the Gilchrist scholarship initially required its finalists to sit exams in India based on the University of London's matriculation exam. In 1888, however, the Gilchrist trustees abandoned this practice after all three candidates failed the Latin portion of the exam.[11] By 1914 the Universities of Oxford, Cambridge, and London had exemptions from their requirements in Latin and Greek for Indians willing to study Asian classical languages, as did the General Council of Medical Education and Registration.[12] Perhaps the first institution to accommodate Indian culture was the Council of Legal Education, founded in 1852 to coordinate requirements among the four Inns of Court. Such policies were encouraged by the India Office, and in Oxford's case enacted after the turn of the twentieth century. They therefore cast in doubt recent assertions that by 1900 British authorities were actively seeking to discourage Indian students from studying in the United Kingdom, for if these institutions had wanted to, they need only have insisted that rules applying to English students' behaviour apply also to Indians.

In spite of the considerable stereotyping of Indian students that occurred in university magazines and the press generally, the accommodation of Indian dress codes and curricular preferences does not fit easily into the practice of pigeonholing other cultures that, according to much recent scholarship, was the dominant aspect of British behaviour toward Indians. Rather British institutional concessions to Indians resulted from the initiatives of Indian students who, valuing their own religion and culture, negotiated the conditions of their study in Britain. Moreover, such concessions are evidence that, at least until the First World War, the British Government encouraged the children of India's elite to study in the United Kingdom. If India Office administrators had truly believed that it was politically expedient for Indians to stay out of Britain, then they would have simply remained silent in the face of institutional intolerance. That they did not demonstrates that they valued the education of a loyal Indian elite in the United Kingdom and considered the ill will that overly rigid culturally-chauvinist policies would create to be more dangerous than tolerating the presence of educated Indians in the imperial metropole. The emphasis, however, must be on the word 'loyal', because this quality became the most important issue, apart from class, to distinguish differences in institutional behaviour toward Indian students.

Assimilation, alienation, and the culture of British higher education

Such official accommodation of Indians did not, however, mean that British students accorded them the same respect. Recent scholarship on Indian students in Britain has emphasised the alienation and bigotry that they experienced, particularly at the hands of British students.[13] There is no need here for a detailed duplication of its analysis. Nevertheless, the institutional response to this issue deserves further attention. Lahiri argues that British authorities declared the presence of Indian students to be a 'problem', because they perceived it as a threat. But this approach makes institutional attitudes toward Indians in Britain appear more hostile than they were, by shifting their focus from the difficulties that Indians encountered in their attempts to receive acceptance into British society to the very presence of Indians in the United Kingdom. The alienation of Indian students resulted more from systemic than institutional reasons. That is, the system of education in Britain made it difficult for outsiders to gain access, and thereafter made it difficult for them to integrate into its society. To the extent that British authorities consciously perpetuated the system in order to limit it to a specific group, they did so mainly to limit it by class within British society. It is for this reason that so many educational reformers argued that India's social improvement must begin with the education of its elite and then work down from there. The problem with this scheme was that the same clannishness that prevented the lower orders of British society from mingling with Britain's elite also prevented India's elite from doing so.

Such exclusionary practices raise important issues of interpretation, since to have attended public schools was a sign of a university student's membership in a club. In India clubs arose along racial lines, from which, Sinha observes, 'there was always a sizeable population of "lower-class" Europeans in India ... who were excluded from the contours of [their] whiteness'. Yet Sinha also acknowledges that 'The popularity of clubs in India was in part a response to the particular demographic challenges of the overseas European population in India.'[14] To the extent, however, that 'whiteness' or Britishness was also a qualification for, and an obstacle to, the acceptance of Indians into university society, class played a much greater role in determining it in Britain than it did in India, because in the social context of the United Kingdom 'clubbability' existed primarily to exclude other Britons according to class. Yet simultaneously, the geographical distance between India and Britain and the inequitable power relationship between the two also played an important role in depriving Indian students of social rank

Indeed, at British universities before the First World War, class and gender considerations dominated the life of an undergraduate, which was markedly different from that of today. During the late nineteenth and early twentieth centuries higher education was overwhelmingly a male pursuit. Women could attend lectures at Cambridge and Oxford from 1870 and 1878 respectively, but neither institution granted the degree title until the early 1920s and Cambridge did not give women graduates full membership rights until 1949. By contrast the University of London was a pioneer in this regard, granting degrees to women from 1880 onwards, and appointing its first female professor in 1912. Among men, however, class remained a profound barrier to acceptance in undergraduate society. In order to study at a British university, a young man needed to have the resources of gentleman from the outset. In

1881 a British student provided the following analysis of expenses at Balliol College, Oxford, for the benefit of potential Indian students reading the *Journal of the National Indian Society*:

Table 1 Annual Expenses at Balliol College, Oxford, 1881[a]

Annual Expenses			
Item	£	s.	d.
Annual Payment to College	77	17	6
Battells (board and furnished lodging)	55	0	0
Tips to Servants	7	10	0
Tailor	30	0	0
Shoemaker	3	0	0
Bookseller	4	0	0
College Club	3	0	0
Hiring Boats	3	3	0
(Student) Union	3	15	0
Total	187	5	6

One-Time Expenses			
Item	£	s.	d.
Matriculation and Degree Fees to University	10	0	0
Examination Fees and Price of Testamurs (certificates of exam passage)	5	4	0
Entrance and Degree Fees	6	4	0
Caution Money (security deposit) at College	21	0	0
Two Fees to Private Tutor	21	0	0
Total	63	8	0

[a]Adapted from G. Sutherland Edwards, 'A student's expenses at the University of Oxford', *JNIA*, 121 (January 1881): 6–13.

These expenses amounted to roughly four times the average 1884 annual wage per capita of £42 14s. and from half again to twice as much as the £100 to £132 that most male school teachers earned in 1884. This standard of living required the Balliol student to have financial resources on a par with the top 1.2 per cent of 1880 British income earners.[15] The presence of expenses such as hiring boats, tips to servants, and membership in the college club and student union, highlight the fact that universities – particularly Oxford and Cambridge – were at least as much places for socialising as learning. To focus on the latter at the expense of the former was to ostracise oneself from university life.

Expenses for students attending the Inns of Court or the University of London were similar. According to Hamid Ali, a student writing for the *JNIA* in 1882, the annual rent for boarding house quarters with separate bedroom and study in a respectable but not fashionable part of town was £174 4s. For a paying guest in a gentleman's family home it was £162 12s. These expenses covered board, lodging, clothing, occasional meals out, and minor entertainment, but not actual educational expenses.[16] For the Inns of Court in 1909 the last consisted of a one-time admission fee of between £127 and £141 plus ongoing private tuition fees to a barrister to study for the Bar exam. Perhaps most expensive were the fees that medical students and solicitors-in-training paid. In 1909 these amounted to a total fee of £315 to become an articled clerk of a law practice for the three to five years of apprenticeship. In addition, the government levied an £80 stamp duty for signing the articles and a £30 5s. fee for taking the Law Society Exam. For medical students at the University of London the total fees in 1909 exceeded £360.[17] Ali claimed that most Indians 'estimate the cost of living in this country very much higher than it really is', but the thirty-six student appeals to the India Office for financial assistance from 1889 to 1915 suggest that Indians sometimes underestimated the costs.[18] For each of these applicants there were presumably many others who lived on the edge of poverty. Indeed the geographical distance between Indian students in Britain and their financial base at home meant that they were more likely than British students to experience a demotion of class position due to insufficient funds or interrupted cash flow.[19] The parliamentary Committee on Distressed Colonial and Indian Subjects noted that

> the death or sickness of the bread winner, an unexpected lawsuit, or the failure of the monsoon, whereby tenants are unable to pay their usual rents – any one of these mishaps may prevent the family from forwarding the monthly or quarterly remittance, and when this disaster occurs, the Indian student with few acquaintances in this country and slender credit is brought to the verge of destitution.[20]

Little wonder that many Indian students lived in housing much more modest than their British counterparts and participated less in social activities. They often lacked the financial resources to live among Britain's middle class. Thus many could not follow Ali's suggestion to live as paying guests in London, in order to 'gain acquaintance with the customs, habits, modes of life, etiquette, disposition and tastes of the English people'.[21]

If financial problems prevented many Indians from taking part in middle-class society, so did lack of experience and cultural literacy. The reasons for such exclusion and the ways in which it occurred were well known by 1907, when the parliamentary committee, quoted above, inquired into the issue. The testimony before them pointed consistently to a narrow set of issues that placed Indians studying in Britain at a social disadvantage. From the very outset their backgrounds were a disadvantage, not only because they were Indian, but because they came from secondary schools of which few British students had heard. Their prior experience, therefore, carried no identifiable social markers with which British students could assess them as they assessed one another. The corollary of this problem was that Indian students rarely had any friends from their secondary school accompany them to their places of education in Britain. Since attendance at prestigious schools, particularly public schools, was the surest way of achieving gentlemanly social rank, students who had arrived straight from India were clearly at a disadvantage. They were totally alone and it was up to them to make inroads into university society. The cause was systemic class discrimination. The effect was racial bigotry. From the 1860s to the 1880s, when the Indian presence on campuses was something new, its very novelty had often overcome British students' ignorance, and Indians had received invitations to join in numerous social events. By 1907, however, as one Indian student testified, 'the idle curiosity of the English [had] long been satisfied',[22] and the educational backgrounds of Indian students was solely a disadvantage in university culture.

The importance of the public school experience is evident in the experiences of the few Indian students who attended them. Jawaharlal Nehru, who had friends from Harrow at Cambridge, describes his life there as 'pleasant years with many friends and some work and some play and a gradual widening of the intellectual horizon'.[23] However, hostile British students could make the public school experience unpleasant for Indian students. N. B. Bonarjee remembers the Dulwich Preparatory School's curriculum which included history lessons in which 'Indians on the whole were not nice people at all, being addicted to burning widows, to incarcerating men and women in Black Holes or murdering them and throwing the bodies into wells, excessive stress being laid on such themes.'[24] Such accounts fuelled the flames of bigotry among British students, one of whom, the son of a former ICS officer, came to blows with Bonarjee after calling him a 'Bengali babu'. But the headmaster did not tolerate official discrimination, as Bonarjee attests:

> At Dulwich 'colour' was not a handicap. Indians (and other coloureds), for example, were not only made prefects, if considered suitable, but were

> also given the rights and privileges that went with a prefect's cap. These included the right of corporal punishment – which was usually inflicted on the delinquent with an O. T. C. [Officer Training Corps] swagger stick.[25]

The contrast of university experiences between the few Indians who had attended public school in Britain and the overwhelming majority who had not, highlights the way in which the inequities of imperial power helped to transform class discrimination into race discrimination. For the disadvantages of background that Indian students experienced in British universities resulted from the fact that they were in Britain to begin with precisely because it was the centre of imperial power. British public schools were therefore prestigious while, to British students, Indian schools were nonexistent.

If most Indian students lacked the necessary social backgrounds, they also lacked the skills and interests that undergraduate culture prized most highly, particularly competitive team sports. Whereas many British students, secure in their prior education and financial support, regarded university mainly as a finishing school for membership in the 'old-boy network', Indian students saw their sojourn in Britain primarily as a means of acquiring qualifications that would make them more competitive professionally at home. While British students often took part in sports and formed their friendships with teammates, Indian students devoted their time to studying. The result was the ostracism of Indian students from college society. Syed Ali Bilgrami, who taught Marathi at Cambridge, observed this development: 'As a rule, however, the British youth prefers as companions those who take an interest in sport rather than in study, and the Indian who is not particularly fond of sport is left more or less to himself. With regard specially to the young men from Aligarh ... I notice with regret the utter absence of interest in games which form such a prominent feature of their own College life.'[26] Similarly a British graduate of Cambridge acknowledged that Indians were 'very hard working, doing far more that the average Englishman'. But this characteristic seemed of little importance to him since he argued that 'the Indian['s] ... devotion to his studies often acts as a bar to intercourse, for it often means that he has no other interests, a state of mind repugnant to the English nature'.[27] Such disinterest in sports was not confined to Indians. As the President of the Cambridge Majlis, a club founded by and for Indian students, pointed out: 'Even in England the cleavage between the "swot" who gets a first, and the sporting man whose goal in life is a Blue, is sufficiently marked.'[28]

The proportion of Indians who participated in team sports, however, was much lower than that of British students. The librarian of the Indian

Institute at Oxford likened them in this regard to Rhodes scholars. A former British student remembered 'an Indian who got on very well at the Union, and also stroked one of our boats. He was an exceedingly popular man.'[29] The 1898 India Office intelligence report referred to a Muslim football player at Oxford and two Muslim cricketers at Cambridge. A Sikh at Edinburgh was a good marksman. One Indian, C. R. Reddy, was even elected Vice-President of the Cambridge Union, the university's official student club-cum-debating society. And there was Ranjitsinjhi. But as the intelligence report stated: 'Ranjitsinjhi stands quite alone.'[30]

In fact, many of these 'exceptions' were not accepted on terms equal to their British fellows, as the initial hostility to Ranjitsinjhi demonstrates. The reason they were not was probably, as an Indian student at Cambridge put it bluntly, because 'the aloofness was due to race prejudice, not any other reason'.[31] The negative view of Indian culture that Cambridge missionaries portrayed in their extracurricular lectures helped to intensify British students' animosity toward Indians as an ethnic group. An Indian student, D. B. Mukherjea, complained: 'Lectures on the Indian "Zenana", on Indian social and religious life . . . seem to convey very inaccurate notions of the actual state of things at home'. A result was the demotion of Indians as a group in British students' informal ranking of the Empire's peoples: 'it is not our fault if some regard us as little better than the Bushmen of Australia'.[32] Racial bigotry of this sort had practical consequences within university life. For instance Reddy found it impossible to advance to the Union's presidency, because of organised opposition from many British students. Moreover, many boarding houses refused to admit Indians. For these acts of prejudice there was no redress, although, in contrast to some other parts of the Empire, neither were there laws enforcing discrimination.

The important issue for the purposes of the present study, however, is the reaction of British authorities. Both the parliamentary committee and, more significantly because of its secrecy, the India Office intelligence report seemed to lament Indian students' lack of participation in sports. They acknowledged that Indian students worked hard and, if anything, were more serious about academic learning than British students. Nevertheless, although an India Office intelligence report denied that much prejudice existed on the part of British students, nowhere did anyone defend racial prejudice on ideological grounds. Those who claimed not to harbour racial prejudice may have been deceiving themselves or simply others. But even this behaviour indicates that to use race openly as a reason for exclusion or discrimination was unacceptable in the British institutions concerned. No laws forbade certain races from studying in British universities as was the case at the time in some parts of the United States, and official discrimination was rarely open.

On the other hand British authorities sometimes treated Indian students' lack of participation in sports, which was in fact often due to financial constraints or bigotry, as a moral failure that justifiably excluded from the ruling class those who did not participate. According to the 1898 report, British polite society's loss of naivety regarding the pretensions of many Indian visitors meant that 'The number of students who have the entrée into good society, and our English life in its best aspects is not large.' The select group who did, the report implied, were 'those Indians who conform to the accepted standard of good manners & good fellowship'.[33] Those not receiving this entrée were excluded 'due rather to Indian ineptitude than English prejudice'.[34] One aspect of this 'ineptitude' was the reluctance of Indians to take part in sports. Instead, they were 'prone to discussion as a recreation', a tendency 'confirmed & encouraged by the course of study for the bar and I. C. S'.[35]

Prejudice on the basis of class could, therefore, be as onerous for Indians studying in Britain as that on the basis of race. Indeed, the former tended to become the latter. A central purpose of Britain's public-school and university curricula and social activities was, after all, to set its recipients as a breed apart from the classes beneath them. By creating a culture that was difficult for Britain's lower, and even middle classes, to enter, it ensured the ascendancy of the elite. This practice was, in fact, a form of ethno-centrism within British society, favouring the descendants of Britain's rulers, who by virtue of birth and rearing were better suited to conform to the public school and university culture. To the extent that Indian students had even greater difficulty conforming to this culture because of the differences between the societies of Britain's and India's elites, official behaviour can be seen as confirming a form of systemic discrimination according to race – but it was a racial discrimination that existed primarily as a by-product of the class discrimination that British authorities endorsed.

The boundaries of official tolerance

If British authorities disapproved of racial discrimination, they did little or nothing to oppose it when it arose from outside forces. Two glaring exceptions to the pattern of official tolerance in the context of unofficial discrimination developed in British higher education between 1900 and 1914. They highlight the limits to which official tolerance of cultural and racial difference extended in the face of pressure from groups more willing to discriminate openly by race.

One was the refusal of some Cambridge colleges to admit Indians simply because they were Indians. Their reasons for doing so were driven more by the bigotry of students than faculty. Such hostility was particularly pronounced at Cambridge, because it was quicker than Oxford or London in allowing Indian students to substitute Sanskrit for Greek. It therefore attracted a larger number of Indian students than other universities. Colleges, such as Downing, Christ's, and St John's, which at the turn of the century accounted for more than half the total number of Indians admitted to the university, acquired a stigma that steered British students toward other colleges. Rather than decry the racism involved, the fellows of Cambridge's colleges restricted the number of Indians they would admit, regardless of their academic potential. That this acquiescence itself could be seen as racist seems not to have occurred to the fellows of the colleges involved. As one fellow put it, without any sense of embarrassment, 'there used to be a strong feeling that St. John's College was overrun with Indians, and the attitude of the English undergraduates was affected thereby. The College therefore adopted a system of selection, and restricted the numbers of Indians.'[36]

Yet faculty could regard even this development, which was one of the most blatant forms of official racial discrimination in Britain, in terms of class. For instance, J. R. Tanner, a fellow of St John's College, Cambridge, distinguished between 'men recommended specially from India' and government scholars. The former, he claimed, had 'turned out' better than the latter, because the 'Government scholar inclined to a hermit's life and tended to be a "smug"'.[37] Similarly, Oscar Browning, a fellow of King's College, Cambridge who had travelled in India, divided Indians at his university into two classes, which he conflated with their moral behaviour:

> Of the better class he thought very highly; he had had very distinguished Indian pupils who had taken high places in the Civil Service examination. He had dined at the 'Majlis' [Indian student society], and could not desire to meet more delightful or more cultivated gentlemen; on the other hand Indians of the worse class were pushing and self-assertive, and were said to be often very immoral.[38]

Such opinions were not confined to Cambridge dons. In its effort to ascertain why Indians appeared to have more positive experiences of Oxford than Cambridge, the Lee-Warner Committee noted that 'more than one Oxford witness suggests ... that the Indians who obtained admission at Oxford belonged on the whole to a better class', thus enabling them to blend more easily into university society.[39]

Yet such restrictions were not forthcoming from the Inns of Court, whose ranks continued to swell with Indian students. Far from limiting the number of Indians they accepted into their ranks, the benchers of the Inns of Court made membership more attractive to Indians by easing the requirements for entry. In 1902 three of the Inns exempted *vakils* from their membership exam and at least four terms of their residency requirement. They did so because, as the Council later acknowledged: 'The English standard for an Indian to be admitted as a Student is a far lower one, although in India an English barrister ranks in position above a Vakil.'[40] This ruling stood in marked contrast to the benchers' decision, at the same meeting, regarding lawyers from New Zealand, whose credentials they would not recognise, because the dominion did not distinguish between barristers and solicitors.

When official discrimination occurred in legal education, the source was not in England. Rather it was British institutions in India, which were more willing than their domestic counterparts to discriminate officially on the basis of race in framing their requirements. Although the Council of Legal Education determined the criteria that students must meet in order to receive a call to the Bar, colonial high courts had great autonomy in determining the requirements for lawyers who could appeal cases in their criminal courts. Furthermore, in spite of their assertion that 'it is not desirable to make any distinction before admission between English, Scotch, and Irish students on the one hand, and Indian, Colonial, and Foreign Students on the other',[41] the Inns of Court sometimes sought the advice of high-court magistrates in India on curricular matters pertaining to barristers training to practice in India. The prejudices of these justices against Indians training for law in Britain, therefore, influenced the behaviour of the benchers of the Inns of Court.

This influence was most evident regarding subjects for the Bar exam. In 1892 the Council of Legal Education created the fields of 'Hindu and Mohammedan' law and Roman Dutch law (the latter applicable in South Africa) 'for students who intend to practice in parts of the Empire where systems of law other than English are the law of the country'.[42] Students could take these options instead of exams on English property law. Attendance at the alternative courses, however, was sparse, with 'Hindu and Mohammedan' law attracting only forty-nine students in 1893, and Roman Dutch law, twenty-seven. By contrast 241 students attended English property law lectures the same year. Reluctant to abandon the project, the Council sought the support of chief justices in India and South Africa. The South African justices endorsed the courses in Roman Dutch law, but the justices in India 'were against any substitution'. The Council, therefore, abandoned the project, albeit with great 'regret' over 'the failure of this experiment', because 'instruction in these subjects ought to be obtainable in this country'.[43] By expunging the study of Indian law from the English legal curriculum, the chief justices in India preserved a clear distinction between English-trained barristers and their Indian counterparts, a distinction that was likely to favour British candidates for Indian positions, since they were less likely to attend the lectures anyway. Ironically, this distinction probably encouraged more Indian students to enroll at the Inns of Court in order to gain the prestige that membership of the English Bar provided in India. In any case, the Council's decision stood for only fifteen years. The increasing number of Indian students led to increasing pressure from these same students to study Indian law. Ultimately, the request for its inclusion in the curriculum came in 1908 from an Indian barrister at the Allahabad high court. It received a favourable endorsement from Morley's reform-minded India Office and from an English legal culture that had favoured the idea in the first place.[44]

A more clearly racist decision raised vehement objections from Indian students and some officials in the India Office. In 1913 the chief justices of the Madras and Allahabad courts required Indian, but not British, members of the English Bar to have studied with an ethnically British barrister for at least one year in addition to the regular three-year course while resident at the Inns. The decision brought immediate protests from Indian barristers, among them the future founder of Pakistan, Muhammad Ali Jinnah. Not only did it require more of Indian students than it did of their British counterparts, but it also placed existing British barristers, those under whom Indian students would be required to study, in a position of greater authority than Indian barristers in England. In a meeting on 24 April 1913 with Indian students protesting this ruling, C. E. Mallet, the India Office's Secretary for Indian students, sided with his audience to resounding cheers. Mallet later declared to his superiors: 'I did not hesitate to say, when challenged, and I should not hesitate to say again, that *if* any Court were to make such a distinction *merely* on the ground of race or colour, I thought it would be wrong, objectionable and unfair.'[45] Secretary of State Lord Crewe agreed, arguing to the Viceroy that the high courts' requirements were 'open to objection'.[46] The Indian courts' requirements effectively transgressed the Inns of Court policy that, regarding the call to the Bar, 'no distinction ... should be made between Indian and other Colonial and Foreign Students'.[47] Yet the benchers of Lincoln's Inn were curiously reticent on the matter. To their Indian students' petition on the issue, they simply replied that 'the Masters of the Bench have no control in the matter'.[48]

This response may appear surprising, because within a year a special committee of Lincoln's Inn protested the Bombay chief justices' exclusion of an Indian member of Lincoln's Inn from its court over a dispute concerning whether the barrister in question intended to practice at the court permanently. Moreover the committee obtained the agreement of the other Inns to launch an investigation as to whether 'the rights of members of the Inns of Court are being unreasonably or unnecessarily curtailed'.[49] From a legal standpoint, however, the two decisions were about significantly different issues. Those of the Madras and Allahabad chief justices were the creation of new rules for admission to their courts, which, however racist they may have been, were, under English custom, the prerogative of their courts. The decision of the Bombay chief justices, on the other hand, was in apparent violation of their own published regulations, and therefore raised the ire of the English benchers.

Institutions in the United Kingdom tried to maintain a policy of racial neutrality in dealing with Indian students. In some cases they accommodated these students' cultural preferences and occasionally even lobbied on their behalf to eliminate discriminatory behaviour toward them. Yet British authorities also often acquiesced in and reinforced discrimination around them, whether it arose among British students or from governing institutions in India. In a society that was still far from imposing anti-discrimination laws on private organisations or individuals, British officials were quick to shrug off racist bigotry among students or even administrators of the Raj as beyond their control. They therefore refused to act, as with the Inns of Court benchers in response to the discriminatory rulings of the Allahabad and Madras high courts, or worse still, adopted discriminatory policies in response to the racist attitudes of the academic marketplace, as with the Oxbridge colleges in response to the preferences of their white students. Such cases revealed tangible limits to the tolerance that British institutions extended to Indians in their midst.

'Immorality' and sexual relations

British authorities even perceived the supposed sexual immorality of Indian students in terms of class. If, as Browning's remarks in the previous section suggest, Britain's elite believed that Indians of lower birth tended toward immorality, then they also thought that the lascivious behaviour of 'the better class' of Indian students resulted from their contacts with lower-class Englishmen and women. Deslandes and Lahiri have emphasised British institutional concern regarding sexual relations between Indian men and British women. This emphasis has complemented other analyses in colonial history, particularly Stoler's.[50]

Much of this writing has focused on concerns over miscegenation. Yet even at public inquiries dealing with the subject, British administrators regarded British lower-class women to be as detrimental an influence on Indian middle- to upper-class men as Indian men in general were on British women.

This attitude is particularly important considering the accusations of sexual immorality that surrounded Indian students. The Cambridge student, P. J. Lewis, believed 'their views on immorality are very different to ours', and referred to a Christian proselytiser's assertion that, although some Indians were 'exceedingly nice men, many of them are men from whom one would in other circumstances hold aloof as much as possible on moral grounds'.[51] Some officials in higher education echoed this sentiment. For instance, referring to Indians studying for the Bar, W. R. Hamilton, a member of Gray's Inn, noted a widespread 'belief that the moral standard of Indians students is not too high',[52] and W. A. Spooner, the warden of New College, Oxford, complained that 'morally, unless they are Christians', Indians were 'apt to deteriorate'.[53] Little wonder, given these attitudes, that British students in 1890s Cambridge barred Indians from attending some dances.[54] Such stereotyping of Indians fits well with a generation of scholarship that has highlighted British portrayals of Indians as sexual predators.

Arguing against such evidence, however, are two issues that historians tend to overlook. One is the attitudes of faculty who regarded Indians to be ethically on a par with Britons of equivalent classes. For example, in the public forum of a parliamentary inquiry on the subject, Rev. J. W. Cartmell, a tutor at Christ's College, Cambridge, declared that 'Indian students had behaved just as well morally at Cambridge as Englishmen; possibly better'.[55] His colleague, A. E. Shipley agreed that 'morally their life is not essentially different from that of other students'.[56] In private correspondence with the India Office, W. R. Hamilton argued that London's potential to corrupt students applied irrespective of race: 'It may be admitted that to set down young men in London without parents or friends is to court disaster. Young Englishmen often go wrong with all the advantages of home and friends, and it is no wonder that Indian youths should go wrong as they do.'[57]

Even more significant is the agreement of many Indians that English society presented sexual temptations that were unusually strong for young men with the social backgrounds of most Indian students. An Indian contributor to the *IMR* related that in conversation with British students at Oxford, 'I discovered that the English boys allow themselves greater liberty in discussing juvenile members of the other sex than could be assumed by a "gentleman" of India. In fact, this feature of English society rather jars upon the sense of social propriety of the

Oriental observer.'[58] Acknowledging that 'a larger number than is tolerable indulge in this vice' of sexual immorality, N. S. Subbarao, the President of Cambridge's Indian Majlis contrasted the 'strong check' that Indian society placed on social relations between men and women outside of their families with 'the liberty so freely granted to women in England'. The latter, he added, was 'at the same time capable of great abuse'. Combined with the depravity of 'light women', it was 'hardly to be expected that the warm-tempered Indian, free from all restraint, would escape the temptation'. Such 'light women' were, of course, from humble backgrounds – 'shop girls' and 'barmaids'.[59]

British authorities were not the only party concerned about these relationships. So were Indian parents, who, according to another Indian student, Naziruddin Hasan, typically complained that their sons had 'become very immoral'. Here again, however, Hasan argued that the situation was worse among students not associated with universities (such as those who studied law), because 'they get their morality from the street'.[60] Such negative Indian assessments of the English working class were nothing new. Indian travel literature routinely decried the moral depravity of England's lower orders. In reflections published for the benefit of both British and Indian audiences, the Indian clergyman, T. B. Pandian, declared that 'England's besetting weakness is a national taste for intoxicating drinks', an evil from which 'all others spring, finding vent in the worst forms of crime and dissoluteness'.[61] And the London stage enabled 'young and pretty actresses to exhibit themselves in costumes and attitudes that would call up deep blushes of shame to the faces of the much maligned dancing girls of my own native land'.[62] Pandian was a Christian, but Hindu parents also took issue with England's moral climate and the negative influence it might have on their youth. In 1886 an Indian contributor to the *IMR* referred to Indian public perceptions regarding the ways in which education in Britain undermined core traditional Indian values:

> Young men [returned from Britain] may be 'atheists' because their conception of Divinity is somewhat different from that entertained by the masses; they may be 'immoral' because they reprobate the subjection of women, and are strong advocates of free intercourse between the sexes.[63]

Many Indians, therefore, believed that the socially conservative upbringing of Indian youths prepared them poorly for the licentious openness of British society.

British and Indian officials agreed. 'The conditions in which the majority of young Indians must of necessity live in London are such as to arouse considerable apprehension in a careful father', declared the

Lee-Warner Committee.

> In a European town the Indian student is confronted with many temptations of which he has had no previous experience; he is supplied with considerable sums of money, and there can be next to no check upon the manner in which he spends it; at the same time he is separated from those domestic and religious influences which in all countries operate as powerful restraints upon young men.[64]

Significantly, the committee cast this problem in terms that likened the interests of parents in Britain and India: 'These are the conditions of life to which we believe no English father would expose his son without considerable misgiving.'[65] And again: 'We are satisfied that the proportion of those who come to grief is not greater than it would be among young Englishmen of the same class, supposing it to be possible that the latter should be placed by their parents in similar circumstances.'[66] Implicit in this last statement is the notion that, if anything differentiated the moral behaviour of young men under similar circumstances, it was not ethnicity but class.

The risks of exposure to lower class morality were not confined to London. Subbarao described Cambridge University's society as divided into 'gentlemen' and 'touts'. Another student, P. N. Dutt, referred to the latter as 'undesirables', many of whom were 'of very low social position'. The problem for an Indian unfamiliar with British society was to know the difference between the two. Since to strike up a friendship with a 'tout' would ostracise him from the 'gentlemen', Subbarao considered the Indian at a disadvantage.[67] The point here is not that male Indians students were in reality more likely to have sexual relations with lower-class women. The evidence suggests that their British counterparts behaved similarly. For instance, as Subbarao pointed out: 'Indians ... find a stimulus in the example of a large number of Varsity men', who used their popularity to solicit sexual favours.[68] The point here is how both British institutions and Indian parents viewed such behaviour. Neither side of the imperial divide approved of it, and both sides regarded it as a symptom of the pernicious presence of lower-class British women.

For Indians more than for Englishmen, however, such emulation could lead to social disaster. None was greater for British authorities or Indian parents than interethnic marriage. The choice of this term is a careful one, because it encompasses the concerns of Britons and Indians more fully than does the word 'interracial'. Race is a Western concept, and in the late nineteenth and early twentieth centuries it could refer to endogamous groupings. This use was obvious in the United States and the white-settler colonies, where formal laws against miscegenation often enshrined societal racism. In no case was the racial barrier clearer than with Queen Victoria's protegé, the Maharaja Duleep Singh. As the deposed King of Punjab, the most powerful Indian state of the early nineteenth century, Duleep received formal honours on a par with the princes of Germany's lesser states. Moreover, he converted to Anglican Christianity shortly after his arrival in England in 1854. Yet to Queen Victoria he complained that he 'could not marry a Heathen, and an Indian who would become a Christian only to please him, would be very objectionable. Were he to marry a European, his children would be half-caste, which would not do.'[69] After he married an Egyptian woman of humble birth in 1861, one of his British acquaintances lamented: 'What we all desired for him was that he might find a nice English wife yet this was no easy matter ... but poor fellow, I have reason to think that he had come to the conclusion that (as he termed it) a "foreigner like himself" was distasteful for our Country women.'[70] If a Christian Indian prince presented such a 'distasteful' potential marriage partner for British polite society, how much less desirable was an Indian student? At an informal level this problem was also present in British society. Little wonder then that when an Indian student married his landlord's daughter, the landlord often disowned her. Other cultural differences, particularly religion, merely intensified the opprobrium at such unions. But in these cases the parents of the Indian student often behaved in a similar manner, because their son had married outside his caste and religion. Of course, the presence of intolerance among Indian parents in no sense diminishes the racism of British society. But the fact that such hostility came from both sides of these ethnic divides relieved British officials of any sense that it was anything other than the natural behaviour of human societies.

British officials were sometimes sympathetic to the victims of such discrimination. This was the case, for instance, with S. A. Mahmoud, who married his landlord's daughter. Together they had three children, whom neither spouse's family would help to support. Curzon Wyllie, the Secretary of State's political *aide-de-camp*, favoured official assistance. But although Philip Hutchins, the secretary of the India Office's Public and Judicial Department, considered the case to be 'very distressing', he voiced the usual concern about the 'inconvenient precedent' that direct aid would set. Instead, he recommended the case to the Charity Organization Society.[71] The official response was similar to Malindranath Mullick, a law student whose mother cut off his allowance when he married a British woman. His wife, Jessie, suffered similar ostracism from her British friends. The fact that the couple had two children only intensified their growing financial distress. As was often the case with destitution, class elicited sympathy. Noting that Malindranath 'seems to be well educated and a highly respectable going [*sic*] man and his wife is also a superior woman', E. G. A. Jackson, the secretary of the Kensington Committee of the Charity Organization Society, sought the India Office's help. 'It seems a pity,' he declared, 'that he should be reduced to seek refuge in the Workhouse if anything can be done to influence his mother and enable him to complete his studies.' Yet at the same time both Jackson and Wyllie accepted the bigotry involved on both sides without any sense of disapproval. The former noted that the Indian's 'difficulties are owing to his own folly as he must have known the opposition that would be raised to his marriage', and the latter stated 'that the husband's friends and relations in India should have discarded him is not unnatural'.[72]

In a manner similar to the acquiescence of college authorities in the racial prejudices of their students, British authorities accepted as a fact of life the endogamous nature of separate cultures. This practice was not simply one that imperial authorities sought to impose on supposedly lesser races. It was one that the subject peoples of India agreed upon with equal enthusiasm to that of British rulers and for their own reasons of ethnic purity. Furthermore, ethnic endogamy was not an invention of orientalist scholarship, since it had existed for centuries, possibly millennia, in India. Ironically, it was the drift of Victorian and Edwardian polite society away from arranged marriage and toward freer interaction between the sexes that created many of the opportunities for interethnic marriage and sexual relations.

It should not be surprising, therefore, that British officials often defined the marriage between an Indian and a Briton in religious rather than biological terms. Religion was the theme of an India Office administrator's pamphlet on marriage published around the time of the cases above. In it Sir Dennis Fitzpatrick, a member of the Council of India, contrasted Christian marriage with non-Christian marriage. The former was 'a union between one man and one woman to the exclusion of all other ... for the joint lives of the parties; and ... based upon the consent of the parties'.[73] The major difference between Christian and non-Christian marriage was that the latter could be polygamous and was, in the case of Islam, often more tolerant of divorce. Both practices, he argued pragmatically, should be tolerated at the civil level, because the 'civil legislator ... is merely allowing the ancient laws of an infidel community to stand, and giving effect to them'.[74] As tolerant as this approach appears, it nevertheless assumed that ethnic groups would tend to remain endogamous. And indeed they did, since marriages between practitioners of different religions were rare in both India and Britain. Fitzpatrick's tolerance was also consistent with over a century of British policy in India, which sought to codify civil law on the basis of traditional communities. The identification of religion as a characteristic of endogamous communities explains the use of the terms 'Hindu' and 'Mohammedan' under the heading 'Race' that appeared on so many Indian administrative forms and in the *IMR* during this period. Its presence is further indication of the tendency among British officials to use race to describe a plethora of social characteristics, in this case conflating religion with ethnicity.

The problem for British officials with the cases above was that they transgressed the boundaries between these differing communities, of which one was Christian-English. More than any other social action, interethnic marriage threatened their ordered view of an imperial society composed of multiple, yet discrete, ethnic communities. Responding in 1888 to an inquiry regarding the legality of a marriage between an Indian man and a British woman, Macpherson, the India Office's Judicial and Public Department secretary, unofficially warned: 'if the gentleman is not a Christian and is entitled by his religion or the custom governing his race to marry more than one wife, it is extremely doubtful whether a marriage with such a person would be good even in England, and it is impossible to say what difficulties might not arise out of England'.[75] The difficulty was that the groom might legally marry a second wife once he returned to India.

But Macpherson raised another point that was perhaps more pertinent to the experience of Indian students in Britain – that most Indians married very young, and were therefore likely already to be married when they arrived in Britain for study. Any subsequent marriage contracted in England would be bigamous under English law. That an Indian student in Britain might remain silent about his wife in India is evident in Gandhi's account of his own friendship with an elderly British woman, who introduced him to potential marriage partners of his own age. Eventually he confessed to her that he was married, adding 'I knew that Indian students in England dissembled the fact of their marriage and I followed suit.'[76]

Perhaps nowhere did British institutions recognise race more clearly than regarding marriage. This barrier is usually the last to fall in encounters between ethnic groups, so the attempts of British officials, and Indian parents, to maintain it is hardly surprising. Yet in doing so, they demonstrated how nebulous was their understanding of the nature of the apparent difference between Indians and Britons. For although in societal practice, physical differences could be a sufficient barrier to an Indo-British marriage, British officials did not highlight them. Rather they focused on religious differences that were insurmountable not only to most British people, but to most Indians as well. Stoler has shown how, for Europeans in the Dutch East Indies, such rhetoric could serve as a cover for opposition to miscegenation based on racial differences.[77] No doubt the same was often the case in Britain as well. It certainly was in India. Yet private correspondence among officials responsible for decisions regarding Indians in Britain suggests that their concerns about religion were sincere. This sincerity, however, did not mean that the institutional response to interethnic marriage bore no traces of biological racism. Rather British officials regarded religion and ethnic origin as so intertwined that it rarely occurred to them that a religious barrier might not exist between an Indian man and a British woman. In spite of the proselytising efforts of inner-city missionaries and the cooperation they received from the India Office, members of the latter tended to treat ethnic groups as endogamous. It is in this context that much of the official response to interethnic sexual relations should be understood. It was often a manifestation of racial intolerance, but it was a form of intolerance that at a cultural level was truly imperial, since it was mutual in its origins and application.

Supervision

The context of mutual ethnic endogamy is one among several issues that requires a reassessment of Lahiri's assertion that British policy toward Indian students was 'surveillance, control and restriction, executed under the cloak of paternalism and protection'.[78] Such a narrow view of British institutional motivation and behaviour only works if one discounts the importance of the civilising mission in institutional thinking and the probable desire of Indian parents to see their children's period of study in the United Kingdom turn to personal advantage. These two motives account for much of the contemporary discussion surrounding supervision. Moreover, even after political rhetoric heightened with the *svadeshi* campaign in the wake of the 1905 partition of Bengal, the presence of legal restrictions on government suppression in the United Kingdom limited options available to British authorities seeking to curb dissent.

British authorities could usually count on the cooperation of Indian parents in the effort to supervise students. Indeed, the numerous examples, cited elsewhere in this book, of Indian students running into financial trouble in Britain, suggest that there was ample reason for concern among Indian parents sending their children off to study in the United Kingdom. Moreover, London's reputation for vice and the unfamiliarity of British surroundings provided these parents with further reason for anxiety. As we have seen, both British and Indian polite society associated much of this vice with Britain's lower classes. Indian students who engaged in it were, therefore, risking their own social standing in both Britain and India. Moreover, some Indians living in Britain suspected that fellow expatriates of lower social standing at home were inventing their backgrounds in order to advance in rank through their British sojourn.

So concerned were some Indians regarding the potential for illegitimate self-promotion that they encouraged the wider use of certificates and references in order to ensure that geographical distance did not in itself permit upward social mobility of their compatriots. In 1893 the Inns of Court required certificates from two barristers in order for a candidate to gain admission. Although these certificates asked for no details of antecedents, they required the signing barrister to declare the candidate 'to be a gentleman of respectability'.[79] But this form was not good enough for one prominent Indian in Britain. Claiming 'special and extensive knowledge of the antecedents of Indians who come to England' to study for the Bar or in universities, S. A. Kapadia, secretary of the Northbrook Society, complained to the treasurer of the Inner Temple that 'Many natives of India whose antecedents render them unsuitable persons to be admitted to Membership of the Inns of Court do obtain such admission and succeed in being called to the Bar.' On the other hand 'respectable Indian students frequently experience serious difficulties in obtaining admission to one of the Inns of Court'. The solution, Kapadia proposed, was 'the appointment by the Inns of Court of a suitable person, whose duty it should be to ascertain the fitness, as regards character, for obtaining the necessary introductions, sureties and proposal for call'. Moreover this officer would 'report upon cases of misconduct or misrepresentation affecting the eligibility of an Indian student for continued membership of his Inn or for Call to the Bar'. Apparently unaware of the irony that he was engaging in his own act of personal self-promotion, Kapadia offered to serve in the office whose creation he proposed.[80] The benchers rejected this proposal for reasons we will examine shortly.

Paternalism and protection were, therefore, no mere 'cloak' to cover the true political motives of British authorities. They were policies that many Indians probably desired for their children in Britain. Anyone acquainted with the administration of overseas studies programmes today knows that parents frequently express concern about their children's behaviour and experiences abroad. There is no reason to believe that this was less the case a hundred years ago, when both Britain and India's societies were more paternalistic than they are today.

Moreover, British authorities believed that Indian parents actually wanted this supervision. Even if these parents disagreed with many aspects of British rule in India, the reasoning went, they were hardly likely to want their children to get into trouble, either for their social behaviour or their political views, while preparing in Britain for careers at home. After all, Indian parents paid handsomely to secure their children career advantages in India by providing them with education in Britain. They did not pay for their children to antagonise the Imperial Government in ways that were likely to become obstacles in their careers. In such cases the personal aspirations of parents for their children were likely to outweigh any political agenda they had. The 1898 India Office intelligence report assumed that such motives were common among Indian parents, who, it claimed, 'would certainly in most cases disapprove of them, not only because they are in the abstract insulting to the British Government, but also because they bring discredit on the youths themselves, and are likely to damage their future prospects'. The government could, therefore, the report assumed, count on parents' assistance in curbing the political activities of their children in Britain: 'It is almost a duty of the authorities in this country to convey friendly information and advice to parents, who are exposed to these risks and at such a disadvantage in the matter of exerting personal control and influence.'[81] Similarly, W. R. Hamilton observed privately to government officials that, faced with examples of Indian youths going astray, Indian parents were 'becoming averse to sending their sons to England'.[82]

The belief among British authorities that Indian parents desired a paternalistic approach toward their children complemented the paternalistic motives of British institutions in encouraging Indians to study in the United Kingdom. The desire to impress Indian students with British civilisation was motive enough for organisations that espoused the civilising mission to try to regulate the behaviour of Indian students in their midst. As with America's Fulbright scholarships for foreign students to study in the United States today, the presence of Indian students in the United Kingdom, whether on scholarships or personal resources, presented an opportunity for British institutions to pursue political and strategic policy through positive reinforcement. The leaders of these institutions were, therefore, at pains to present the best face of British society to their young Indian visitors. If these students were to serve as an elite through which Britain could run its empire, then they must come to admire British society rather than despise it.

It was this combination, of parental paternalism and imperial paternalism, that accounted for much of the desire to supervise Indian students in the United Kingdom at the turn of the twentieth century. Even before Indian nationalist protest during the 1890s and 1900s raised British concerns about Indian dissent, institutions in Britain (some of which numbered Indians among their leaders) offered parents the reassurance of greater supervision of their children studying in the

United Kingdom. From their very foundations, organisations espousing Britain's civilising mission in India, such as the NIA, the East India Association and the Northbrook Society, sought to provide social venues for Indians to discover Britain and mix with Britons interested in India. Starting in 1885, however, the NIA supplemented its ad hoc arrangements with an organised procedure for supervising Indians studying in Britain. In return for an advance payment of £200 per annum for a student's expenses, plus a one-time, refundable deposit of £100, the NIA agreed 'to arrange a reception of the Student; to provide a suitable School or College, according to his age and requirements; and generally to supervise, befriend, and direct him during his stay in England'. In addition the association promised to 'endeavour to make the Student acquainted with the best side of English life and manners'. To oversee these activities it appointed a 'superintendent of students', initially one Algernon Brown, a barrister and member of the Northbrook Society who had 'lately visited India, and has had successful experience training Indian youths'.[83] The NIA's governing committee of seven, which conceived this act of paternalism, was overwhelmingly Anglo-Indian in composition. In addition to Elizabeth Manning, the association's secretary, it included three former senior British members of the ICS and a recent member of India's legislative council. It also included M. M. Bhownagree, who would later serve as a Conservative Member of Parliament.[84]

Nevertheless, as the turn of the twentieth century approached, the NIA, the East India Association, and the Northbrook Society lost their appeal for Indian students. Two developments account for this decrease in interest. Since its political implications were a major concern of the India Office, its interpretation of them was important. One development was the increase in the number of students in Britain. As the testimony before the 1907 parliamentary committee on Indian students suggests, Indians no longer had the exotic allure for the polite society of turn-of-the-century England that they had held a generation earlier. The lack of welcome offered to many, probably most, Indian students only exacerbated their tendency, as is often the case with students studying in another country, to seek out people of similar cultural backgrounds – in this case, other Indian students. The growth of organisations, such as the Cambridge Majlis, London Indian Society, and Edinburgh Indian Association, run mainly by Indian students, was a response to this ostracism, but it also helped to perpetuate it. However, the more that Indian students limited their society to fellow Indians, the more British students came to resent them, even though the disinterest and hostility of British students had contributed significantly to the Indian students' clannishness in the first place.

The other development was the increasing vehemence of Indian nationalist rhetoric both in India and Britain. By highlighting British exploitation of India's economy, Indian nationalists undermined the legitimacy of the civilising mission that was the ideological basis for the existence of the NIA, East India Association, and Northbrook Society. Most active in this effort was the British Committee of the Indian National Congress, whose ideas Indian students in Britain read regularly in the committee's weekly journal, *India*. Unfortunately, from the British Government's perspective, the organisations that Indian students preferred to attend were much more open to Indian nationalist influence than those espousing the civilising mission.

The important issue here, though, is that even amid their concerns about dissent, British authorities continued to believe in the civilising mission as a powerful reason to tolerate and even encourage the presence of Indian students in British universities and technical colleges. Such thinking lay at the heart of British administrators' fears, since they believed that the education of India's elite, or for that matter, any country's elite, was such a potent force in shaping its society. Thus the 1898 intelligence report warned: 'In view of the important part these youths are destined to play in the social & political development of India, Governments cannot be indifferent to the conditions under which some of their most impressionable years are passed.'[85]

Further evidence of the importance of the civilising mission can be found in British responses to Indian dissent which, at least in the United Kingdom, were remarkably restrained for a government relying on authoritarian rule to subjugate another population. The 1898 report's proposals for remedying the situation were:

1. Interfere with funding distribution in the United Kingdom of dissident literature – a goal to be achieved merely 'by letting those donors know that Gov't disapprove';
2. Enlist the aid of 'older Indian residents in London', who, for the most part, were presumably loyal to the Empire;
3. Inform parents, whom authorities believed would discourage their children's supposedly seditious activities;
4. Dissuade British institutions of higher education from appointing politically radical lecturers who might raise the ire of Indian students against the Raj;
5. Encourage British polite society to put aside any prejudices it might have against 'the best Indian students'; and
6. Provide compensation for the unfavourable rupee–sterling exchange rate that Indians in the ICS struggled against when their sons were receiving educations in Britain.[86]

None of these solutions involved a heavy-handed crackdown on dissent or prevention of Indians from studying in Britain. All of them involved direct or indirect attempts to steer Indian students back toward the goals of the civilising mission that had initially motivated British institutions to support the education of India's elite in the United Kingdom. Only against the last of these options did Lee-Warner advise, probably due to its expense.

The intelligence report was confidential. But Lee-Warner's official commission expressed similar opinions in public nine years later. This time, however, it hinted at strategic reasons to welcome Indians studying in Britain:

> It is obvious that for many years to come the educated classes of India will find it necessary and beneficial to visit Europe or America; and as long as this tendency exists, it is clearly best for the young men to come to England where, besides understanding the language, they will find a considerable number of persons predisposed to take a sympathetic interest in their welfare.[87]

The reason the commission gave for Indians to prefer Britain was questionable, particularly given the testimony it had heard on the subject, but it fitted once again with the civilising mission that British authorities continued to pursue. Unstated was the fear that Indians would encounter even greater criticism of the British Empire in the United States and Europe than they did in the United Kingdom. As with technical education, therefore, the fear of Indian hostility developing beyond their control outweighed the fear of it developing in their midst.

The civilising mission also delayed the creation of a London hostel for Indian students until 1920. The India Office first considered the idea seriously in 1902, when the East India Association's H. C. Richards raised it in an article in *East and West*. W. R. Hamilton, who as we have seen, regarded the London environment as the principal cause of student misbehaviour, whether Indian or British, saw class-related benefits in making residence in a hostel mandatory for Indians studying at the Inns of Court. Doing so would 'tend to check impecunious and undesirable persons from joining the Bar'. If Indian students suffered unusually from the temptations of London, the solution was still to be found in weeding out the social wheat from the chaff: 'There is a belief that the moral standard of Indian students is not too high, and anything that would tend to raise this standard and to restrict the Bar to a higher class of men would not be unwelcome.'[88]

Sir Henry Cotton, however, opposed the proposal, arguing that it would discourage Indian students from mingling with British society and would, therefore, undermine the benefits for Britain in having them study in the United Kingdom. Likening Indian students and their parents to their British counterparts, he argued:

> These young men ... come to learn the English language, to acquire English manners and customs, and to saturate themselves with English spirit and sentiments so as to enable them to meet Englishmen on equal terms on their return to India ... Consider the case of Englishmen when they send their sons abroad to learn French and German. We should not wish our sons to live in an English boarding house at Bonn, Heidelberg, or Paris.[89]

British officials could easily approve of this objection, since it shared the goal of the civilising mission.

The other major reason for Indian students' disapproval of a hostel was fear of surveillance. As the existence of Lee-Warner's intelligence report demonstrates, such concerns were justified. Yet India Office administrators and officials of the Raj recognised that even to appear to monitor Indian students for political purposes would likely backfire. When considering ways to persuade Indians travelling to Britain to procure certificates of identity, the viceroy's council warned that their 'Resolution should not ... make any allusion to political movements' and that government and educational authorities 'should be instructed not to refuse certificates in any case, but merely dissuade persons from attempting the journey when the means seem to be insufficient'.[90] Such advice was more likely to discriminate according to class than political views. To the extent that politics was an issue, the Indian Government wanted to avoid giving that impression – so much so that the policy was less effective as a political tool than it might otherwise have been, since eight years later British authorities were still unable to arrive at an exact figure of the number of Indians studying at universities in the United Kingdom.[91] The Lee-Warner Committee reflected such private opinions in public when, in 1907, it proposed the creation of a 'Bureau of Information' for Indian students planning to study in Britain. In doing so the committee warned that 'to introduce an element of compulsion into the scheme would be both undesirable and impracticable ... it must always remain for the students themselves, and more especially for their parents, to decide whether or not to avail themselves of the opportunities offered'.[92]

One reason for so mild a response was administrative uncertainty as to how serious the level of dissent among Indians in Britain was. The same paternalism that led British institutions to encourage the education of India's elite in the United Kingdom also led them to dismiss much of the rhetoric among these students as harmless follies of youth. Regarding the anti-imperial rhetoric of Indian students at Edinburgh University, Wyllie remarked in 1903:

> Most of the members, although not all, are probably of the National Congress type. They doubtless at times talk a good deal of stuff that sounds disloyal, or at any rate discontented, against the official Englishman in India and the Government there so far as these officials represent it. But the sound is worse than the meaning, and I don't quite see how the talk is to be checked or prevented, even if it were worth while trying to do so.[93]

Reminiscing about this period in his education, Jawaharlal Nehru echoed Wyllie's assessment of such rhetoric:

> In the Majlis and in private talks Indian students often used the most extreme language when discussing Indian politics. They even talked in terms of admiration of the acts of violence that were then beginning in Bengal. Later I was to find that these very persons were to become members of the Indian Civil Service, High Court judges, very staid and sober lawyers, and the like. Few of these parlour firebrands took any effective part in Indian political movements subsequently.[94]

Like Nehru later, Wyllie recognised that dissenting speech did not necessarily translate into dissenting action.

Besides playing down the importance of political rhetoric, Wyllie's remarks point to an equally important aspect of dissident activity in Britain – unlike its equivalent in India, it was protected under law. Even when he expressed concern over the tone of the Edinburgh Indian Association's lectures and debates, his options were limited to refusing to fund their activities when they petitioned for support from the India Office. Similarly, the Lee-Warner commission made clear that there was little the government could do to prevent Indians in the United Kingdom from criticising Britain's occupation of India. Rather it sought the assistance of sympathetic Indians living in Britain to set for students an alternative example to that of the Indian National Congress. Furthermore, in keeping with the paternalistic attitude of the age, it argued that 'extremist' attitudes were an ailment of youth that time would heal: 'But experience can only come with years; it is an element of political wisdom in which youth must always be deficient, and which it is therefore useless to expect in young men from India or any other country.'[95]

In this context, from the government's perspective, a fortuitous by-product of overtly violent acts, which the government abhorred, was the opportunity to suppress dissident organisations that British law would otherwise protect. Such an opportunity arose with the assassination of Wyllie at a meeting of the National Indian Association in 1909. Not only did British authorities prosecute, and ultimately execute, the assassin, Madan Lal Dhingra, who was an engineering student at University College, London, but they also used his association with India House to close this institution, which had served as a meeting place for opponents of Britain's occupation of India.[96]

British institutions, however, occasionally refused to monitor students as a matter of principle. The benchers of the Inns of Court turned down Kapadia's offer to monitor Indian students on the grounds that it would be prejudiced against Indians on the basis of their ethnicity. Stated Ralph Neville, the committee's chairman: 'In their opinion the duties of any such official as Mr. Kapadia suggests would have to extend to all classes of His Majesty's subjects alike. They also feel that an official of the character suggested would in the case of natives from India be vested with inquisitorial power, which might be used oppressively.'[97] This policy held even after the India Office created the Bureau of Indian Students in 1909. In 1913 the benchers declared it 'not advisable that all Indian Students should obtain the Certificate from the Secretary for Indian Students'. Rather they made an exception for Indian students with at least a year's educational experience in Britain, who were required instead to produce 'a Certificate from the Head of his School or College, or from his Tutor'.[98]

Although the minutes of the meeting do not explain the motives for this exemption, three were likely. First, the benchers of the Inns of Court were not in the habit of following the lead of civil servants or even elected ministers of state. This exemption maintained, at least symbolically, their independence from the India Office when dealing with Indian students. Second, they probably trusted tutors and headmasters in the United Kingdom more than they did magistrates and administrators in distant India. Finally, to exempt from production of the India Office certificate students who had received some education in Britain allowed them to argue that they were not treating Indians on a different basis from native Englishmen. Rather, students received treatment that differed on the basis of whether they had prior educational experience in Britain. The records do not indicate how the Inns treated Europeans who had received their education only in India. Nonetheless, this caveat is further evidence of the benchers' desire to shy away from any suggestion that they treated their students differently according to their race.

Supervision of Indian students in Britain, therefore, remained a paternalistic project in the most literal sense of the word. When the Lee-Warner Committee suggested the creation of a committee to advise the

India Office on matters concerning Indian students, it described the position of the committee's members as *'in loco parentis'*. The Lee-Warner Committee called for the advisory committee to be 'predominantly Indian in character, which shall be recognised to be, and in fact be, representative of the Indian parents who are unable directly to superintend the education of their sons in this country'.[99] There is no evidence to suggest that the Lee-Warner Committee intended to discourage Indians from studying in Britain. To discourage Indians from coming to Britain would only encourage many of them to go to Britain's strategic rivals, such as the United States or Germany, where their exposure to criticism of Britain's occupation of India might be greater. Moreover, to encourage or at least allow Indians to study in Britain was consistent with the goal of a civilising mission which, in theory, was the reason for Britain's continued occupation of India. The solution to any 'problem' with Indian students, therefore, was not to exclude them, but to make sure that they came under the influence of the right British and Indian hosts in the United Kingdom. In such a political climate, British authorities continued to hope in the years preceding the First World War that the presence of Indians studying in Britain would strengthen rather than undermine the British Empire.

Recent scholarship has reinforced the personal aspect of the encounter between Indians and British institutions by highlighting the ways in which the racism of British students fuelled the resentment of their Indian peers. Of equal importance to the behaviour of British students is that of the governmental, academic, and philanthropic authorities that supervised the education of Indians in Britain. The rhetoric of these institutions implied a willingness on the part of British authorities to treat Indians as equals of their social counterparts in Britain and to share responsibility with India's elite for the governance of the Raj. In so doing these institutions reinforced the logic of imperial British subjecthood described in Chapter 5. This rhetoric presented a stark contrast to the racial prejudice that Indian students actually experienced in the company of British students and in their attempts to obtain employment, either in government service in India or in professions in Britain.

Less clear is the extent to which administrators in the United Kingdom discouraged such racism or reinforced it through their own personal behaviour. British institutions were ambivalent toward the careers of Indian students, because their administrators held conflicting views on the matter. Some of this ambivalence lay in a shift among British officials during the late Victorian and Edwardian periods from more positive to more negative attitudes regarding Indian students in the United Kingdom. Two major reasons account for this shift. One was the sheer volume of Indian students. Lahiri points out that, in a case of apparent familiarity breeding contempt: 'The first generation of students and visitors excited interest from the host population rather than the hostility encountered by later arrivals, when the novelty had worn off.'[100] The volume of students competing for positions that middle-class British candidates sought in the professions and imperial administration increased the hostility of British students who may have seen their Indian counterparts as threats to their careers. In this case, the racial prejudice of British students probably started out in just as personal a way as Indian efforts to secure administrative positions, before the aspirations of both groups became ideological.

The other major reason for a shift in the attitudes of British administrators was the growth of hostility to British rule among the professional classes in India. This hostility, born in part from the frustration of so many individual careers and opportunities for advancement in the racially privileged setting of the British Raj, made British administrators particularly suspicious of any political activity among Indians in the United Kingdom. It was in Britain that Indians could most easily test the reality of their supposedly common subjecthood with their British rulers, and it was in Britain that they could push the boundaries of the supposed indifference to race within British institutions. The period under discussion witnessed a process that led indirectly to British hostility toward the presence of Indian students in the United Kingdom. This process began with British racism outside official institutions in the United Kingdom, either in the Anglo-Indian administration of the British Raj or, in Britain, among the British students and workers. All three groups, in their own ways, regarded Indians as competitors for personal wealth and power. This behaviour encouraged Indian students to band together and politicise their grievances while studying in Britain. The India Office and local police responded to this political activity in turn with alarm and suspicion.

Such a shift, however, did not mean that British administrators abandoned the class-based social hierarchy as an important component of their behaviour toward Indians. Rather they defined other aspects of individual Indian students, such as loyalty to the Empire, prowess in sport, personal wealth, quality of speech, and personal demeanour, in terms of class. That narrow ethnically-based, cultural biases often informed the definitions of these qualities does not negate the importance of class as the primary register of this discourse. It was the rhetoric of class and the model of gentlemanly behaviour that it embodied that simultaneously became the greatest source of hope and disappointment for Indian students in Britain. Official racial blindness in the United Kingdom set a standard that the rest of the Empire and British society did not live up to. The difference, all the more apparent because administrators of British institutions sometimes tried to meet the standard, undermined British authority in India during the early twentieth century.

Notes

1 'Hindu ladies', *JNIA*, 30 (June 1873): 358.
2 Bernard Cohn, 'Representing authority in Victorian India', in Eric Hobsbawm and Terence Ranger (eds), *The Invention of Tradition* (Cambridge: Cambridge University Press, 1983), 193.
3 J. L., 'The Queen and Indian ladies', *JNIA*, 116 (August 1880): 463.
4 Burton, *At the Heart of the Empire*, 61.
5 IOR L/PJ/2/36 No. 41, Horace Mann to the Undersecretary of State, India Office, 24 October 1868.
6 IOR L/PJ/6/897 No. 3835, D. W. Douthwaite, Steward and Under-Treasurer, Gray's Inn, to Colin G. Campbell, 17 December 1908. For the India Office's request for a positive response see Campbell, draft letter to the treasurers of Inner Temple, Middle Temple, Lincoln's Inn, and Gray's Inn, 25 November 1908, in *ibid*. The record of Lincoln's Inn adding this provision as a permanent policy can be found in PRO PRO 30/77/21, fo. 275, Lincoln's Inn 'Black Book', 25 November 1908.
7 PRO PRO 30/77/21, 'Black Book', minutes, petition by K. V. R. Swami, 5 October 1910, fo. 526.
8 *Ibid.*, petition by Divijendra Nath Basu, 13 March 1906, fo. 522.
9 PRO PRO 30/77/19, 'Black Book', minutes, 25 November 1895, petition by Balwant Singh Garwal, 21 November 1895, fo. 224.
10 G. Beckerlegge, 'Professor Friedrich Max Müller and the missionary cause', in *Religion in Victorian Britain*, Vol. 5 (Manchester: Manchester University Press, 1988), 183 and 188.
11 IOR L/PJ/6/225 No. 626, Arthur Milman, Registrar, University of London, to Godley, 26 April 1888; and IOR L/PJ/6/251 No. 1958, 'Gilchrist Indian Scholarships – draft heads of scheme based on the letters and dispatches from India and from the Secretary of State, and prepared by Professor Stuart, M.P. and Rt. Hon., Sir M. Kay Shuttleworth, Bart., M.P., for submission to the other Gilchrist trustees', December 1888.
12 *CIS*, 16; and 'Medical Students from India', *JNIA*, 127 (August 1881): 363.
13 See Deslandes, '"The foreign element"'; and Lahiri, *Indians in Britain*, 103–7 and 198–201.
14 Sinha, 'Britishness, clubbability', 188 and 185.
15 Figures are from Leone Levi, *Wages and Earnings of the Working Classes: Report to Sir Arthur Bass, M.P.* (London: J. Murray, 1885), 4 and 51.
16 Hamid Ali, 'The cost of living in London', *JNIA*, 134 (February 1882): 88–92.
17 Committee of the National Indian Association, in Conjunction with the Advisory Committee, India Office, *Handbook of Information for Indian Students Relating to University and Professional Studies, Etc., in the United Kingdom* (London: J. S. Phillips, 1909), 6–7 and 39–40.
18 Ali, 'Cost of living', 89. The number of destitute students is calculated from 'Précis of Precedents'.
19 Lahiri makes this point in *Indians in Britain*, 65–71.
20 Cd. 5133 (1910) *Committee on Distressed Colonial and Indian Subjects*, 17.
21 Ali, 'Cost of living', 92.
22 'Written statement by Mr. Naziruddin Hasan, Downing College, Cambridge', 18 May 1907, *CIS*, 210.
23 Jawaharlal Nehru, *Toward Freedom: The Autobiography of Jawaharlal Nehru* (New

York: John Day Company, 1942), 33.

24 N. B. Bonarjee, *Under Two Masters* (Oxford: Oxford University Press, 1970), 40.

25 *Ibid.*, 50. For the name-calling incident, see 44.

26 'Written statement by Mr. Syed Ali Bilgrami, Teacher of Marathi, Cambridge University', 19 May 1907, *CIS: Minutes*, 190.

27 'Written statement of Mr. P. J. Lewis, B.A., St. John's College, Cambridge', 17 May 1907, *CIS: Minutes*, 189.

28 'Written statement by Mr. Namjangud Subbarao Subbarao, St. John's College Cambridge, President of the Indian "Majlis"', n. d. (May 1907), *CIS: Minutes*, 196. A Blue is a term of honour used to describe students at Oxford or Cambridge who play for their university team against the other university.

29 'Written Statement of Mr. P. J. Lewis, B.A., St. John's College, Cambridge', 17 May 1907, *CIS: Minutes*, 188.

30 IOR L/PJ/6/363 No. 1875a, minute, 'The position of young Indians sent to England for Education'.

31 'Evidence of Mr. Jagannath Lunmon Sathé, St. John's College, Cambridge', 16 May 1907, *CIS: Minutes*, 193.

32 'Written statement by Mr. Deva Brata Mukherjea Emmanuel College, Cambridge', 23 May 1907, *CIS: Minutes*, 206.

33 'Indians in England', fo. 783.

34 *Ibid.*, fo. 815.

35 *Ibid.*, fo. 791.

36 'Written statement by Dr. J. R. Tanner, Tutor of St. John's College, Cambridge', *CIS: Minutes*, 77.

37 'Evidence of Dr. J. R. Tanner, St. John's College, Cambridge', 16 May 1907, *CIS: Minutes*, 178.

38 'Evidence of Mr. Oscar Browning, King's College, Cambridge', 17 May 1907, *CIS: Minutes*, 184.

39 *CIS*, 17.

40 PRO PRO 30/77/21, 'Black Book', Macnaghten, 'Report of the Council of Legal Education of the Four Inns of Court', 8 November 1909. For the benchers' decision to exempt *vakil*s from some requirements for admission to the Inns of Court, see PRO PRO 30/77/20, 'Black Book', report of the Joint Committee of the Duties, Interests and Discipline of the Bar, 27 December 1902, 1, fo. 153. The ruling on New Zealand lawyers is on p. 4, f. 156. For the petition regarding *vakil*s, see PRO PRO 30/77/20, 'Black Book', petition by R. K. Soobramania Sastri on behalf of the Madras High Court Vakils' Association, 17 January 1901, 1–2, fos. 39–40.

41 PRO PRO 30/77/19, 'Black Book', report of the Joint Committee of the four Inns of Court, 15 February 1893, enclosed in council minutes, 21 February 1893,

42 London, Archive of the Institute for Advanced Legal Studies, A. CLE 2/6, 'Minutes of the proceedings of the Council of Legal Education', 26 July 1892, in *Consolidated Regulations of the Several Societies of Lincoln's Inn, the Middle Temple, the Inner Temple, and Gray's Inn as to the Admission of Students, the Mode of Keeping Terms, the Education and Examination of Students, the Calling of Students to the Bar, and the Taking out of Certificates to Practise Under the Bar* (London: Cassell, Peter and Galpin, December 1875), 1. I am grateful to the Institute for Advanced Legal Studies for permission to use this collection.

43 PRO PRO 30/77/19, 'Black Book', Council of Legal Education report to the Inns of Court, 18 January 1894, attached to Council minutes, 31 January 1894.

44 Dubé to Secretary of State for India, 20 October 1908; and IOR L/PJ/6/901 No. 3923, Judicial Department minute paper, Campbell, 'Greater facilities re[quired?] for Studying Indian law in England', 20 October 1908.

45 IOR L/PJ/6/1067 No. 706, 'Copy note by Mr. C. E. Mallet, Secretary for Indian Students, dated 31st December 1913', enclosed in Public No. 49, attached to the Marquess of Crewe, 4 December 1914. This document is not an exact copy of the original letter.

46 IOR L/PJ/6/1067 No. 706, Public No. 146, Crewe to His Excellency the Right

Honourable the Governor General of India in Council, 6 June 1913.

47 PRO PRO 30/77/19, 'Black Book', 'Report of the Joint Committee of the four Inns of Court', 15 February 1893, enclosed in council minutes, 21 February 1893.

48 PRO PRO 30/77/21, 'Black Book', council minutes, 9 June 1913, fo. 324.

49 PRO PRO 30/77/22, 'Black Book', 'Report of the Special Committee re: a communication from an Indian Barrister', 18 May 1914, fo. 476.

50 See Deslandes, '"The Foreign Element"'; Paul Deslandes, *Oxbridge Men: British Masculinity and the Undergraduate Experience, 1850–1920* (Bloomington: Indiana University Press, 2005), 209–24; Shompa Lahiri, 'British policy towards Indian princes in late-nineteenth and early twentieth-century Britain', *Immigrants and Minorities*, 15:3 (1996): 214–32; Lahiri, *Indians in Britain*, 121–3; and Ann Laura Stoler, *Carnal Knowledge and Imperial Power: Race and the Intimate in Colonial Rule* (Berkeley and Los Angeles: University of California Press, 2002), 79–111.

51 'Written statement of Mr. P. J. Lewis, B.A., St. John's College, Cambridge', 17 May 1907, *CIS: Minutes*, 189.

52 L/PJ/6/642 No. 1638, note by Mr Hamilton, n. d., in Confidential Correspondence, 'Indian Hostel in London', Note to Sir Charles Lyall by Sir Curzon Wyllie, 31 December 1902.

53 'Written statement by the Warden of New College, Oxford [W. A. Spooner]', 23 May 1907, *CIS: Minutes*, 226.

54 'Indians in England', fo. 815.

55 'Evidence of the Rev. J. W . Cartmell, Tutor of Christ's College, Cambridge', 18 May 1907, *CIS: Minutes*, 181.

56 'Written statement by Mr. A. E. Shipley, Christ's College, Cambridge', 4 May 1907, *CIS: Minutes*, 185.

57 Note by W. R. Hamilton.

58 'First impressions of Oxford: By an Indian student', *IMR*, 423 (March 1906): 73.

59 'Written statement by Mr. Namjangud Subbarao Subbarao, St. John's College Cambridge, President of the Indian "Majlis"', n. d. (May 1907), *CIS: Minutes*, 198.

60 'Written statement by Mr. Naziruddin Hasan, Downing College, Cambridge', 18 May 1907, *CIS: Minutes*, 210.

61 T. B. Pandian, *England to an Indian Eye: or English Pictures from an Indian Camera* (London: Elliot Stock, 1897), 91.

62 *Ibid.*, 93.

63 Bishan Narayan Dar, 'Some characteristics of Indian English-educated youths, a paper lately read before the Indian Society (a Society in London, consisting almost exclusively of Indian gentlemen)', *IM*, 191 (November 1886), 572.

64 *CIS*, 11.

65 *Ibid.*

66 *Ibid.*, 13.

67 'Evidence of Mr. Namjangud Subbarao Subbarao, St. John's College, Cambridge', 17 May 1907, 200, and 'Evidence of Mr. P. N. Dutt, Christ's College Cambridge', 17 May 1907, *CIS: Minutes*, 203.

68 Evidence of Subbarao.

69 Quoted in Michael Alexander and Sushila Anand, *Queen Victoria's Maharajah: Duleep Singh, 1938–93* (New York: Taplinger, 1980), 65.

70 *Ibid.*, 105.

71 IOR L/PJ/6/732 No. 2615, Judicial and Public Department Minute Paper, 'Appeal by Rev. B. W. Pullinger on behalf of S. A. Mahmood', 24 August 1905.

72 IOR L/PJ/6/953 No.1246, E. G. A. Jackson to the Secretary, the India Office, 31 March 1909, and W. H. C. Wyllie to Sir Charles Lyall, Pol. ADC Reference Paper, 2 April 1909.

73 Sir Dennis Fitzpatrick, *Non-Christian Marriage* (no publication information, reproduced in the Henry Morse Collection: Pamphlets on Political Science and Jurisprudence), 1fn.

74 *Ibid.*, 47.

75 IOR L/PJ/227 No. 889, A. G. Macpherson to A. S. Wieland, 22 June 1888.

76 Mohandas K. Gandhi, *An Autobiography: The Story of My Experiments with Truth*, trans. Mahadev Desai (Boston: Beacon Press, 1957), 65.
77 Until 1848 Dutch law in the East Indies forbade marriages between Christians and non-Christians. See Stoler, *Carnal Knowledge*, 101; and Ann Laura Stoler, 'Making empire respectable: The politics of race and sexual morality in 20th-century colonial cultures', *American Ethnologist* 16:4 (November 1989): 637–9.
78 Lahiri, *Indians in Britain*, 116.
79 PRO PRO 30/77/19, 'Black Book', 'Report of the Joint Committee of the Four Inns of Court', 15 February 1893, enclosed in council minutes, 21 February 1893.
80 PRO PRO 30/77/20, 'Black Book', S. A. Kapadia to Treasurer, Honourable Society of the Inner Temple, 13 January 1902, in report of the Joint Committee on the Duties, Interests and Discipline of the Bar, 16 July 1903, 1–2, fos. 237–8.
81 'Indians in England', fo. 827.
82 Note by Mr. Hamilton.
83 'Superintendence of Indian students in England', *JNIA*, 177 (September 1885): 405.
84 Besides Manning and Bhownagree these members were Thomas H. Thornton, former member of the Legislative Council of India; Major-General R. M. MacDonald, former director of public instruction, Madras; C. R. Lindsay, former judge of the Chief Court of Judicature, Punjab; and Lieutenant-General Charles Pollard, former secretary for the Government of Punjab. Also on the committee was M. Brandreth, whose biographical details remain unidentified.
85 'Indians in England', fo. 763.
86 IOR L/PJ/6/363 No. 1875a, Secret Department minute, W. L.-W. [William Lee-Warner], 'The position of young Indians sent to England for education', 29 March 1898.
87 *CIS*, 21.
88 Note by Mr Hamilton.
89 Reply from Sir Henry Cotton to Sir Curzon Wyllie, 2 April 1903, enclosed in 'Indian Hostel in London'.
90 IOR L/PJ/6/515 No. 1381, Public No. 41, Curzon *et al.* to Hamilton, 6 July 1899.
91 *CIS*, 9.
92 *Ibid.*, 40.
93 IOR L/PJ/6/625 No. 193, W. H. C. Wyllie to Sir Charles Lyall, 19 January 1903.
94 Nehru, *Toward Freedom*, 35.
95 *CIS*, 58–9.
96 Visram, *Asians in Britain*, 161.
97 PRO PRO 30/77/21, 'Black Book', Ralph Neville, resolution in Report of the Joint Committee on the Duties, Interests and Discipline of the Bar, 17 June 1913, 2.
98 Report of the Joint Committee, fo. 335.
99 *CIS*, 31.
100 Lahiri, *Indians in Britain*, 194.

CHAPTER NINE

Conclusion: a hierarchical empire

At the Imperial Conference of 1911, Secretary of State for India Lord Crewe addressed the prime ministers of the white-settler dominions gathered in London. His concern was legislation in their countries that either prevented Indians from entering their territories, discriminated against them while they were there, or both. He reminded these prime ministers that it was 'difficult for statesmen who have seen Indians represented only by manual labourers and petty traders' to appreciate the complexity, antiquity, and 'importance to the Empire as a whole' of India. 'If the question were not so grave,' he declared 'it would be seen to be ludicrous that regulations framed with an eye to coolies would affect ruling princes who are in subordinate alliance with His Majesty, and have placed their troops at his disposal, members of the Privy Council of the Empire, or gentlemen who have the honour to be His Majesty's own Aides-de-Camp.'[1]

Crewe was commenting on a fundamental difference in the ways that administrators in Britain and those in the dominions perceived their shared hierarchical empire. The Secretary of State's perspective reflected the discourses of social hierarchy that British institutions applied to Indians in the United Kingdom. He began with an implicit contrast between the experience of officials in Britain and those in the dominions. Whereas the latter tended to encounter Indians only from the lowest social ranks, the former did so from a wide variety of backgrounds. He might have added that British society was itself more widely stratified than were those of the dominions. The confluence of these two realities, the stratification of society generally in Britain and among Indians visiting and residing there, governed the Indian encounter with institutions in the United Kingdom. The result was the interpretation of India's social ranks into British equivalents, a process in which both British administrators and Indian visitors and residents participated. Equally important, this process occurred within a legal framework that treated most Indians as subjects of the British monarch, whose relationship to him or her was defined largely in terms of social rank.

The process of interpreting such ranks from their Indian to British equivalents drew on a variety of apparent hierarchical differences among Indians. An obvious one was wealth. British institutions responded to Indians with financial means more favourably than to those without. The reasons for this bias are equally obvious, for the administrators of Britain's institutions valued what wealth could buy: education, demeanour, financial generosity, and financial security. The education that Britain's elite valued most – that of the public school – was expensive. Demeanour arose from education, but also from the ability to afford good clothing and proper hygiene. Similarly, financial generosity, which was a marker of gentlemanly status, required money. Most Indian members of the NIA were men and women of financial means, often through their families, and could thus afford to participate in polite society. Indeed, it was those students who exhausted their financial resources who were most likely to descend the ladder of social rank by living in more modest housing and participating less in elite social events than was necessary for them to maintain the aura of respectability. It was logical, therefore, that many Indians, in filling out their certificates of identity, stated their own, or their father's, annual income, even though these forms rarely requested such information.

Nevertheless, actual wealth was not the sole measure of an Indian's social standing in Britain. For instance, British institutions valued Indians from rural over urban areas. Princes, *zamindars*, and even dispossessed Punjabi smallholders all received consideration as members of ranks equivalent to Britain's traditional rural aristocracy, gentry, and yeomanry. This consideration did not arise exclusively, or even mainly, from an attempt to emphasise the supposedly inferior static nature of India's society in contrast to the superior adaptable nature of Britain's. Rather it extended from the tendency of Britain's elite to romanticise its own rural culture and interpret what it perceived to be India's into these British equivalents. The pages of the *JNIA* and its successors attest to this romantic and nostalgic view of both British and Indian societies, a view that both British and Indian intellectuals expressed. In practice this view translated into the British institutional reception of what officials considered to be the Indian equivalent of its aristocracy and gentry, the groups that the terms 'gentlemen' and 'ladies' had originally defined.

Another important measure of social rank was education, particularly one that emphasised the social skills valued by Britain's elite. For this reason, Indians with public school backgrounds were more likely to gain acceptance in university society than were students who embarked on a course of study with no such background. Furthermore, the British public school emphasis on sport carried over into the university setting to plague any Indian focused solely on academic study. Even Indians temporarily without money were more likely to receive India Office aid because of their education and resulting demeanour. Inasmuch as the approved educational background was steeped in a British cultural context, then British officials indulged in a form of cultural chauvinism that privileged British over Indian culture. However, because class was the register of this discourse, skin colour was not an absolute barrier to Indians seeking acceptance in British polite society.

Since education often defined one's occupation, the latter also played an important role in the process of interpreting rank. If the landowning occupations ranked highly among British institutions, the educated professions were not far behind, particularly those that usually required a public school education. Institutions generally held those employed in medicine, law, education, and the civil service in high regard, so long as they came to these professions with the proper gentlemanly credentials and background. The perception that an Indian pursued a 'respectable' or even intellectual calling often led to special consideration from India Office administrators, as in the cases of Ramabai and Panwalker. Such consideration extended to Hindu and Islamic religious teachers, whom India Office administrators respected, not so much for their religious beliefs as for their education and, in the case of Hindus, caste. Even technical students and businessmen could acquire gentlemanly status in the context of other increasingly respectable professions. Perhaps the best example of this rule was Wagle, whom managers and workers alike regarded as a gentleman in the context of his effort to acquire a technical education.

Education was an important method of determining the social rank of Indians because it was for Britons as well. But it was even more important in the context of Indians visiting Britain, because it was so central to British elite beliefs in the Empire's *raison d'être*. For it was through the education of India's elite that the administrators of British institutions hoped to spread their culture and cement their dominance over India. Education of the elite made the whole imperial enterprise, which might otherwise have appeared a tawdry exercise in economic exploitation, seem morally noble. An educated, loyal Indian was therefore a sign of this mission's success.

British elitist attitudes toward education help to explain much of the institutional antipathy toward the 'babu class' of Indian students who came to England seeking positions in the ICS. This antipathy grew out of what was originally the purely British context of the prejudice of public school alumni against British civil service candidates who were not. Indeed, the government reformed the ICS in 1853 in order to favour public school alumni. Subsequent tinkering with examination eligibility age limits were attempts primarily to exclude from the service non-public school alumni, whether British or Indian. In this context institutional contempt for urban middle-class Indian candidates was as much an issue of class prejudice as it was of race, albeit evidence of how the former could become the latter. The British Government's miscalculation that competitive exams would restrict the ICS to Britain's public-school educated elite extended to Indian society as well, because it was the urban professional and business classes of India, rather than the aristocracy and *zamindars*, who most sought posts in the service. Overt and official racial discrimination in India rankled administrators of institutions committed to the civilising mission. Thus the Gilchrist trustees terminated their award for Indians studying at the Universities of London and Edinburgh, and the India Office continued uneasily to pursue the contradictory policies of defending discriminatory hiring for the ICS while funding a select few Indian students to study in Britain, ostensibly in order to join the ICS.

So far, all of these methods of measuring rank may appear to have been straightforward, inasmuch as they were methods used by Britain's elite to measure social rank for Britons and justify their own society's inequities. But India also had another system of social ranking – caste – which recent scholarship has claimed to have appeared utterly alien to Britain's elite. Yet the actual institutional treatment of Indians in Britain suggests that British officials considered castes to be analogous to Britain's social ranks. Whether or not they believed that these castes were immutable and occupationally defined – and there is considerable evidence that they did not – they treated them as if they were; translated them into British equivalents; and ranked them accordingly. Central to this process were the efforts of Indians themselves, in keeping with practice dating in India from at least the seventeenth century, to highlight their caste pedigree, either through simple reference to their lineage, or, as was particularly the case with *brahmans*, through the observance of behavioural restrictions that set them off from the rest of the population. Thus, even the most impoverished and socially unconnected *brahmans* could force British authorities to treat them exceptionally by refusing to do certain types of work or eat certain forms of food.

British authorities could have remained unmoved in the face of such behaviour, and simply ostracised the Indians in question or allowed them to starve. After all, many of these same administrators (particularly in the India Office) were capable of such indifference regarding the plight of millions in India stricken by famines at the time.[2] In Britain, and in the immediate presence of Indians, however, British administrators did not behave this way. Rather they recognised the Indian elite discourse of caste and treated those who claimed *kshaitrya* or *brahman* lineage as deserving special treatment. Usually this recognition took the form of acceptance into polite society, such as the reception that the NIA (sometimes in concert with the India Office) provided to Indian 'gentlemen' and 'ladies' visiting or studying in the United Kingdom. Less frequently the translation of upper-caste to gentlemanly status occurred through emergency assistance in time of need, and without the normal requirement of manual labour. Indeed the frequent references to caste in the *JNIA* and its successors is evidence of an elite subculture of Indians in Britain who, although usually professing to abhor caste, nevertheless often referred to their own and one another's upper-caste backgrounds as a means of establishing their membership in British polite society.

The behaviour of British institutions toward Indian women in the United Kingdom was somewhat more problematic than was their behaviour toward men, because Britain's elite disapproved of the very behaviour that was often considered the mark of elite womanhood in India. The practice of purdah prevented Indian women from participating in social events that their British counterparts normally attended. Moreover, the purported tendency of Indian men to neglect the importance of education among women eroded their gentlemanly status in British eyes. Indians in Britain, both male and female, reacted to such criticisms in two ways. One was for women to abandon purdah altogether and take part in British social events. Many Indian men encouraged their wives to do so. The adoption of Western dress often accompanied such decisions, but not always. Some Indian women, such as Ramabai and Sorabji had never practised purdah anyway. The other response was to argue that purdah was an acceptable marker of respectability in Indian society and should be treated as such in Britain. Some members of Britain's elite accepted this argument, as did some Indian women visiting Britain. The 'Misanthrope' correspondence in the *JNIA* is testament to the importance of feminine honour, whether defined in Indian or British terms, in the maintenance of the gentlemanly status of Indian and British men. Whichever way they constructed it culturally, both Britain's elite and India's elite in Britain accepted the central role in civilised society of the 'lady' as the guardian of domestic purity.

The use of purdah in the translation of rank is just one among many examples of the role that accommodation of cultural difference played in the Indian encounter with institutions in the United Kingdom. In the light of recent scholarship this accommodation raises serious questions of motive. Was the tolerance of the Sikh turban at Oxford University and Muslim abstention from alcohol and prayers at the Inns of Court evidence of institutional acceptance of cultural diversity? Or were these policies evidence instead of a desire to mark Indian visitors as cultural curiosities and highlight the differences that set them apart from the supposedly civilised rulers of the Empire? The answer to these questions is complex. The projection of imperial authority was an important motive behind the royal family's encouragement of the wearing of indigenous clothing and the holding of indigenous titles. To interpret all institutional accommodations of Indian cultural difference in terms of imperial power is, however, particularly problematic when Indians clearly approved of or actively sought it. Religious beliefs and practice defined many of the cultural restrictions that Indians refused to break, whether in matters of diet, dress, or even names. It was in these areas that British institutions, perhaps conscious of the cultural arrogance that contributed toward the Indian Rebellion, most readily accommodated Indian cultural difference. In doing so they recognised differences between their culture and India's, but did not regard them as necessarily diminishing the social ranks of their observers when translated into British equivalents. The accommodation of cultural differences highlighted the institutional tolerance of religious differences, for it was over religious issues that Indians usually sought such accommodations and British institutions made them. Because such differences arose from religious beliefs and practice, British institutions responded to them in ways that differed dramatically according to their goals. Since the major goal of the India Office was to administer and preserve British rule, its personnel opposed behaviour toward Indians that might excite opposition to Britain's occupation. Although most India Office administrators were at least nominal Christians, they were reluctant to appear to discriminate in favour of Indians on the basis of their Christianity. Indeed so anxious were they to avoid this charge that in some cases, such as Ramabai's, they may have discriminated against Indian Christians at an official level partly because they were Christian.

On the other hand, since Christian missions sought to convert Hindus, Muslims, and Sikhs away from their religions and to Christianity, they were obviously less likely to respect Indian practices than were more secular institutions. Salter's disdain for the diet and music of the Indians he encountered in London is a good example of this tendency. Yet even Salter regarded much of the moral depravity that he found in Indians to be a result of contamination from England's urban poor, so it is difficult to tell how much of his disapproval was based on race or class. Indeed a rough parallel across social strata is evident when comparing the behaviour of some missionaries toward lower-class Indians in Britain and that of some social improving organisations toward middle-class Indians. The primary goals of both groups was the improvement of the Indian people, as opposed to the exploitation of them and their country's resources. Both missionaries and social improvers, therefore, conflicted occasionally with British groups and institutions committed to using the Empire for personal enrichment. For British missionaries, these institutions were the private shipping companies that exploited lascars. For social improvers it was private businesses and government agencies that discriminated against educated Indians.

In fact, cultural accommodation fitted well within British institutional attitudes toward rank – for although British institutions recognised the equivalence of Indian and British ranks, they did not believe that such recognition made Indians interchangeable with their British counterparts. Here again institutional thinking in this regard was complex. On the one hand, Indians could rise very high in British society, so long as they had the necessary social background and acted in ways that were recognised as markers of gentlemanly or ladylike behaviour: Ranjitsinjhi's sporting skills overcame racist opposition to his membership of England's cricket team and even enhanced his already high status in India; Nehru's public school experience allowed him to fit into British university life more easily than many of his Indian colleagues did. On the other hand, British officials joined the rest of society as a whole in frowning on interethnic marriage, although Parliament passed no law against it. Even Duleep Singh, as a Christian and the highest born Indian in the United Kingdom, could not find a bride among Britain's elite. Lower down the social ladder, male Indian students who married British women often incurred the wrath of their own parents and those of their British wives.

This mutual taboo against exogamy, however, did not prevent Indians from taking part in many other aspects of British society. Nor did it lessen the tendencies of British institutions to translate Indian social ranks into British equivalents. British poor law guardians and India Office administrators may not have felt as much affinity to upper-caste Hindus and Punjabi plaintiffs as they did to British gentlemen and yeomen, but they helped these Indians to avoid manual labour, a fate that they considered quite appropriate for Britain's labouring classes. British officials behaved this way because they acknowledged their own position in a multi-ethnic, socially stratified empire, in which each culture had its own hierarchy of roughly analogous social ranks. Most of them believed that it was their mission, working through its elite, to lift India's society up to the superior level that they thought Britain's occupied. This belief highlighted rather than lessened their sense of gradations of rank among Indians they encountered in the United Kingdom.

Class hierarchy was able to play such an important role in the Indian encounter with institutions in the United Kingdom, because these institutions still regarded loyalty in pre-nationalist terms. Since inhabitants of the British Isles were officially subjects of the monarch rather than citizens of the British nation, it was possible for British institutions to describe and treat Indians as British subjects too. Since the sense of Britishness among Britain's elite was based on class as much as ethnicity, they could welcome Indians into their society when the latter met their standards for membership, which nonetheless sprang from British cultural norms. Queen Victoria's accession proclamation of 1858 was more than mere ceremonial window dressing. Its statements of religious toleration and racial equality set the standard against which Indians, and many British reformers, held institutions in the United Kingdom until the First World War. If all Indians were British subjects, then British institutions should treat them on a par with ethnic Britons. Ultimately, this ideal became one of the arguments that the Indian National Congress used against British rule in India. Indians in Britain were able to use the absence of formal discriminatory laws against them to exercise political rights that their British counterparts held – but only when they were in Britain. The political geography of the British Empire resembled pre-Reform Act England, in which different boroughs had vastly different franchises and privileges. That system was a holdover from the Middle Ages and fitted well the concept of dynastic allegiance that was still the language of British law. Indians, therefore, had vastly different rights and privileges depending on where they lived in the Empire. In Britain these rights were limited formally, as they were for Britons, by wealth and gender. Informally they were also limited by the willingness of British institutions, and polite society generally, to recognise individual Indians' gentlemanly status.

If the effort to define subjecthood allowed British authorities to attempt, rather unsuccessfully, to monitor the movement of Indians in and out of the United Kingdom, it also empowered Indians to establish their social rank upon arrival. The India Office encouraged Indians to use certificates of identity partly in order to monitor their movements and partly to ensure that they would receive a favourable impression of the centre of imperial power. But as with so many efforts to categorise, this one became the opportunity for Indians to assert, or even change, their social rank as they crossed geographic space. The result sometimes led to disputes when British officials suspected that these credentials exaggerated the holder's rank. For instance, the 1893 trial of Punjabi oculists focused on whether or not they were real physicians, and Indian students at Cambridge defended themselves somewhat awkwardly against their own lack of recognisable public school credentials. When such accusations arose, class, rather than race, was the acceptable criterion for discrimination. Indeed, Britain's elite regarded the racism of the British lower and middle classes as a reason why they were unfit to run the Empire, and India Office administrators, who were certainly not free from racial prejudice concerning ICS appointments, bemoaned the bigotry of industrial workers toward Indian technical students. It is, of course, commonplace today for those who use race as a judgmental category to deny it and to decry it in others, but it is worth noting that even in the more overtly racist environment of Victorian and Edwardian Britain, the same practice could apply.

Significantly, charges of class prejudice were rare. Few British officials regarded discrimination according to social rank as wrong. British officials developed and refined rules of eligibility for sitting the ICS exams specifically and openly in order to restrict the service to the public-school elite, but denied that they intended to discriminate by race. They also included questions of parentage and caste in certificates of identity that they encouraged Indians to obtain – questions that they then used to rank Indians in British society.

For Indians, the process of translating rank from their society to Britain's presented both risks and opportunities. On the one hand students used their sojourns in Britain to elevate themselves socially and economically in India. Ranjitsinjhi is probably the most extreme example, since he used his popularity in England to ascend the throne of a princely state. More common were the examples of Indian students who gained an edge over their competition back home with the social cachet that a British education provided. In order to gain access to British universities and the Inns of Court, these students knew that they should highlight their family's social status. Thus the numerous claims on certificates of identity and university application forms of prospective students' upper-caste and landowning status. The cult of the village, which was a dominant feature of British institutional values in both India and the United Kingdom, benefited students who claimed a genteel, and often rural, parentage. Combined with the aura surrounding India's *kshaitrya* and *brahman* castes, the maintenance of which British authorities assisted, the process of translation from *zamindars* to gentlemen was a fairly easy one.

On the other hand, the sojourn in Britain could become a nightmarish experience for Indians who failed to establish genteel status. Many students fell into destitution only to receive the disdain of India Office administrators, because they did not fit the preconceived profile that these officials had of the public-school educated member of the governing class. Moreover the process of translating ranks sometimes worked against Indian visitors to the United Kingdom. A *hakim* did not command the respect in Britain that he did in India, partly because the increasingly influential British medical profession sought a monopoly over the marketing of its skills. Failure to receive such social recognition often resulted in financial ruin, as it did for the Punjabi oculists. For destitute students and practitioners such as these, the stay in Britain became a degrading experience that actually harmed their social standing.

The potential hazards to Indians of the social mobility available through travel to the United Kingdom underscore British institutions' easy acceptance of social inequity and the degradation that often accompanied it. The fact that institutions did not practise extensive social levelling in their encounter with Indians does not exonerate British imperialism from responsibility for the harm it caused beyond Britain's shores or within them. Nor does it mean that racial bigotry was not an important part of the experience of Indians in Britain. The rhetoric and actions of the institutions that Indians most frequently encountered in the United Kingdom were not consistent with the behaviour of a wide swath of British society which treated Indians increasingly with suspicion and hostility. Nor were they consistent within governing institutions which encouraged India's elite to study in Britain while preventing it from participating fully in the ICS, the career that often brought these students to Britain's shores in the first place. Indeed, because primary motives of involvement with Indians differed among institutions, individuals working for two of these organisations at the same time sometimes experienced a tension between their conflicting goals.

Moreover, the class consciousness that so pervaded Victorian and Edwardian Britain perpetuated profound social inequities, many of which were based on the environment into which a person was born. The hierarchy of rank was hardly fairer than that of race. It maintained the power of Britain's elite and those whom its members perceived to be their counterparts in India. Just as Britons in the rest of the Empire often defined their ethnic identity in contrast to 'other' supposedly lesser ethnic groups, so did polite society in the metropole define much of its identity in contrast to 'other' supposedly lesser social ranks that it encountered. In a society where an upper-middle-class Anglo-Indian could describe London's East End as 'a very long way off from civilised London', there was little need to construct an 'orient' in order to secure the dominance of Britain's ruling elite. The register of class provided a sufficient hegemonic discourse. In this context, the socially improving philosophies of British universities, the NIA, the Gilchrist Trust, and, to a lesser extent, the India Office hardly meet the standards of modern democratic societies – for they all assumed the superiority of the gentlemanly classes, whether British or Indian, over the rest of their societies, and behaved as if only through this elite could either society improve. Add to this elitism the cultural chauvinism that assumed the superiority of British over Indian culture, and such organisations appear doubly condescending. Indeed, as the history of the Gilchrist Award demonstrates, such class elitism, in the context of the unequal economic and political power relationship between Britain and India, could actually thwart the best intentions of British social improvers toward Indians and indirectly reinforce racial discrimination. When institutions assisted lower-class Indians in Britain (rather than middle- or upper-class Indians lacking money), it was clearly a matter of charity rather than any sense of the recipients' entitlement to assistance. Private donations to lower-class Indians, therefore, reinforced, rather than undermined, the social hierarchy, keeping Britain's elite and India's secure in their superiority over the lower orders of both lands.

The coexistence of racial and social hierarchies, however, did undermine the position of Britain's elite with regard to India's. It is no accident that many of the leaders of India's national movement, and of post-independence India and Pakistan, received education in Britain. The institutional rhetoric of British subjecthood and class hierarchy jarred with the actual experiences of many Indians in Britain, and more importantly, with the obvious racial discrimination of British administrators in India. The negative effect of imperial hypocrisy might not have been so damaging to British interests if British officials had merely been using the rhetoric of class hierarchy and common British subjecthood as a smokescreen to cover conscious efforts to exploit the Indian people whatever their social rank. In this case they would have been more careful not to point out the hypocrisy to one another, either privately or publicly. But in Britain at least, the behaviour and confidential correspondence of officials indicate that their respect for Indians whom they designated 'gentlemen' or 'ladies' was no simple cover for racial discrimination. Rather it arose out these officials' daily participation in a society profoundly stratified by social rank. However condescending were the ideas of Victorian and Edwardian social improvers, they were, for the most part, sincerely condescending. This sincerity led reforming institutions, which normally cooperated with governing ones, occasionally to clash with them and highlight the inconsistencies and hypocrisy of British rule in India. The fact that Britain's institutions were far from monolithic and pursued different goals through the Empire, meant that even imperialists might embarrass the government through criticism. The presence of Indians in

Britain, and their encounters with these institutions, therefore, served as a catalyst for a debate about the Empire which ranged from the confidential correspondence of the India Office to the public positions of the NIA's members and journal readers. The resulting ambivalence revealed a society that would not long remain a centre of imperial power.

Notes

1 Cd. 5745 (1911) 54:501, *Imperial Conference, 1911 – Papers Laid Before the Conference*, 396.

2 The 1901 Famine Commission actually described British assistance to starving Indians as 'excessive'. See Davis, *Late Victorian Holocausts*, 175.

Bibliography

Primary sources

Unpublished papers

Archive of the Institute for Advanced Legal Studies, London:
Council of Legal Education files

Birmingham University Library, Special Collections, Birmingham:
Church Missionary Society Archive

Bodleian Library, Oxford:
Oxford University Archives, Admission Records

British Library, London – India Office Records:
Government of India: Crown Representative: Political Department Indian States Records
India Office: Public and Judicial Department Records
India Office: Political and Secret Department Records

British Library, London – Private Collections:
Kilbracken, Arthur Godley, 1st Baron Collection
Curzon, George Nathaniel, Marquess Collection

London City Mission:
Minutes of Committee Meetings
Minutes of Disciplinary Committee

London Metropolitan Archives:
Central Criminal Court, Minutes of Evidence (microfilm)

National Archives of the United Kingdom, Kew:
1881 British Census and National Index: England, Scotland, Wales, Channel Islands, Isle of Man, and Royal Navy, CD-ROM set. Salt Lake City: Church of Jesus Christ of Latter Day Saints, 1999
1901 Census (online) www.1901census.nationalarchives.gov.uk/
Board of Trade files
Home Office files
Lincoln's Inn 'Black Book' (microfilm)

St John's College Archives, Cambridge:
Admission Records
Delhi Mission Papers

University College Library Special Collections, London:
Gilchrist Educational Trust Collection

Journals and newspapers
Evangelical Magazine
Indian Magazine
Indian Magazine and Review
Journal of the National Indian Association
London City Mission Magazine
St James Gazette
The Standard
The Times

Official and institutional publications

Association for the Advancement of Scientific and Industrial Education of Indians. *Report of the Association for the Advancement of Scientific and Industrial Education of Indians*, 1908.

Baines, J. A. *Census Commissioner For India: Report for 1891*. London: HMSO, 1893.

Chamier, F. E. A. *Report of the Regular Settlement of the Bara Banki District*. Allahabad: North-Western Provinces and Oudh Government Press, 1879.

Committee of the National Indian Association, in Conjunction with the Advisory Committee, India Office. *Handbook of Information for Indian Students Relating to University Etc. Professional Studies, Etc., in the United Kingdom*. London: J. S. Phillips, 1909.

Committee of the National Indian Association. *Handbook of Information Relating to University Etc. Professional Studies, Etc., for Indian Students in the United Kingdom*, 7th edn. Westminster: Archibald Constable and Company, 1893.

Committee on Distressed Colonial and Indian Subjects, Cd. 5133. 1910.

Gilchrist Educational Trust. *The Gilchrist Educational Trust: Pioneering Work in Education, 1865–1930*. Cambridge: Cambridge University Press, 1930.

Imperial Conference, 1911 – Papers Laid Before the Conference, Cd. 5745. 1911.

Keith, A. Barriedale (ed.). *Speeches and Documents on Indian Policy, 1750–1921*. Oxford: Oxford University Press, 1922.

Levi, Leone. *Wages and Earnings of the Working Classes: Report to Sir Arthur Bass, M.P.* London: J. Murray, 1885.

Macaulay, Thomas Babington Macaulay, Baron. 'Minute Recorded in the General Department', 2 February 1835, in Lynn Zastoupil and Martin Moir (eds), *The Great Indian Education Debate: Documents Relating to the Orientalist-Anglicist Controversy, 1781–1843*. London: Curzon Press, 1999.

Report and Minutes of the Committee Appointed by the Secretary of State for India to Inquire into the Position of Indian Students in the United Kingdom. London: Eyre and Spottiswoode, 1907.

Risley, Herbert Hope. *Census of India*, Vol. 1, *Ethnographic Appendices: Being the Data Upon Which the Caste Chapter of the Report is Based*. Calcutta: Office of the Superintendent of Government Printing, India, 1903.

Strangers' Home for the Natives of India, Arabia, Africa, China, Straits of Malacca, the Mosambique, and the Islands of the South Pacific, *Annual Report for the Year 1886*. N.p., 1887.

—— *Annual Report for 1900*. London: Edwin Sears and Co., 1901.

—— *Fortieth Annual Report*. N.p., n.d.

United Kingdom, House of Commons. *Parliamentary Debates*, 4th series.

Weyland, John Matthias. *Our Veterans: Life-Stories of the London City Mission*. London: S. W. Partridge and Co., 1881(?).

Books, pamphlets and articles

Aeschylus. *Agamemnon*, trans Herbert Weir Smyth. Loeb Edition, 1926. Reprint: Cambridge, MA: Harvard University Press, 1999.

Bonarjee, N. B. *Under Two Masters*. Oxford: Oxford University Press, 1970.

Browning, Oscar. *Impressions of Indian Travel*. London: Hodder and Stoughton, 1903.

Burne, Owen Tudor. *Memories*. London: Edward Arnold, 1907.

Fitzpatrick, Sir Dennis. *Non-Christian Marriage*. N.p, n.d. Reproduced in the Henry Morse Collection, Pamphlets on Political Science and Jurisprudence.

Gandhi, Mohandas K. *An Autobiography: The Story of My Experiments with Truth*, trans. Mahadev Desai. Boston: Beacon Press, 1957.

Hodgson, Pratt. *University Education in England for Natives of India: Considered with a View to Qualify Them for the Learned Professions or the Public Service; and to Create a Class Who Shall Mediate Between the Indian People and Their English Rulers*. London: James Ridgway, 1860.

Hutchinson, H. G. (ed.). *Private Diaries of the Rt. Hon. Sir Algernon West, G. C. B.* London: John Murray, 1922.

Kilbracken, Arthur Godley, First Baron. *Reminiscences of Lord Kilbracken*. London: Macmillan, 1931.

Lyall, Alfred C. *Asiatic Studies: Religious and Social*. London: John Murray, 1907.

Lyall, Charles James. *Translations of Ancient Arabian Poetry: Chiefly Præ-Islamic*. N.d.; Reprint. New York: Columbia University Press, 1930.

Maine, Henry Sumner. *Village-Communities in the East and West: Six Lectures Delivered at Oxford to Which Are Added Other Lectures Addresses and Essays*. New York: Henry Holt and Company, 1880.

Nehru, Jawaharlal. *Toward Freedom: The Autobiography of Jawaharlal Nehru*. New York: John Day Company, 1942.

Oxford and Asquith, Earl of. *Memories and Reflections, 1852–1927*. London: Cassell and Co., 1928.

Pandian, T. B. *England to an Indian Eye: or English Pictures from an Indian Camera*. London: Elliot Stock, 1897.

Patel, J. M. Framjee. *Stray Thoughts on Cricket*. Bombay: Times Press, 1905.

Ramabai, Pandita. *The Letters and Correspondence of Pandita Ramabai*, ed. A. B. Shah. Bombay: Maharashtra State Board of Literature and Culture, 1977.

—— *The High-Caste Hindu Woman*, 2nd edn. Philadelphia: Jason B. Rogers Printing Co., 1888.

Risley, Herbert Hope. *The People of India*. 2nd edn 1915; reprint, Delhi: Oriental Books Reprint Corporation, 1969.

Salter, Joseph. *The Asiatic in England: Sketches of Sixteen Years Work Among Orientals*. London: Seeley, Jackson, and Halliday, 1873.

—— *The East in the West, or Work Among the Asiatics and Africans in London*. London: S. W. Partridge and Company, 1895.

Sen, Keshub Chunder. *Keshub Chunder Sen in England: Diaries, Sermons, Addresses, and Epistles*, ed. Prem Sundar Basu, 4th Indian edn. Calcutta: Writers Workshop, 1980.

Strachey, John. *India*. London: Kegan Paul, Trench, Trübner and Co., 1894.

Trevelyan, G. O. *The Competition Wallah*. London: Macmillan, 1866.

Warren, Max. *To Apply the Gospel: Selections from the Writings of Henry Venn*. Grand Rapids, MI: William B. Eerdmans, 1971.

Secondary sources

Adas, Michael. *Machines as the Measure of Men: Science, Technology, and Ideologies of Western Dominance*. Ithaca: Cornell University Press, 1989.

Alexander, Michael and Anand, Sushila. *Queen Victoria's Maharajah: Duleep Singh, 1938–93*. New York: Taplinger, 1980.

Ali, Imran. *The Punjab Under Imperialism, 1885–1947*. Princeton: Princeton University Press, 1988.

Anderson, Benedict. *Imagined Communities: Reflections on the Origins and Spread of Nationalism*, 2nd edn. New York: Verso, 1991.

Arnesen, Eric. 'Whiteness and the historians' imagination',

International Labor and Working-Class History, 60 (Fall 2001), 3–32.

Arnold, David. *Colonizing the Body: State Medicine and Epidemic Disease in Nineteenth-Century India*. Berkeley and Los Angeles: University of California Press, 1993.

—— (ed.). *Imperial Medicine and Indigenous Societies*. Manchester: Manchester University Press, 1988.

—— *Science, Technology and Medicine in Colonial India*. In *The New Cambridge History of India*, Series 3, Vol. 5. Cambridge: Cambridge University Press, 2000.

Arnstein, Walter L. 'The myth of the triumphant Victorian middle class', *Historian*, 37:2 (1975): 205–21.

Bartrip, Peter. *Themselves Writ Large: The British Medical Association, 1832–1966*. London: BMJ Publishing Group, 1996.

Bayly, Susan. *Caste, Society and Politics in India from the Eighteenth Century to the Modern Age*. Cambridge: Cambridge University Press, 1999.

Beckerlegge, G. 'Professor Friedrich Max Müller and the missionary cause', in *Religion in Victorian Britain*, Vol. 5, *Culture and Empire*. Manchester: Manchester University Press, 1997.

—— 'Followers of "Mohammed, Kalee and Dada Nanuk": The presence of Islam and South Asian religions in Victorian Britain', in *Religion in Victorian Britain*, Vol. 5, *Culture and Empire*. Manchester: Manchester University Press, 1997.

Best, Geoffrey. *Mid-Victorian Britain, 1851–1875*. London: Weidenfeld and Nicolson, 1971.

Bhattarcharya, Neeladri. 'Lenders and debtors: Punjab countryside, 1880–1940', in *Credit, Markets and the Agrarian Economy of Colonial India*. Delhi: Oxford University Press, 1994.

Bonnett, Alastair. 'How the British working class became white: The symbolic (re)formation of racialized capitalism', *Journal of Historical Sociology*, 11:3 (September 1998): 316–40.

Brawley, Sean. *The White Peril: Foreign Relations and Asian Immigration to Australasia and North America, 1919–78*. Sydney: UNSW Press, 1995.

Briggs, Asa. *The Age of Improvement, 1783–1867*. London: Longmans, Green, 1959.

Brown, Judith. *Modern India: The Origins of an Asian Democracy*. Oxford: Oxford University Press, 1985.

Buchighnani, Norman and Indra, Doreen M. *Continuous Journey: A Social History of South Asians in Canada* . Toronto: McClelland and Stewart, 1988.

Burton, Antoinette. *At the Heart of the Empire: Indians and the Colonial Encounter in Late-Victorian Britain*. Berkeley and Los

Angeles: University of California Press, 1998.
—— *Burdens of History: British Feminists, Indian Women, and Imperial Culture, 1865–1915*. Chapel Hill: University of North Carolina Press, 1994.
—— 'Institutionalizing imperial reform: *The Indian Magazine* and late-Victorian colonial politics', in David Finkelstein and Douglas M. Peers (eds), *Negotiating India in the Nineteenth-Century Media*. Basingstoke, UK: Macmillan Press, 2000.
Cannadine, David. *Ornamentalism: How the British Saw Their Empire*. Oxford: Oxford University Press, 2001.
—— *The Rise and Fall of Class in Britain*. New York: Columbia University Press, 1999.
Cartwright, Frederick F. *The Development of Modern Surgery*. New York: Thomas Y. Crowell, 1967.
Chakravarti, Uma. *Rewriting History: The Life and Times of Pandita Ramabai*. New Delhi: Kali for Women, 1998.
Chandrasekhar, S. *From India to Canada: A Brief History of Immigration; Problems of Discrimination, Admission and Assimilation*. La Jolla, CA: Population Review, 1986.
Cohn, Bernard S. 'Representing authority in Victorian India', in Eric Hobsbawm and Terence Ranger (eds), *The Invention of Tradition*. Cambridge: Cambridge University Press, 1983.
—— 'The census, social structure and objectification in South Asia', in *An Anthropologist Among the Historians and Other Essays*. Delhi: Oxford University Press, 1987.
Colley, Linda. 'Britishness and otherness: An argument', *Journal of British Studies*, 31:4 (1992): 309–29.
Compton, J. M. 'Indians and the Indian Civil Service, 1853–1879: A study in national agitation and imperial embarrassment', *Journal of the Royal Asiatic Society of Great Britain and Ireland*, 3/4 (1967): 99–113.
—— 'Open competition and the Indian Civil Service, 1854–1876', *English Historical Review*, 83:327 (April 1968): 264–84.
Cox, Jeffrey. *Imperial Fault Lines: Christianity and Colonial Power in India, 1818–1940*. Stanford: Stanford University Press, 2002.
—— 'Religion and imperial power in nineteenth-century Britain', in Richard Helmstadter (ed.), *Freedom and Religion in the Nineteenth Century*. Stanford: Stanford University Press, 1997.
—— *The English Churches in a Secular Society: Lambeth, 1870–1930*. Oxford: Oxford University Press, 1982.
—— 'The missionary movement', in D. G. Paz (ed.), *Nineteenth-Century English Religious Traditions: Retrospect and Prospect*. Westport, CT: Greenwood Press, 1995.

Crossick, Geoffrey. 'From gentlemen to residuum: Languages of social description in Victorian Britain', in Penelope J. Corfield (ed.), *Language, History and Class*. Oxford: Basil Blackwell, 1991.

Crow, Duncan. *The Victorian Woman*. London: Allen and Unwin, 1971.

Crowther, M. A. *The Workhouse System, 1834–1929: The History of an English Social Institution*. Athens, GA: University of Georgia Press, 1982.

D'Cruze, Shani. 'Women and the family', in June Purvis (ed.), *Women's History: Britain, 1850–1945*. New York: St Martin's Press, 1995.

Davis, Mike. *Late Victorian Holocausts: El Niño Famines and the Making of the Third World*. London: Verso, 2001.

Deslandes, Paul R. '"The foreign element": Newcomers and the rhetoric of race, nation, and empire in "Oxbridge" undergraduate culture, 1850–1920', *Journal of British Studies*, 37 (1998): 54–90.

—— *Oxbridge Men: British Masculinity and the Undergraduate Experience, 1850–1920*. Bloomington: Indiana University Press, 2005.

Dewey, C. J. 'The education of a ruling caste: The Indian Civil Service in the era of competitive examination', *English Historical Review*, 88:347 (1973): 262–85.

Dirks, Nicholas. 'The invention of caste', *Social Analysis*, 25 (1989): 42–52.

Elshtain, Jean Bethke. *Public Man, Private Woman: Women in Social and Political Thought*. Princeton, NJ: Princeton University Press, 1981.

Emsley, Clive. *Crime and Society in England, 1750–1900*, 2nd edn. London: Longman, 1996.

Fischer, Louis. *The Life of Mahatma Gandhi*. Toronto: Macmillan, 1950.

Fisher, Michael H. *Counterflows to Colonialism: Indian Travellers and Settlers in Britain, 1600–1857*. Delhi: Permanent Black, 2004.

Green, Jeffrey. *Black Edwardians: Black People in Britain, 1901–1914*. London: Frank Cass, 1998.

Gorin, George. *History of Ophthalmology*. Wilmington, DE: Publish or Perish, 1982.

Grover, B. L. *A Documentary Study of British Policy Towards Indian Nationalism, 1885–1909*. Delhi: Shri Kishan, 1967.

Guha, Ranajit. *A Rule of Property for Bengal: An Essay on the Idea of Permanent Settlement*. Durham, NC: Duke University Press, 1996.

—— *Subaltern Studies I: Writings on South Asian History and Society*. Delhi: Oxford University Press, 1982.

Hamer, D. A. *John Morley: Liberal Intellectual in Politics*. Oxford: Clarendon Press, 1968.

Hardy, Anne. *Health and Medicine in Britain Since 1860*. New York: Palgrave, 2001.

Harrison, Mark. 'Was there an oriental renaissance in medicine? The evidence of the nineteenth-century medical press, *The Indian Magazine* and late-Victorian colonial politics', in David Finkelstein and Douglas M. Peers (eds), *Negotiating India in the Nineteenth-Century Media*. Basingstoke: Macmillan Press, 2000.

Hasian, Marouf Arif. *The Rhetoric of Eugenics in Anglo-American Thought*. Athens, GA: University of Georgia Press, 1996.

Herz, Nicole. 'It's personal before it's political: Ambition and angst in the lives of Indian civil servants, 1880–1950', *Essays in History*, 40 (1998): http://etext.lib.virginia.edu/journals/EH/EH40/herz40.html (accessed 8 November 2005).

Hobbes, Thomas. *Leviathan*. London: J. M. Dent and Sons, 1914.

Hobsbawm, E. J. *The Age of Revolutions, 1789–1848*. London: Weidenfeld and Nicolson, 1962.

Honey, J. R. de S. *Tom Brown's Universe: The Development of the English Public School in the Nineteenth Century*. New York: Quadrangle, 1977.

Howe, Stephen. *Ireland and Empire: Colonial Legacies in Irish History and Culture*. Oxford: Oxford University Press, 2000.

Hudson, Pat. 'Women and industrialization', in June Purvis (ed.), *Women's History: Britain, 1850–1945*. New York: St Martin's Press, 1995.

Hunt, James D. *Gandhi in London*. New Delhi: Promilla and Co., 1978.

Huttenback, Robert A. *Racism and Empire: White Settlers and Colored Immigrants in the British Self-Governing Colonies, 1830–1910*. Ithaca: Cornell University Press, 1976.

Ignatiev, Noel. *How the Irish Became White*. New York: Routledge, 1995.

Inden, Ronald. 'Orientalist Constructions of India', *Modern Asian Studies*, 20:3 (1986): 401–46.

Jasanoff, Maya. *Edge of Empire: Lives, Culture and Conquest in the East, 1750–1850*. New York: Alfred A. Knopf, 2005.

Jensen, Joan M. *Passage from India: Asian Indian Immigrants in North America*. New Haven: Yale University Press, 1988.

Journal of Colonialism and Colonial History, 3:1 (2002).

Joyce, Patrick. *Visions of the People: Industrial England and the Question of Class, 1848–1914*. Cambridge: Cambridge University Press, 1991.

Kaminsky, Arnold P. *The India Office, 1880–1910*. Westport, CT: Greenwood Press, 1986.

Karatani, Rieko. *Defining British Citizenship: Empire, Commonwealth and Modern Britain*. London: Frank Cass, 2003.

Keith, Arthur Berriedale. *A Constitutional History of India, 1600–1935*, reprint of 2nd edn. London: Methuen, 1969.

Kirk-Greene, Anthony. *Britain's Imperial Administrators, 1858–1966*. New York: St Martin's Press, 2000.

Kolff, Dirk. *Naukar, Rajput and Sepoy: The Ethnohistory of the Military Labour Market in Hindustan, 1450–1850*. Cambridge: Cambridge University Press, 1990.

Lahiri, Shompa. *Indians in Britain: Anglo-Indian Encounters, Race and Identity, 1880–1930*. London: Frank Cass, 2000.

—— 'British policy towards Indian princes in late-nineteenth and early twentieth-century Britain', *Immigrants and Minorities*, 15:3 (1996): 214–32.

Lane, Joan. *A Social History of Medicine: Health, Healing and Disease in England, 1750–1950*. London and New York: Routledge, 2001.

Lawrence, Christopher. *Medical Theory, Surgical Practice: Studies in the History of Surgery*. London: Routledge, 1992.

Lengel, Ed. 'A "perverse and ill-fated people": English perceptions of the Irish, 1845–52', *Essays in History*, 38 (1996): http://etext.virginia.edu /journals/EH/EH38/Lengel.html (accessed 1 January 2008).

Lindeborg, Ruth. 'The "Asiatic" and the Boundaries of Victorian Englishness', *Victorian Studies*, 37:3 (1994): 381–404.

Lorimer, Douglas. 'Reconstructing Victorian racial discourse: Images of race, the language of race relations, and the context of black resistance', in Gretchen Holbrook Gerzina (ed.), *Black Victorians/ Black Victoriana*. New Brunswick, NJ: Rutgers University Press, 2003.

Mackenzie, John M. *The Empire of Nature: Hunting, Conservation and British Imperialism*. Manchester: Manchester University Press, 1988.

—— 'The imperial pioneer and hunter and the British masculine stereotype in late Victorian and Edwardian times', in J. A. Mangan and James Walvin (eds), *Manliness and Morality: Middle-Class Masculinity in Britain and America, 1800–1940*. Manchester: Manchester University Press, 1987.

Magubane, Zine. *Bringing the Empire Home: Race, Class, and Gender in Britain and Colonial South Africa*. Chicago: University of Chicago Press, 2004.

Mallet, Bernard. *Sir Louis Mallet: A Record of Public Service and Political Ideals*. London: James Nisbet and Co., 1905.

Mangan, J. A. *Athleticism in the Victorian and Edwardian Public School: The Emergence and Consolidation of an Educational Ideology*. Cambridge: Cambridge University Press, 1981.

—— *The Games Ethic and Imperialism: Aspects of the Diffusion of an Ideal*. London: Viking, 1986.

Marshall, P. J. *Bengal: The British Bridgehead: Eastern India, 1740–1828*. Cambridge: Cambridge University Press, 1987.

Martin, Briton, Jr. *New India, 1885: British Official Policy and the Emergence of the Indian National Congress*. Berkeley: University of California Press, 1969.

Mathur, Saloni. 'Living ethnological exhibits: The case of 1886', *Cultural Anthropology*, 15:4 (November 2000): 492–524.

McClintock, Anne. *Imperial Leather: Race, Gender, and Sexuality in the Colonial Contest*. London: Routledge, 1995.

McLeod, Roy and Lewis Milton (eds). *Disease, Medicine, and Empire: Perspectives on Western Medicine and the Experience of European Expansion*. London: Routledge, 1988.

Mehrotra, S. R. *The Emergence of the Indian National Congress*. Delhi: Vikas Publications, 1971.

Metcalf, Thomas R. *The Aftermath of Revolt: India, 1857–1870*. Princeton: Princeton University Press, 1964.

—— *Ideologies of the Raj*. Cambridge: Cambridge University Press, 1997.

—— *Land, Landlords, and the British Raj: Northern India in the Nineteenth Century*. Berkeley and Los Angeles: University of California Press, 1978.

Misra, B. B. *The Bureaucracy in India: An Historical Analysis of Development up to 1947*. Delhi: Oxford University Press, 1977.

Moir, Martin I. *et al.* (eds). *J. S. Mill's Encounter with India*. Toronto: University of Toronto Press, 1999.

Nicholson, Reynold A. *Sir C. J. Lyall, 1845–1920*. London: Oxford University Press, n. d.

Noiriel, Gérard. *The French Melting Pot: Immigration, Citizenship, and National Identity*, trans. Geoffrey de Laforcade. Minneapolis: University of Minnesota Press, 1996.

Omissi, David. '"Martial races": Ethnicity and security in colonial India, 1858–1939', *War and Society*, 9:1 (1991): 1–27.

Pacey, Arnold. *Technology in World Civilizations: A Thousand-Year History*. Oxford: Oxford University Press, 1990.

Parry, Noel and José. *The Rise of the Medical Profession: A Study of Collective Social Mobility*. London: Croom Helm, 1976.

Parsons, Gerald. 'Rethinking the missionary position: Bishop Colenso of Natal', in John Wolffe (ed.), *Religion in Victorian Britain*, Vol. V *Culture and Empire*. Manchester: Manchester University Press, 1997.

Peers, Douglas M. '"The habitual nobility of being": British officers and the social construction of the Bengal army in the early nineteenth century', *Modern Asian Studies*, 25:3 (1991): 545–59.

Perkin, Harold. *The Rise of Professional Society: England Since 1800*. London and New York: Routledge, 1989.

Perkin, Joan. *Victorian Women*. London: John Murray, 1993.

Ramdin, Ron. *The Making of the Black Working Class in Britain*. Aldershot: Gower Publishing Company, 1987.

Roper, Michael and John Tosh (eds). *Masculinities in Britain since 1800*. London: Routledge, 1991.

Schneer, Jonathan. *London 1900: The Imperial Metropolis*. New Haven: Yale University Press, 1999.

Scott, Joan W. 'Gender: A useful category of historical analysis', *The American Historical Review*, 91:5 (1985): 1053–75.

Searle, G. R. *Eugenics and Politics in Britain, 1900–1914*. London: Noordhoff International Publishing, 1976.

Sen, Satadru. *Migrant Races: Empire, Identity and K. S. Ranjitsinjhi*. Manchester: Manchester University Press, 2005.

Sherif, M. A. *Searching for Solace: A Biography of Abdullah Yusuf Ali, Interpreter of the Qur'an*. Kuala Lumpur: Islamic Book Trust, 1994.

Shorter, Edward. *Doctors and Their Patients: A Social History*. New Brunswick, NJ: Transaction Publishers, 1985.

Simon, Bian and Ian Bradley (eds). *The Victorian Public School: Studies in the Development of an Educational Institution*. Dublin: Gill and Macmillan, 1975.

Sinha, Mrinalini. 'Britishness, clubbability, and the colonial public sphere', in Tony Ballantyne and Antoinette Burton (eds), *Bodies in Contact: Rethinking Colonial Encounters in World History*. Durham, NC: Duke University Press, 2005.

—— *Colonial Masculinity: The 'Manly Englishman' and the 'Effeminate Bengali' in the Late Nineteenth Century*. Manchester: Manchester University Press, 1995.

Stanley, Brian. *The Bible and the Flag: Protestant Missionaries and British Imperialism in the Nineteenth and Twentieth Centuries*. Leicester: Apollos, 1990.

Stokes, Eric. *The English Utilitarians and India*. London: Clarendon Press, 1959.

Stoler, Ann Laura. 'Making empire respectable: The politics of race and sexual morality in 20th-century colonial cultures', *American Ethnologist*, 16:4 (November 1989): 634–60.

—— *Carnal Knowledge and Imperial Power: Race and the Intimate in Colonial Rule*. Berkeley and Los Angeles: University of California Press, 2002.

—— *Race and the Education of Desire: Foucault's History of Sexuality and the Colonial Order of Things*. Durham NC: Duke University Press, 1995.

Tabili, Laura. 'The construction of racial difference in twentieth-century Britain: The Special Restriction (Coloured Alien Seamen) Order,

1925', *Journal of British Studies*, 33(1) (1994): 54–98.

—— '"Keeping natives under control": Race segregation and the domestic dimensions of empire, 1920–1939', *International Labor and Working-Class History*, 44 (1993): 67–78.

Thompson, E. P. *The Making of the English Working Class*. London: V. Gollancz, 1964.

Torpey, John. *The Invention of the Passport: Surveillance, Citizenship and the State*. Cambridge: Cambridge University Press, 2000.

Tsuzuki, Cshushichi. *H. M. Hyndman and British Socialism*. Oxford: Oxford University Press, 1961.

Visram, Rozina. *Ayahs, Lascars and Princes: Indians in Britain, 1700–1947*. London: Pluto Press, 1986.

—— *Asians in Britain: 400 Years of History*. London: Pluto Press, 2002.

Ward, Peter W. *White Canada Forever: Popular Attitudes and Public Policy Toward Orientals in British Columbia*. Montreal: McGill-Queen's University Press, 1974.

Wilde, Simon. *Ranji: A Genius Rich and Strange*. London: Kingswood Press, 1990.

Williams, Donovan. *The India Office, 1858–1869*. Hoshiapur, India: Vishveshvaranand Vedic Research Institute, 1983.

Wolpert, Stanley. *Morley and India, 1906–1910*. Berkeley: University of California Press, 1967.

—— *A New History of India*, 6th edn. Oxford: Oxford University Press, 2000.

Yule, Henry and Burnell, A. C. *Hobson-Jobson: a glossary of colloquial Anglo-Indian words and phrases, and of kindred terms, etymological, historical, geographic and discursive*, 2nd edn. London: Murray, 1903.

Index

Note: 'n.' after a page number indicates the number of a note on that page

Abdul Hamid II, Sultan of the Ottoman Empire 149
Africa and Africans 6, 7, 16, 18, 22n.9, 22n.10, 35, 52, 64, 69, 71–2, 74, 81, 83, 85, 101
Ahmed, Aziz 52
Aliens Act (1905) 105
Aliens Restriction Act (1836) 105
Ali, Hamid 203
Ali, Hidayat (Mohamed Nazir) 139–40
Ali, Imran 135
Ali, Yusef 55, 59
Aligarh University 199
All Souls College, Oxford *see* Oxford University
analogy, construction of 8–9, 17, 22n.12, 27, 35–6, 39–41, 50, 55–6, 60, 81, 110, 160–3, 168, 173, 236, 239
  see also categories and categorisation, construction of; difference, construction of
Anglo-Indians (Britons connected with India) 9, 11, 48, 56, 170, 172, 187, 221, 228, 242
Ankuram, case of 146
Arabia and Arabs 72, 84, 159
Arabic 35–6, 83, 113, 149, 192n.57, 199
Argyll, George Douglas Campbell, First Duke of 168–70
army, discrimination against Indians in 6, 102, 168
Arnold, T. W. 186
asceticism 129
Association for the Advancement of Scientific and Industrial Education of Indians 186
Australia 1, 3–5, 101, 105, 206
Ayahs 13, 17, 22n.10, 33, 125
Ayahs' Home 13, 125
  see also Strangers' Home for Asiatics, Africans and South-Sea Islanders

'babu' stereotype 157, 166–7, 204, 235
Baine, J. A. 109
Balliol College, Oxford *see* Oxford University
Banerjea, Surendranath 169, 191n.38
Banerjee, Sasipada 53–4
Bar, English
  attire, required for 197
  exam 158–9, 203, 207, 209
  Indians called to 53, 158, 197, 209–10, 219, 223
  prestige of 158, 209
  study for 207, 209, 212, 219

Basu, Divijendra Nath 198
Bayley, Steuart C. 115–18
Bayly, Susan 45n.16, 107
Beale, Dorothea 133
Bendall, Cecil 54
Bernard, Charles E. 138–9, 142, 176
Bethune School, Calcutta 181
Bhagavad Gita 130
Bhore, Mary 180–1
Bhownagree, M. M. 221
Bilgrami, Syed Ali 205
Bilgrami, Syed Husain 139, 148, 187
Birdwood, George 185
Black Books of Lincoln's Inn 197
Bodington, I. V. 184
Bodley, Rachel 134
Bonarjee, N. B. 204–5
Bose, Pramatha Nath 50–1
Boyne, Stapleton 143–4
Brahmins *see* caste, *brahman*
British society
  as a constituent part of the Empire 9, 75, 92, 99, 168
  as distinct from India 9, 209
  importance of class ranking in 9, 31–3
  see also class; 'gentleman' and 'gentlemen'; 'lady' and 'ladies'; women
British subjects and subjecthood 5, 6, 13, 28, 49, 53, 79, 99–107, 119, 130, 137, 143, 150, 158, 163, 186
  benefits of 6, 102–4, 106, 240
  dynastic concept of 13, 99–102, 234, 240
  equality of 5, 22n.9, 79, 99–102, 106, 158, 226–8, 240, 243
Brown, Algernon 221
Browning, Oscar 180, 208, 211
Bureau of Indian Students 226
Bureau of Information 224
Burne, Sir Owen Tudor 30, 39
Burnie, R. J. D. 124
Burton, Antoinette 22n.10, 23n.21, 48–9, 58, 132, 154n.23
Butler, W. G. 187
Butler, William 182

Cama and Company 82–3
Cambridge Majlis 205, 208, 213, 221, 225
Cambridge University
  Christ's College 212
  Indian students at 54–5, 164, 168, 176, 204–6, 212–13, 241
  King's College 208
  mission to India 164
  Ranjitsinjhi and 1–4
  restrictions on number of Indian students at 164, 208
  St. John's College 164, 168, 208
  social background of administrators and 34
  society 214
  see also education; universities
Campbell, Colin G. 31
Campbell, Reginald John 86
Canada 5, 100
Cannadine, David 8–9, 17, 40
  see also analogy, construction of
Cardus, Neville 2
Carpenter, Mary 48, 58, 60
Cartmell, J. W. 212
caste
  Baidya 41
  brahman ('brahmin' in older usage) 10, 37–8, 41, 51, 53–6, 108, 126–35, 144, 147, 151–2, 153n.9, 169, 236–7, 241
  brahman mystique 53–4, 126–31, 152, 236, 241
  gotra 37, 108
  jati 37–8, 108
  Kayasth 41, 56, 109
  kshaitrya 37, 128, 148, 169, 237, 241

occupational definition of 41, 51, 56, 89–92, 136, 151, 236
racial origins 38–9, 50–2
Rajput 4, 10, 11, 37, 40–2, 128, 136, 148, 153n.9
Ranjitsinjhi's 4
restrictions 127, 146, 236, 238
shudra 37, 51, 132
vaishya 37, 136
varna 37–8, 51, 54, 108, 130–1, 136
categories and categorisation, construction of 7, 11, 16, 18–19, 36, 38, 41, 63, 89, 102, 108, 240–1
see also analogy, construction of; difference, construction of
censuses
of England 31, 33
of India 37, 41, 109, 131
certificates of identity 102–10, 113, 117–19, 140–1
identifiers of social rank 106–10, 219, 234, 241
instruments of control 103, 119, 120n.8, 226, 240
reasons for acquisition 104, 107–10, 119, 224
see also British subjects and subjecthood; passports
Chakravarti, Uma 132
Challis, Abraham 83–8, 92, 148
attitude toward the Quran 86
disciplinary proceedings against 84–6
see also London City Mission; Salter, Joseph; Strangers' Home for Asiatics, Africans and South-Sea Islanders
Chamier, F. E. A. 89–92, 115, 128–30, 139, 146
preference for Hindus over Muslims 90–1, 128
service in India 89–91
see also land usage and ownership; Strangers' Home for Asiatics, Africans and South-Sea Islanders
charity 14, 83, 139–42, 144–5, 215–16, 243
as a measure of social rank 81–2, 92, 125, 140, 142, 243
Charity Organization Society 215–16
Cheltenham Ladies' College 132–3
China 72, 79, 187
Chinnappa, Mersha 180
Christians and Christianity
as basis of ethics 69, 77, 80–1, 212
conversion to 12, 14, 82–3, 88–9, 132, 145–6, 227, 238
doctrine 76, 85–6, 88, 92, 133, 148
marriage and 216–17
official attitudes toward 145–8, 157–2, 182, 238
Westernization and 52, 75–8
see also Challis, Abraham; Church Missionary Society; London City Mission; Salter, Joseph; Strangers' Home for Asiatics, Africans and South-Sea Islanders
Christ's College, Cambridge *see* Cambridge University
Churchill, Lord Randolph Henry Spencer 133–4, 171, 179
Churchill, Winston Spencer 39
Church Missionary Society 52, 71, 83
see also Christians and Christianity; London City Mission; Strangers' Home for Asiatics, Africans and South-Sea Islanders
citizenship *see* British subjects and subjecthood
City Temple 86
civilising mission 5, 12, 75

feminine virtues and 57, 60
religion and 75
role of education in 14, 159–90, 199, 218–27, 236
see also education; women
class
acceptance of as legitimate hierarchy 56, 64, 178
consciousness 3–7, 18–21, 28, 32, 71, 172, 242
economic nature of 15–20, 40–3, 126
occupational definition of 19–20, 56, 92, 106, 117, 125, 128, 130–1, 141, 152, 235
racialisation of 15, 18, 23n.18, 38, 141–2, 165, 179
role as paradigm 15–16
see also caste; 'gentleman' and 'gentlemen'; 'lady' and 'ladies'; race
clubbability 32, 201–2, 206
Cobden, Richard 33
Cohn, Bernard 38, 107, 196
Coldstream, William 186
College of Calcutta 168
Colonial Office 29
Coloured Seamen Order (1925) 6, 105
Commonwealth Immigration Act (1962) 6
Cornwallis, Charles, First Marquess Cornwallis 43
Cotton, Henry 223–4
Council of India *see* India Office
Cox, Jeffrey 73, 77
Crewe, Robert Offley Ashburton Crewe-Milnes, Marquess of 210, 233
Critchett, George Anderson 112
cult of domesticity *see* domesticity, cult of
Curzon, George Nathaniel, Marquess Curzon of Kedleston 104, 107
Cust, Robert Needham 52–3, 66n.16, 78, 82, 89

Das, Bilash Chandra 109
Davar, Dinsha 61, 63
Deshmukh, Krishanara Gopal 53, 57
Deslandes, Paul 21n.8, 211
destitute Indians 14, 33, 47, 71–6, 89, 92, 105–6, 115–16, 124–53, 175, 203, 215–16, 241–2
see also Challis, Abraham; legal appeals of property and inheritance; London City Mission; poverty and the poor; Salter, Joseph; Strangers' Home for Asiatics, Africans and South-Sea Islanders
Dhingra, Madan Lal 226
difference, construction of
by class 9, 15–19, 32, 39, 78, 80, 163, 185, 214, 234
by ethnicity and race 8, 15, 22n.12, 27, 35–9, 78–80, 102–3, 131–2
by gender 17, 20, 32, 196
see also analogy, construction of; categories and categorisation, construction of
difference, cultural
accommodation of 14, 127, 195–7, 200, 207, 237–9
superficiality of 62
difference in administrative experiences in India and the United Kingdom 34, 65, 233
difference in power 11, 17, 19
Dirks, Nicholas 38
Distressed Colonial and Indian Subjects, Parliamentary Committee on 203
diversity, institutional tolerance of 99, 158, 161, 196, 238

domestic life
of India Office administrators 31–3
of women in India 58–9, 180–1
see also domesticity, cult of; women
domesticity, cult of 57–62, 79, 90–2, 150–1, 181, 214, 237
see also women
Dorasami, J. 143–4
Dravidians 38
Dublin College 114
Dufferin and Ava, Frederick Temple Hamilton-Temple-Blackwood, first Marquess of 171
Dufferin Fund, Lady 134
Durham Report (1839) 101
Dutt, P. N. 214

East End *see* London's East End; poverty and the poor
East India Association 13, 47–8, 52, 221–3
East India Company 29, 30, 34, 42, 76, 99, 162, 168–9, 199
economy
agrarian 42, 135–7, 161, 180
as context of Indo-British encounter 69, 74, 79, 119, 135, 183–4, 190, 235, 241, 243
India's place in imperial 42–3, 135, 178, 183–6, 222, 235, 243
theories of 33, 43–4, 135
see also class; destitute Indians; land usage and ownership; legal appeals of property and inheritance
Edinburgh Indian Association 221, 225
Edinburgh University 175, 206, 221, 225, 236
see also education; students in Britain, Indian; universities
education 6, 14, 157–241
caste and 52–3, 55
fees 202–3
importance in social background 12, 19–21, 31, 34–6, 41, 75, 83, 99, 129, 135, 177, 204–6, 234–5
legal 209–12, 226–7
policy 157–77, 198–9, 223–4
technical 183–9, 222–3
women and 20, 50, 57–62, 132–4, 146–51, 179–83, 201, 237
see also Cambridge University; civilising mission; Edinburgh University; Inns of Court; Latin and Greek; Oxford University; public schools; Sanskrit; universities
Edward VII, King of Great Britain and Ireland, Emperor of India 108, 129–30
Edwards, Herbert 167
Egypt 101, 215
Elphinstone College, Bombay 199
emigrationist policy 105
eugenics and Social Darwinism 39, 41, 126
'euthanasia of a mission', concept of 73–4

Fergusson, J. H. 95n.69, 127
Fitzgerald, Gerald 115, 118, 134, 139, 146, 150, 154n.29
Fitzpatrick, Gerald 216–17
Fowler, H. H. 124
France 40, 87 161
franchise
in Britain 6, 19, 29–30, 101–2
in India 6
in settler colonies 101
see also race
French (language) 149, 160–1, 224
Fulbright scholars in the United

States, comparison to Indian students in Britain 220

Gandhi, Mohandas K. 157, 217
gender 5, 8–9, 15–17, 20, 32, 60, 62, 179–82, 201, 240
  in domestic workforce 32
  gendered language 8, 15, 20–1, 57, 148, 166–7
  see also race; women
'gentleman' and 'gentlemen'
  application to Indians 4, 21, 48–50, 55, 61–4, 80–1, 91–2, 108, 129–30, 151–2, 157–9, 163–4, 167–77, 185, 204, 208, 212–19, 228–9, 233–43
  'players' (in cricket) 2–3
  usage and meaning of term 3, 19–20, 31–2, 53, 61–4, 112–13, 151, 167–72, 175, 185, 201–4, 212–19, 228–9, 234–6
  see also class; 'lady' and 'ladies'; public schools; race; sports; women
Germany 199, 215, 224, 227
Gilchrist, John Borthwick 173
Gilchrist Trust 173–80, 183, 187, 189–90, 199, 236, 242–3
  destroyed correspondence with India Office 193n.67
  intent to award scholarships only to wealthy Indians 174–5
  partnership with India Office 175–6
  partnership with National Indian Association 177
  scholarships for women 177–9
  termination of scholarship 176–7, 189–90, 236
  see also Cambridge University; civilising mission; Edinburgh University; education; Indian Civil Service; Oxford University; universities
Ginwalla, N. S. 61, 63
Gladstone, William Ewart 31, 33, 168
Godley, Sir Arthur (later Lord Kilbracken) 116–18, 135
  duties as Permanent Undersecretary for India 30–1
  education 34, 135
  political opinions 33–4
  social status 31
  see also India Office
Gopal, Pandit Ram 146–7
gotra *see* caste
Gourama, Princess of Coorg 146
Government of India *see* Indian government
Greek *see* Latin and Greek
Gupta, Krishna Govind 33, 187

Habermas, Jürgen 103, 120n.11
Haileybury College 34, 199
Hamilton, Lord George Francis 104, 106–8, 183
Hamilton, W. R. 212, 220, 223
Harris, George Canning, Fourth Baron 2
Hasan, Naziruddin 213
Hastings, Warren 37
Hindus 80, 82, 138, 187, 235
  cultural traits 55, 57, 75, 80, 85, 90–1, 113, 169
  dietary restrictions 54, 197
  ethnic category 49, 84, 108–9, 147–8, 217
  law 209
  loyalty 151
  parents 213
  philosophy and beliefs 86, 132, 147–8
  women 58–9, 181
  see also caste
Hindustani Ghadr movement 186

Hindustani language 75, 83, 127, 173, 192n.50
Hobbes, Thomas 125
Hodgson, Pratt 162–3
Holderness, T. W. 184
Home Office 22n.9, 29
Hughes, R. Marsh 75, 79, 81–3, 92
Hutchins, Philip Percival 30, 115–18, 141–2, 149, 215
Hyndman, H. M. 48, 66n.2, 135

Ilbert, C. P. 169
Ilbert Bill 170
'immorality' of Indians 78, 80, 208, 211–13
 see also 'gentleman' and 'gentlemen'; marriage; women
Inden, Ronald 38
India Act (1858) 29–30
India House 226
India Office 12–14, 27–44, 47–8, 71–4, 89, 101–9, 173–8, 181–90, 197, 200, 210, 212, 215–18, 220–1, 223–9, 236–9, 244
 administrative structure 28–30
 aid to Indians 115–19, 124–59, 181–3, 203, 235–6, 241
 authority and importance of 27–30, 101, 103, 106, 118, 206, 223–7
 Council of India 29–35, 39, 43, 47, 129–31, 139, 144, 150, 170, 186–7, 216
 female staff 32
 financial independence 29
 Judicial and Public Department 28, 30, 31, 35, 37, 89, 115, 129, 133, 141–2, 175–6, 217
 orientalist expertise 28, 34–44, 50, 51, 182
 policy on repatriation 117, 124–6, 129–31, 138–9, 143, 150–1
 Political and Secret Department 28, 30, 31, 39, 115, 135, 138, 150, 151
 political views 33–4
 social background of officials and staff 27–8, 31–3, 34, 57, 175, 239, 241
 see also Indian government; orientalism and orientalists
Indian Civil Service (ICS) 164–77, 188–90, 235–6
 barriers to Indian membership in 104, 236, 241–2
 covenanted and uncovenanted service in 172
 exams 34, 104, 158, 165–73, 176, 188, 191n.38, 236, 241
 officers 55, 80, 89–91, 166–7, 172, 187, 204, 221
 recruitment 165–72, 177, 190
 reform 165, 170–3, 188, 236
 social rank of officers 165–71, 188, 235
 see also Indian government
Indian Emigration Acts 6, 105, 140
Indian government (Government of India, the Raj) 4, 10, 90–2, 146, 162–4, 172–95, 224–8
 administrators 4, 10, 90–2, 172–3, 211, 224
 India Office and 28–9
 land policy 43–4, 135–6, 139
 loyalty to 91
 opposition to 48, 186, 222
 racial discrimination of 102, 158, 164, 168–88, 195, 211, 227–8
 see also Indian Civil Service; India Office
Indian Institute, Oxford 171, 199
Indian Mutiny *see* Indian Rebellion of 1857–58
Indian National Congress 48, 148,

170, 225, 240
British Committee of the 48, 52, 64, 222
Indian nationalists and nationalism 6, 21, 44, 49, 92, 102, 107, 147–8, 183–4, 186, 191n.38, 220–2
Indian Rebellion of 1857–58 (Indian Mutiny, Sepoy Rebellion) 14, 29, 89, 99, 135, 146, 161, 167, 169, 188, 238
Inns of Court 158, 197–211, 219, 238, 241
benchers 197, 209, 226
expenses for students at 203
policy on restricting admissions 209–11, 219, 225–6
relations with Indian judiciary 209–11
residency requirements 158
tolerance of cultural difference 197–200, 238
see also education; law; students in Britain, Indian
Iredale, Frank, journalist 3
Ireland and the Irish 7, 16, 18, 39, 209
Islam *see* Muslims

Jackson, E. G. A. 216
Japan 72
Jasanoff, Maya 137
Jaswantsinjhi, Jam Sahib of Nawanagar 4
jati *see* caste
Jehanghir, Lady J. C. 60
Jinnah, Muhammad Ali 210
Jones, William 199
judges
Indian 6, 53, 57, 147, 164, 170, 225
opinions regarding Indian law students 209–11
see also education; Inns of Court; law; students in Britain, Indian
Judicial and Public Department *see* India Office

Kapadia, S. A. 219, 226
Karim, Abdul 142
Kayasth *see* caste
Kay-Shuttleworth, Ughtred J. 175
Khalil, Mustafa 149–51
Khan, Abdul 145
Khan, Mohammed Yusef 114
Khan, Syed Ahmad 163
Kimberley, John Wodehouse, First Earl of 115–18, 171
King's College, Cambridge *see* Cambridge University
Kolasker, M. S. 130–1
kshaitrya *see* caste

'lady' and 'ladies'
application to Indians 49, 50, 53, 58–61, 133, 146, 150, 180–2, 237, 243
usage and meaning of term 20, 32, 59, 81, 179–81, 234, 237
see also class; gender; 'gentleman' and 'gentlemen'; women
Lahiri, Shompa 17, 21n.8, 120n.8, 167, 200, 211, 228
Land Alienation Act (1900) 136, 139
land usage and ownership 40–4, 55–6, 89, 91, 101, 108–9, 127–8, 135–40, 146, 151–2, 164, 165, 168–9, 173, 235, 241
Lang, Marshall 83
lascars 17, 22n.10, 73, 79, 80, 85–7, 125, 239
Lascar Transfer Officer, title for Honorary Secretary of Strangers' Home 73

Latin and Greek
cultural literacy in 135
influence on civilisation 161
requirements in education 174, 199, 208
see also education; Gilchrist Trust; Sanskrit; universities
Laurie, Maxwell 141–2
Laurie, Werner 141–2
law
as academic subject 174–5, 182–3
British 22n.9, 35, 105–6, 110–17, 161, 206, 209, 211, 217, 225–6, 239–40
in dominions 215
equality before 99, 102, 106
Indian 35, 37, 161, 197, 199, 209, 215, 217
marriage 90, 216
Roman 34, 209
students 57, 63, 131, 159, 197, 210, 213
suits 76, 141, 203
theory of 104
see also British subjects and subjecthood; Inns of Court; race; students in Britain, Indian
Law Society Exam 203
lawyers
in India 198, 209, 225
Indian in Britain 127, 209, 225
New Zealand 209
see also Inns of Court
League of Progressive Thought 86
Lee-Warner, William 130, 135, 148–51, 154n.31
career 30
Committee 208, 213–14
intelligence report 148–51, 206–7, 220, 222–4
see also Muslims; race; students in Britain, Indian
legal appeals of property and inheritance 76, 127–8, 135–9
Legal Education, Council of 199–200, 209
legal profession 126, 235
see also Inns of Court; law
Lewis, P. J. 212
Lincoln's Inn *see* Inns of Court
Lindeborg, Ruth 79–80
Liverpool Mosque and Muslim Institute 148–51
see also Muslims
Locke, John, influence in development of British concepts of landholding 42
London and Counties Medical Protection Society 111, 113
London City Mission 69, 71, 74–5, 83–8
leadership 85–6
missionaries' social background 75, 83
missionary fields 74, 83–4
see also Challis, Abraham; Christians and Christianity; destitute Indians; poverty and the poor; Salter, Joseph; Strangers' Home for Asiatics, Africans and South-Sea Islanders
London Indian Society 221
Long, J. 64
Lyall, Sir Alfred Comyn 35–41, 166
social status 144, 147
views on Indian society 35, 38, 40–1, 160
see also caste; orientalism and orientalists
Lyall, Sir Charles James 144, 147
scholarship 35–6
see also orientalism and orientalists

Macaulay, Thomas Babington Macaulay, Baron 159–63, 167, 172–3, 175, 177, 188–90, 199

see also civilising mission; class; education
Macpherson, Sir Arthur George 31, 138, 146, 217
Mahmoud, S. A. 215
Maine, Sir Henry Sumner
orientalist credentials 34–5
social status 32, 34
views on Indian society 40, 54–6, 136, 160
see also caste; orientalism and orientalists
Majlis *see* Cambridge Majlis
Mallet, C. E. 210
Mallet, Sir Louis 103
career 30–1
political views 33–4, 44
Mallick, B. N. 176
Manning, Elizabeth 221
marriage
arranged 57, 91, 216
child 59
interethnic 51, 214–18, 232n.77, 239
see also caste; race; women
masculinity 20–1, 57, 166–7
see also gender; women
Mathur, Saloni 81, 137
Medical Act (1858) 113
Medical Education and Registration, General Council of 199
medicine and surgery 110–18
fees for 112
see also oculists; physicians and surgeons
Mental Deficiency Act (1913) 39
Mercantile Marine Department of the Board of Trade 73
Merchant Shipping Acts 6, 73
Metcalf, Thomas R. 22n.14, 39
Minto, Gilbert John Elliot Murray Kynynmound, Fourth Earl of 186–7
'Misanthrope' correspondence 61–4, 237
Misra, B. B. 169
Mittra, R. 52–3, 57
Monier-Williams, Sir Monier 59, 170–1, 199
Morison, Theodore 186–7
Morley, John, Viscount Morley of Blackburn 187, 210
Morris, Henry 80–1
Mughal Empire 11, 40–2, 51, 107
Mukherjea, D. B. 206
Mullick, Jessie 215–16
Mullick, Malindranath 215–16
Muslim Institute (Liverpool) 149
Muslims 37, 40, 52, 75–6, 91, 128, 148, 206, 235
Christian proselytization of 71, 74–6, 86, 238
cultural traits 69, 75–6, 80, 84–5, 90–1, 113, 169
dietary restrictions 126, 146, 197, 238
ethnic category 84, 136, 148, 217
law 209
loyalty 148, 151–2
marriage 90–2, 216–17
medicine 113
missionary activity of in Britain 148–52
philosophy and beliefs 84, 86, 136, 148, 150–2
see also Lee-Warner, William; students in Britain, Indian

Naoroji, Dadabhai 44, 49, 52, 66n.2, 135, 142, 191
National Indian Association
goals and services 47, 163, 180, 221–2, 237, 242–4
journal 48–50, 53–6, 58, 61, 64–5, 78, 82, 90, 163, 174, 180, 183–4, 189, 195–7, 202–3, 212–13, 217, 234, 237, 244

membership 47, 49–50, 52, 163, 234
membership fees 163
paternalism 49
relationship with government 47–8
supervision of students 163, 221–2
views on women 56–62, 180, 182–3, 189, 195–7
nationality
role of class in determining 10
role of race in determining 7, 100–2, 119, 240
role of religion in determining 92, 148–51
see also British subjects and subjecthood; difference, construction of
Nehru, Jawaharlal 157, 204, 225, 239
Neville, Ralph 226
New Zealand 5, 105, 209
Noiriel, Gérard 104
Northbrook Society 13, 47–9, 219, 221–2
Northcote, Stafford 165, 167

objectification
of Indians 185
of women 196
see also difference, construction of
oculists 110–19, 124–6, 157, 240, 242
India Office aid to 115–18
portrayal of as 'quacks' 111–13
surgical procedures of 111
trial of 110–15, 121n.30, 121–2n.32, 122n.33, 122n.34
translation of hakim 113
see also destitute Indians; law; medicine and surgery; physicians and surgeons
orientalism and orientalists
among missionaries 71–2, 83, 85, 127
assumptions and expectations of 130, 152, 185
debate with Anglicists 198
in higher education 47
in the India Office 12–13, 34–7, 51
in the National Indian Association 12–13, 47–8, 51, 55, 59, 63, 66, 196
postcolonial critique of 35, 55, 216
see also India Office; National Indian Association
Orientalist-Anglicist debate 198–9
see also Macaulay, Thomas Babington Macaulay, Baron
Oxford University
All Souls College 164
Balliol College 174, 202
faculty 59, 133, 163, 170–1, 180, 199
Indian Institute at 171, 199, 205–6
Indian students at 212, 238
New College 212
scholarships to 182–3
see also education; universities

Pacey, Arnold 113
Pandian, T. B. 213
Panwalker, Rajaram Bhasker 130–1, 133, 147, 150–1, 235
Parker, Joseph 86
Parliament
commissions 163, 171, 203–4, 206, 212, 221
elections 29
Indian institutions analogous to 54
Indians serving in 2, 6, 66n.4, 221
legislation 39, 76, 168, 171, 239

Members of 39, 188
oversight of India Office 28–30
Parsis 2, 52, 58, 60, 61, 82–4, 148
passports 102–8, 119
see also British subjects and subjecthood; certificates of identity
paternalism
class 12, 17
cultural 17, 49, 220–1, 224–6
toward students 218–21, 224–7
see also India Office; National Indian Association
Peninsular and Oriental Shipping Company 87, 92
Permanent Settlement (1793) 136
Permanent Undersecretary of State for India, responsibilities of 30–1
Persia 38, 69, 89
Persian (language) 41, 89, 199
see also Sanskrit
Phear, J. B. 55
physicians and surgeons 41, 111–14, 118, 121–2n.32–3, 192n.50, 240
see also medicine and surgery; oculists
Political and Secret Department *see* India Office
Poor Law 105–6, 115, 239
post-colonial analysis 16, 117, 157, 160
see also categories and categorisation, construction of; difference, construction of
poverty and the poor
among Indians in Britain 12, 48, 69–81, 92, 104, 106, 143, 167, 181, 203
as a characteristic of India 51, 54, 59, 126, 132
genteel 40–1, 134
London's East End and 49, 63, 64, 78, 242
as an object of charity 81, 92, 119
'othering' of 8, 17, 63–4, 79, 242–3
solutions to 33–4, 43–4
see also destitute Indians; London City Mission; Strangers' Home for Asiatics, Africans and South-Sea Islanders
princes, Indian
charitable donations from 82, 149
construction of identity as 1–4, 11, 241
gentlemanly status of 1–4, 37, 47, 91, 107–8, 110, 169, 215, 233–4
residing in United Kingdom 75–6, 82, 215
social value of 37, 47
public schools
background among government officials 34, 164
clubbability and 201, 204, 234–5, 239, 242
curricula 49, 204, 207
expense 234
importance in gentlemanly credentials 20, 165, 167, 170, 188, 204, 207, 235–6, 241–2
racism and 204–5, 236
see also clubbability; 'gentleman' and 'gentlemen'; universities

Quilliam, William Henry (Abdullah) 148–51
see also Muslims

race
Aryan 38, 40, 50–1, 55–6
bigotry based on 2, 5, 14, 18, 75
in Britain 1–9, 16–17, 21n.8, 104
characteristics of 2, 39, 62, 90–1,

117, 134, 168, 212, 217, 238
conflation of religion with 217
in determining social rank 2–3, 5, 8–10, 15–17, 21, 21n.8, 32, 39, 44, 55, 64, 87, 105, 119, 126, 141–2, 158, 167–9, 178, 185, 205, 241–2
definition of 18, 39, 90, 217
discourse of 15, 62–5, 168, 206, 217–18, 241
discrimination by 5–6, 13–17, 63, 75, 101–2, 104–5, 117, 157–8, 164–9, 172–3, 176–9, 188–90, 195, 201, 204–11, 216, 218, 226–8, 236, 239, 241, 243
effect of location on attitudes toward 5, 7, 9, 11, 27, 49, 65, 163
elite perception of middle- and lower-class bigotry based on 165–7, 190, 241
equality of each 63, 99, 228
feminisation of 167
in India 6, 9, 164–5, 228
intermarriage between *see* marriage, interethnic
as origin of caste and class 38–9, 50–2
in the settler dominions 5–6, 16–17, 101, 215, 233
superiority of white 13, 38, 50, 52, 63, 118, 196, 216
theories of 38, 41, 52, 75, 198–9
in the United States 16, 33, 206–7, 214–15
see also caste; class; gender; orientalism and orientalists
racism *see* race
Raj *see* Indian government
Rajia, P. A. 143–4
Rajput *see* caste
Raleigh, W. A. 163–4
Ramabai, Pandita 132–5, 147
caste and 133–5
Christianity and 132–3, 147
early life 132
female education and 132–4, 182
purdah and 237
respectability of 134, 235
see also caste; Christians and Christianity; education; Hindus; women
Ramayana 59
Ranjitsinjhi, Kumar Shri 1–5, 7, 11, 206, 251, 253
career in England 1–5, 206
skill as cricketer 1–2
social background 3–4
see also Cambridge University; clubbability; princes, Indian; sports; universities
Ratnagar, N. J. 54, 65
Ray, Ran Dulal 64
Reddy, C. R. 206
religion *see* Christians and Christianity; Hindus; Muslims; Sikhs
repatriation
cost of 33, 73, 106, 124, 131, 138–9, 142, 150
dependent on class 116, 129–31, 138–9, 143, 151
of lascars 73, 125
responsibility for 88–9, 106
policy on 117, 124–6, 129–31, 138–9, 141, 150–1
see also certificates of identity; destitute Indians; India Office; passports; students in Britain, Indian
Richards, H. C. 223
Ripon, George Frederick Samuel Robinson, First Marquess of 170–1
Risley, Sir Herbert Hope 37–8, 40, 41, 50, 131
see also caste; orientalism and

orientalists; race
Ritchie, Richmond T. 31, 116, 118
Roberts, Frederick Sleigh Roberts, First Earl 142
Roy, Mrs. P. L. 58
Royal College of Surgeons 111
rupee-sterling exchange rate 178, 222
Russia 160–1
ryots 42, 55, 66n.2, 64
 see also land usage and ownership; zamindars

Said, Edward 9, 35
 see also difference, construction of; post-colonial analysis
St. John's College, Cambridge *see* Cambridge University
St. Stephen's College, Delhi 164
Salisbury, Robert Arthur Talbot Gascoyne Cecil, Third Marquess of 169–70
Salter, Joseph 74–84, 86, 87, 88, 92, 186, 238
 social background and education 77
 see also Challis, Abraham; Strangers' Home for Asiatics, Africans and South-Sea Islanders
Sandhurst 13
Sanskrit
 as alternative to Latin or Greek 174, 199, 208
 professors of 47, 54–5, 59, 133, 170–1, 199
 scholarships 171
 see also education; Gilchrist Trust; Latin and Greek; universities
Satthianadhan, S. 54
Secretary of State for India
 aid to destitute Indians in Britain 115–16, 124, 133–4, 146
 behaviour toward Indians in the dominions and 233
 Indian Civil Service appointments and 176
 petitions to 48
 requirements for Indians called to the Bar and 210
 role in India Office administration 29–30
 supervision of Indian students in Britain and 104
 scholarships for Indians studying in Britain and 165, 168, 171, 179, 187
 scholarships for women and 187
 see also Indian government; India Office
Sen, Keshub Chunder 48
Sen, Satadru 5
separate spheres *see* domesticity, cult of
Sepoy Rebellion *see* Indian Rebellion of 1857–58
servants
 household 31–4, 59, 180, 202
 Indian, in Britain 31–3
 see also class
Sharfuddin, Syud 63
Sharma, Ajoodhia Prashad 129–31, 133
Shipley, A. E. 212
shudra *see* caste
Sikh Educational Conference, Gujranwalla 197
Sikhs 42, 71, 82, 84, 136, 138, 148, 186, 206, 238
 characteristics 136, 238
 dress code 197, 238
 opposition to British rule 82, 186
 title 'Singh' 198
 see also difference, cultural
Singh, Duleep, Maharaja of Punjab 71, 82, 215, 239
Singh, Girwal 127
Singh, Jawan 145–6
Singh, Raja Ram Pal 56

Singh, Ranjit, Maharaja of Punjab 42
Singh (Garwal), Balwant 198
Sinha, Mrinalini 23n.21, 32, 167, 172, 201
Small, George 127–8, 145
socialism and socialists 33, 48, 64, 66n.2, 66n.4
social levelling 7, 33, 63–4, 105, 109, 242
social rank
  local and regional context 9–10
  registers of 8–10, 13, 18, 56, 62, 111, 195, 228, 235, 242
  see also class; gender; 'gentleman' and 'gentlemen'; 'lady' and 'ladies'; race
Sorabji, Cornelia 179, 182, 196, 237
Sorabji, Mary 182
Sorabji, Pheroze 182
South Africa 52, 64, 209
  see also class; construction of difference; race
South Asians in Britain, number of 3, 7, 17, 22n.10, 32, 72, 104–5, 108, 135, 153, 163, 179, 208–9, 221, 224
  see also destitute Indians; students in Britain, Indian; Strangers' Home for Asiatics, Africans and South-Sea Islanders
Spooner, W. A. 212
sports
  'amateurs' and 'gentlemen' 3
  cricket 1–5, 206, 239
  equestrian 166
  importance in establishing social rank 1–4, 205, 228, 235, 239
  Indian unfamiliarity with 166, 205–7
  rowing 206
  see also clubbability; public schools; Ranjitsinjhi, Kumar Shri; universities
Squires, H. C. 81, 83
Stanford University 186
Steel, Flora Annie 60
Stoler, Ann Laura 61, 211, 217–18
Strachey, Major General Richard 43
Strachey, Sir John 35, 40, 43–4
Strangers' Home for Asiatics, Africans and South-Sea Islanders 12–13, 47, 49–50, 69–92, 115, 124–30, 135, 137–8, 145, 152, 175
  annual reports 69–70
  contributors to 72–3, 82–3, 152
  discrimination on basis of caste and class 127–9, 137–8
  ethnic composition of inmates 72
  Honorary Secretary, role of 74, 88–9, 124
  missions 74, 77, 79, 81–2, 84, 87–8, 92
  relationship to British government 72–4, 92, 124–5, 175
  structure 71
  see also Challis, Abraham; Chamier, F. E. A.; Christians and Christianity; destitute Indians; London City Mission; Salter, Joseph
students in Britain, Indian 1–2, 14–17, 54–7, 63, 66n.4, 157–90, 195–229
  adviser to 48
  age of eligibility for Indian Civil Service exams 169
  applications to university 15, 164
  British stereotypes of 62
  destitute 147, 167
  difficulty apprenticing with British firms 184–6
  discrimination against 2, 157, 168, 187, 189, 195

evidence of social rank 163–4
expenses 163, 175
female 58, 134, 179–83, 189
hostel for 223–4
importance of 157
insufficiently elite 163
lack of social skills 166
monitoring of 103–7, 163, 218–29
motives for migration 158–9, 183
number of 22n.10, 104, 158
passage to Britain 174
radicalisation of 104
scholarly analysis of 17
social rank 109, 130–1
superintendent of 221, 226
technical 183–7, 189–90
see also education; Gilchrist Trust; public schools; universities
Sturt, W. Neville 129–30
Subbarao, N. S. 213–14
subcaste *see* jati
subjecthood *see* British subjects and subjecthood
surgeons *see* physicians and surgeons
surgery *see* medicine and surgery
Svadeshi Movement 184, 186, 190, 218
Swami, K. V. R. 198

taluqdars 41, 91
Tanner, J. R. 208
Tari 128–9, 139
Thakur, Sripad Babaji 169
Thakur Khemchund 128–9, 139, 153n.9
Times, The 54, 110, 119, 121n.30, 121n.32, 141
Torpey, John 103, 120n.11
trade unions 183–5
Treasury 29
Trevelyan, C. E. 166
Trevelyan, E. J. 164
Trevelyan, G. O. 166–7

ulema, importance of in establishing customary law 37
United States of America 16, 33, 100–2, 133–4, 186, 207, 214, 220, 223, 227
universities
admission restrictions for Indians applying to British 164, 208
application forms 164, 168, 241
expenses at 201–3
graduation attire 197, 200, 236
Indian faculty in British 6, 205
orientalist scholarship and 35, 47, 55, 59
number of Indian students in British 158, 224
quality of Indian 57
women at 201
university society 15, 21n.8, 201–2, 234, 239
see also education; Gilchrist Trust; sports
University College, London 174, 226
University of London 176, 199, 201, 236

vaishya *see* caste
vakils 159, 209
varna *see* caste
Venn, Henry 71, 73–4, 83, 93n.8
Vibhaji, Jam Sahib of Nawanagar 3–4
Victoria, Queen of Britain and Ireland, Empress of India
adoption of title, 'Empress of India' 137
anonymous contribution 142
Indian performances before 140, 144
jubilees 108

loyalty to 79–82, 138–9, 149–50
proclamation of accession over India 99, 176, 240
reception of Indians 196, 215
subjects of 53, 78, 119
sympathy toward Indian converts to Christianity 145–6
see also British subjects and subjecthood
village, cult of 34–5, 40–1, 54–6, 59, 78–9, 136, 180, 241
Vivekananda, Narendranath Datta, Swami 148

Wagle, Nikanth B. 184–6, 235
Walpole, Horace 31, 146
War Office 6, 29
Westernization 75, 112
'whiteness', construction of 16, 18, 20, 61, 201
see also categories and categorisation, construction of; class; difference construction of; race
Wilson, H. H. 199
Wilson, James J. 57
women 56–62, 179–83
in Ayah's Home 13
caste and 38, 51, 132
considered 'ladies' 20, 32, 62
detrimental influence of lower-class, on Indian men 212–14
education of 179–83, 189
entertainers 140–1
grant recipients 177, 179, 189
in higher education 179–80, 182–3, 201
illiteracy of 181
in India Office 32
male behaviour toward 61–2, 195–6
in male roles 132
in National Indian Association 49, 234, 237
objectification of 196
organisations 133
professional barriers against 132, 179, 189
role in defining polite society 56–61, 90–1
seclusion of 50, 57, 59–61, 81, 180, 182, 206, 213, 237
traditional dress of 196–7
at universities 201
see also domesticity, cult of education; gender; 'lady' and 'ladies'
Women's Medical College, Philadelphia 134
Wyllie, William Hutt Curzon 129–30, 139, 143–4, 147, 153n.16, 215–16, 225
assassination of 48, 226

yeoman class, comparison with Indian social ranks 40, 136–8, 151, 234, 239
Yorkshire College, Leeds 183–4

zamindars 10, 41–3, 55, 91, 108, 139, 152, 164, 168, 234, 236, 241
see also class; land usage and ownership; ryots; yeoman class, comparison with Indian social ranks

CPSIA information can be obtained at www.ICGtesting.com
Printed in the USA
BVOW06s2102130216

436636BV00003B/10/P

9 780719 089084